The Cambridge Companion to the Latin American Novel

The diverse countries of Latin America have produc̄
evolving tradition of novels, many of which are read
the world. This Companion offers a broad overview
and analyzes in depth several representative works by,
García Márquez, Machado de Assis, Isabel Allende and
The essays collected here offer several entryways into the ̲ ̲ng and
appreciation of the Latin American novel in Spanish-speaking America and
Brazil. The volume conveys a real sense of the heterogeneity of Latin American
literature, highlighting regions whose cultural and geopolitical particularities
are often overlooked. Indispensable to students of Latin American or Hispanic
studies and those interested in comparative literature and the development of
the novel as genre, the Companion features a comprehensive bibliography and
chronology and concludes with an essay about the success of Latin American
novels in translation.

THE CAMBRIDGE
COMPANION TO
THE LATIN
AMERICAN NOVEL

EDITED BY
EFRAÍN KRISTAL
University of California, Los Angeles

CAMBRIDGE
UNIVERSITY PRESS

CAMBRIDGE UNIVERSITY PRESS
Cambridge, New York, Melbourne, Madrid, Cape Town, Singapore, São Paulo

Cambridge University Press
The Edinburgh Building, Cambridge CB2 2RU, UK

Published in the United States of America by Cambridge University Press, New York

www.cambridge.org
Information on this title: www.cambridge.org/9780521532198

© Cambridge University Press 2005

First published 2005

Printed in the United Kingdom at the University Press, Cambridge

A catalogue record for this book is available from the British Library

ISBN-10 0 521 82533 4 hardback
ISBN-10 0 521 53219 1 paperback
ISBN-13 978 0 521 82533 7 hardback
ISBN-13 978 0 521 53219 8 paperback

CONTENTS

NOTES ON CONTRIBUTORS

PIERS ARMSTRONG is an Australian-born Brazilianist. He has taught at UCLA and USC in California, and at the Federal University of Bahia and at the State University of Feira de Santana in Brazil. Since 2002 he has been Assistant Professor at Dartmouth College in New Hampshire. His first book, *Third World Literary Fortunes* (1999), contrasts the international receptions of Brazilian literature, Spanish American literature, and Brazilian popular culture. His second book, *Cultura Popular na Bahia & Estilística Cultural Pragmática* (2002), is an introduction to cultural studies in the context of Bahia.

DANIEL BALDERSTON is Professor of Latin American Literature at the University of Iowa. Recent publications include *Borges, realidad y simulacros* (2000) and *El deseo, enorme cicatriz luminosa: ensayos sobre homosexualidades latinoamericanas* (2004). He is also the co-editor of *Voice-Overs: Translation and Latin American Literature* (2002) and the *Encyclopedia of Latin American and Caribbean Literature, 1900–2003* (2004).

ROY C. BOLAND OSEGUEDA is Professor of Spanish in La Trobe University, Honorary Professor of Spanish in the University of Queensland, and Director of the Centre of Galician Studies of Australia. He has been Visiting Professor in many universities, including UCLA, Complutense, Santiago de Compostela, and Lund. He has published widely on Latin American literature and is the current editor of *Antipodas*, the Journal of Hispanic and Galician Studies of Australia and New Zealand. His most recent books are *Culture and Customs of El Salvador* (2001) and *Una rara comedia. Vision and revision de las novelas de Mario Vargas Llosa* (2003).

STEVEN BOLDY teaches at the University of Cambridge. He has published widely on Latin American narrative, including *The Novels of Julio Cortazar* (1980) and *The Narrative of Carlos Fuentes* (2002).

CATHERINE DAVIES is a Professor in the Department of Hispanic and Latin American Studies at the University of Nottingham. Her research addresses issues relating to cultural production, gender, and nationalism in Spain and Spanish America in the nineteenth and twentieth centuries. She is currently working on nineteenth-century Latin American literature and history, in particular the Wars of Independence, and is preparing gendered readings of independence discourse (the writings of Simón Bolívar and Andrés Bello among others). She is Director of the Arts and Humanities Research Board project "Gendering Latin American Independence" (2001–2006). Her numerous publications include the following books: *A Place in the Sun? Women Writers in Twentieth-Century Cuba* (1997), *Spanish Women's Writing* (1849–1996), ed. with Anny Brooksbank Jones (1998), *Latin American Women's Writing: Feminist Readings in Theory and Crisis* (1996).

MICHELLE CLAYTON is Assistant Professor of Comparative Literature, and Spanish and Portuguese at the University of California, Los Angeles. She has published several articles on modern Peruvian and Southern Cone writers and is currently preparing a manuscript on Cesar Vallejo's *Trilce*.

BRIAN GOLLNICK is Assistant Professor in the Department of Spanish and Portuguese at the University of Iowa, specializing in Mexican literature, regionalism, and subaltern studies. He has published several articles on contemporary Latin American Literature and Cultural Studies. His current research focuses on literature from the southern Mexican state of Chiapas.

STEPHEN HART is Professor of Hispanic Studies at University College London, England, and holds an honorary doctorate from the Universidad Nacional Mayor de San Marcos, Lima. He was recently awarded the "Orden al Merito por Servicios Distinguidos" by the Peruvian Government. He is co-editor of the Critical Guides series and commissioning editor of Tamesis. His main publications are *A Companion to Spanish American Literature* (1998), *Contemporary Latin American Cultural Studies* (2003), and *Cesar Vallejo: autografos olvidados* (2003). He is currently preparing a book on Latin American film.

JOHN KING is Professor of Latin American Cultural History at the University of Warwick. He has authored and edited some ten books on Latin American cinema, literature, and cultural history. His most recent publications include *Magical Reels: A History of Cinema in Latin America* (expanded edition, 2000) and *The Cambridge Companion to Modern Latin American Culture* (2004).

EFRAÍN KRISTAL is Professor of Spanish and Comparative Literature at UCLA. He is author of *The Andes Viewed from the City: Literary and Political Discourse on the Indian in Perú* (1987), *Temptation of the Word: The Novels of Mario Vargas Llosa* (1998), and *Invisible Work: Borges and Translation* (2002).

SUZANNE JILL LEVINE is a distinguished translator and Professor of Latin American Literature at the University of California in Santa Barbara. Her most recent book is a literary biography *Manuel Puig and the Spider Woman: His Life and Fictions* (2000), published in Spanish in 2002. Her other publications include an early study of *One Hundred Years of Solitude* (1975) and *The Subversive Scribe: Translating Latin American Fiction* (1991), as well as numerous essays, articles, chapters, interviews, reviews, and creative translations of major Latin American and Hispanic writers. Her honors include a Guggenheim Fellowship, the PEN Award for Career Achievement in Hispanic Studies, and several grants and fellowships from the National Endowment for the Arts and from the National Endowment for the Humanities.

NAOMI LINDSTROM is a Professor of Spanish and Portuguese and affiliated with Comparative Literature at the University of Texas at Austin. Her numerous publications include *The Social Conscience of Latin American Writing* (1998) and *Early Spanish American Narrative* (2004).

WILLIAM LUIS Professor of Spanish at Vanderbilt University, is the author of several books, including *Literary Bondage: Slavery in Cuban Narrative* (1990), *Dance Between Two Cultures: Latino Caribbean Literature Written in the United States* (1997), *Culture and Customs of Cuba* (2001), and *Lunes de Revolución: Literatura y cultura en los primeros años de la Revolución Cubana* (2003). He has held teaching positions at Dartmouth College, Washington University in St. Louis, SUNY Binghamton, and Yale University. Born and raised in New York City, he is widely regarded as a leading authority on Latin American, Caribbean, Afro-Hispanic, and Latino US literatures.

ISMAEL P. MÁRQUEZ is Professor and Chair of the Department of Spanish and Portuguese at the University of Wisconsin, Milwaukee. His research interests include Spanish American literature, Peruvian narrative, Andean narrative, and *indigenista* literature. He is author of *La retórica de la violencia en tres novelas peruanas* (1994) and of edited volumes on Julio Ramón Ribeyro, Alfredo Bryce Echenique, and Edgardo Rivera Mártinez.

MARTA PEIXOTO is Associate Professor in the Department of Spanish and Portuguese, New York University. In addition to several articles on Brazilian poetry and fiction, she has published two books: *Poesia com coisas: uma leitura de Joao Cabral de Melo Neto* (1983) and *Passionate Fictions: Gender, Narrative and Violence in Clarice Lispector* (1994), the latter forthcoming in Portuguese as *Ficcoes apaixonadas*.

PHILIP SWANSON is Professor of Hispanic Studies at the University of Sheffield, UK. He has published extensively on Latin American literature, including books on the New Novel, José Donoso, and Gabriel García Márquez. His most recent books are *Latin American Fiction: A Short Introduction* and the edited volume *The Companion to Latin American Studies*. He is currently completing a book on Isabel Allende. Professor Swanson has taught in a number of universities in Europe and the USA.

JOSÉ J. MARISTANY is the author of *Narraciones peligrosas: Resistencia y adhesión en las novelas del Proceso* (1999) and co-editor of several collections on Argentine literature and culture, as well as of the journal *Anclajes*. He teaches Argentine literature and literary theory at the Universidad Nacional de La Pampa and at the Instituto del Profesorado Joaquín V. González in Buenos Aires.

CLAIRE WILLIAMS is Lecturer in Portuguese and Brazilian Studies at the University of Liverpool. Her research has focused mainly on lusophone women's writing, particularly Clarice Lispector, Maria Gabriela Llansol, and Lília Momplé. Wider interests include storytelling and virtual orality, maternal genealogies, and literary representations of the Brazilian favela. Recent publications include the co-edited volume *Closer to the Wild Heart: Essays on Clarice Lispector* (Oxford: Legenda/European Humanities Research Council, 2002) and the forthcoming *The Encounter Between Opposites in the Works of Clarice Lispector* (2004). Dr. Williams is an assistant editor of the *Bulletin of Hispanic Studies* and vice-president of Women in Spanish, Portuguese, and Latin American Studies (WiSPS).

ACKNOWLEDGMENTS

I would like to express my gratitude to the contributors of this volume for their knowledge and insight. I would also like to thank Ray Ryan and Alison Powell at Cambridge University Press for their editorial guidance, and Jacqueline French for her sedulous, skillful copy-editing. A UCLA Faculty Senate Grant supported the project, as did the Institute for Advanced Study at La Trobe University in Australia, where I worked on the project as a Visiting Fellow. Carole Viers offered indispensable assistance with the final page-proof corrections. Special thanks to Romy Sutherland, John King, Deborah Cohn, Roy C. Boland Osegueda, Suzanne Jill Levine, Kelly Austin, Ryan Kernan, and José Luis Passos for their advice and support.

NOTE ON TRANSLATIONS

The titles of original works in the text are followed by an English translation in parentheses. Dates refer to the first publication unless indicated otherwise. A literal translation is provided in quotation marks for those works where no published translation is available. Quotations from original works are followed by the relevant page numbers of the cited edition and an English translation in parentheses. The corresponding page numbers of published translations are also given. Where translations are those of the individual contributors to this volume, this is noted in the text.

CHRONOLOGY

1810–28	Independence of most Latin American Nations with the exceptions of Cuba and Puerto Rico
1816	*El Periquillo Sarniento* (*The Itching Parrot*) by José Joaquín Fernández de Lizardi (Mexico, 1776–1827).
1823–72	Slavery is abolished with the exceptions of Cuba and Brazil
1841	*Sab* by Gertrudis Gómez de Avellaneda (Cuba, 1814–73)
1845	*Facundo* by Domingo Faustino Sarmiento (Argentina, 1811–88)
1846–48	Mexican–American War concluding with the annexation of California and other South Western states to the United States; Texas had already been annexed in 1845
1855	*Amalia* by José Marmol (Argentina, 1817–71)
1862	*Martín Rivas* by Alberto Blest Gana (Chile, 1830–1920)
1863	*La peregrinación de Bayoán* ("Bayoan's pilgrimage") by Eugenio María de Hostos (Puerto Rico, 1839–1903)
1865	*Iracema* by José de Alencar (Brazil, 1829–79)
1867	*María* by Jorge Isaacs (Colombia, 1837–95)
1879	*Cumandá* by Juan León de Mera (Ecuador, 1832–94)
1882	*Cecilia Valdés, o La loma del Angel* (*Cecilia Valdés, or Angel's Hill*) by Cirilio Villaverde (Cuba, 1812–94); *Enriquillo* (*The Cross and the Sword*) by Manuel de Jesús Galván (Dominican Republic, 1834–1910)
1886	Abolition of slavery in Cuba
1888	Abolition of slavery in Brazil
1889	Brazil becomes a Republic; *Aves sin nido* (*Birds without a Nest*) by Clorinda Matto de Turner (Peru, 1852–1909)
1898	Spanish American War; USA occupies Cuba and Puerto Rico
1899	*Dom Casmurro* by Joaquim Maria Machado de Assis (Brazil, 1839–1908)
1902	Cuban independence: *Os Sertões* (*Rebellion in the Backlands*) by Euclides da Cunha (Brazil, 1866–1909)

1903	The province of Panama breaks away from Colombia and becomes an independent nation with the support of the United States
1911–20	Mexican Revolution
1915	*Los de abajo* (*The Underdogs*) by Mariano Azuela (Mexico, 1873–1952)
1919	*Raza de bronce* ("Race of bronze") by Alcides Arguedas (Bolivia, 1879–1946)
1924	*La vorágine* (*The Vortex*) by José Eustasio Rivera (Colombia, 1889–1929)
1926	*Don Segundo Sombra* by Ricardo Güiraldes (Argentina, 1886–1927); the United States deploys troops in Nicaragua; resistance by Sandino will follow; Sandino will be assassinated in 1936
1928	*Macunaíma* by Mario de Andrade (Brazil, 1893–1945)
1929	*Doña Bárbara* by Rómulo Gallegos (Venezuela, 1884–1969)
1931	*Las lanzas coloradas* (*The Red Lances*) by Arturo Uslar Pietri (Venezuela, 1906–2001)
1932–35	The Chaco War between Bolivia and Paraguay
1934	*Huasipungo* (*The Villagers*) by Jorge Icaza (Ecuador, 1906–78)
1937	Getulio Vargas establishes an authoritarian regime in Brazil
1938	*Vidas secas* (*Barren Lives*) by Graciliano Ramos (Brazil, 1892–1953); *La amortajada* (*The Shrouded Woman*) by Maria Luisa Bombal (Chile, 1910–80; Mexican Government expropriates foreign oil companies
1941	*El mundo es ancho y ajeno* (*Broad and Alien is the World*) by Ciro Alegría (Peru, 1909–67); *El jardín de senderos que se bifurcan* ("The garden of forking paths") by Jorge Luis Borges (1899–1986)
1943	Military coup in Argentina sponsored by General Perón who will win the Argentine elections in 1946
1945	The Organization of American States is founded
1947	*Al filo del agua* (*The Edge of the Storm*) by Agustín Yáñez (Mexico, 1904–1980)
1948	Civil war in Colombia
1949	*Hombres de maíz* (*Men of Maize*) by Miguel Angel Asturias (Guatemala, 1899–1974); *El reino de este mundo* (*The Kingdom of this World*) by Alejo Carpentier (Cuba, 1904–80)
1950	*Vida breve* (*A Brief Life*) by Juan Carlos Onetti (Uruguay, 1909–94)

1952	Evita Perón dies; Puerto Rico becomes a "free associated state" of the United States
1955	*Pedro Páramo* by Juan Rulfo (Mexico, 1918–86)
1956	*Grande sertão: veredas* (*The Devil to Pay in the Backlands*) by João Guimarães Rosa (Brazil, 1908–67)
1958	*Los ríos profundos* (*Deep Rivers*) by José María Arguedas (Peru, 1911–69); *Balún Canán* (*The Nine Guardians*) by Rosario Castellanos (Mexico, 1925–74)
1959	Cuban Revolution
1961	Assassination of Trujillo after a thirty-year dictatorship of the Dominican Republic
1962	Cuban missile crisis; *La muerte de Artemio Cruz* (*The Death of Artemio Cruz*) by Carlos Fuentes (Mexico, b. 1929)
1963	*La ciudad y los perros* (*Time of the Hero*) by Mario Vargas Llosa (Peru, b. 1936); *Rayuela* (*Hopscotch*) by Julio Cortázar (Argentina, 1914–84)
1964	*A paixão segundo G. H.* (*The Passion According to G. H.*) by Clarice Lispector (Brazil, 1925–77)
1964–85	Brazil is ruled by a military dictatorship
1965	*Tres tristes tigres* (*Three Trapped Tigers*) by Guillermo Cabrera Infante (Cuba, b. 1929); US military intervention in the Dominican Republic
1966	*Paradiso* by José Lezama Lima (Cuba, 1910–76)
1967	Death of Che Guevara in Bolivia; Nobel Prize in literature awarded to Miguel Angel Asturias; *Cien años de soledad* (*One Hundred Years of Solitude*) by Gabriel García Márquez (Colombia, b. 1928); *Dona Flor e seus dois maridos* (*Dona Flor and Her Two Husbands*) by Jorge Amado (Brazil, 1912–2001); *Morirás lejos* (*You Will Die in a Distant Place*) by José Emilio Pacheco (Mexico, b. 1939)
1968	Tlatelolco massacre in Mexico
1968–80	Military government in Peru
1969	*Hasta no verte jesús mío* (*Here is to you Jesusa!*) by Elena Poniatowska (Mexico, b. 1932)
1970	*El obsceno pájaro de la noche* (*The Obscene Bird of the Night*) by José Donoso (Chile, 1924–96); *Un mundo para Julius* (*A World for Julius*) by Alfredo Bryce Echenique (Peru, b. 1939)
1971	Military coup led by General Banzer Suárez in Bolivia
1973–90	Military dictatorship in Chile led by General Augusto Pinochet
1974	*Yo el Supremo* (*I the Supreme*) by Augusto Roa Bastos (Paraguay, b. 1917)

1975   *Soñe que la nieve ardía* (*I Dreamt the Snow was Burning*) by
        Antonio Skármeta (Chile, b. 1940)
1976–83 Military dictatorship in Argentina
1976   *El beso de la mujer araña* (*The Kiss of the Spider Woman*) by
        Manuel Puig (Argentina, 1932–90); *Entre Marx y una mujer
        desnuda* (*Between Marx and a Naked Woman*) by Jorge E.
        Adoum (Ecuador, b. 1923); *La guaracha del macho Camacho*
        (*Macho Camacho's Beat*) by Luis Rafael Sánchez (Puerto Rico,
        b. 1936)
1977   *El último juego* ("The last game") by Gloria Guardia (Panama,
        b. 1940)
1979   Sandinistas overthrow Somoza dictatorship in Nicaragua;
        regime lasts until 1990
1980   Military repression in Guatemala resulting from guerrilla
        activity; *Respiración artificial* (*Artificial Respiration*) by Ricardo
        Piglia (Argentina, b. 1941); *La biografía difusa de Sombra
        Castañeda* ("The diffused biography of Sombra Castañeda") by
        Marcio Veloz Maggiolo (Dominican Republic, b. 1936)
1981   *La guerra del fin del mundo* (*The War of the End of the World*)
        by Mario Vargas Llosa; *En breve cárcel* (*Certificate of Absence*)
        by Sylvia Molloy (Argentina, b. 1938); *Las genealogías* (*The
        Family Tree*) by Margo Glantz (Mexico, b. 1930)
1982   *La casa de los espíritus* (*The House of the Spirits*) by Isabel
        Allende (Chile, b.1942); Nobel Prize in literature awarded to
        Gabriel García Márquez
1983   *Los perros del paraíso* (*The Dogs of Paradise*) by Abel Posse
        (Argentina, b. 1939); *Cola de Lagartija* (*Lizard's Tail*) by Luisa
        Valenzuela (Argentina, b. 1938)
1983   *Lumpérica* (*E. Luminata*) by Diamela Eltit (Chile, b. 1949)
1984   *A república dos sonhos* (*The Republic of Dreams*) by Nélida
        Piñón (Brazil b. 1936); *La nave de los locos* (*Ship of Fools*) by
        Cristina Peri Rossi (Uruguay, b. 1940)
1985   Democracy is restored in Argentina, Brazil, and Uruguay; five
        years later in Chile; this date signals to many the return to
        democracy in Latin American nations that had suffered
        dictatorships, and the rise of neo-liberal economic policies;
        Stella Manhattan by Silviano Santiago (Brazil, b. 1936)
1987   Oscar Arias plan for peace in Central America; on that same
        year the statesman from Costa Rica wins the Nobel Prize for
        Peace; *Maldito Amor* (*Sweet Diamond Dust*) by Rosario Ferré
        (Puerto Rico, b. 1938)

1988	*Domar a la divina garza* ("The taming of the divine stork") by Sergio Pitól (Mexico, b. 1933); *La mujer habitada* (*The Inhabited Woman*) by Gioconda Belli (Nicaragua, b. 1935)
1989	*El jaguar en llamas* ("The jaguar in flames") by Arturo Arias (Guatemala, b. 1950); *Relato de um certo oriente* (*The Three of the Seventh Heaven*) by Milton Hatoum (Brazil, b. 1950); *As horas nuas* (*Naked Hours*) by Lygia Fagundes Telles (Brazil, b. 1923)
1990	Mario Vargas Llosa is defeated by Alberto Fujimori in the Peruvian presidential elections
1991	*La liebre* ("The hare") by César Aira (Argentina, b. 1949)
1992	Nobel Peace Prize awarded to Rigoberta Menchú; *Doña Inés contra el olvido* (*Doña Inés Vs. Oblivion*) by Ana Teresa Torres (Venezuela, b. 1945)
1993	*La loca de Gandoca* ("The madwoman of Gandoca") by Ana Cristina Rossi (Costa Rica, b. 1952); *Madrugada: El Rey del Albor* ("Dawn: the king of Albor") by Julio Escoto (Honduras, b. 1946)
1994	Zapatista revolt begins in Chiapas (Mexico); *No se lo digas a nadie* (*Don't Tell Anyone*) by Jaime Bayly (Peru, b. 1965)
1995	*Santa Evita* by Tomás Eloy Martínez (Argentina, b. 1945)
1996	*Las rémoras* ("The obstacles") by Elroy Urroz (Mexico, b. 1967)
1997	*Café nostalgia* ("Nostalgia café") by Zoé Valdés (Cuba, b. 1959); *Cidade de Deus* ("City of God") by Paulo Lins (Brazil, b. 1958); *Cartilha do siléncio* ("Manual of silence") by Francisco J. C. Dantas (Brazil, b. 1941)
1998	*Aprendiendo a morir* ("Learning to die") by Alicia Yánez Cossío (Ecuador, b. 1928)
1999	*En busca de Klingsor* (*In search of Klingsor*) by Jorge Volpi, (Mexico, b. 1968); *Salón de Belleza* ("Beauty parlor") by Mario Bellatín (Peru/Mexico, b. 1960)
2000	President Vicente Fox is elected President of Mexico and for the first time since its foundation after the Mexican Revolution, the PRI ("Revolutionary Institutionalized Party") is defeated in Mexican election; *Sirena Selena vestida de pena* (*Sirena Selena*) by Mayra Santos-Febres (Puerto Rico, b. 1966)
2001	*La materia del deseo* (*Matter of Desire*) by Edmundo Paz Soldán (Bolivia, b. 1967); *Libro de mal amor* ("Book of bad love") by Fernando Iwasaki (Peru, b. 1961)

2002   *Sombras nada más* ("Nothing but shadows") by Sergio Ramírez
       (Nicaragua, b. 1942); *Dias e dias* ("Days and days") by Ana
       Maria Miranda (Brazil, b. 1951)
2003   *Las películas de mi vida* (*The Movies of my Life*) by Alberto
       Fuguet (Chile, b. 1964); *Budapest* by Chico Buarque (Brazil,
       b. 1944)
2004   *2666* by Roberto Bolaño (Chile, 1953–2003)

EFRAÍN KRISTAL

Introduction

The Latin American Novel encompasses a rich body of literary works written primarily in Spanish and Portuguese. Its main corpus is drawn principally from the over twenty Spanish-speaking countries of the Western Hemisphere and from Portuguese-speaking Brazil. The *Companion to the Latin American Novel* is intended to underscore literary contributions while offering a broad overview of the novel's history, and a sense of its heterogeneity, highlighting regions whose cultural and geopolitical particularities are often overlooked in general reference or introductory works. This volume should make it evident that there are as many commonalities and differences between Spanish- and Portuguese-language novels as between those of different regions and ethnic constituents in Latin America, and it includes women writers throughout while also recognizing the significance of the gender and sexuality approach which has become fundamental to many critics and literary historians. It also recognizes the growing interest in translation studies in Latin American literary and cultural studies.

On "Latin America"

The term "Latin America" has been controversial since it was first coined by the French to justify their colonial designs on the Western Hemisphere after the Napoleonic invasion of the Iberian Peninsula in 1807. It became useful, especially in the twentieth century, to group together historical, political, cultural, and artistic phenomena that cut across national boundaries.[1] The label is readily used today in the United States, the Commonwealth, France, and Germany, while in Spain there is a preference for the term *Hispano América* ("Spanish America") to single out literary works in the Spanish language. Outside Latin America, therefore, even specialists of national literatures – those who work primarily on Argentine or Mexican literature for instance – usually teach within the academic confines of the broader Spanish American or Latin American label at their institutions. It is not surprising, on the other hand, that in Spanish America and in Brazil, the local novel is primarily studied in the context of national literatures. That being said, the more inclusive approach – advocated by Emir Rodríguez Monegal, Angel Rama, Bella Jozef, Gerald Martin, Earl Fitz, Antonio Candido, and others – has gained considerable ground. In recent years universities in Argentina, Peru, Brazil, and elsewhere have begun to offer degrees in Latin American literature as an alternative to the study of their respective national literatures.

An essentialist view of "Latin America" would be as misguided as a view that rejects the label altogether. The notion of Latin America as a literary category has been constituted by unresolved tensions between nationalistic imperatives, political considerations, and personal preferences, as they play themselves out in academic institutions, journalism, and the publishing world. Even though the numerous approaches to the Latin American novel that abound – the esthetic, political, postmodern, gender, ethic, ethnic, culturalist, postcolonial, etc. – are not always reconcilable, there is a general agreement, all the same, regarding the benefits of studying the novel across national boundaries. An engagement with the Latin American label, of course, does not preclude the study of national or regional literatures. Most scholars of the Latin American novel move effortlessly from national to broader geographical or theoretical concerns, and there are good reasons to approach the same novel from more than one perspective and in different contexts. It is illuminating, for example, to read *Cien años de soledad* (*One Hundred Years of Solitude*, 1967) by Gabriel García Márquez, as Raymond Leslie Williams has proposed in *The Colombian Novel 1844–1987*, in the context of the historical and regional peculiarities of a nation.[2] This reading highlights the significance of García Márquez's novel as the culmination of a long tradition of writing in Colombia's Caribbean coast, and of the novelist's take on historical events addressed by other Colombian authors. But it is equally enriching, as Williams has also done in *The Twentieth-Century Spanish American Novel*, to read the works of García Márquez in the context of a literary moment in which the Peruvian Mario Vargas Llosa, the Mexican Carlos Fuentes, the Brazilian Clarice Lispector, and the Argentine Julio Cortázar are concurrently making substantial contributions.[3]

It is productive to think of the Latin American label as an umbrella for a process – involving ongoing debates and controversies – whereby pasts are invented and recovered as the various literary genres are rehearsed.[4] It was not until the twentieth century that the notion of Latin American literature was championed by Latin American intellectuals themselves, but as soon as it was, literary critics began looking back to the nineteenth century, and even to the Colonial past, for works of literature that might be construed as legitimate expressions of Latin America's literary heritage. The notion of literary continuity in Latin America can be misleading if one claims that every literary development led to every other one in a necessary causal chain, or even in a strict chronological sequence; but it would be just as misleading to ignore the fact that many novelists, including García Márquez, Vargas Llosa, Carlos Fuentes, Guimarães Rosa, Alejo Carpentier, Darcy Ribeiro, and Juán José Saer, willfully rewrote historical or anthropological works in the fiber of their novels to stress real, imagined, ironic, or playful continuities with the Spanish, Portuguese, indigenous, or African heritage of the heterogeneous populations that comprise their visions of Latin America. The typologies and concepts with which literary historians have organized their overviews have shifted and changed in the light of new kinds of novels and new critical approaches that have urged a reconsideration of the canon.

Indigenous and African cultures are prominently represented in the Latin American novel, and in the current scholarship there is an influential approach – pioneered by Angel Rama, Antonio Cornejo Polar, Regina Harrison, and others – in which novelists such as José María Arguedas in *Los ríos profundos* (*Deep Rivers*, 1958), Rosario Castellanos in *Balún Canán* (*The Nine Guardians*, 1958), and Miguel Angel Asturias in *Hombres de Maíz* (*Men of Maize*, 1949), are understood as "translators" of indigenous cultures. This approach is represented in several places in the *Companion*, especially in the essays devoted to the regional novel, the Andean novel, the Caribbean novel, the Brazilian novel, and the Central American novel.

A note on the significance of Brazil

Many accounts of the Latin American novel either exclude Brazil (as with Stephen Hart's useful and informed *A Companion to Spanish-American Literature*) or include it in a separate section (as with the monumental *The Cambridge History of Latin American Literature* edited by Roberto González Echevarría and Enrique Pupo Walker).[5] The main barrier to the smooth incorporation of the Brazilian novel in general studies of Latin American literature is linguistic. And yet, the unique historical events that shaped the Brazilian nation, its cultural peculiarities, and the fact that its literature is written in Portuguese rather than Spanish, hardly justify excluding the Brazilian narrative from a study of the commonalities of the Latin American novel. The historical and cultural differences between any two Spanish American nations can be just as great or even greater; and Brazil's commonalities with certain Spanish American regions can be illuminating. Given the shared heritage of slavery, for example, the literatures of the Caribbean may have more in common with Brazil than with Chile.

It should be of interest to any reader of the Latin American novel to learn that the Brazilian South (and not just the Argentine or Uruguayan Pampas) had a tradition of literary works featuring the gaucho, including *O gaúcho* ("The gaucho," 1870), a novel by José de Alencar, Brazil's premier Romantic novelist. Brazilian novels that feature distinct regional landscapes can be fruitfully studied next to Spanish American novels that do the same. Writers like Jorge Amado, who shared a similar kind of commercial and literary success as his Spanish American counterparts in the 1960s, can offer an eye-opening perspective on the period in which the Latin American novel came into world prominence. It should be interesting to readers of the *Companion* to notice that in Brazil – as in the Caribbean, Central America, and the Andean region – African and indigenous themes, cultures, and literatures play a considerable role in the novel. Any study on gender theory and on queer studies in Latin America will certainly be enriched by taking into account both Brazilian and Spanish American texts. Finally, any account of the Latin American novel in English translation should cover both Brazilian and Spanish American novels. Indeed, publishers in the USA and the UK include Brazilian and Spanish American titles in their Latin American lists as a matter of course.

Notwithstanding the commonalities, the Brazilian novel is also informed by distinct phenomena that require separate treatment: unlike Spanish America, Brazil was the seat of an empire (when the Portuguese court moved to Rio de Janeiro after the Napoleonic invasion of the Iberian Peninsula); unlike Spanish America, Brazil became a monarchy on seceding from the Portuguese Crown; and unlike Spanish America, the transition from aristocratic to Republican rule took place without a war of independence. These historical events inform themes, events, and even literary structures in Brazil. If a masterplot of the Spanish American novel involves the brother–sister incest motif, an equivalent masterplot in the Brazilian novel is the absent father motif.[6] Brazil also developed some distinct literary phenomena that do not have counterparts in Spanish America such as a peculiar brand of Romanticism with indigenous themes, its own brand of modernism, or narratives in which national identity is represented as a fusion of European, African, and indigenous cultures and ethnicities.

Historical overview

Hundreds of novels have been published in Latin America since the early nineteenth century, when the ban against the Romance of Chivalry and other secular narrative genres was first loosened, and finally abolished, by virtue of independence from Spain and Portugal. That being said, there are important narrative works published before the Republican periods of Spanish America and Brazil that can be studied as antecedents to the Latin American novel. Indeed, a number of major works from the Colonial period have been read as novels, at least in part, even though they were not written as such.[7]

In the nineteenth century most Latin American novelists, from José Marmol in Argentina and Alencar in Brazil to Clorinda Matto de Turner in Peru, wrote with the awareness that their novels would contribute to establishing their respective national literatures, and with openly acknowledged feelings of inferiority regarding the European novel. Two exceptions are the Colombian Jorge Isaacs, and the Brazilian Joaquim Maria Machado de Assis. Isaacs's *María* (1867), a precursor to Gabriel García Márquez's *Cien años de soledad*, was the only Latin American novel in the nineteenth century to gain a sizeable reading public beyond its national boundaries. The saga of two chaste star-crossed lovers, set in the agricultural heartland of Colombia, was edited many times, and acclaimed both in Spanish America and in Spain. Machado de Assis, the grandson of freed slaves, is another exception, not because he was well known outside Brazil, but because of his extraordinary literary qualities which set him apart as the only world-class nineteenth-century Latin American novelist. He was recognized as a force in Brazilian literature from the outset, but it took over a century before he was acknowledged as a writer of international stature. In recent years he has been celebrated by prominent intellectuals including Susan Sontag, Jorge Edwards, Roberto Schwarz, and Carlos Fuentes.

The nineteenth century did produce classic novels within national contexts. *Cecilia Valdés, o La Loma del Angel* (*Cecilia Valdes, or Angel's Hill*, 1882) by the Cuban Cirilio Villaverde, *Iracema* (1865) by the Brazilian Alencar, *Enriquillo* (*The Cross and the Sword*, 1882) by the Dominican Galván, *Aves sin nido* (*Birds Without a Nest*, 1889) by the Peruvian Clorinda Matto de Turner, *Cumandá* (1979) by the Ecuadorian Juan León de Mera, and *La peregrinación de Bayoán* ("Bayoan's pilgrimage," 1863) by the Puerto Rican Eugenio María de Hostos are examples of works that continue to be read by school children in their respective nations today.

In the 1920s, with an upsurge of novels exploring regional themes and local customs, it became possible, for some critics and observers, to begin to discuss the Latin American novel as a meaningful concept. It is worth noting, however, that the first major literary history devoted to the Spanish American novel, written by Fernando Alegría, was not published until 1959.[8] Before the first histories of the Latin American novel were written, therefore, the regional novelists believed they were making original contributions to literature by depicting geographical regions, ways of life, and social predicaments germane to Latin America, never before explored in literary works. Jean Franco generalized this rational for the originality of Latin American literature in her early books – which introduced the history of Latin American literature to the English-speaking world – as perhaps its most distinguishing feature.[9] The regional novel proper left indelible visions of the landscape on the Latin American imagination, whether in the depiction of the Amazonian jungle in José Eustasio Rivera's *La vorágine* (*The Vortex*, 1924), the endless and rugged plains of Venezuela in Rómulo Gallegos's *Doña Bárbara* (1929), the Brazilian backlands (known as the sertão) in Graciliano Ramos's *Vidas secas* (*Barren Lives*, 1928), the Argentine Pampas as the home of the gaucho in Ricardo Guiraldes's *Don Segundo Sombra* (1926).

Even though they shared similar concerns, the regional novelists did not write with a sense of collective purpose. It was the pioneering Puerto Rican literary critic, Concha Meléndez, who recognized the significance of the regional novel in retrospect. The label "regional" was reconsidered by some literary critics to accommodate works such as Mariano Azuela's *Los de abajo* (*The Underdogs*, 1915), set in harsh terrains during the Mexican Revolution, or Ciro Alegría's *El mundo es ancho y ajeno* (*Broad and Alien is the World*, 1941), set in the Peruvian Andes.[10] Even as the regional novel gained prominence in Latin America as its most representative contribution to literature, many writers, such as Juan Carlos Onetti in Uruguay and Martín Adán in Peru, were producing a kind of experimental novel whose significance was not recognized in its own time.[11]

Before the 1960s, the Latin American novel was considered a marginal literary expression. Latin American poetry, on the other hand, had not been banned during the Iberian Colonial period, and had been in the limelight since the beginning of the twentieth century. Remarkable poets such as Rubén Darío, Pablo Neruda, Octavio Paz, Carlos Drummond de Andrade, Gabriela Mistral, and César Vallejo had received the sort of international recognition which had eluded even the most locally prominent of Latin American novelists. With few exceptions, therefore, Latin American novelists wrote for national audiences even when writing against the nationalistic grain; and few Latin American novels found an audience beyond their own national borders. The situation changed dramatically in the 1960s when Gabriel García Márquez, Carlos Fuentes, Julio Cortázar, Mario Vargas Llosa, Guillermo Cabrera Infante, and José Donoso burst onto the international literary scene. Inspired as much by Joyce, Woolf, Mann, Conrad, Faulkner, and Proust as they were by the Cuban Revolution, many of the greatest exponents of the new Latin American novel wrote convinced that their narrative fiction had come of age artistically, and was poised to play a role in the social and political transformation of the Western Hemisphere. These European-based writers knew each other, read each other's manuscripts, and wrote essays about each other's novels with a sense of common purpose. They even mentioned each other and included one another's characters in their novels. Their self-confidence was accompanied by an unprecedented level of critical and popular success that made it possible, for the first time, to think of a Latin American novelist as a world-class writer who could measure up to or surpass the greatest contemporary exponents of the genre in literary quality and commercial reach.[12] After influential books by Emir Rodríguez Monegal and José Donoso, these writers came to be known as the novelists of "the Boom," a term suggesting both an explosion in literary riches and an economic phenomenon of unprecedented proportions for any literary genre in Latin America.

Julio Cortázar wrote a sophisticated brand of novel that challenged the generic conventions of narrative fiction, and even the assumptions regarding the way a reader may progress from one chapter to the next.[13] In *Rayuela* (*Hopscotch*, 1963), considered by many to be the most experimental of all Latin American novels, Cortázar invites readers to jump from one chapter to another according to alternative schemes that produce different readings of the same work. Cortázar also engaged in a subtle dialogue with surrealism, existentialism, the musical forms of jazz, and the Western fascination with oriental philosophy.

Gabriel García Márquez, Mario Vargas Llosa, and Carlos Fuentes expanded the possibilities of Faulknerian techniques in novels where spatial and chronological planes are superimposed, where a single story can be narrated from various contradictory points of view, and where mystery and intrigue depend not only on the plot but also on intentional ambiguity, and on the fact that information may be concealed from the reader. This arsenal of technical refinement allowed for some of the most memorable depictions of social conflict, in settings as distinct as the Amazonian jungle in Vargas Llosa's *La casa verde* (*The Green House*, 1964), the Mexican Revolution in Fuentes's *La muerte de Artemio Cruz* (*The Death of Artemio Cruz*, 1963), or the invented region of Macondo in the novels of García Márquez, where the commonplace has the feel of the extraordinary and the fantastic the feel of the ordinary.

José Donoso wrote novels in which the everyday was transformed into grotesque and even nightmarish worlds, as he explored the decline of Latin American aristocracies with a Proustian sensibility, and the rise of contemporary dictatorial regimes with bitter detachment. *Casa de campo* (*A House in the Country*, 1978), for example, is an oblique allegory about Pinochet's dictatorship in the guise of a rewriting of William Golding's *Lord of the Flies* (1954).

Most of the first accounts of the Boom were generated by the novelists themselves. They tended to agree with the prevailing critical views that disparaged their predecessors, especially the regional novelists. It must be said, however, that the Boom novelists went to great personal lengths to recognize some writers of quality or cultural significance who had been widely ignored outside their national contexts. It is worth noting therefore that, by and large, the most important writers of narrative fiction before the Boom gained their international acclaim only in the afterglow of the Boom. Among these writers one could cite Jorge Luis Borges, Alejo Carpentier, Guimarães Rosa, José María Arguedas, Juan Rulfo, and Juan Carlos Onetti who were admired in their respective countries, but overlooked elsewhere except in rarified contexts.

Borges never wrote a novel, and yet he had a transforming effect on the way the Spanish American novel was written.[14] Years before his international fame, he was a writer's writer. Borges was studiously read by many who followed in his footsteps, introducing fantastic touches, irony, philosophical ideas, technical sophistication, literary self-reflection, and a mixing of genres, many of which he was personally responsible for introducing to a wide reading public (Borges was the editor of the pioneering and most influential anthologies of fantastic and detective fiction in Spanish America). Borges also raised the once rhetorical, stylized prose of Latin American narrative fiction to standards that are yet to be surpassed. García Márquez famously acknowledged that despite loathing Borges's political views, he read him every night.

Borges's fictions were not focused on the historical and political predicaments of Latin America in ways García Márquez could have appreciated, but the same cannot be said of the Mexican Juan Rulfo. His *Pedro Páramo* (1955) is considered by many critics and writers to be a landmark of the Spanish American novel due to its disarming pathos, technical sophistication, mythological underpinnings, persuasive mixture of realistic and otherworldly elements, psychological insights, and relevance as a work of social criticism. The tale of an illegitimate son seeking his father across a devastated landscape in the wake of the Mexican Revolution was hailed by a poll of literary critics in the Spanish newspaper *El País* as the most important book (not just a novel) written in the Spanish language in the twentieth century.[15]

The Cuban Alejo Carpentier, a premier novelist of Latin America, was responsible for the exploration of the apparently fantastic elements in Latin American reality.[16] He was masterful in handling narrative time to suggest the simultaneity of contradictory experiences. He pioneered the mode of writing fiction that came to be known as "magical realism." Carpentier did not coin the term as such but did identify the concept in the original prologue to his novel *El reino de este mundo* (*The Kingdom of this World*, 1949).[17] The novel depicts the slave revolts that ushered in Haiti's independence, in such a way that historical events often feel like wild imaginings. The prologue is considered a manifesto for a phenomenon Carpentier identified as "*lo real maravilloso*" ("the marvelous real"): Latin America as a place where the real has the feel of the marvelous. Inspired by his ideas, and using his novels as prime examples, other literary critics used the term "magical realism" to suggest either a peculiar Latin American sensibility to realism, or the sense that Latin American reality seems fantastic to those who see it with the conventions of other lands. Today the term has been rejected by many Latin Americans, and by some postcolonial critics, as the internalization of demeaning exoticizing tendencies by Third World writers. It has also been questioned, and even parodied, by a new breed of novelists, including the Chilean Alberto Fuguet and the Bolivian Edmundo Paz Soldán, for whom the realities of Latin America in a globalized world ought not to be taken as exotic or extravagant. The characters in their novels include worldly cosmopolitan denizens of the polluted and overcrowded Latin American cities: they are often travelers or expatriates well versed in more than one language, in popular culture, and in the new technologies. That being said, "magical realism" remains a label with significance to many, and it is still the most distinctive term applied to the Latin American novel. Writers from Salman Rushdie to John Updike have underscored magical realism as a distinct contribution by Latin American authors to the contemporary literary idiom; and Fredric Jameson has argued that this literary mode broke new ground, making it possible to reintroduce historical considerations into the world-novel after an impasse brought about by the modernist aesthetic framework with its emphasis on heightened subjectivism.

After the initial "Boom," a second wave of worldwide interest in the Latin American novel was generated, almost single-handedly at first, by Isabel Allende whose critical and commercial success opened the way for the recognition of women writers. The interest in contemporary writing by women was due in part to the literary quality achieved by writers such as Clarice Lispector from Brazil, Elena Poniatowska from Mexico, and Rosario Ferré from Puerto Rico; but also by the scholarship of feminist critics who have unearthed many works of consequence by unrecognized or underappreciated female writers. Many women writers of the recent past, such as María Luisa Bombal from Chile and Rosario Castellanos from Mexico, are now standard reading in courses of Latin American literature. Critics have also been underscoring forgotten contributions by many women novelists of the nineteenth century, such as the Argentine Juana Manuela Gorriti and the Peruvian Mercedes Cabello de Carbonera. The latter's *El conspirador*

("The conspirator," 1892) was probably the first novel about a Latin American dictator, a theme that has inspired major novels including Miguel Angel Asturias's *El Señor Presidente* (1946), García Márquez's *El otoño del patriarca* (*The Autumn of the Patriarch*, 1975), the Paraguayan Augusto Roa Bastos's *Yo el Supremo* (*I, the Supreme*, 1974), and Vargas Llosa's *La fiesta del Chivo* (*The Feast of the Goat*, 2000). All fictional depictions of the Latin American "strong-man," it must be noted, have an important antecedent in Domingo Faustino Sarmiento's *Facundo* (1845), a work written as a sociological treatise. Its depiction of the brutal life and pathetic solitude of a dying despot has become a prominent staple of Latin American narrative fiction until today; and even novels that mix personal and political intrigue – such as Edmundo Paz Soldán's *La material del deseo* (*Matter of Desire*, 2002) about the political coming of age of a young Bolivian who has to come to terms with the Hugo Banzer Suárez dictatorship, or Alonso Cueto's *Grandes Miradas* ("Lofty gazes," 2003), a novel exploring the dilemmas of a judge caught in the miasma of Alberto Fujimori's regime in Peru – owe an indirect debt to the Argentine classic.

By the time the significance of women writers was recognized, the relative sense of collective purpose shared by the writers of the Boom had become diffused. The harmonious relationship of these writers with each other, and with the Cuban Revolution, was irreparably damaged in the aftermath of a controversy that followed the 1971 incarceration, and subsequent public humiliation, of the Cuban poet Heberto Padilla.[18] Vargas Llosa, Fuentes, García Márquez, and many others deplored the fate of the poet, but some were reluctant to embarrass the Cuban regime by making public their dissatisfaction. As a result of the controversy, Cuban cultural institutions and literary journals reconsidered their enthusiasm for the Boom novel and began to promote a kind of testimonial novel based on interviews with the exploited peoples of America. Roberto Fernández Retamar's essay *Caliban* constituted the manifesto of this proposal, and Miguel Barnet's *Biografía de un Cimarrón* (*Esteban Montejo: Biography of a Runaway Slave*, 1966) – based on taped interviews with the protagonist of the book – became its model. Rather than displacing the more imaginative Latin American novel, the novel of testimony extended the range of possibilities open to Latin American writers.

The rift between the cultural leaders of the Cuban Revolution and some of the Boom writers generated divergent literary responses which coincided with the ambition of other novelists to explore new possibilities. Donald Shaw points to Antonio Skármeta's *Soñe que la nieve ardía* (*I Dreamt the Snow Was Burning*, 1975) as a novel that signals a departure from a Boom to a Post-Boom esthetic.[19] Shaw has also argued that it is no longer possible to privilege any single dominant tendency. Indeed, since the 1980s the concerns of the Latin American novel have amplified to a dizzying degree. It is no longer as persuasive (as it was in the 1960s for the Boom writers) to produce manifestos purporting to encompass the concerns of an entire generation of Latin American novelists. No single manifesto could cover the testimonial novels of Elena Poniatowska, the fictional biography by Tomás Eloy Martínez; the fusion of cinematic discourse and the novel of Manuel Puig and Rubem Fonseca; the melding of magical realism with gastronomy in Laura Esquivel's *Como agua para chocolate* (*Like Water for Chocolate*, 1989), or with cyberspace in Zoé Valdés's *Café nostalgia* (1997); the anti-historical historical novels of Ana Teresa Torres, Fernando del Paso, and Moacyr Scliar; the humorous novels of social parody and self-irony by Alfredo Bryce Echenique; the Slavic-inspired carnavalesque tour de force by the vastly underrated Sergio Pitól in *Domar a la divina garza* ("Taming the divine stork," 1988); the Germanic novels by José Emilio Pacheco, Ignacio Padilla, and Jorge Volpi; or the recent trend in Brazil to write novels set in non-Brazilian settings including Chico Buarque's *Budapest* (2003). Writers such as Edgardo Rivera Martínez in Peru are revitalizing the Andean novel with informed nods to psychoanalytical thinking, while Ricardo Piglia and others have been intentionally blurring the boundaries between fiction, historical discourse, philosophical biography, journalistic accounts, and other nonfictional genres. As a counter statement to the literary trends inspired by poststructuralism, Jorge Volpi has added a measure of humor and irony to his explorations of European culture in *El fin de la locura* ("The end of madness," 2003), a satirical novel about the engagements of a Mexican psychoanalyst with politics and the ideas of French master thinkers including Lacan, Foucault, and Althusser. Meanwhile several writers consecrated in the 1960s continue to publish vigorously. Carlos Fuentes has been reorganizing his novels and publishing new ones according to a grand literary scheme called *La edad del tiempo* ("The age of time") intended to rival Balzac's *Comédie humaine*; and Mario Vargas Llosa has continued to alternate between ambitious political statements in novels such as *The Feast of the Goat* and his ongoing dialogues between narrative fiction and the visual arts in *El paraíso en la otra esquina* (*The Way to Paradise*, 2003).

Clearly, the most salient development in recent years is the central place that women writers, such as Diamela Eltit and Nélida Piñón, now occupy in the panorama of Latin American literature. Not too long ago it was common to read entire books about the Latin American novel without mention of a single female author. Today this is no longer the case, but it is also not possible to pigeonhole the contribution of women writers. Their output is vast, and their works range from fictional biographies and historical novels to the ironic self-reflexive text.

Another development of interest to students of the Latin American novel is the growing number of writers as grounded in the culture of the United States as in their own. A number of novels that highlight the experience of Latin Americans in the United States have been published in Spanish or Portuguese including Silviano Santiago's *Stella Manhattan* (1985) and Alberto Fuguet's *Las películas de mi vida* (*The Movies of my Life*, 2003). There is also a growing number of novels written in English by Latino writers engaged, as William Luis has put it in a pioneering book, in a "dance between two cultures."[20] The novels of Julia Alvarez, Oscar Hijuelos, and Cristina García are examples of this trend.

The work of Lois Parkinson, Doris Sommer, Earl Fitz, Djelal Kadir, and Debborah Cohn is emblematic of a related direction in scholarship which aims to study the literature of the Americas in ways that relate several languages and regions. Literary critics have been attempting to find productive ways to engage the works of writers from North and South America, those of Spanish America with Brazil (as we are attempting to do in this *Companion*), and to explore the literatures of the Caribbean in English, Spanish, and French.

In recent years scholars have been revisiting novels once regarded as minor or insignificant, and rereading nonfictional works as products of the literary imagination. They have also been rethinking the Latin American novel in terms of approaches to literature such as postmodernism, queer theory, and hybridity studies. In this climate, a general picture of the history of the Latin American novel has emerged in which the novels of the nineteenth century are being reread for new insights into the cultural history of the hemisphere; the regional novel has gained in the estimation of prominent critics; the Boom novel is seen as a closed chapter that opened the way to many developments as yet not fully assessed.[21] Some scholars who once directed their attention primarily to literary analysis have shifted their interest towards the concerns of media, cultural, and postcolonial studies, no longer giving pride of place to the novel, and yet the number of novels published in Latin America is greater today than at any other period in the history of the genre.[22]

Organization of the *Companion*

This collective work aims to acknowledge the commonalties, heterogeneity, and diversity of the Latin American novel while offering close readings of some representative works. The contributors represent a cross-section of scholars at various stages in their careers. They have been chosen for their capacity to offer informed and original perspectives.

"History," the first section of the *Companion*, offers an overview of seminal developments and turning points in the Latin American novel from the beginning of the nineteenth century until the present: the nineteenth-century novel; the regional novel; the Boom novel; and the Post-Boom novel. The first essay by Naomi Lindstrom covers the rise of national literatures, including the social and historical concerns of the most salient nineteenth-century novels. This essay address works considered classics in the context of national literatures, and accounts for new directions of research in nineteenth-century Latin American literary studies. Brian Gollnick's essay on the regional novel covers a body of literature published mostly in the 1920s and 1930s, which gave considerable attention to human and social dramas informed by distinct geographical regions. These works include literary explorations of the Amazonian jungle, the Brazilian backlands, the Venezuelan plains, the Argentine Pampas, and the rough Mexican terrains during its revolutionary period. The third essay by John King covers the advent of the Boom novel, whose major exponents include García Márquez, Jorge Amado, Carlos Fuentes, José Donoso, Julio Cortázar, and Mario Vargas Llosa. The essay explores the range and depth of their contributions to literature, their political concerns, their fictional depictions of Latin America's social predicaments, their innovative literary techniques, and their literary engagements with history, myth, popular culture, and intellectual history. The final essay in the historical section, by Philip Swanson, covers the novel of the Post-Boom. It follows the trajectories of a number of writers who gained notoriety in the period of the Boom while exploring more recent developments including the prominence of Latin American women writers, the New Historical novel, and the advent of postmodern constituencies.

"Heterogeneity," the second section of the volume, explores some regions not usually covered in histories of Latin American literature. It addresses issues of ethnicity, pays special attention to pre- and non-European traditions, and to the fruitful dialogue between the novel and developments in the anthropology and the heritage of non-Western populations. Writers of African descent are covered in the sections on Brazil, the Caribbean, and Central America, and the significance of the indigenous populations in the sections on the Andes, Brazil, and Central America.

The essay on the Brazilian novel by Piers Armstrong concentrates on Brazil's multicultural heritage across distinct sociopolitical regions. It addresses Brazil's history, and its unique expressions of African and indigenous cultures. The essay accounts for literary movements unique to Brazil, including its distinct concept of modernism, whose most representative expression is found in Mario de Andrade's *Macunaíma* (1928). William Luis's essay on the Caribbean novel focuses on the literatures of Cuba,

Puerto Rico, and the Dominican Republic but suggests themes and issues that have a bearing on the literature of other Caribbean nations such as Venezuela and Colombia. The Caribbean was the focal point of slave trade to Spanish America. Along with Brazil it is, therefore, a privileged vantage point from which to explore the African contribution to the Latin American novel. The Caribbean was historically an area of rich exchange, flow, and conflict between several European powers, the United States, Africa, and the New World. This complex historical situation might explain in part why notions such as magical realism and the Latin American baroque were first developed there. Ismael Márquez's essay on the Andean region pays special attention to the literatures of Peru, Bolivia, and Ecuador. It underscores the many attempts by novelists to engage the novel with the culture, predicaments, and even language of the Quechua, Guaraní, and Aymara indigenous populations. The core of this essay is a study of literary *indigenismo*, a corpus of novels exploring the cultural and social situation of the indigenous populations from both political and anthropological perspectives.[23] The essay explores the attempts of novelists to incorporate non-Western elements of Latin American culture into the novel, including indigenous literary traditions. It also investigates the rise of urban literatures in the context of mass migration of indigenous and *mestizo* populations from rural areas into the milieus of the city.

Roy C. Boland Osegueda's piece on the Central American novel concentrates on the literatures of Nicaragua, Guatemala, Honduras, El Salvador, Panamá, and Costa Rica. Its centerpiece is an analysis of Miguel Angel Asturias, the first Latin American novelist awarded a Nobel prize. Asturias is lauded for his explorations of Guatemala's Mesoamerican roots, the contemporary Maya Quiché populations, and Central American dictators. The essay addresses the literary representation of the Mesoamerican indigenous populations and explores the representation of civil wars, dictatorships, and revolution, including the role of literature in the political history of the region. The essay covers the novels of insurgence by the Salvadorian Manlio Argueta; the peculiar blend of lyrical magical realism and politics in the novels of the Nicaraguan Sergio Ramírez; and the relevance of the peace activist Rigoberta Menchú for students of Latin American fiction.

"Gender and sexuality," the third section of the book, is intended to explore a dimension that has engaged literary scholars since the rise of feminism in Latin American literary studies. In her essay, Catherine Davies summarizes an approach to reassess the Latin American novelistic canon from the perspective of gender studies, while acknowledging a new academic climate in which the contributions of women novelists and literary critics have moved from the periphery to the center of literary studies. Davies explores the feminist critique of Latin American patriarchy, and the constructions and deconstructions of the gendered subject in the novel. The piece by Daniel Balderston and José Maristany on the "Lesbian and gay novel" is a carefully documented account of a corpus which has enriched the panorama of the Latin American novel. Partly as a result of developments in both social movements of liberation, and the rise of gender and queer studies in academia, the contributions by lesbian and gay novelists are taking on an increasingly prominent role. They have challenged homophobic stereotypes in *machista* societies and produced some of the most compelling novels of the last forty years, including Manuel Puig's *El beso de la mujer araña* (*The Kiss of the Spider Woman*, 1976) and Reinaldo Arenas's parodic subversion of Cuban literary classics. The Uruguayan Cristina Peri Rossi and the Argentine Sylvia Molloy have broken new ground exploring lesbian desire in novels that undermine the distinctions between sexuality, writing, and the body. Innovative literary critics have also been "queering" the Latin American novel, offering readings of novels whose engagements with sexuality had been previously overlooked.[24]

After exploring historical, regional, and gender issues, the *Companion* includes close readings and detailed analysis of six works widely considered among the most seminal or representative Latin America novels. Marta Peixoto explores Machado de Assis's *Dom Casmurro* (1899), a tale of jealousy and ambiguous self-delusion. It has been read as an historical parable, as a shrewd rewriting of Shakespeare's *Othello* and Sterne's *Tristram Shandy*, and as a postmodern novel *avant la lettre*. Major books have been dedicated to this single novel in Brazil and abroad, and one can trace important developments in the critical approaches to the novel by studying the critical responses to this novel over the last century. Jason Wilson offers a reading of *Pedro Páramo* by Juan Rulfo. The tale of an illegitimate son in search of his father, from the world of the living into the world of the dead, is a searching exploration, without sentimentalism, of a rural people in the aftermath of the Mexican Revolution, only indirectly mentioned in the novel. Stephen Boldy offers a fresh reading of *Cien años de soledad* by Gabriel García Márquez. The single most famous and bestselling Latin American novel of all time explores the saga of the Buendía family in the imaginary city of Macondo, a microcosm of Colombian and, indeed, Latin American history. Stephen Hart analyzes *La casa de los espíritus* (*The House of the Spirits*, 1982), the breakthrough novel by Isabel Allende, which adopts some of García Márquez's literary structures while subverting his sexist bias by introducing both a feminine point of view and feminine concerns. Allende's novel moves beyond magical realism by incorporating sections of journalistic prose that foreground the immediacy of unfolding historical events. Michelle Clayton offers a critical interpretation of Mario Vargas Llosa's *La guerra del fin del mundo* (*The War of the End of the World*, 1981), considered by Ángel Rama as the only novel in a position to challenge García Márquez's *Cien años de soledad* for its fusion of popular and literary art.[25] It is an historical novel set in Brazil at the end of the nineteenth century, a novel that makes a statement akin to the one we are trying to put forward in this volume, for in it, the historical and cultural traditions of Brazil become one with those of Spanish America. Claire Williams offers a sensitive reading of Clarice Lispector's *A paixão segundo G. H.* (*The Passion according to G. H.*, 1964), one of the most probing novels of human consciousness in Latin America: a novel that explores the unbearable dilemma between social conformity that annihilates individuality, or individuality condemned to shattering solitude; its literary and philosophical complexities have inspired major critics and theorists alike.

The volume concludes with Suzanne Jill Levine's essay on the Latin American novel in English translation. Levine, a literary scholar and one of the most distinguished translators of Latin American literature, explores the history and role of translation in the reception of the Latin American novel in the English-speaking world. She discusses the criteria with which some novels have been translated and others have not, as well as the ways in which translators have often adjusted the tone and connotations of works for their Anglo-American readerships.

Conclusion

There is a consensus within and beyond Latin America that the study of national literatures can be enriched by an understanding of the similarities and differences among Latin American nations. This collective work does not mean to be comprehensive – the length of the *Companion* would simply not allow it – but it aims to offer several entryways into the understanding and appreciation of the Latin American novel in both the Spanish- and the Portuguese-speaking realms.

NOTES

1. On "Latin America" as a literary category see Elzbieta Sklodowska, "Latin American Literatures," in Philip Swanson (ed.), *The Companion to Latin American Studies* (Oxford University Press, 2003), pp. 86–106. For an historical context to situate the Latin American novel, the best place to start is Edwin Williamson's *Penguin History of Latin America* (London: Penguin Books, 1992).

2. Raymond Leslie Williams, *The Colombian Novel 1844–1987* (Austin: University of Texas Press, 1991).
3. Raymond Leslie Williams, *The Twentieth Century Spanish American Novel* (Austin: University of Texas Press, 2003). Even though Williams's primary focus is on Spanish language novels, there are many moments in his analysis where it becomes quite natural to focus on Brazil, as when he discusses the work of Lispector along with her Spanish American counterparts. He is not alone in this move. The Larousse dictionary of Spanish American writers, for example, includes entries on Guimarães Rosa, Machado de Assis, and other Brazilian authors. See *Diccionario de escritores hispanoamericanos*, ed. Aarón Alboukred and Esther Herrera (Buenos Aires: Larousse, 1992).
4. Efraín Kristal, "The Degree Zero of Spanish-American Cultural History and the Role of Native Populations in the Formation of Pre-Independence National Pasts," *Poetics Today* 15, 4 (Winter 1994): 587–603.
5. An indispensable history of twentieth-century Latin American narrative fiction which integrates Brazilian and Spanish American novels is Gerald Martin's *Journeys through the Labyrinth: Latin American Fiction in the Twentieth Century* (London and New York: Verso, 1989).
6. I thank José Luiz Passos for the observation regarding the import of the absent father motif in Brazilian narrative. For the significance of the brother–sister motif in Spanish American narrative, see Efraín Kristal, "The Incest Motif in Narratives of the United States and Spanish America," in Udo Schöning (ed.) *Internationalität nationaler Literaturen* (Göttingen: Wallestein Verlag, 2000), pp. 390–403.
7. Enrique Pupo Walker has made a compelling case for exploring the development of Spanish American narrative fiction in connection to major historical works of the Colonial period in his book *La vocación literaria del pensamiento histórico en América. Desarrollo de la prosa de ficción: siglos XVI, XVII, XVIII y XIX* (Madrid: Gredos, 1982).
8. Fernando Alegría, *Breve historia de la novela hispano-americana* (Mexico City: De Andrea, 1959). In the same year Alberto Zum Felde published a major book on Spanish American narrative (*Indice crítico de la literatura hispanoaméricana* (Mexico City: Editorial Guarania, 1959), and five years earlier Enrique Anderson Imbert had published a history of literature covering all genres: Enrique Anderson Imbert's *Historia de la literatura hispano-americana* (Mexico City: Fondo de Cultura Económica, 1954).
9. Jean Franco, *The Modern Culture of Latin America: Society and the Artist* (New York: F. A. Praeger, 1967).
10. Arturo Torres-Rioseco was one of the critics responsible for expanding the canon of the regional novel to include writers such as Mariano Azuela. See his *Seis novelistas de la tierra: Mariano Azuela, Rómulo Gallegos, Ricardo Güiraldes, Benito Lynch, Carlos Reyles, José Eustasio Rivera* (Berkeley and Los Angeles: University of California Press, 1941).
11. Vicky Unruh contextualizes the vanguard experimental novel in *Latin American Vanguards: The Art of Contentious Encounters* (Berkeley and Los Angeles: University of California Press, 1994).

12. In his subtle, understated, and informed readings, Alfred Mac Adam demonstrates the transition, in Latin American literature (primarily in narrative), from the incorporation of forms generated elsewhere, to its participation in creating new ones. See his *Modern Latin American Narratives: The Dreams of Reason* (Chicago University Press, 1977); and the essays on Donoso, Arenas, Borges, and Vargas Llosa in *Textual Confrontations: Comparative Readings in Latin American Literature* (University of Chicago Press, 1987).

13. Carlos Alonso (ed.), *Julio Cortázar: New Readings* (Cambridge University Press, 1998).

14. See Jaime Alazraki, "Borges and the New Latin-American Novel," *TriQuarterly* 25 (1972): 379–98.

15. *El País*, May 5, 2001.

16. Roberto González Echevarría, *Alejo Carpentier: The Pilgrim at Home* (Austin: University of Texas Press, 1990).

17. Carpentier's essay is included in Lois Parkinson Zamora and Wendy B. Farris (eds.), *Magical Realism: Theory, History, Community* (Durham and London: Duke University Press, 1995).

18. For an account of the "Padilla case" see Seymour Menton's *Prose Fiction of the Cuban Revolution* (Austin: University of Texas Press, 1976).

19. See Donald Shaw L, *Nueva narrative hispanoamericana: Boom. Posboom. Posmodernismo* (Madrid: Cátedra, 1999), p. 287. See also Donald Leslie Shaw, *Antonio Skármeta and the Post Boom* (Hanover, NH: Ediciones del Norte, 1994).

20. William Luis, *Dance Between Two Cultures* (Nashville: Vanderbilt University Press, 1997). See also William Luis's essay "Latino US Literature," in Philip Swanson (ed.), *The Companion to Latin American Studies* (Oxford University Press, 2003), pp. 122–53.

21. For an engaging discussion of new directions in the Latin American novel written by some of the protagonists of the new generation, see *Palabra de America*, Barcelona: Seix Barral, 2004. This collective work includes essays by Roberto Bolaño, Jorge Franco, Rodrigo Fresán, Santiago Gamboa, Gonzalo Garcés, Fernando Iwasaki, Mario Mendoza, Ignacio Padilla, Edmundo Paz Soldán, Cristina Rivera Garzo, Ivan Thays, Jorge Volpi. The book includes assessments of recent developments in a prologue by Guillermo Cabrera Infante and in an epilogue by Pere Gimferrer.

22. See Jean Franco's essay "Remapping Culture," in Alfred Stepan (ed.), *Americas: New Interpretative Essays* (Oxford University Press, 1992); and the book by William Rowe and Vivian Schelling, *Memory and Modernity: Popular Culture in Latin America* (London and New York: Verso, 1991).

23. Márquez's approach to *indigenismo* underscores the literary and critical project of overcoming superficial takes on the reality of the Indian. I have taken a different line of research, namely, to study the extent to which *indigenismo* narrative in the nineteenth and early twentieth centuries, is mediated by political debates about the indigenous peoples that took place in urban settings. See Efraín Kristal, *The Andes Viewed from the City: Literary and Political Discourse on the Indian in Peru (1848–1930)* (New York: Peter Lang, 1987).

24. William David Foster opened up new directions in this area of study. See his *Sexual Textualities: Essays on Queering Latin American Writing* (Austin: University of Texas Press, 1997).

25. "The high standards reached by Latin American literature in the last few decades have been raised by [*The War of the End of the World*]. It will be difficult to surpass it in the sort of fusion between the popular novel and literary art that was established by this novel's only rival, [Gabriel García Márquez's] *One Hundred Years of Solitude*," in Ángel Rama, "La guerra del fin del mundo: una obra maestra del fanatismo artístico," *Eco* 45/6, 246 (1982): 600. The translation is mine.

I

HISTORY

I

NAOMI LINDSTROM

The nineteenth-century Latin American novel

As the nineteenth century began, Latin American writers had not yet produced a work that fully qualified as a novel, though many had written lengthy narratives with certain literary features. One reason for the delay was Spain's ban on novels in its American colonies, though this ruling had proven difficult to enforce. In 1539, Mexico City came to house the first press in the New World, and Lima acquired a press in 1584, but these outlets were highly regulated. Authorized printing was controlled by the colonial government and was limited to official business and works with religious content. Privately owned presses operated outside these restrictions; unauthorized printing became increasingly widespread in the later years of the Colonial period.

Another obstacle to the development of the novel, even after the independence movements of the early nineteenth century, was the low prestige of the genre in comparison with such forms as heroic poetry. The reading of novels was associated in many people's minds with idleness and escapism. The first Spanish American text that most critics consider a novel is the 1816 *El Periquillo Sarniento* (*The Itching Parrot*) by José Joaquín Fernández de Lizardi (Mexico, 1776–1827). For some time thereafter, novels appeared at a slow rate. Around mid-century, the genre assumed a more prominent place in Latin American literature and more examples of it came into being. During the final two decades of the nineteenth century, a great number of novels, many of lasting significance, held the attention of Spanish American readers.

El Periquillo Sarniento was an outgrowth of Lizardi's newspaper *El Pensador Mexicano* ("The Mexican thinker"; the newspaper's title came to be applied to its publisher as well). In February 1816, Lizardi began serializing *El Periquillo Sarniento* at the rate of two chapters a week. With this work, he sought to show that novels could serve a worthy purpose, providing readers with moral uplift and sound advice, particularly about molding young people into good citizens. Pedro, the narrator of this four-volume novel, somewhat resembles a picaresque protagonist as, during his early adulthood, he wanders from one unsavory master to another. Yet, unlike the conventional rogue, he is no hardened miscreant, but a young man weakened by maternal overindulgence and a lack of practical skills. Through resolve and Christian faith, he reforms and subsequently makes a positive contribution to society. At the time Pedro narrates his life, he is an elderly man eager to pass on his hard-won wisdom to his offspring. The reader of *El Periquillo Sarniento* is placed in the situation of one of Pedro's children.

During the greater part of the nineteenth century, the development of the Spanish American novel was closely associated with nationalism. Lizardi's celebrated novel appeared partway through Mexico's struggle to break with Spain, when the author was not yet openly supporting independence. Yet he expresses nationalism in other ways.

Nancy Vogeley has researched Lizardi's outlook on colonial relations in *The Itching Parrot*. This scholar's thorough analysis shows that Lizardi was still sorting out his own thoughts on colonial rule when he composed his best-known work. The novel's message concerning Mexico's colonial status is not uniform throughout, but in certain passages, such as those describing an ideal society, readers may glimpse a critique of imperialism. For example, Vogeley finds that the discussion of work in the Utopian episode "reproaches . . . colonial economic notions; the concept of colonial territories as part of the *real patronato* ["royal patronage," my translation], the theory of wealth as bullion from American mines, Spanish monopolistic control of the colonies represented as protection, even the sordid trade based on slavery."[1] Lizardi is concerned with making Mexico more disciplined and robust by improving the habits of its citizens. Through his mouthpiece Pedro, he faults a number of widespread customs that weaken Mexicans, such as keeping irregular hours, overindulgence in food and drink, and allowing children to lounge around the house. Lizardi advocates consistent schedules, a healthful diet, sobriety, and fresh air and exercise.

Lizardi also hopes to discourage harmful concepts that Mexicans have inherited from Spain, especially the ideal of an aristocracy exempt from manual labor. Pedro's troubles begin when his mother, who views herself and her descendants as nobles, prevails over her husband's desire to have Pedro learn a trade. She is convinced that practical work diminishes the dignity of a well-born man. As a result, Pedro acquires an ornamental humanistic education that allows him to spout impressive Latin phrases but gives him no honest way to earn a living, much less help strengthen the nation.

It is difficult to set a starting date for the Brazilian novel, owing to the publication in the 1830s of a number of works that could be considered either long short stories or short novels. The earliest Brazilian novel that generally appears on required-reading lists is *A moreninha* ("The little brunette," 1844) by Joaquim Manuel de Macedo (1820–82). Popular in its time, this novel exemplifies one variant of literary nationalism, the portrayal of characters and customs typical of a given nation.

Memórias de um sargento de milícias (both English translations are entitled *Memoirs of a Militia Sergeant*) by Manuel Antônio de Almeida (1831–61) may be the earliest Brazilian novel easily appreciated by today's readers. (Though the protagonist is eventually named a militia sergeant, military themes are not as prominent as the title might suggest.) *Memórias* first appeared in installments in 1852–53 in the *Correio Mercantil*. The author was publicly identified only as "a Brazilian," even when the novel was published in two volumes in 1854 and 1855. After Almeida died in a shipwreck, his name appeared on subsequent editions.

Memórias de um sargento de milícias appeared at the height of Romanticism, but is closer to the realist fiction that would gain ascendancy later in the century. It somewhat resembles a picaresque novel, although it departs in many ways from that tradition. The loosely knit plot, narrated by a garrulous third-person observer, follows the checkered career of the freewheeling Leonardo from his conception on board an immigrant ship from Portugal through his feckless childhood in Rio de Janeiro up to his marriage. Leonardo wanders through life, indolent and with no special talent beyond cleverness and a prankster's gift for stirring up excitement. His dimwitted, impulsive father, also named Leonardo, appears and disappears in the son's life. Both Leonardos are constantly involved in scrapes. Although the youthful protagonist does little to deserve success, fortune favors him. Good luck often arrives through well-placed protectors. Young Leonardo's godparents intercede for him with their own connections, who are in turn able to involve higher-ups, until an entire network of obligatory loyalties is mobilized on his behalf. By the end of the novel, he effortlessly attains wealth and escapes an untrustworthy flirt to marry a proper young widow whom he has always fancied.

Current-day readers turn to *Memórias* not only for its literary features but also for the information it contains about Rio in approximately the 1810s and 1820s. The novel offers a comic but informative portrait of the police and judicial systems. As well as the two Leonardos and the godparents, *Memórias* features many other characters. The great majority are lower-class white people, with the exception of a free mulatto who is a paid troublemaker. Ruling-class Brazilians and slaves barely appear. The large cast includes Portuguese immigrants and their descendants, a gypsy girl, and a *caboclo* (mestizo) from whom the elder Leonardo seeks magical assistance. The characters spend considerable time exchanging gossip and speculating about unfolding events. Lengthy passages are dominated by dialogue that, rather than advancing the plot, comments upon the behavior and motives of characters. These observations provide insight into the inner workings of society.

Unlike the classical picaresque novel, whose first-person narrator illustrates sinful behavior, *Memórias* takes a lenient view of human failings. The bemused, at times almost nonjudgmental, narrator views the characters as rascals rather than sinners and their actions as deviltries or escapades instead of anything more reprehensible. Antonio Candido, the Brazilian critic who greatly stimulated modern interest in the novel, describes it as portraying "a world that seems free of the weight of error and of sin. A universe without guilt and even without repression, except for the external repression [of authorities]."[2] In Candido's analysis, while the novel exhibits scant preoccupation with the struggle between good and evil, it continually draws attention to the tension between order and disorder. Young Leonardo emerges from the chaos of his early years to become a solid citizen.

Spanish American writers had for some time been acquainted with the Romantic movement, which would come to hold sway over much of nineteenth-century culture. Romantic rhetoric appears sporadically in Spanish American writings of the very early nineteenth century. A well-known example is Simón Bolívar's 1815 *Carta de Jamaica* ("Jamaica letter") with its passionate, emotive style. Yet a Romantic movement did not emerge until the disruption of the wars of independence (1810–24) had considerably subsided. Then, in John S. Brushwood's summation, "Almost all the fiction in the years following the achievement of independence is romantic."[3]

One of the earliest and most accomplished of Romantic novelists is the Cuban-born Gertrudis Gómez de Avellaneda (1814–73). This widely respected poet, playwright, and fiction writer made her career in Spain but continued to employ Cuban settings and references in many of her texts. *Sab* (1841), her first novel, is a skillfully composed work that treats jointly the themes of slavery and of women's exploitation in marriage. This narrative follows, in Romantic fashion, tales of unrequited love. The central attachment is that of the slave Sab to Carlota, the beautiful heiress whom he serves. In turn, Carlota is besotted with an opportunist who is too shallow to return her love. Sab is loved by a poor relation of Carlota's who serves as her companion.

The character Sab is designed to make the point that the institution of slavery is inherently wrong. Sab, the informally recognized son of Carlota's uncle, has received a good education and been spared the hardship of fieldwork. Nearly indistinguishable from his masters, he feels more sharply the injustice of his enslavement to them.

Romantic novels appeared in ever-increasing numbers throughout the mid-century period. In Spanish American literature, Romanticism has links with the political struggles of the period following independence, such as the effort to overthrow the dictatorships that often replaced Spanish Colonial rule. A celebrated example is the novel *Amalia* (incompletely serialized 1851–52; published in book form 1855) by José Mármol (full name José Pedro Crisólogo Mármol; Argentina, 1817–71). The writing of *Amalia* was part of Mármol's campaign, from exile in Montevideo, to topple the authoritarian government of Juan Manuel de Rosas. So closely was *Amalia* tied to anti-Rosas opposition that, as soon as Mármol realized that the dictatorship was falling, he rushed back to Argentina, leaving his novel unfinished for three years. *Amalia* contrasts good characters with evil ones and refined Argentines with coarse rustics, although there are also in-between figures whose potential virtue is suppressed by a noxious environment. Such schematic characterization reflects both the Romantic love of extremes and the polarized outlook of the anti-Rosas exiles. Readers today are apt to find *Amalia* lacking in subtlety, especially in its portrayal of its doomed lovers, Amalia and the noble resistance fighter whom she seeks to shelter from Rosas's agents. In recent years, increased concern with nationalism in Spanish American literature has drawn more attention to *Amalia* as a novel that illustrates its author's vision of Argentina and what the nation needs in order to join the progressive world.

Some serialized novels later appeared in book form; a few of these went on to attain major status. Many more, though, were only published in installments. Recent research has included these novels that never became books. A noteworthy example is *Pirate Novels: Fictions of Nation Building in Spanish America* (1999) by Nina Gerassi-Navarro. Gerassi-Navarro's goal in bringing such works of, at times, pulp fiction into her discussion, along with better-known published texts, is "to expand the literary corpus on which recent studies on nation building have focused when analyzing postindependence literature in Spanish America."[4]

After mid-century, the Romantic style had not yet lost its appeal, but realism was coming into vogue. Realism sought to portray existence as human beings ordinarily experience it. In this sense it moved away from Romantic fiction, which frequently showed extreme situations, exotic or ancient settings and supernatural phenomena. Realists sought to diminish the subjective element highlighted in Romantic writing. Though the two tendencies seem distinct when described, in practice Spanish American writers fused them. During this period, a number of novels drew both upon the Romantic tradition, especially the melodramatically eventful plots typical of this tendency, and upon such realistic conventions as the use of unexceptional characters with everyday concerns.

An example of the rise of realism is *Martín Rivas* (1862), which has enjoyed critical esteem along with popularity. It is regarded as a landmark in the development of the Chilean novel. By far the best-known work of Alberto Blest Gana (Chile, 1830–1920), *Martín Rivas* first appeared, as did many nineteenth-century novels, as a serial. Published in the Santiago newspaper *La Voz de Chile*, the novel gripped readers with a complex plot full of secrets, revelations, and sudden reversals of fortune.

Martín Rivas is essentially a success story. While the eponymous hero suffers setbacks, at the end he has fared very well in both love and finance. The protagonist is from the northern mining regions of Chile. He is viewed as a country bumpkin by the other characters, longtime residents of the nation's capital where he has just arrived. His goal is to become a lawyer and support his family, whose finances have suffered a disaster. Martín must overcome, through determination and sound thinking, numerous obstacles. He is an assiduous positive thinker who, when he experiences insecurity, forces himself to be resolute: "the voice of reason persuaded him to abandon his childish discouragement before it dampened his spirits."[5] He at first endures snobbish rejection for his provincial ways and lack of means. For most of the novel, Martín suffers from unrequited love for Leonor, the imperious daughter of the rich man who is providing him lodging. Though the family members are hardly welcoming, Martín places himself at their service, helping the father with his business and freeing the son from entrapment by an opportunistic young woman.

The use of Romantic conventions to further a nationalistic program is evident in *Iracema: Lenda do Ceará* (*Iracema*, 1865) by José de Alencar (Brazil, 1829–77). Alencar, who had a career in public life as well as in literature, was preoccupied with the nation's indigenous past as a source of Brazilian identity. Alencar based his fiction on research. He was an amateur scholar of indigenous Brazilian languages who published a lexical guide to the *Língua Brasílica*. This study was part of Alencar's nationalistic program for Brazilian literature, since he believed that "knowledge of the indigenous language is the best criterion for the nationalization of literature."[6] Alencar published three novels in his Indianist manner, featuring indigenous characters and incorporating into Portuguese words from native languages: *O Guarani* ("The Guarani," 1857), *Iracema* (1865), and *Ubirajara* (1874). Of these, the second has attracted the most attention.

Composed in highly poetic language, *Iracema* is, as the Portuguese subtitle indicates, presented as a legend (*lenda*) of the origins of Brazil. However esthetically pleasing readers find Alencar's lyrical prose, they find it hard to overlook the novel's ideological skew. Its plot follows the love of Martim, a Portuguese soldier exploring what would become the state of Ceará, and Iracema, a young beauty who, as the daughter of a holy man, is a sacred virgin in the Tabajara tribe. Iracema takes Martim under her wing and seeks to shelter him in her own community, but when it becomes clear that he cannot live among the Tabajaras she leaves her tribe to follow the foreigner. Martim eventually loses interest in Iracema and she dies of heartbreak.

The novel shows this ill-fated love as producing a positive outcome, the birth of a mestizo. The narrator designates Moacir, the son of Martim and Iracema, as "the first child born in Ceará."[7] Obviously, many indigenous children have already been born in the region, but the narrator implies that the newborn mestizo is the first to participate in Brazilian history. The novel presents an allegory in which the birth of Moacir corresponds to the beginning of the Brazilian nation. No doubt many readers had already noticed what the critic Afrânio Peixoto observed in 1931: Iracema's name is an anagram of *America*.[8] Moacir is born of America, but to thrive and progress he needs the culture that the Portuguese have brought. Iracema, who is in decline, cannot produce enough milk to nourish the boy, but he prospers once Martim takes charge of him. The indigenous woman, having served her purpose, can now fade out of the picture, leaving the future to the new Brazilians of mixed heritage and Christian faith.

In real-world Brazilian history, the Portuguese invaded and took over lands previously held by indigenous communities. In *Iracema*, though, the Portuguese soldier is a perfect Christian gentleman who struggles not to offend his native hosts or to defile Iracema's sacred purity. Iracema pursues Martim, who shies away citing the honor code of "the warriors of my blood."[9] The conception of a new Brazilian race only becomes possible after Iracema drugs Martim. A further sign of Martim's respect for native peoples is his desire to learn their traditions and master their languages.

María, the 1867 novel by Jorge Isaacs (Colombia, 1837–95) is by all accounts the most widely read work of Spanish American Romanticism. By Donald McGrady's estimate, in the first hundred years after its initial publication, *María* went through some 150 editions.[10] The novel's widespread appeal, especially to sentimental readers, has at times diminished its critical reputation. *María* can easily seem to be a work contrived merely to elicit tears from its audience. In recent years, though, students of Spanish American literature have come to appreciate the complexity of the novel. In addition, as critics have taken a closer look at issues of gender, race, and class, more attention has gone to works like *María*, which offer clues to contemporary views on these topics.

María is a story of loss. The most prominent plot line features the decline and death of the eponymous heroine, narrated many years later by Efraín, whom she leaves bereaved. A note indicates that Efraín has since died, leaving his siblings an account of his great love and grief. In Efraín's telling, María's illness and death are linked to another narrative about watching much-loved things decline. During Efraín's childhood and adolescence, his family is among the most established and respected in the region. As well as owning a large ranch house, family members enjoy roaming over a stretch of the Cauca Valley, whose scenic beauty is lovingly evoked, and being treated with deferential affection by the workers (including some slaves) who have long been associated with the landowners. The family suffers reverses and ends up losing its beloved homestead.

The ranch, named El Paraíso, is for Efraín an Eden that he is forced to leave to carry out his studies. His great desire is never to be separated from the family home. His absences, demanded by a father who is determined that his son exercise a profession, heighten Efraín's idealization of El Paraíso. In Sylvia Molloy's analysis, when Efraín imagines what it is like to be back on the ranch, he is envisioning "a life suspended outside of time," a bucolic rural world where little changes except the seasons. In his nostalgic mind, going home for good would be "the reintegration of the son into the family community," "getting back to the origin."[11] Finally, Efraín permanently loses the possibility of returning home when the family estate becomes the property of strangers.

John S. Brushwood condenses into a single sentence the relation between María's death and the old estate passing out of the hands of Efraín's family: "*Efraín suffers the loss of María and the region to which he belongs* [italics in original]. The expansion of this statement repeatedly associates María with the region as the protagonist's sense of separation develops."[12] Although *María* is a short novel, it contains a secondary narrative (Chapters 40–43) that is almost a novel in itself. Efraín is recalling the final days of Feliciana (born Nay), a freed slave who raised María. This event leads to an account of Nay's life back in Africa, where she was the daughter of a noble warrior, on a slave ship, and in South America. Isaacs's fictional Africans stand out for their magnificently luxurious personal adornment and festivities. They are capable of great love and altruism. But in the vision that Isaacs presents, Africans, like all human beings, are incapable of forming a good society without the guidance of Christianity. Christian doctrine is needed to restrain the Africans' warlike tendencies and to end such practices as human sacrifice and slavery. The sole theme of Chapter 41 is the conversion of Nay and her soon-to-be husband to the Christian faith.

In the latter parts of this narrative, Nay and her husband are captured, sold as slaves, and permanently separated. Her fortunes improve when Efraín's father purchases her freedom and then employs her, but she never recovers from the loss of her great love and of Africa. Isaacs provides a vivid description of the inhuman conditions on slave ships and emphasizes the grief and despair of slaves. While these chapters are the most closely focused on slavery, the "peculiar institution" appears several times in *María* when Efraín and his father interact with slaves on their estate. The theme of slavery in an 1867 novel is perhaps surprising in that this practice had already been abolished in Colombia in 1852. Still, the debate over slavery was raging in other American countries. The novel's antislavery message is softened by the portrayal of Efraín and his father as big-hearted masters who empathize with their slaves' plight, share in their joys and sorrows, and are loved by them.

As well as representing Spanish American Romanticism, which typically co-occurred with realistic elements, *María* provides abundant examples of the tendency known as *costumbrismo*. *Costumbrismo*, which flourished in both Spanish and Spanish American literature, is the characterization of the folkways and typical habits of a given country or region. Efraín demonstrates his devotion to the province of Antioquia and, even more, to the Cauca Valley by recalling in detail, years later, the dress, sayings, and other cultural traits of local people. Lower-class characters rooted in their localities are most often the subjects of Efraín's portrayals in the *costumbrista* manner. For example, Efraín remembers (Chapter 9) a trip to the little house of the peasant José. His account of the long-ago visit includes numerous observations about the modest family's customs of hospitality, the cleanliness and décor of their home, and the refreshments offered, as well as a very detailed description of the daughters' dress and hairstyles. Rustic merrymaking especially fascinates Efraín, and he several times characterizes local music and festivities.

This Colombian novel has very notable links to French writing, most obviously to a highly influential essay of 1802, *Le Génie du Christianisme* (*The Genius of Christianity*) by François René de Chateaubriand (1768–1848). When Efraín home-schools his sister and María (Chapter 12), they study this treatise written in defense of the superiority of Christianity. Efraín is convinced that Chateaubriand's thought has made María more beautiful (13). For recreation, the three read Chateaubriand's 1801 *Atala*, a romantic tale of ill-fated love set against wild and exotic American scenery (Chapter 13). *María* also echoes *Paul et Virginie* (1788) by Jacques-Henri Bernardin de Saint-Pierre (1737–1814), which exalts primitive innocence and landscape unmarred by human hand; this novel also centers on a doomed couple. Many parallels may be traced between the plot of *María* and the events of the two French narratives.

Although Romanticism lost ground to realism around the mid-1800s, it continued to be a force; Romantic novels still appear late in the century. One such work, Juan León Mera's *Cumandá, o un drama entre salvajes* ("Cumandá [the heroine's name], or a drama among savages," 1879) is often referred to as the first Ecuadorian novel, and is undeniably the earliest one to make a mark. Such claims as "first national novel" can never be established with certainty, since many nineteenth-century novels were serialized and forgotten. The narrative, whose third-person narrator interrupts his story to expound his views on social issues, is set in the eastern part of Ecuador. Its characters are either white missionaries or members of Amerindian tribes, and the interaction between the two groups in the novel is a model for how whites and Amerindians can come together and heal the wounds of a nation divided along ethnic lines.

To end on a note of reconciliation, the novel takes its characters through a melodramatic plot involving forbidden intercultural love, revelations about the characters' true identities and relationships, and the ritual killing of the heroine. Doris Sommer explains the logic of the novel's conclusion: "The sacrifice was Cumandá, the woman over whose dead body Spanish and Indian fathers can love each other."[13]

During the 1880s, the most important figure in Brazilian literature entered his period of greatest originality. Joaquim Maria Machado de Assis (1839–1908) not only made significant innovations in his writing but also played an important role in the nation's cultural life; he founded the Brazilian Academy of Letters. Machado had been publishing fiction since the 1860s, starting out in a predominantly Romantic vein. As he moved away from his early Romanticism, he developed the distinctive narrative manner for which he is celebrated. Whether related in first or third person, his mature novels are ironic, mocking, skeptical, and quick to draw attention to their own fictional devices.

While Machado's novels won acclaim by contemporary standards, to later generations of readers they seem ahead of their time, resembling the metafiction of the late twentieth century. The ideal of many nineteenth-century realists and naturalists was to hide the process of writing. Ideally, if readers could momentarily forget that they were dealing with a written document, the novel would be like a window opened onto social realities. Machado utilizes a number of devices to draw attention to the fact that a narrative has been deliberately constructed, with an author choosing among such options as chronological succession versus leaps backward and forward in time. In addition, Machado's fictional world is full of ambiguities and uncertainties.

Contemporary reactions to Machado's novels indicate that the Portuguese-language public of the time read them in a more straightforward and unambiguous manner than is common today. The way that Machado's fiction has been understood presents an example of how successive readings and interpretations of literary works enrich meaning.

Best appreciated today are the novels that Machado published beginning with *Memórias póstumas de Brás Cubas* (translated as *Epitaph for a Small Winner* and as *The Posthumous Memoirs of Brás Cubas*). The novel first appeared in installments in the *Revista Brasileira* (March–December 1880), then in book form in 1881. The first-person narrator states that, although dead, he has been able to compose the text that we are reading. He offers an account of his outwardly conventional life as an upper-class man who attains some success on the cultural and political scene of Rio de Janeiro and conducts a lengthy affair with a married woman. Throughout his life, Brás Cubas harbors thoughts whose eccentricity and disaffected irony reveal that, under his conformist exterior, he is a misfit who does not share his society's preoccupation with maintaining appearances and displaying public achievements. He ends his story by identifying the accomplishment that gives him greatest satisfaction: "I had no children, I haven't transmitted the legacy of our misery to any creature."[14] His memoirs are interspersed with posthumous reflections on literary and philosophical questions and bleak observations about humankind.

The text that conveys Brás Cubas's jaded outlook is fragmented into very brief chapters, not all of which tie directly into the story of the narrator's life. Satire, parody, and wry humor mark his approach. These features function together with the narrator's (and Machado's) expectation that the reader perform some of the work of completing the story. A much-noted example of Machado's playfulness is Chapter 55, "The old dialogue of Adam and Eve." The dialogue is rendered using nothing but ellipses, question marks, and exclamation points. Besides being surprising and amusing, this arrangement offers the reader the opportunity to exercise his or her imagination by filling in the dialogue. Chapter 139, "How I Didn't Get to Be Minister of States," contains only lines of elliptical dots. The following chapter explains that some things are better left unsaid. Brás Cubas comments on the decisions he made in constructing his memoirs and refers the reader from one chapter to another in search of clues. The *Posthumous Memoirs* take aim at a variety of satirical targets. Many are literary habits. In suggesting a more participatory role for the reader, Brás Cubas implicitly snickers at writers who, expecting little of the literary public, spoon-feed their audience. At various moments, Brás Cubas makes sport of the all-too-typical practices of Romanticism, realism, and naturalism, the main literary currents found in the literature of his time.

The novel's satire is not restricted to literary matters. Many of the narrator's observations serve to mock the stodginess, conformity, and obsession with respectability that characterized upper-class existence in nineteenth-century Rio de Janeiro (as in many places). Though the love between Brás Cubas and his mistress is passionate, it does not preclude constant worry about public opinion. In other cases, the issue is a universal human failing, particularly the cold-hearted self-interest that seems to have especially fascinated this novelist. A character who prides himself on driving a hard bargain expends his last gasping breaths on negotiations over the price of a house. While he is an extreme case, many other characters cannot repress their drive to emerge the winner in financial dealings. Affection and friendship are frequently commingled with a desire to profit from the other party. Being dead, Brás Cubas has nothing to lose by pointing out the flattery, feigned cordiality, and sheer greed that he has witnessed and of which he has been guilty.

It is impossible for a brief summary to do justice to Machado's mature novels, which continued to appear throughout the late years of the nineteenth century and the early twentieth. For a fuller treatment of this novelist's work, please see two other contributions to this volume: that of Piers Armstrong, on the Brazilian novel, and that of Marta Peixoto, on Machado's much-noted novel of 1899, *Dom Casmurro*.

In Cuba, the abolition of slavery in 1880 brought to light a number of novels that, for their critical treatment of the institution, had been withheld from general circulation. The most important, the lengthy and intricate *Cecilia Valdés, o La Loma del Ángel* (*Cecilia Valdés, or Angel's Hill*) by the Cuban Cirilo Villaverde (1812–94), has a complicated history of rewritings. In 1839, Villaverde published a short story entitled "Cecilia Valdés," centered on a beautiful, ill-fated mulatto child. That same year, the author brought out the first version of the novel *Cecilia Valdés*. It was not until 1882 that the definitive version of the work appeared in New York. The 1882 *Cecilia Valdés*, the one read and studied today, is different from its predecessors in focusing attention on the question of slavery and its effects, not only on slaves, but on Cuban society as a whole.

The degree to which *Cecilia Valdés* constitutes an antislavery novel remains open to debate. Beyond doubt, the novel denounces the ill treatment of slaves on sugar plantations and slave ships. While these passages give the impression of an antislavery novel, *Cecilia Valdés* also portrays a tobacco plantation where slaves enjoy a garden-like environment and adore their benevolent, fair-minded mistress. Researchers have sought to identify the position that, in real life, Villaverde took toward slavery. The author moved in upper-class progressive circles in Cuba. These liberals, whose personal wealth often depended in part upon slaves, considered a number of ideas for improving the lot of slaves yet not actually ending slavery, at least not during their lifetimes. These half-measures included a ban on the slave trade, outlawing the beating of slaves, and various plans for phasing out slavery. From Villaverde's favorable portrayal of servitude under a kindly owner and good conditions, one might imagine that he also hoped that slavery could be reformed. After reviewing the evidence, though, William Luis believes that "Villaverde explicitly embraced the antislavery cause."[15]

Though its verdict on the future of slavery is unclear, *Cecilia Valdés* portrays Cuba as collectively diseased by slavery as currently practiced. This malaise is epitomized by the biracial extended family of Cándido Gamboa, whose illegitimate daughter is Cecilia Valdés. The Gamboas are financially dependent on the worst aspects of slavery; Don Cándido owns a slave ship and his wife a sugar plantation where slaves lead a hellish existence. The white Gamboas use slaves as wet nurses and nannies, and the white males consider both female slaves and free black women as potential mistresses, so the family has come to include both white and black members, though the former try to avoid recognizing the latter as kin. The white Gamboas keep life tolerable by closing their eyes to what strike the reader as obvious facts; for example, the mother maintains her ignorance of the horrors that take place aboard slave ships, while the son denies the obvious fact that Cecilia, who is identical to his legitimate white sister and strongly resembles his father, is his half sister. The suggestion is that white Cubans, to live with slavery and its accompanying racial system, must practice assiduous denial of how their society maintains itself.

The Gamboas and Cecilia have ties to many other acquaintances, friends, admirers, rivals, subordinates, and hangers-on. *Cecilia Valdés* contains nearly one hundred characters. Among them they represent all of Cuba's social classes and racial and ethnic categories, as well as individuals born on the island, in Spain, and in Africa. These many interconnected characters make a portrait of Cuban society as a vast multiracial family.

The desire to create a myth of national origin is vividly present in another late Romantic novel, *Enriquillo* (1882). The work of the Dominican Manuel de Jesús Galván (1834–1910), this novel was translated into English by the poet Robert Graves as *The Cross and the Sword* (1954). *Enriquillo* is the novel-length elaboration of an episode in the *Historia de las Indias* (probably composed 1527–60s) by Bartolomé de las Casas (1474–1566). Enriquillo is an indigenous nobleman converted to Christianity, the overseer on a

Spanish-owned estate. Though Enriquillo is peaceable and law abiding, the abusive treatment that he and his wife suffer from the Spanish landowner drives him to escape. Enriquillo becomes the leader of a band of indigenous workers who have fled virtual slavery. Las Casas emphasizes that Enriquillo avoids bloodshed and seeks peace with justice.

Subsequent generations of readers have pointed to distortions of historical fact in *Enriquillo*. One of the principal complaints is that, while Las Casas shows the cruelty of the conquerors, Galván portrays the Spanish as, with exceptions, humane. Another objection is that Galván creates a national myth in which Dominicans arise from the indigenous legacy, leaving African origins unmentioned. Antonio Benítez Rojo summarizes: "Although a great part of the [Dominican] population was black and mulatto . . . nationalistic practices sought the explanation for the more or less dark color of the people in a fictional indigenous ancestry, an approach which *Enriquillo* strengthened."[16]

During the late nineteenth century, naturalism made rather limited inroads into Spanish American writing. In the Spanish-language literary world, there was considerable fascination with French naturalism, epitomized by the novels and proclamations of Emile Zola, who viewed the novelist as ideally a scientific observer. Many believed that naturalism, which showed behavior as the product of heredity and environment, was unsuited for a Catholic society that valued free will. In addition, naturalist fiction often featured harsh descriptions that upset many Spanish-language readers. Over the winter of 1882–83, Countess Emilia Pardo Bazán (1851–1921), the respected yet controversial Spanish novelist, published a series of essays on the topic. Her reflections, which first appeared in periodical form and then in a much-reprinted pamphlet, were entitled *La cuestión palpitante* ("The burning issue"). She recommended that, for Spanish-language readers, naturalism be made compatible with a Christian vision according to which human beings can transcend their circumstances.

As Enrique Laguerre observes, few novels written in Spanish qualify as naturalist fiction in the strict sense. If one includes texts in which naturalism co-occurs with realism, though, many Spanish-language novels can be included at least partially in the category.[17] The Spanish American novel most often labeled naturalistic is *Sin rumbo* ("Without direction," 1885) by Eugenio Cambaceres (1843–89), the Argentine writer and political progressive. This short novel follows a jaded member of the Argentine landed class over the last three years of his life. Throughout *Sin rumbo* Andrés, in Noé Jitrik's words, "occupies the entire narrative structure, which pales in comparison."[18] Whether on his sheep ranch or living the high life in Buenos Aires, he exhibits pervasive boredom and scant tolerance for his fellow human beings. In the country, he conquers and abandons the daughter of one of his most loyal hands. While the ranch woman annoys him with her simplicity, he becomes equally irritated with his next lover, an acclaimed soprano who is the quintessence of artifice and theatricality.

During this first part of the novel, Andrés manifests few appealing qualities. He is not just a womanizer, but an irresponsible landowner. Cambaceres, who looked to the Argentine elite to guide the nation's ranch lands into a progressive future, makes Andrés an example of failure to exercise leadership. In its early chapters, the novel shows Andrés unable to focus his attention consistently on his sheep-raising operation, which nearly runs into financial ruin for lack of oversight. Although he spends much of the year in the country, he at times seems unfamiliar with its ways, as when he insists on fording a swollen creek. Even as he depends on longtime hands to run the ranch, Andrés speaks insultingly to the help. The workers who have been with Andrés's family accept the young master's verbal abuse, but a hired man rebels.

The shorter second part of the novel reveals the protagonist's previously hidden positive qualities. Andrés discovers that his rustic conquest has given birth to their daughter and died. He suddenly throws himself into the role of loving father. Though he now has a purpose in life, the frenetic quality of his paternal devotion makes the reader doubt that he is really on a steady course. The clues that Andrés has not achieved stability are confirmed when he commits suicide after his daughter's death.

Many Argentine readers of the 1880s found *Sin rumbo* too far from the decorum that was still widely observed at the time. The novel contains several violent passages, starting with a scene of careless shearing that leaves the sheep wounded. By far the most memorable are the closing episodes. The narrator first provides a gory description of an unsuccessful tracheotomy performed on Andrés's daughter. There follows an account of Andrés's self-disembowelment, which requires extracting his entrails with both hands. In the narrator's unsparing description: "Un chorro de sangre y de excrementos saltó, le ensució la cara, la ropa, fue a salpicar sobre la cama el cadáver de su hija, mientras él, boqueando, rodaba por el suelo . . ." ("A torrent of blood and excrement leapt out; it soiled his face, his clothes, it splattered his daughter's cadaver on the bed, while he, gasping, writhed on the floor . . .")[19]

Many Spanish American novels could be read either as naturalistic or realistic, depending on which passages receive greatest attention and how strict a definition of naturalism is applied. An example is *La charca* (translated at different times as *La Charca* and *The Pond*) by Manuel Zeno Gandía (Puerto Rico, 1855–1930). Zeno Gandía was a physician and a public figure eager to spread his views on the problems confronting Puerto Rico; *La charca* is, among other things, an effort to communicate his outlook on the nation to the novel-reading public. Benigno Trigo's new reading of the novel focuses on its promotion of scientific hygiene and rationalistic analysis of the country's situation, seeking its implied statements about class, gender, identity, and subjectivity. In Trigo's analysis, the novel reduces its most prominent woman character, an exploited young peasant, to little more than a female body harboring disease. At the same time, "following traditional gender-coded oppositions," the principal male figure, an intellectual landowner, "decorporealizes into a series of personal and national memories to become an ethereal consciousness."[20]

Brazilian readers and writers turned to naturalism in the last two decades of the nineteenth century. While Spanish and Spanish American naturalism was usually an attenuated variant of the French movement, Brazilian naturalism could be bold. David T. Haberly asserts that "neither [Zola] nor his French disciples were as frank, in their descriptions of sexuality, as the Brazilians."[21] The work that critics most frequently name to exemplify Brazilian naturalism is *O cortiço* (*A Brazilian Tenement*, 1890) by Aluísio Azevedo (1857–1913), which exercised a great influence on turn-of-the-century Brazilian literature. The tenement to which the title refers is a vast and constantly growing rental and commercial property in Rio de Janeiro. It is the creation of João Romão, a Portuguese immigrant and ruthless empire-builder. Many of the characters are Romão's tenants. One set, however, is a respectably bourgeois family that, living next to the expanding domains of Romão, eventually accepts the rising businessman as an in-law.

O cortiço conveys a pessimistic view of Brazilian society. A particular cause for apprehension appears to be the crumbling of the traditional social order and the new upward mobility of hard-driving newcomers. Many readers have seen in the novel a nostalgic longing for the days of an established elite.

Clorinda Matto de Turner (Peru, 1852–1909) drew considerably upon contemporary progressive thought in her fiction. Her 1889 novel *Aves sin nido* (translated into English as *Birds Without a Nest* and *Torn from the Nest*) is dedicated to the charismatic pro-Amerindian reformer Manuel González Prada (1848–1918) and illustrates some of his central concepts.

Aves sin nido set off a furor when it appeared and continues to be debated. As Ana Peluffo notes: "Even though *Aves sin nido* (1889) today has a canonical status as the first work of *indigenismo* and had a massive circulation in the nineteenth century, as demonstrated by the three simultaneous editions that sold out and its almost immediate translation into English, the publication of this novel generated an acute controversy in the literary world."[22] While Matto's most famous novel is not very sophisticated in style or narrative construction, it continues to interest scholars for the response it provoked and for its information about social problems and progressive thought in nineteenth-century Peru. *Aves sin nido* is the first widely read (though not actually the first) novel to represent literary *indigenismo*, that is, writing designed to raise awareness of the problems facing native populations of the Americas.[23] In addition, researchers are fascinated by Matto's dramatic life as a woman intellectual with daringly advanced opinions and the ability to wield influence. In Mary G. Berg's summary, "Burned in effigy, excommunicated, the presses of her feminist print shop smashed and her manuscripts burned by mobs just before her hasty flight from Lima in 1895, Clorinda Matto de Turner may have been the most controversial woman writer of nineteenth-century Latin America."[24]

In the early 1880s, a new tendency, *modernismo*, emerged in Spanish American writing. Unlike Romanticism, realism, and naturalism, *modernismo* was originated by Spanish American writers. The *modernistas* who attained the greatest international renown are José Martí (Cuba, 1853–95) and Rubén Darío (real name Félix Rubén García Sarmiento; Nicaragua, 1867–1916). *Modernistas* wanted to make greater use of the repertory of techniques and devices available in literary Spanish. They let the artifice inherent in literature stand out more visibly. The fundamental goal, though, was not to make literary Spanish artificial, but to make it more beautiful and melodious by utilizing to greater advantage the rhythmic qualities of the language. The hallmarks of *modernista* writing include unusual adjectives, allusions to ancient history and mythology, exoticism, and sensuality.

Modernismo is best known for producing poetry and poetic prose with little plot. Yet some late nineteenth-century novels are *modernista*. Martí wrote one novel, known at various times as *Amistad funesta* ("Ill-fated friendship") and *Lucía Jerez* (1885), under a pseudonym. But the outstanding *modernista* novel of the nineteenth century is *De sobremesa* ("After-dinner conversation") by the Colombian José Asunción Silva (1865–96). The final version of the novel was completed the year of the author's suicide, but until 1925 only excerpts were published.

De sobremesa is closely focused on José Fernández, a wealthy, cultivated Colombian. After his early success as a poet, Fernández has frittered away his energy on various pursuits, ranging from amateur archeology to erotic adventures to imagining how Colombia would progress under his dictatorship. Fernández suffers from a malaise that has some positive qualities. Sensory impressions register so powerfully upon the hypersensitive young man that he is easily overwhelmed, especially by art or female beauty. He experiences life intensely and is aware of the esthetic dimension, but he cannot organize his ideas coherently.

In a framing story, Fernández invites select friends to his house, decorated with exotic but tasteful sumptuosity, and after dinner reads aloud from his diary. The text of the diary occupies most of the novel. It tells of Fernández's aimless travels through Europe and his pursuit of beautiful women and paintings, two entities that are commingled in his outlook. For the most part, Fernández chooses women who are sexually knowledgeable, demimondaines or aristocratic libertines. But amidst this dissipation, the protagonist falls in love with an adolescent to whom he attributes the greatest innocence and purity, although he has never spoken with her and knows little about her. His European trip then becomes a quest for an ideal being who less resembles a real-life woman than a Pre-Raphaelite painting. Though he mourns her death, he is uncertain that she has ever existed.

Readers have reached varying understandings of what Fernández represents. During the time when fragments of Fernández's diary were published out of context, it was easy to assume that the views he expresses were those of Silva himself. Looking at the entire novel, though, it is clear that Fernández must stand for some more general category of people. He is a South American gentleman who enjoys such advantages as poetic talent, appreciation of beauty, knowledge of high culture, and like-minded friends. Yet he remains a dabbler, because he has not yet been able to organize an intellectual life in which issues and ideas could be developed and resolved. In the summary of Aníbal González, Fernández is "a Spanish American writer on the eve of his transformation into an intellectual."[25]

As the nineteenth century ended, writers were still extending the lines of development started during the 1880s and 1890s. Machado had yet to publish two of his mature novels, ironic and open to interpretation: in 1904, *Esaú e Jacó* (*Esau and Jacob*) and in 1908 *Memorial de Ayres* (*Counselor Ayres' Memorial*). Some *modernista* novelists published most of their work in the new century, among them Manuel Díaz Rodríguez (Venezuela, 1871–1927), José María Vargas Vila (Colombia, 1860–1933), and Enrique Larreta (Argentina, 1873–1961). Federico Gamboa (Mexico, 1864–1939) draws considerably, though not exclusively, upon naturalism in his much-read *Santa* (1903); naturalistic elements continue to appear in novels published throughout the early 1900s.

Throughout the twentieth century and into the twenty-first, writers and readers of Latin American fiction remained aware of the nineteenth-century novel, whether they sought to reject it or to learn from it. During the middle of the twentieth century, Spanish American writers representing the new narrative of 1940–70, and especially the 1960s Boom, were often viewed as rescuing the Spanish American novel from the stodginess of traditional nineteenth-century fiction. In the waning years of the twentieth century, the new narrative was upstaged by yet newer developments and lost some of its exceptional status. Many readers no longer viewed the Spanish American novel of the mid-twentieth century as inherently superior to its predecessors. Interest rose in both the Post-Boom of the late twentieth and early twenty-first centuries and in fresh readings of nineteenth-century fiction. Machado de Assis continued to be the dominant figure in Brazilian literature, but highly original new interpretations kept the reading of his novels in perennial evolution.

If one feature gives greatest originality to the Latin American novel of the nineteenth century, it may well be authors' ability to fuse diverse literary tendencies, including those that in European writing would be less likely to co-occur. To give an example, Romanticism and realism are by no means inherently incompatible, but in French writing certain writers are associated with the Romantic school and others are regarded as realists. In Spanish American fiction, it is the norm for romantic novels to contain realistic elements and vice versa. Beyond the commingling of these two major movements in nineteenth-century narrative, the Spanish American novel brings into the mix such other tendencies as *costumbrismo*. In the late years of the century, *modernismo* enters the literary scene, often joined with existing novelistic currents to produce a highly original blend.

Also distinctive in Latin America is the intimate relation between nationalism and the development of the novel. Nation-building was the greatest single concern among Spanish American thinkers from the outset of the nineteenth century, when independence movements were gathering momentum, until the late 1800s. The campaign to construct identities and goals for the newly independent countries, or in some cases for Spanish America collectively, was a shaping force behind many Latin American novels. Though by the 1880s nationalistic themes began to wane in importance, over the greater part of the century Latin American writers strove to showcase the distinguishing features of Latin America, including its indigenous heritage, its diverse peoples, its landscape, and the special problems it confronted, by means of the novel.

NOTES

1. Nancy Vogeley, *Lizardi and the Birth of the Novel in Spanish America* (Gainesville: University Press of Florida, 2001), p. 114.
2. Antonio Candido, "Dialectic of Malandroism," in Howard S. Becker (ed. and trans.) *Antonio Candido: On Literature and Society* (Princeton University Press, 1995), p. 97.
3. John S. Brushwood, *Genteel Barbarism: New Readings of Nineteeth-Century Spanish-American Novels* (Lincoln: University of Nebraska, 1981), p. 4.

4. Nina Gerassi-Navarro, "Introduction," *Pirate Novels: Fictions of Nation Building in Spanish America* (Durham: Duke University Press, 1999), p. 9.

5. Alberto Blest Gana, *Martín Rivas*, trans. Tess O'Dwyer (New York: Oxford University Press, 2000), p. 15.

6. José de Alencar, "Letter to Dr. Jaguaribe," in his *Iracema*, trans. Clifford E. Landers (New York: Oxford University Press, 2000), p. 134.

7. Alencar, *Iracema*, p. 111.

8. Afrânio Peixoto, *Noções de história da literatura brasileira* (Rio de Janeiro: F. Alves, 1931), p. 163.

9. Ibid., p. 23.

10. Donald McGrady, "Introducción," Jorge Isaacs, *María* (Madrid: Cátedra, 1986), p. 13.

11. Sylvia Molloy, "Paraíso perdido y economía terrenal en *María*," *Sin Nombre* 14, 3 (1984):39.

12. John S. Brushwood, *Genteel Barbarism: New Readings of Nineteenth-Century Spanish-American Novels* (Lincoln: University of Nebraska Press, 1981), p. 86.

13. Doris Sommer, "Starting from Scratch: Late Beginnings and Early (T)races," in her *Foundational Fictions: The National Romances of Latin America* (Berkeley and Los Angeles: University of California Press, 1991), p. 240.

14. Joaquim Maria Machado de Assis, *The Posthumous Memoirs of Brás Cubas*, trans. Gregory Rabassa (New York: Oxford, 1997), p. 203.

15. William Luis, *Literary Bondage: Slavery in Cuban Narrative* (Austin: University of Texas Press, 1990), p. 107.

16. Antonio Benítez Rojo, "The Nineteenth-Century Spanish American Novel," in Roberto González Echevarría and Enrique Pupo-Walker (eds.), *The Cambridge History of Latin American Literature* (Cambridge University Press, 1996), Vol. II, p. 467.

17. Enrique Laguerre, "Prólogo," Manuel Zeno Gandía, *La charca* (Caracas: Ayacucho, 1978), pp. xxiv–xxvi.

18. Noé Jitrik, "Cambaceres: adentro y afuera," in his *Ensayos y estudios de literatura argentina* (Buenos Aires: Galerna, 1970), p. 37.

19. Eugenio Cambaceres, *Sin rumbo* (Buenos Aires: Editorial Abril, 1983), p. 150; my translation.

20. Benigno Trigo, "The Crisis of Memory: Remembering Machines and Self-Government," in his *Subjects of Crisis: Race and Gender as Disease in Latin America* (Hanover, NH: Wesleyan University Press / University Press of New England, 2000), p. 111.

21. David T. Haberly, "Aluísio Azevedo," in Carlos A. Solé and Maria Isabel Abreu (eds.), *Latin American Writers* (New York: Scribner's, 1989), Vol. II, p. 336.

22. Ana Peluffo, "El poder de las lágrimas: sentimentalismo, género y nación en *Aves sin nido* de Clorinda Matto de Turner," in Mabel Moraña (ed.), *Indigenismo hacia el fin del milenio. Homenaje a Antonio Cornejo-Polar* (Pittsburgh: Biblioteca de América, 1998), p. 119.

23. Luis Mario Schneider, "Clorinda Matto de Turner," in Matto, *Aves sin nido* (New York: Las Américas, 1968), pp. xx–xxi, cites as earlier indigenista novels *El padre Horán* (1848) by Narciso Aréstegui and *La trinidad del indio o costumbres del interior* (1885) by José T. Itolarres (real name José Torres y Lara).

24. Mary G. Berg, "Writing for Her Life: The Essays of Clorinda Matto de Turner," in Doris Meyer (ed.), *Reinterpreting the Spanish American Essay: Women Writers of the Nineteenth and Twentieth Centuries* (Austin: University of Texas Press, 1995), p. 80.
25. Aníbal González, *La novela modernista hispanoamericana* (Madrid: Gredos, 1987), p. 106.

FURTHER READING

Brushwood, John S., *Genteel Barbarism: Experiments in Analysis of Nineteenth-Century Spanish-American Novels*, Lincoln and London: University of Nebraska Press, 1981.

Castagnaro, R. Anthony, *The Early Spanish American Novel*, New York: Las Americas, 1971.

Kirkpatrick, Gwen, "Spanish American Narrative 1810–1920," in John King (ed.), *The Cambridge Companion to Modern Latin American Culture*, Cambridge University Press, 2004, pp. 60–83.

Lewis, Bart. L., "Recent Criticism of Nineteenth-Century Latin American Literature," *Latin American Research Review* 2 (1985): 182–88.

Lindstrom, Naomi, *Early Spanish American Narrative*, Austin: University of Texas Press, 2004.

Pedraza Jiménez, Felipe B. (ed.), *Manual de literatura hispanoamericana. II. Siglo XIX*, Navarra: CENLIT Ediciones, 1991.

Picón Garfield, Evelyn and Ivan A. Schulman, *Contextos: literatura y sociedad latinoamericanas del siglo XIX*, Urbana: University of Illinois Press, 1991.

Reyes, Lisa D. "The Nineteenth-Century Latin American National Romance and the Role of Women," *Ariel* 8 (1992): 33–44.

Sommer, Doris, *Foundational Fictions: The National Romances of Latin America*, Berkeley and Los Angeles: University of California Press, 1991.

González, Aníbal, *La novela modernista hispanoamericana*, Madrid: Gredos, 1987.

2

The regional novel and beyond

The regional novel from the first decades of the twentieth century marks a turning point in Latin American narrative. In the 1960s, Latin American writers became world leaders in combining technical innovation with commercial success and critical acclaim. However, what came to be known as the Boom novel would not have been possible without advances made in the preceding decades. Beginning in the last third of the nineteenth century, Latin America experienced economic expansion and relative political stability. These changes were accompanied by the consolidation of liberal political institutions that eliminated many vestiges of Colonial society. The regionalist writers of the early twentieth century came to grips with these changes by drawing on international influences and local cultures to generate new narrative forms. The eminent Uruguayan critic Ángel Rama's outline of this phenomenon remains the most important social periodization of Latin American narrative in the early twentieth century, and his work usefully suggests that the regional novel can be defined in part through its engagement with the complex dynamics of inclusion and exclusion that structure models of citizenship and cultural belonging.

The corpus of texts to be addressed under "regionalism" is not obvious. The most apparent inclusion would be the *novelas de la tierra*, or telluric novels, that describe local realities through nature, rural life, and cultural traits understood as peculiar to Latin America. In the 1930s, Concha Meléndez had already identified this body of works, now established in the literary canon. As Carlos Alonso has argued, even if these novels rely on problematic concepts of representation, they played a crucial role in defining Latin America's cultural modernity, particularly as a response to US Pan-Americanism and as an expression of revitalization one hundred years after independence. However, these novels of the land represent only a portion of early twentieth-century Latin American narrative. Conceiving the regional novel more broadly expands its meaning and permits wider historical analysis. In this broader sense, the regional novel may be defined as inclusive of texts written during the first three or four decades of the twentieth century with a direct concern for the relationship between local and national structures, particularly as the latter worked to incorporate the former through processes of modernization and national consolidation.

Regional novels within this definition can be subdivided by their efforts to represent diverse social subjects and collective cultural projects. In most of the canonical regional novels, the national project appears as a process of domination leading towards homogenization, often allegorized through the landscape and rural life. Against that framework, a different set of writers perceived more ambiguous relations between emerging social subjects and the nation. While these writers were usually less heralded in their own time, their work largely defines the regional novel as a crucible of innovation still relevant today.

A survey of the canonical novel of the land can begin with its archetype, *Doña Bárbara* (1929), by Venezuelan writer Rómulo Gallegos (1884–1969). *Doña Bárbara* employs a polished realist technique to narrate the conflict between two characters who allegorize possibilities for national development: the eponymous villain, whose name literally refers to barbarity, and her male counterpart, Santos Luzardo, whose first name means "saints" and whose surname derives from "light." Gallegos's novel thus seems to repeat the conflictive formula of Domingo Faustino Sarmiento (1811–88), whose classic political essay, *Facundo* (1845), presents Argentina as trapped between the civilizing force of European culture and the barbarity incarnate in Latin America's untamed nature. Gallegos's protagonists live out similar categories as they struggle for supremacy on Venezuela's *llanos* or interior plains, with Santos Luzardo triumphing through a plan to rationalize territorial organization and agriculture under an enlightened authority which contrasts to Doña Bárbara's black magic and despotic charisma.

Unlike Sarmiento, Gallegos does not resolve the allegorical conflict in *Doña Bárbara* by annihilating one of its terms. Instead, his novel employs a model Doris Sommer has called the "foundational fiction," that is, a plot which resolves social conflicts symbolically through romance. In the end, Santos Luzardo marries Doña Bárbara's renegade daughter, suggesting a synthesis. Moreover, Doña Bárbara herself is a complex villain, whose will to power is explained through a troubled past that includes the murder of her first lover and her subsequent rape by his killers. In the end, she too falls in love with Luzardo but withdraws to avoid harming her daughter as she herself was harmed. This background story again suggests a symbolic union of Venezuelan society, and that message points to Gallegos's complex treatment of rural culture.

Doña Bárbara employs direct, third-person realism. As critics have noted, this creates an omniscient perspective and a linguistic hierarchy between the characters' rural dialects and the narrator's "standard" Spanish, but some minor characters manage to articulate a different treatment of oral tradition. One is "Pajarote," a ranch-hand who helps Santos Luzardo regain control of his family's land. Pajarote is a storyteller, and his tales register a strong engagement with orality. Often infused with a sense of the fantastic, Pajarote's stories allow rural folk traditions to take center stage against the novel's emphasis on rationalization and progress. Santos Luzardo specifically tries to reform the rustic Spanish spoken by Doña Bárbara's daughter, but Pajarote's yarns offer a playful sense of orality that is a less threatening version of Doña Bárbara's irrational worldview. Pajarote's voice can thus be seen as one way in which the regionalist novel introduced devices developed by later Latin American writers into innovative narrative forms such as "magical realism."

Even before *Doña Bárbara*, other regional writers had employed similar techniques. Most famously, Ricardo Güiraldes (1886–1927) created a popular Argentine *gaucho*, the hero of *Don Segundo Sombra* (1926), who bestows folk wisdom on a male apprentice from the city while spinning a nostalgic vision of the Pampas around Buenos Aires. Although Güiraldes lived most of his adult years in Paris, his novel returns to his youth on his family's ranch. Beatriz Sarlo has noted that *Don Segunda Sombra* does not recreate the historical world of the Pampas at the turn of the century, but an idealized rural life prior to the influx of immigrants in the late nineteenth century and the modernization of agriculture. This nostalgia creates a falsely harmonious image of the past and the present so that a new Argentine identity can be imagined through the fusion of idealized rural values and modern urban culture. As Sarlo concludes, the novel's esthetics follows a similar model by treating Argentina's landscape with a French-influenced style.

A counterpoint to the successful domination of nature in *Doña Bárbara* and the celebration of rural life in *Don Segundo Sombra* can be found in the best-known regional novel set in the jungle, *La vorágine* (*The Vortex*, 1924), by Colombian writer José Eustasio Rivera (1888–1928). *La vorágine* is the most experimental telluric novel, and Rivera uses a first-person narrator, Arturo Cova, to tell his own story as a dissolute socialite who flees Bogotá with his lover and ersatz muse, Alicia. The couple makes a desperate voyage across the Colombian interior to the Amazon basin's booming rubber economy. Only the second and third sections of this complex novel are set in the jungle, but that landscape powerfully defines the work and gives it its title. In part, *La vorágine* presents a dramatic condemnation of chaotic development in the region between Colombia, Venezuela, and Brazil. Rivera knew this reality firsthand through his work as an inspector for Colombia's border with Venezuela, and the jungle appears in his novel as a no man's land inhabited by a rapacious cast of international figures intent on getting rich and leaving. A lack of social controls suggests the absence of the nation as a political entity capable of defining and managing its interior spaces. No state has sovereignty at the end of *La vorágine*, and the jungle territory emerges as a quasi-independent zone straddling three nations but controlled from the Brazilian city of Manaus, the hub of the Amazonian economy. This unruly area is never brought under control, and Rivera's work follows the downward trajectory of Cova's declining mental condition. Ostensibly presented as Cova's "memoirs," *La vorágine* becomes an increasingly troubled tale in which the narrator pursues his ambitions with maniacal determination, and the jungle's tormented landscape is as much a projection as a cause of his insanity.

It is difficult to read *La vorágine* except with Cova as an unreliable narrator, and his disturbed subjectivity undermines the constructive values championed by a figure like Santos Luzardo. In Rivera's hands, rationality, self-restraint, and moral compunction – central elements in Gallegos's allegory of a renewed national culture – are all tied to destructive forces. The latter emerge both from modern literary explorations of the human psyche and from the damage done to progressive visions of history by World War I. In *La vorágine*, efforts to channel nature's power seem a thin façade for violence and self-gratification. Cova and Luzardo are equally convinced that their cause is just, but *La vorágine* invites the reader to question that faith. Correspondingly, there is no happy reunion for Cova and Alicia, and *La vorágine* suggests a counter-paradigm to Gallegos's successful national romance. In this sense, Rivera's novel exemplifies what Brazilian critic Antônio Cândido identified as a central feature in Latin American literature from the first decades of the twentieth century: a growing awareness that far from the promise of abundance and prosperity, the region's natural resources represented a great weakness for societies that lacked strong nation-states to counter foreign interests. The national project remains an inescapable point of reference for Rivera, but his novel suggests that the forces driving national development are also generating fragmentation.

Despite their differences, *Doña Bárbara* and *La vorágine* are more similar than different in their presentation of the nation-state as a presence felt primarily through domination, and both novels allegorize that process as the control of nature. This marginalizes questions like the role of popular culture in national consolidation, and a narrative of development from a non-dominant perspective becomes possible only through minor characters or subordinate narrative modes. Ironically, Cova's irrational voice in

La vorágine is even more impenetrable to alternative subjectivities than the third-person style of *Doña Bárbara*. A different option emerged in *Vidas sêcas* (*Barren Lives*, 1938), the most well-known novel by Brazilian writer Graciliano Ramos (1892–53).

Ramos's early novels made innovative use of first-person narrators and offer a stark perspective on the lives of social outcasts. *Vidas sêcas* uses a third-person narrator, but it retains psychological density in telling the story of Fabiano and Vitória, parents in a family of migrant workers struggling to survive on the *sertão*, Brazil's draught-stricken interior plain. Ramos's novel is thematically reminiscent of its contemporary from the United States, *The Grapes of Wrath* (1939), but Steinbeck's novel is an optimistic epic of class consciousness whose protagonists seem inevitably tied to the collective agency of larger social networks. In contrast, Ramos's sparse prose reflects the emotional states of his characters in the harshness of their daily lives. He presents the family as extremely isolated, both from each other (the two children are never referred to by name) and, crucially, from the other poor farmers and workers who share their fate. The novel ends as it begins, with Fabiano and Vitória looking for work after abandoning a spare plot of land. Ramos's intense pessimism bears some comparisons to French existentialism, but a more apt comparison might be to Norwegian novelist Knut Hamsun (1859–52) or Sweden's Pär Lagarkvist (1891–1974). As Ángel Rama noted, these authors appealed to Latin American writers like Mexican novelist Juan Rulfo (1917–86) because the Scandinavians wrote about the devastation of rural life and traditional values in countries that also experienced modernization from the peripheries of the great world powers. Hamsun in particular gained international renown for depicting the hopeless longing of peasants trapped by urbanization, and Ramos occupies a similar space in Latin American literature.

The family's crisis in *Vidas sêcas* arises when the estate where they had long lived is taken over by an absentee landlord whose harshness contrasts strongly in Fabiano's mind to the previous owner's benevolent control. The new landlord schemes to extract more labor and money from his workers, and this change implies a growing insertion of the rural economy into market structures that eroded traditional forms of patronage and control. At times the desperation of the protagonists' lives seems to derive from the harshness of the land itself, but that impression is both nihilistic and partial. Working against the novel's circular plot and static tone, the underlying narrative of a changing rural society implies that the characters' fate results less from climatic extremes of drought and flash-floods than from a dysfunctional social system. This concern firmly inserts *Vidas Sêcas* into the regionalist problematic of economic modernization and its impact on national and local cultures. What separates Ramos's work from much literature of the 1930s is the emotional intensity achieved in his stark language.

Ramos's prose is spare throughout *Vidas sêcas*, and one of the novel's greatest strengths is its ability to create emotional and psychological contours through action. What the characters do often reveals more about their experience and motivations than what they say or think. Particularly in the novel's opening chapters, the result is a deceptively direct style that seems to mimic the characters's laconic nature while forcing the reader to engage with the text in ways that a more elaborated narrative would not. Similarly, much of the novel's backstory comes through Fabiano's own reflections, further drawing the reader into his perspective. Ramos's ability to avoid an externalized view of his characters and the novel's underlying history of economic change separates *Vidas sêcas* from a great deal of regional fiction, but the same focus on the immediacy of action also generates a central limitation. Ultimately, the novel seems to indicate that the struggle for subsistence so overwhelms the rural poor that they are incapable of imagining any alternative social outcome other than a return to the idealized good landowner. In the final pages, Fabiano and Vitória speak of moving to the city, where their children might be educated and so avoid the hard life of the *sertão*. This dream offers a dim alternative, but it also functions within the dominant system and its promise of social advancement for the poor. Moreover, the hope of upward mobility emerges only in the final pages and seems more the sign of a false hope or a deception than the possibility of a forward-looking solution to the problems of the countryside.

In addition to Ramos's focus on the rural poor, gender offers an important point at which different perspectives on Latin American society emerged in the regionalist writing of the 1920s. The nineteenth-century national romance persists in novels like *Doña Bárbara*, and gender relations remain central in *La vorágine*. The gender-based schemes that sustain the allegorical frameworks of these works have long been questioned by women intellectuals, including prominent figures like Venezuelan writer Teresa de la Parra (1891–1936). De la Parra's impressionistic novel, *Las memorias de Mamá Blanca* (*Mama Blanca's Memoirs*, 1929), responds directly to the patriarchal worldview expressed in a book like *Doña Bárbara*, but De la Parra's criticism emerges from nostalgia for the rural oligarchy, a social class being undermined by economic changes since the late nineteenth century. A different kind of feminist writing can be found in the work of Chilean author María Luisa Bombal (1910–80), whose stylistic innovations are tied to a critique of women's marginalization.

Like De la Parra, Bombal was born into privilege, but her work moves into subjective and fantastic narratives in a mode pioneered by Brazilian novelist Machado de Assis (1839–1908) and Uruguayan writers Felisberto Hernández (1902–64) and Juan Carlos Onetti (1909–93). Bombal's second novel, *La amortajada* (*The Shrouded Woman*, 1938), follows Machado's *Memórias póstumas de Brás Cubas* (*The Posthumous Memoirs of Brás Cubas*, 1880) in narrating from the perspective of a dead protagonist, in Bombal's case a woman who remembers her life as family members pay their respects to her body. Bombal combines this surprising perspective with a style influenced by post-*modernista* poetry. She was a close friend of Pablo Neruda (1904–73), Latin America's dominant poet in the first half of the twentieth century, and her controlled language generates unusual psychological depth. This is particularly important for her depictions of feminine subjectivity. In both *La amortajada* and her first novel, *La última niebla* (*The House of Mist*, 1935), Bombal implies a strong critique of domestic abuse, abortion, and women's subordination. Most incisively Bombal expresses feminine sexuality well outside the accepted terrain of marriage and maternity. Today, she is rightly seen as a major writer whose influence was recognized by novelists as important as Juan Rulfo.

Doña Bárbara exemplifies the telluric novel as national romance, while writers like Rivera and Bombal undermined the social force of that allegory by introducing alternative narrative subjects. In a similar vein, Ramos engaged the problem of social class, but *Vidas Sêcas* finally denies a collective agency to his protagonists. From this perspective, a separate starting point can be identified for the regional novel: the years 1914–15, in the semi-arid landscape of west-central Mexico. Here Mariano Azuela (1873–1952), a small-town doctor, embarked on a dangerous political flirtation that would sweep him out of his familiar environment and lead to deep changes in his style as a novelist. A supporter of Francisco I. Madero, the first leader of the Mexican Revolution (1910–20), Azuela served in the revolutionary government established for the state of Jalisco by Pancho Villa. When the Villista regime in Jalisco collapsed, Azuela followed its troops north and spent a brief period in El Paso, Texas. Desperate for cash, he pulled together a short work from his notes on recent events. The result was *Los de abajo* (*The Underdogs*, 1915), a novel that became a turning point in Latin American narrative.

For many years, *Los de abajo* was lost in the tumult of Mexico's civil war, but critics rediscovered it in the mid-1920s and its rapid canonization as the central novel of the revolution marked the consolidation of a new intellectual class. Artistic activity had been strong in the years before the Mexican Revolution, and many dissenting writers became foundational figures for a post-revolutionary cultural establishment that transformed the iconography of Mexico's national history. Their work focused on a vindication of popular traditions in contrast to the Europeanizing philosophy of the pre-revolutionary government. Azuela was active in local intellectual circles before joining the Villista movement, and his early literature reflects the pre-revolutionary fervor. *Los de abajo* itself is centered on Demetrio Macías, a small-time rebel who becomes a Villista general. Critics in the 1920s praised the realism and sympathy with which Azuela depicts his lower-class protagonists, but as the novel progresses, Demetrio falls victim to a feckless advisor who amasses a fortune and quickly abandons him. It has subsequently been noted that the novel's trajectory follows an inverse arch: the more Demetrio strays from his home and the higher he rises in the rebel army, the more he losses his morality and the more his understanding of the revolution fails. The reader is left to conclude that the lower classes could not comprehend political changes they themselves helped to initiate, and *Los de abajo* can be seen as a work whose final message is that the common people cannot govern themselves. That message meshed with the post-revolutionary elite's efforts to construct a centralized and paternalistic state, but *Los de abajo* functioned in this role only because of its unprecedented inclusion of popular culture and oral traditions.

Los de abajo continues to show the influence of earlier narrative forms, particularly a tendency inherited from French naturalism to tie moral and social development to environmental factors. What is new in *Los de abajo* is Azuela's use of dialogue, which reduces the narrator's interventions to telegraphic descriptions. The story's driving force thus seems to come from the characters themselves rather than a heavy-handed allegory imposed by an omniscient narrator. The novel also derives its sense of having faithfully captured the revolution and its protagonists through Azuela's use of regional and class-specific dialects. In contrast to Gallegos, Azuela does not always mark these forms of popular speech as clearly inferior to his third-person narration. A two-edged dynamic results. On the one hand, Azuela's use of orality lends credibility to a narrative that is otherwise hostile to the aspirations of its own anti-heroes. On the other hand, the range of expression which Azuela opens around his lower-class characters sometimes exceeds the ideological structure of the novel. While the dominant allegory of *Los de abajo* denies that the lower-class revolutionaries had their own political agenda, Azuela's dialogue allows the careful reader to construct a counter-narration of the revolution from a more popular perspective. This is particularly true for the figure of Pancho Villa. While Villa is not present as a character, his fame exercises a powerful charisma over Demetrio and his men. When these moments are reassembled from different points in the novel, it is possible to outline a set of aspirations counter to the overall depiction of the rebels as lacking a social agenda independent of their educated but self-serving advisors.

Along with Azuela, many of Mexico's most important post-revolutionary intellectuals wrote about the armed conflict. These included José Vasconcelos (1882–1959), whose cultural nationalism was influential across Latin America, and Martín Luis Guzmán (1887–76), whose *La sombra del caudillo* ("The shadow of the caudillo," 1929) is an outstanding example of the urban novel in early-twentieth-century Latin America and whose memoir, *El águila y la serpiente* (*The Eagle and the Serpent*, 1928), offers a vivid document of the period. While post-revolutionary literature was peaking in the 1930s, a different kind of work was created by the only woman considered a canonical novelist of the Mexican Revolution, Nellie Campobello (1900–86). Campobello was well known as an innovator in modern dance, and her literature was read but not widely understood until recently. Her first novel, *Cartucho* (1931), is fragmentary to the point of questioning standard definitions of the novel. For many years, it was considered innovative primarily for using the first-person voice of a young girl whose moral detachment long defied analysis. As Blanca Rodríguez has noted, the lack of critical engagement with Campobello owes a great deal to the fact that she defied all the norms of feminine culture in her day. The young woman who narrates *Cartucho* assails such stereotypes as women's passivity and moral superiority, long tied to idealized images of maternity and sentimental education. In addition, Campobello articulates a historical perspective invalidated in a work like *Los de abajo*. Azuela's novel limits its protagonists' political and social ambitions through a national perspective on the revolution: Demetrio seems unable to understand the revolution as a national movement, and this failure condemns him to corruption and defeat. By contrast, *Cartucho* is uncompromisingly regional, and the young narrator's celebration of violence and death can best be explained through the specific history of Campobello's home in north-central Mexico, where a long tradition of local autonomy created friction with the central government.

Campobello's regionalism is inescapably tied to her engagement with popular cultural and oral traditions. She quotes from folk ballads (*corridos*) but, more importantly, she depicts events and personages as *corridos* treated and popularized them. Also influential in *Cartucho* are lithographic prints (*estampas*) such as those of José Guadalupe Posada (1852–1913), which are reflected in Campobello's condensed character sketches and her fragmentary sense of action, as well as her subordination of plot to moral codes. Like figures in *estampas*, Campobello's characters are icons of behavioral norms, such as loyalty, courage, daring, treason, devotion, and cowardice. These norms are not defined through ethics, or models of behavior with universal value, but through regional identity. In *Cartucho*, a character's worth depends on loyalty to this regional identity, not abstract notions of good and evil. For Campobello, the Mexican Revolution is, then, not a failed attempt to effect national integration. It is a failed effort to defend local structures against an intrusive national state. This aspect of Campobello's work exemplifies a strong regionalist subcurrent whose significance has become clear only as the nation-state has ceased to function as an unquestioned principle for organizing Latin American cultural history.

The recalcitrant regionalism expressed in a novel like *Cartucho* represents a new focus on social elements which resist a homogenous national culture. One of the most influential branches of Latin American literature to address similar issues in the early twentieth century focused on the experience of the working classes. In Spanish America, the short stories of Chilean writer Baldomero Lillo (1867–1923) offer the most important announcement of a proletarian literature. Lillo's collections *Sub terra* (1904) and *Sub sole* (1907) depict the working conditions of rural Chile and its copper mines. Even more strongly than Azuela, Lillo's work demonstrates the ongoing influence of naturalism, but it also illustrates the move of Latin American intellectuals towards political and social stances critical of the dominant order. A more elaborated example can be found in *El tungsteno* (*Tungsten*, 1931), the only novel by Peruvian poet César Vallejo (1892–1938). *El tungsteno's* direct realism contrasts to Vallejo's hermetic and experimental poetry, and *El tungsteno* followed a shift away from the established Latin American ideologies of liberalism and conservatism in favor of new political formulations drawn from nationalism, anti-imperialism, anarchism, and Marxism.

Like Vallejo, many left-leaning intellectuals in the 1930s began to engage with systematic political analyses but also with new literary forms. An incisive example is *Los que se van* ("The ones who go away," 1930), a collection of short stories by Ecuadorian writers Demetrio Aguilera Malta (1909–82), Joaquín Gallegos Lara (1911–47), and Enrique Gil Gilbert (1912–75). They formed the core of the "Guayaquil Group" and their work strove to create a politically engaged description of Ecuadorian society focused on that country's Pacific coast. *Los que se van* is a superb example of programmatic literature which demonstrates strongly shared political and esthetic tenets. The most striking innovation is a sustained engagement with popular modes of speech. In this, their work is superficially similar to Azuela's or Campobello's, but Ecuadorian history lacked the unifying theme which the Mexican Revolution provided, and the specificity of oral discourse registered in *Los que se van* is so idiosyncratic that it now serves less as a mechanism for legitimating the author's realism than as an off-putting device that renders the text opaque to many readers. The Guayaquil Group's reputation has correspondingly suffered, and their attempts to create a convergence of radical politics and new narrative techniques did not generate a sustained influence.

The proletarian fiction with greater staying power has tended to address working-class problems through individual psychology and more complex narrative structures. A clear example is Mexican writer José Revueltas (1914–76), whose long career and conflicted relationship with the Mexican Communist Party defined him as a figure ill at ease with the official life of the state and with its institutional opposition. Revueltas's work spans Marxist social theory from Stalinist orthodoxy in the 1940s and 1950s to the cultural rebellion of the 1960s. His novelistic output is similarly diverse, but it is united by the psychology of alienation. This topic led Revueltas into theories of language, consciousness, and the role of culture in political change, as can be seen in *El luto humano* (*Human Mourning*, 1943), his first novel. This short masterpiece brings together Revueltas's interests in a compact narration of an agricultural strike in northern Mexico. In part a meditation on the strike as a political tool, *El luto humano* penetrates deeply into its protagonists' psychology in order to suggest that class consciousness can be understood only through popular culture and through local and regional identities. Some of Revueltas's best-known subsequent novels, such as *Los días terrenales* ("Earthly days," 1949), chronicle his conflicts with the Mexican Communist Party, and while Revueltas's reputation has been rooted in his profile as an activist intellectual, his work made pioneering adaptations of the interior monologue while exploring such unexpected themes as homosexuality. Only recently has Revueltas transcended his status as a cult figure in Mexico to become a writer of international profile. Such is not the case for Jorge Amado (1912–2002), Brazil's most recognized author and an important narrator of working-class struggles.

Amado worked as a labor activist and his literature is influenced by the social philosophy and rural politics of Brazil's northeast. In the 1930s and 1940s, he wrote prolifically about coastal life in northeastern Brazil and its dependence on the agricultural export-economy. As Neil Larsen argues, Amado's novels like *Cacau* (1933), *Suor* (1934), *Jubiabá* (1935), and *Terras do sem fim* (*The Violent Land*, 1943) offer accomplished realist narratives that move beyond racial or geographic explanations for social conflict. Instead, Amado attributes social crises to historic and economic problems tied to the international economy. His early works thus engage with a non-deterministic historical framework through sympathetic treatments of working-class culture and its role in the development of class consciousness and political organization. Amado moved in a different direction with the highly acclaimed *Gabriela, cravo e canela* (*Gabriela, Clove and Cinnamon*, 1959), which is based on eroticism and fantasy. This change emerged from Amado's personal political dissatisfactions, but it is indicative of broader trends as Latin American novelists turned with increasing sophistication to the problems of social heterogeneity embodied particularly in ethnicity. This turn proved particularly influential in the *indigenista* novel.

Indigenista fiction treats Latin America's native populations, but it often recreates the paternalism and racial hierarchies which it seeks to question. This is true even in progressive writers like Ecuadorian novelist Jorge Icaza (1906–78). Icaza's best-known novel, *Huasipungo* (*The Villagers*, 1943), is a scathing condemnation of Ecuador's insertion into the global economy and the brutal exploitation of indigenous workers. However, Icaza portrays his native protagonists as so thoroughly crushed under the dominant economic system that they seem incapable of taking effective action on their own behalf. His descriptions infantilize and animalize the native characters, and Icaza reduces their speech to primitive enunciations built around nouns and gerunds. The result makes indigenous cultures appear deficient in analytical categories and historical perspective.

Other *indigenista* writers were more nuanced, such as Guatemalan novelist Miguel Ángel Asturias (1899–1974), whose short stories in *Leyendas de Guatemala* (*Legends of Guatemala*, 1930) had already moved beyond the pitfalls of *Huasipungo*. Ironically, however, Asturias's efforts to engage with Maya culture drew heavily on European surrealism, which Asturias experienced in Paris during the 1920s. A different technique was adopted by the other great *indigenista* writer of the mid-twentieth century, Peruvian novelist José María Arguedas (1911–69).

Raised bilingually in Quechua and Spanish, Arguedas, almost alone among Latin American writers, possessed a high level of colloquial proficiency in a native language. As a result, rather than using European innovations to depict Latin American culture, Arguedas altered the esthetic systems of the dominant literature according to linguistic and social codes drawn from Quechua-speaking Peruvians. Arguedas's early short-story collection, *Agua* (1935), offered the first example of a technique developed more fully in his first novel, *Yawar fiesta* (1941). Both *Agua* and *Yawar fiesta* employ an idiosyncratic Spanish altered at the level of syntax to reflect how native speakers of Quechua express themselves in a second language. Arguedas abandoned this technique for esthetic and sociological reasons, eventually settling on less direct alterations to the novelistic form. The best-known example is his semi-autobiographical work *Los ríos profundos* (*Deep Rivers*, 1958), which tells the story of a bilingual narrator who resists assimilation into the dominant society of his boarding school. Less linguistically challenging than Arguedas's earlier fiction, *Los ríos profundos* continues a Quechua-influenced perspective on social relations through deeply contextualized moral codes. Few authors have used popular traditions to leverage the dominant form of the novel as successfully as Arguedas, but his work also

includes problematic treatments of gender. It is only in the work of Rosario
Castellanos (1925–74), Latin America's most important woman author of
indigenista fiction, that a critical portrayal of national and regional consolidation appears within categories inflected by both ethnicity and gender.

Perhaps more than any other writer, Castellanos illustrates how aspects
of the regional novel operated well into the 1960s. Born to a wealthy family from southern Mexico, Castellanos achieved fame as a feminist, poet,
narrator, and essayist. Both of her *indigenista* novels, *Balún-Canán (The
Nine Guardians,* 1957) and *Oficio de tinieblas (The Book of Lamentations,*
1962), center on gender categories as markers for regional and native identities. *Balún-Canán* focuses on a land-owning family whose social standing is
eroded by reforms from the national government. This history is allegorized
through the incapacity of the family to sustain its patriarchal line. When her
sickly brother dies, the novel's protagonist, a young girl, becomes the sole
heir, threatening the continuation of the family name. That crisis produces
a sense of stagnation, and the indigenous peasants' face-off with the girl's
father in a conflict that ultimately drains both sides. Caught in the middle,
Castellanos's young narrator portrays how powerful forces of socialization,
particularly the Church, break the girl's identification with the local Maya
culture in order to mold her according to dominant models of feminine
subjectivity.

Oficio de tinieblas is a more ambitious novel centered on an indigenous
rebellion in the mid-nineteenth century. Castellanos transfers this history to
the 1930s, when the government of Lázaro Cárdenas implemented a wide-
ranging program of land reform in Mexico. An epic narrative, *Oficio de
tinieblas* draws together characters from various sides of the conflict and
focuses on a famous but apocryphal local event: the crucifixion of an indigenous child, slain by his own people to found a native Christian church.
As Cynthia Steele has noted, Castellanos's depictions of this event reproduce many stereotypes about the savagery of indigenous culture, but *Oficio
de tinieblas* remains a noteworthy achievement for its portrayal of indigenous women as crucial to popular insurrection. Like *Balún-Canán, Oficio
de tinieblas* defends regional history and the ambiguity it expresses about
the nation-state as a vehicle for modernization.

Conclusion

The time has long passed when the regional novel could be taken to represent the maturity of Latin American literature through the successful expression of national identities. Such accounts rest on overly optimistic historical assessments and on a teleological imperative in which national cultures

operate as singular entities, each with a past, present, and future that can be told as a coherent whole. That fact does not, however, deny the importance of understanding the regional novel as part of a cultural history in which the first decades of the twentieth century are both a transition from the past and a groundwork for the future. The best way to understand the importance of the regional novel within that transition may not be its efforts to adopt new narrative devices or its elaboration of specific political themes. Instead, the periodization of regional narrative may best be derived from its appearance at the moment in which the novel came to occupy a central place in Latin American intellectual life. Virtually all of the writers examined here wrote with the supposition that their works would participate in broad dialogues on the major issues of their day, including the meaning of local history and its relationship to international politics and national development. A similar sense that the novel held a central place in such debates reached its peak with the Boom writers of the 1960s and early 1970s. Since that time, the social significance of the novel has seemingly declined. This decline derives from the growth of Latin American social science, which has assumed many of the critical functions previously associated with artists. The decline of the novel's importance also responds to the growth of civil societies that have attenuated the role of public intellectuals, but the most important factor contributing to the loss of social standing for the Latin American novel is the growth of the mass media, which have steadily eroded the importance of literature and the other arts as central to the definition of collective identity, cultural citizenship, and shared social destiny. The novel's place in Latin American intellectual life is now assuming a profile markedly different from its role in the first decades of the twentieth century. This new profile has yet to assume a definite form, but it is clearly tied to a transnational literary marketplace that mediates the form and content of the novel in ways unanticipated by previous generations of writers. Ultimately, the institutional and social space afforded to literature within a public sphere dominated by the international media and its literary marketplace will determine, more than innovations in language or form, how future readers will measure the distance that separates them from the cultural environment in which the Latin American regional novel emerged as a rich and significant body of work.

FURTHER READING

Alonso, Carlos, *The Spanish American Regional Novel*, Cambridge University Press, 1990.

Franco, Jean, *An Introduction to Spanish American Literature*, Cambridge University Press, 1994.

González Echevarría, Roberto, "*Doña Bárbara* Writes the Plain," in Roberto González Echevarría, *The Voice of the Masters: Writing and Authority in Modern Latin America*, Austin: University of Texas Press, 1985, pp. 33–63.

Henríquez Ureña, Pedro, *Literary Currents in Hispanic America*, Cambridge, Mass: Harvard University Press, 1945.

Neil Larsen, *Reading North by South*,University of Minnesota Press, 1995.

Martin, Gerald, "Literature, Music, and the Visual Arts, 1870–1930," and "Literature since 1920," in Leslie Bethell (ed.), *A Cultural History of Latin America*, Cambridge University Press, 1998, pp. 47–227.

Meléndez, Concha, "Tres novelas de la naturaleza americana: *Don Segundo Sombra, La vorágine, Doña Bárbara*," *Revista Bimestre Cubana* 28 (1931): 82–93.

Ordóñez, Montserrat (ed.), *La vorágine: textos críticos*, Bogotá: Alianza Editorial Colombiana, 1987.

Rama, Ángel, *Transculturación narrativa en América Latina*, Mexico City: Siglo XXI, 1982.

Robe, Stanley, *Mariano Azuela and the Mexican Underdogs*, Berkeley and Los Angeles: University of California Press, 1979.

Rowe, William, *Mito e ideología en la obra de José María Arguedas*, Lima: Instituto Nacional de Cultura, 1979.

Sarlo, Beatriz, "Responses, Inventions, and Displacements: Urban Transformations and Rural Utopias," in Ricardo Güiraldes, *Don Segundo Sombra*, ed. Gwen Kirkpatrick, trans. Patricia Owen Steiner, University of Pittsburgh Press, 1985, pp. 245–56.

Sommer, Doris, *Foundational Fictions*, Berkeley and Los Angeles: University of California Press, 1991.

Steele, Cynthia, *Literatura indigenista en los Estados Unidos y México*, Mexico City: Insitituto Nacional Indigenista, 1985.

3

JOHN KING

The Boom of the Latin American novel

Mapping the field

Beginnings are notoriously difficult to define: what we have in literature are continuities and breaks with the past. Did the "Boom" of the Latin American novel begin in 1958, when Carlos Fuentes (b. 1928) published his innovative, multilayered exploration of Mexico City in the 1940s and 1950s, *La región más transparente* (*Where the Air is Clear*)? Or in 1962, when Mario Vargas Llosa (b. 1936) won the Biblioteca Breve Prize (offered by the Spanish publishers Seix Barral) for his manuscript *Los impostores* ("The impostors"), that would later be re-titled *La ciudad y los perros* (*Time of the Hero*)? Or in 1963, when Julio Cortázar (1914–84) published *Rayuela* (*Hopscotch*), his extraordinary Baedeker of the new? Or in 1967, when Gabriel García Márquez (b. 1928) brought out *Cien años de soledad* (*One Hundred Years of Solitude*), initiating a worldwide interest in magical realism? Whatever inaugural date different critics might propose, this chapter deals with developments from the late fifties to the early seventies.

Two different political projects helped to modernize and radicalize the political and cultural climate: the Cuban Revolution and the rhetoric and realities of what economists at the time called "developmentalism." We should not, with over forty years of hindsight and in a very different political climate, underestimate the achievements and also the hope offered by the Cuban Revolution. It was held by most at the time in Latin America to be an exemplary nationalist and anti-imperialist movement that seemed to demand an intellectual and practical commitment and offered the utopian promise of uniting the artistic and political vanguards. In the early years at least, Cuba invited young writers to visit the island, awarded literary prizes, published new work in their journal *Casa de las Américas*, and organized symposia and round-table discussions. There is no doubt that writers such as Carlos Fuentes and Mario Vargas Llosa sympathized with this early promise of social and cultural change. Carlos Fuentes wrote part of *La muerte de Artemio Cruz* (*The Death of Artemio Cruz*, 1962) – his quintessential "Boom" novel – while in residence in Havana, while Vargas Llosa would persuasively argue in his acceptance speech at being awarded the Rómulo Gallegos Prize in 1967 – evocatively and significantly entitled "Literature is fire," a statement that could almost be read as a manifesto of a group – that the underdevelopment of Latin America could be solved only through radical means.[1] While history would take a different turn to that imagined by Vargas Llosa, the passion and commitment of the argument remain as a testament to that specific time.

Fear of another Cuba would, of course, dominate US foreign policy in the 1960s in Latin America, and would lead to policies that form part of any overall definition of the Boom. These policies ranged from support for "modernizing," non-revolutionary regimes such as those of Frondizi in Argentina, Frei in Chile, or Kubitschek in Brazil, to the development of support of certain forms of modern art by cultural foundations such as Ford and Rockefeller, to the establishment of centers of study on Latin America in the USA and in Europe – that were fundamental in generating critical works on the Boom and on many other aspects of politics and culture – to the support of translations of Latin American fiction. Later in this book, Suzanne Jill Levine discusses the politics of translation and the promotion of Latin American literature in the USA, while Jean Franco's 2002 study – and Franco, it must be acknowledged, was an important disseminator of knowledge about Latin American literature from the sixties, along with higher profile academics of the time like Emir Rodríguez Monegal who actively disseminated the works of the Boom in his magazine *Mundo Nuevo* and in subsequent publications – gives a reading of Spanish American literary texts in the context of the Cold War.[2] This context is clearly important to our overall understanding of the internationalization of the Boom writers, but it would be wrong to label their work as "export-led" or to construe their importance merely as a US marketing strategy. Before the novelists had a visibility in world markets, they had found their own Latin American audiences.

The sixties, sandwiched in Latin America between populist regimes of the forties and fifties and a wave of military dictatorships in the early to mid-seventies, showed many signs of cultural innovation and modernization (to use another term of the time). Some snapshots of the period must suffice as illustrations. The most impressive, perhaps overblown, symbol of the new was the building of the city of Brasília. In a project led by the enthusiastic and charismatic president of Brazil, Juscelino Kubitschek – who promised his country "fifty years of progress in five" – and designed by the architects Oscar Nieymeyer and Lúcio Costa, Brasília took shape from the late 1950s and through the 1960s. The ambition and beauty of the project caused Kubitschek to herald it in 1960 as an extraordinary *Brazilian* achievement:

> We imported neither architects nor town planning experts to design Brasília. We planned and built it with our own native talents – Niemeyer and Costa – and the laborers who erected it, from the contractor down to the "candango" . . . were all our own people. That is why Brasília depicts, more eloquently than words can convey, our level of civilization and our enterprising spirit.[3]

Here is an early expression of the optimism of the time, which could be summed up in Octavio Paz's famous phrase that Latin Americans were now contemporaries of all mankind, sharing the banquet of civilization on equal terms. The Boom, in the same way as Kubitschek described Brasília, would be both formally innovative and "rooted" in a Latin American experience.

Moving to another city, Buenos Aires, the late fifties and early sixties were marked here by innovations in many fields, from the selling of washing machines and washing powders, to new wave cinema, to the introduction of television and mass media advertising, to the growth of psychotherapy and analysis. The word "Boom," of course, is intimately associated with marketing, with the launching of new products. Critic Angel Rama has provided revealing figures of sales of Cortázar's novels in the 1960s. If an expected print run was one or two thousand copies for a novel published in 1960, by the end of the decade, sales for each novel would be in the tens of thousands or, in the case of García Márquez's runaway success, *Cien años de soledad*, in hundreds of thousands.[4] The Boom helped to cause but also benefited greatly from this growth in middle-class readership in Latin America.

A number of factors contribute to this increase apart from obvious demographic changes and growth in urbanization. The story of the Boom is linked to the open and aggressive policies of certain publishing houses, in Spain and throughout Latin America. In Barcelona, Carlos Barral set up the Biblioteca Breve prize, which guaranteed widespread distribution for the winner's novel. Within Latin America, some of the larger houses, especially in Argentina and in Mexico – Losada, Sudamericana, Espasa Calpe – increased their representation and distribution of Spanish American texts and smaller publishing houses grew up and supported contemporary authors. In Buenos Aires, the university press EUDEBA began to produce cheap copies of classics in print runs of tens of thousands. Of course, there had been distribution throughout Latin America before the sixties. In an autobiography as full of fable as of fact, García Márquez spoke of the traveling salesmen who would arrive in Baranquilla in the late forties with books from Argentine publishers such as Losada and Sur: "Thanks to them we were early admirers of Jorge Luis Borges, Julio Cortázar, Felisberto Hernández and the English and American novelists, well translated by Victoria Ocampo's group."[5] But such distribution was infrequent and print runs were small.

A brief look at the relationship between García Márquez and his publishers helps to reveal this shift in the marketplace. In his memoir he talks of writing his third novel, *La mala hora* (*In Evil Hour*, 1962), in a rundown residence in the Latin Quarter in Paris in 1960, waiting, like the Colonel in his earlier novel, *El coronel no tiene quien le escriba* (*No One Writes to the Colonel*, 1958) "for a check that never arrived." He bound the manuscript with a tie and then forgot about it for two years, until he was asked to submit it for the Esso Colombia literary prize. He sent the only copy of the manuscript to the jury, and won the $3,000 US, a small fortune in a world of penniless authors. The novel was published in Madrid but the author found that it had been "dubbed" into the dialect of Madrid, with laughable consequences. He was forced, he claims, to have this edition withdrawn and to "retranslate" it into Caribbean Colombian Spanish, since the original was the one used and abused for the "Spanish" version.[6] This success gave him some security, but he would still spend a number of years in the sixties in precarious conditions, writing film scripts in Mexico for movies that no one wanted to make, until he decided to put all his discarded scripts together and expand the world of Macondo that he had been developing in his earlier tales. He sent the resulting manuscript, *Cien años de soledad*, to the Argentine publishers Sudamericana whose modest initial print run was sold out in hours. Cultural journalist and later bestselling writer Tomás Eloy Martínez remembers taking García Márquez to the theater at the Di Tella Institute – the hub of "swinging Buenos Aires" – a few weeks after the publication of the novel. The entire audience stood up when they entered the auditorium and began clapping and shouting their approval.[7] García Márquez had "arrived" and would never again leave the center stage. The initial print run in Spanish for his next novel *El otoño del patriarca* (*The Autumn of the Patriarch*, 1975) would be half a million copies.[8]

Tomás Eloy Martínez would be a key figure in the dissemination of the Boom as the main cultural journalist, along with Ernesto Schóo, of the newsweekly magazine *Primera Plana* that, in the style of *Time* or *Newsweek*, offered a new style of political and cultural commentary in the 1960s in Argentina: other magazines would subsequently copy its format all over the continent. From its first issue in November 1962 that carried on its front cover an image of J. F. Kennedy, the magazine exuded sophistica-tion and modernity and was up to date with all the latest fashions. In the section on books, the world of authors and books became news, beyond the domain of small literary groups or *cénacles*. And what could be more fashionable than this seemingly new writing coming from all over Latin America, or the success of home-grown talents? In *Primera Plana*, primacy was given to the interview, to highlighting the writer as "star." In line with the marketing connotations of the word Boom, the author would become a brand name, a mark of industrial quality, by which new products could be sold. The journalism was, at the same time, of the highest standard. Perhaps the most striking illustration for our purposes is a 1967 issue of the jour-nal that displays García Márquez on the front cover, followed inside by an interview and an extract from the yet to be published, *Cien años*.

The Chilean writer José Donoso would write his own "personal history" of the Boom in 1972.[9] In it he repeatedly emphasizes the centrality of this vibrant city Buenos Aires in his literary formation, as he escaped from what he experienced as the claustrophobia of cultural life in Chile. He also argued that the literary journal *Mundo Nuevo*, established in Paris in 1966 by the Uruguayan critic Emir Rodríguez Monegal, was a key factor in promoting the Boom. Unlike the Cuban journal *Casa*, *Mundo Nuevo* avoided discus-sion of concrete political commitment and treated contemporary novelists as part of a cultural renaissance, free from ideological disputes. It favorably reviewed the latest texts, conducted interviews with authors – the first issue in July 1966 had a long interview with Carlos Fuentes – and printed short extracts of new work. It chimed with the US cold war support of literary modernism and it perhaps came as no surprise when the body support-ing the magazine, the Congress for Cultural Freedom, was found to receive its funds from the CIA. As we have argued above, this is a further exam-ple of the Boom attracting, for the space of a decade, the support of both politically engaged and culturally modernizing groups. The honeymoon, in particular with Cuba, would end quite abruptly, for some, in the early seventies.

Precursors to the Boom

The Boom novelists were also in some cases indefatigable literary critics, who gave a clear sense of how their work resonated with other authors. In *Rayuela,* that compendium of literature, certain River Plate writers are offered as required reading: Roberto Arlt, Juan Carlos Onetti, and Leopoldo Marechal, while Borges constantly haunts its pages. *Cien años de soledad* has direct and oblique references to Rulfo, Borges, and Carpentier, amongst others. Carlos Fuentes's *La nueva novela hispanoamericana* of 1969 offers a lineage going back to the 1920s but gives prominence to Borges and to Carpentier. Even Mario Vargas Llosa's trenchant essay of 1968, with its pugnacious title, "Primitives and creators," had space to acknowledge that certain writers before the "creative" Boom had value. He registers the birth of the "modern" novel in 1939, with the publication of Onetti's *El pozo* (*The Well*). This is the moment for Vargas Llosa when the novel

> ceases to be "Latin-American", it breaks free from its servitude. It no longer serves reality, but serves itself from reality . . . Some of them [the new novelists] like the Mexican Juan Rulfo . . . , the Brazilian João Guimarães Rosa in his only novel *Grande Sertão: Veredas* (1956) or the Peruvian José María Arguedas in *Los ríos profundos* (1959) make use of the same themes as the primitive novel, but in these novelists they are no longer ends in themselves, but literary means, experiences which their imagination renews and objectifies in words.[10]

Of all these writers, Borges and Carpentier can be perhaps be seen as the most important to the Boom writers in terms of literary and thematic concerns. They take their place alongside the innovators of literary modernism, Joyce, Woolf, and Faulkner in particular, as *auteurs phares*, to use a phrase of Baudrillard: the guiding lights of a group. Space precludes a detailed discussion of influences. Gerald Martin has analyzed the impact of Joyce in Latin America.[11] The discussion about Virginia Woolf has concentrated to date on her relationship with Victoria Ocampo, her most diligent and committed translator and publisher in Spanish America, and the importance of Woolf's proto-feminist texts like "A Room of One's Own" for subsequent generations of women writers. But her interest for the Boom writers is still largely to be analyzed: for example the fascination of García Márquez and Vargas Llosa with the novel *Mrs. Dalloway*. When García Márquez first began working as a journalist for *El Heraldo* in Baranquilla in 1950, he used the pseudonym Septimus after the troubled character from *Mrs. Dalloway*, Septimus Warren Smith. Vargas Llosa has also dedicated an essay to the novel, in which he analyzes in particular the effortless complexity of the narrative point of view – in particular the blending of the *style indirect libre* and the interior monologue – which would be one of the hallmarks of his own writing in the 1960s.[12]

But it is William Faulkner who would be most often on the lips of the Boom writers when they spoke of narrative and thematic influences, for Faulkner was both modern and southern. Fuentes sums up the attraction of Faulkner:

So I feel that Faulkner had and has a great lesson for us and it is not only a formal lesson, of the modern use of the baroque, it is a profound historical lesson on how to face defeat, to admit the tragic possibility in history, it is also a profoundly literary lesson, which is the discovery of the novel through the novel, the discovery of the story by telling the story, the discovery of the characters by letting the characters act, all these magnificent lessons which I think had a profound influence on the literature of Latin America. Certainly many of the more modern novelists, García Márquez, Mario Vargas Llosa, myself, were very influenced by Faulkner.[13]

It is likely that García Márquez first read Faulkner in a translation by a writer who would become one of his mentors, Jorge Luis Borges. Borges translated *The Wild Palms* for Sudamericana publishing house in 1940, although, characteristically, he claimed that his mother did most of the work. Borges and Faulkner are the two most quoted and commented upon precursors of the Boom writers. But whereas the topics and issues in Faulkner's southern writing could offer fertile points of departure for later writers, Borges was viewed in the main as a stylistic innovator. One aspect of Borges's work caught the general mood of the sixties: his lack of deference to models, his eclectic and voracious readings across cultures, and his early claim that the tradition of Latin American literature was not confined behind autarkic national barriers but was the whole of Western culture. In a subsequently much repeated phrase, he argued that, "I believe that we South Americans can deal with all European themes without superstition, with an irreverence that can have, and already does have, fortunate consequences."[14] In this he echoed, albeit less aggressively, the Brazilian "Cannibalist Manifesto" of the 1920s, in which it was argued that, following a long tradition of anthropophagic practices dating back to the sixteenth-century Tupinambá Indians, the best way to deal with foreign influences was to ingest them and discard anything non-nutritious.

Jorge Luis Borges never wrote a novel and spent a great deal of time debunking the pretensions of modern narrative fiction, but his essays and short stories, in particular *Ficciones* (*Fictions*, 1944) and *El Aleph* (*The Aleph*, 1949), were to become enormously influential firstly to writers and later, in the sixties, to readers all over the world. Borges's rejection of realism and nationalist symbols, his definition of literature as verbal artifice, his use of the purified motifs and techniques of detective fiction and fantastic literature that emphasized the primacy of imagination over lived experience, and his praise for the role of the reader all found an attentive audience. Cortázar has stated that Borges taught him to eliminate flowery phrases, repetition, and the habit of saying in one page what could be said in one line, while Fuentes, in his influential overview of the new novel and the Boom published in 1969, stated: "The end effect of Borges's prose, without which there simply would not be a Spanish American novel, is to attest, first of all that Latin America lacks a language and consequently that it should create one. To do this, Borges shuffles the genres, rescues all traditions, eliminates the bad habits and creates a new order of rigorousness."[15]

Less attention was paid to Borges's political views, except for embarrassment at some of his less fashionable thoughts on Cuba in the sixties and the early Pinochet regime in 1973 and beyond. Most agreed with Octavio Paz, that Borges was not much interested in history and that his political opinions were either moral or esthetic judgments, based on little knowledge. A more complex and nuanced analysis of Borges's views on history and politics awaits its historian.[16]

Not all River Plate writers subscribed to Borges's metaphysical fantasies of the forties, although a close group of friends and colleagues, Adolfo Bioy Casáres (1914–99), Silvina Ocampo (1903–94), and José Bianco (1908–86) would develop his interests, and the early short stories of Julio Cortázar, in particular *Bestiario* (*Bestiary*, 1951), *Final del juego* (*End of the Game*, 1956), and *Las armas secretas* (*Secret Weapons*, 1959) would show the Borges mark of carefully crafted, rather knowing, fictions in which the fantastic could erupt suddenly into the everyday, where the boundaries of the normal were marked by a porous "other side," – unknown, threatening, and always beckoning – where doubles abounded and mysterious links appeared across time and space, where literature and reading was a game, albeit on occasion a dangerous one.

Someone who had little time for Borges politically was Leopoldo Marechal (1900–70), a Catholic and a supporter of Perón, whose populist regime, an alliance between the military, the working classes, and elements of national capital, governed Argentina between 1946 and 1955. Most writers were staunch anti-Peronists, seeing Perón as a fascist dictator: the usually mild-mannered Borges wrote virulent anti-Peronist articles and short stories. In Marechal's sprawling novel set in the 1920s, *Adán Buenosaires* (*Adam Buenosayres*, 1948) – a Joycean novel par excellence, in which Marechal attempts to write his own version of Ulysses using *Genesis* as Joyce had used *The Odyssey* – he portrays Borges as something of a blundering, myopic buffoon. Marechal's ambitious work charts the Dantesque journey of the eponymous hero through the streets of Buenos Aires over forty-eight hours. This novel, with its broad sweep, its use of the city as a space of hope and nightmare, its mixing of genres and of languages, and its playful movement between high seriousness and childish knockabout – the novel ends with the phrase, "solemn as an Englishman's fart" – blew its own *petard* at the liberal literary establishment. It also served as an inspiration for Cortázar's own depiction of the city in *Rayuela,* together with the scabrous novels of the Argentine Roberto Arlt (1900–42). The high seriousness and somewhat gloomy existentialist writings of another Argentine writer, Ernesto Sábato (b. 1911), would not have the same appeal to other writers or to wider readers, even though his most important novel, *Sobre héroes y tumbas* (*On Heroes and Tombs,* 1961), was another homage to the city of Buenos Aires. Its exploration of dark, obsessive, psychic disturbance did not capture the imagination, especially of the young, to the same degree, as we shall see, as Cortázar's playful, effortless, cosmopolitanism.

Across the River Plate, a Faulknerian universe was developing in the writing of Juan Carlos Onetti (1909–94), in the fictional port town of Santa María, "founded" as an amalgam of Argentine and Uruguayan coastal towns, in the novel *La vida breve* (*A Brief Life,* 1950), and occurring in his major fictions until its destruction by fire some forty years later in *Déjemos hablar al viento* (*Let the Wind Speak,* 1979). The reclusive Onetti would probably not have found his way to the public limelight which was relished by some of the Boom's protagonists: his world was bounded in the main by the walls of his bedroom, writing surrounded by limitless books, imagining, like his characters, other worlds, other lives as compensation for the dreariness of the everyday.

It is a long way from the mists and gloom of Santa María, in the far south of the continent, to the suffusion of light that illuminates the fictional worlds of Alejo Carpentier (1904–80), in the "marvelous real" of the Caribbean. To his short novel about slave uprising and revolution in eighteenth- and early nineteenth-century Haiti, *El reino de este mundo* (*The Kingdom of This World,* 1949), Carpentier added a prologue, where he discusses the concept of "lo real maravilloso americano," American marvelous reality. Carpentier had been close to the surrealists in the late 1920s and early 1930s in Paris and shared their interests in freeing the "marvelous" from the dead hand of rationality. By the time of his prologue, however, he felt that surrealism was a mere literary game and that the pursuit of the marvelous could be found in the geography and history of Latin America, and in the mythmaking narrators and storytelling of oral cultures. An exhausted Europe was contrasted to the exuberance and vitality of Latin America.

The search for this elusive Latin American identity and for a language to describe it could not be achieved by a writer abjuring his responsibility and turning his back on modernity as Carpentier's next novel *Los pasos perdidos* (*The Lost Steps,* 1953) would make clear. Here, a musicologist tries to turn away from the modern city and retrace his steps back to an earlier, more "civilized" moment, when he could find the wellsprings of creativity. Living outside one's own time is a brief illusion: the only comfort for

Carpentier's hyper-cultivated narrators is that they can draw on the wealth of heterogeneous cultures that make up the continent to enrich their experience of modernity. One cannot step into another's skin, although at times in *El reino* the narrator becomes so close to certain characters, in particular the slave everyman, Ti Noel, that he seems to blend with his consciousness, thus allowing movement between very different planes of reality: a rational discourse and a "magical" appreciation of the world where lycanthropy or escape from execution at the stake become possible through the *faith* of the different observers. These narrators had an Adamic task, in Carpentier's words, to name the continent, with such baroque excess in his case, that the "orderly" nature of Cartesian logic would be smothered by the exuberance of the New World. A number of paths lead from Carpentier to the Boom novelists: the search for identity; the appreciation of the heterogeneity of the continent; the dialectic between Europe and America; the blending of "high" culture and oral culture that would be at the heart of the practice that became known as magical realism; the use of baroque language as an appropriate form to do justice to the exuberance and boundless possibilities – in Carpentier's terms – of the Latin American landscape and its heterodox identities.

Of course we are using Carpentier here not as an isolated precursor, but rather as shorthand for similar tendencies taking place throughout the continent. In 1949, the year that Carpentier published *El reino*, the Guatemalan Miguel Angel Asturias (1899–1974), as other chapters analyze, brought out his magisterial "magical realist" *Hombres de maíz* (*Men of Maize*) about native Mayan resistance and defeat, blending different histories, myths, and folklore. In 1956, the Brazilian João Guimarães Rosa (1908–67) published his extraordinary *Grande sertão: veredas* (*The Devil to Pay in the Backlands*), set in the *sertão* or backlands around Minas Gerais. This work, in a more radical manner than in Carpentier's novels, blends many different sources as Riobaldo, a retired gunman, tells his story to what we take to be an urban gentleman. This bewildering narrative, with its constantly shifting viewpoint, its radical depiction of time and space – the story, unbroken by chapters, spreads out before our eyes like the overwhelming space of the *sertão*, episodes range forward and backward in time without the anchoring safety of chronology – its incorporation of the techniques of medieval romance into a modernist text, its Faustian frame, and its profoundly ambiguous, restless quest for meaning or truth, can be seen as Brazil's most ambitious and complex novel. Much like Borges in Argentina and in Spanish America, Rosa marks a divide: in Brazilian narrative there is a distinct "before" and "after" Rosa. It is clear, however, that his novel had only a limited resonance in the Spanish-speaking countries. Charles Perrone has pointed out that

Rosa's, "place in the 'boom' of contemporary Latin American narrative has not received full recognition. The fervor Rosa stirs and the respect he commands in Brazil have not had truly Pan-American repercussions."[17] Perrone attributes this to what he calls the "lamentable" separation of Spanish American and Brazilian cultural affairs but also to the stylistic extravagance of his novels, that makes translation, into Spanish or English, say, a very complex matter. Rosa and other Brazilian writers, as we shall see, were somewhat marginal to the broad marketing enthusiasm of the Boom. Rosa's *Devil to Pay in the Backlands* was published by Knopf in New York in 1963, the year when, for many, the Boom began with the publication of *Rayuela*.

The Boom novels of the 1960s

Most critics would include Julio Cortázar, Carlos Fuentes, Gabriel García Márquez, and Mario Vargas Llosa in any discussion of the Boom. These writers have dominated the literary scene since the early sixties and their influence shows no signs of diminishing as this chapter is penned in 2004. In the new millennium, for example, Vargas Llosa's "dictator" novel, *La fiesta del chivo* (*The Feast of the Goat*, 2000) sold close to one million copies in the Spanish language, while his complex intertwining of the lives of Flora Tristán and Paul Gaugin, *El paraíso en la otra esquina* (*The Way to Paradise*, 2003), put Vargas Llosa on the bestseller list in France for the first time in his life in the summer of 2003. This chapter does not follow these writers over forty years but rather focuses more narrowly on that decade when their reputations became established and unshakeable.

Rayuela enchants and "creates" its readers from the opening lines of the "normal" reading that begins with Chapter 1. As we follow the narrator Oliveira's quest for La Maga – the muse, the sorceress, the woman, the "other" – across the bridges of Paris, we are convinced by the end of the paragraph that we will never settle our world to the chronology of dates and appointments, we are not the sort of people who need lines on writing paper, or who squeeze our toothpaste from the bottom of the tube. We are Cortázar's readers: engaged, modern, experimental, hip. And what could be more experimental than for the *lector cómplice* ("accomplice" or active reader), in the novel's terms, to follow the Table of Instructions in the novel, and begin with Chapter 73, a dense discussion about literature and reality and the need to find the "other side of habit," then work back to Chapters 1 and 2 and on to Chapter 116. But even this reading is thwarted as one is trapped, between Chapters 58 and 131, to repeat the same order ad infinitum. And what of the "expendable" chapters, from Chapter 57, that comprise a third of the book, where Morelli, a rather pompous alter ego of the narrator/novelist, endlessly discusses culture and reading/writing and berates the laziness of the "lector hembra" the "female" passive reader (a term that Morelli/Cortázar could still get away with at the time), who would always look for narrative coherence, "assimilation in time and space, an ordering to the taste of the female reader."[18] The last word in the Table of Instruction is "search," a search following the meditation guide of a mandala (Cortázar's earlier title for the novel) or perhaps a rather more arbitrary search dependent on where the stone lands in the children's game of hopscotch.

Oliveira's quest for his "kibbutz of desire" takes him through the streets of Paris and Buenos Aires, into the cafes and apartments where his friends, the "Serpent's Club" meet to talk endlessly, to drink, and listen to jazz. How to step out of one's own deadening culture? Sex, drink, the improvisations of music, using literature for its ludic potential offer glimpses of the other side, where the world is not bounded by the laws of rational consciousness and logic, but in the end leave the narrator suspended, quite literally, on a ledge in an asylum, contemplating the possible final leap of the hopscotch, "paff, the end" (Chapter 56). The search for freedom is both existential and profoundly literary: the need to un-write the novel, to free it from convention and high seriousness – the solemnity and pomposity of much of national literatures – to play the game with grace and intelligence. It was this freshness and irreverence, the limitless cultural breadth, the eroticism – if, as Philip Larkin wrote, sexual intercourse began in 1963, its boundaries might not be marked in Argentina by the Chatterly ban and the Beatles' first LP, but rather by the publication of *Rayuela* – and the dialectic between Paris and Buenos Aires that attracted new readers, at first in Buenos Aires and later throughout Latin America. If, as the River Plate artists Torres García and Nicolás Uriburu would depict in paintings – Joaquín Torres García, "Our North is the South," 1936; Nicolás Uriburu, "Utopía del Sur," 1993 – the map of Latin America could be turned upside down, the south becoming north, then those sitting with their copies of *Rayuela* in the cafés in Buenos Aires in the mid-sixties, listening to artists and intellectuals such as Oscar Masotta talking about happenings or *art informel*, would in reality, Cortázar's reality, be sitting in the same café in Paris listening to talk of happenings and *art informel*. For a time, it seemed that that conjuring trick had been carried off and that Buenos Aires or Mexico City could live at the same pace, to the same pulse, as Paris or New York.

Cortázar would continue to be at the vanguard of experimentalism in the sixties. His next novel, *62: modelo para armar* (*62: A Model Kit*, 1968) would take the idea of the *lector cómplice* a stage further by offering the building blocks for a narrative that needed to be assembled by the reader. At the same time, he became more radicalized politically, adhering more closely to the Cuban political project and becoming involved in the events of May 1968 in Paris as well as keeping a close eye on events in Argentina, where a military coup in 1966 had led to a radicalization of politics and, in the early seventies, the growth of guerrilla groups. But his literary concerns crossed political divides. In 1964, the Cuban writer Guillermo Cabrera Infante (b. 1929) won the Biblioteca Breve prize in Spain for a novel in progress with the seemingly optimistic title of "Vista del amanecer en el trópico" ("A view of dawn in the Tropics"). By the time he rewrote it for publication, its title had become a tongue twister, *Tres tristes tigres* (*Three Trapped Tigers*, 1965) and its themes chimed with those of Cortázar: a group of friends endlessly talking, punning to hide pain, listening to music (boleros rather than jazz), exploring the limits of language and literature (for Morelli read Bustrófedon), parodying earlier literary traditions by having famous Cuban writers pen their own versions of Trotsky's death, and sustaining a constant humor as the world collapses around the characters. Cabrera would soon take up permanent residence in London and from 1968 – in an article published in *Primera Plana* – would begin a relentless attack on the Cuban regime. Cuba would soon offer a very public parting of the ways for the Boom.

The regime's treatment of writers would later take center stage with the Padilla affair, but the publication and subsequent criticism of José Lezama Lima's gargantuan *Paradiso* in 1966 was a sign of things to come. Lezama's eroticism, his hermeticism, and his discussion of homosexuality did not find favor with an increasingly moralizing regime but did find avid readers worldwide, including Julio Cortázar, who remarked famously that Lezama knew more about Ulysses than Penelope herself.[19]

A writer that the Cubans would pillory in the early seventies but wooed in the early sixties was the Mexican writer Carlos Fuentes. Throughout his writing career Fuentes would be preoccupied with an earlier revolution in Mexico and its legacy in society. His first novel, *La region más transparente* (*Where the Air is Clear*, 1958) incorporated the techniques of Faulkner and Dos Passos in a sweeping evocation of Mexico City in the 1940s and 1950s, the period when the dream of the revolution had given way to the dictates of savage capitalism. Fuentes's ambitious scope in this interweaving of the many voices of Mexico was in stark contrast to Mexico's other major novelist of the 1950s, Juan Rulfo, whose *Pedro Páramo* (1953) deals instead in silences, gaps, ellipses. *Pedro Páramo* would be Rulfo's only novel, while Fuentes went on to build up a body of work that he now organizes as a *Comédie Humaine*, a wide-ranging study of nineteenth and in particular twentieth-century Mexico across many novels. Fuentes was the opposite of the rather retiring and taciturn Rulfo, an ideal person to both lead and celebrate the Boom. Cosmopolitan, polyglot – with perfect English, that would make him a natural interlocutor for writers and intellectuals in North America – well versed in modernism, especially Anglo-American, politically engaged, and very articulate, Fuentes was a key figure in the sixties. His Boom novel par excellence was *La muerte de Artemio Cruz* (1962).

As Artemio Cruz lies dying, twelve days of his life come into his memory, twelve moments of choice when he survived at the expense of others, to reach the zenith of his power as a corrupt big-businessman. Cruz's account is divided into three voices, the "I," "You," and "He" that narrate in the present, future, and past tenses. As Stephen Boldy remarks: "Temporal succession is shuffled dizzily as the twelve episodes are recounted out of chronological order which allows Fuentes to sow and the reader to develop in his mind a fascinating, multi-directional web of different formal links and echoes between the periods."[20] Cruz's journey from illegitimate landowner's son before the Mexican Revolution to his death in April 1959, just before the triumph of the Cuban Revolution, affords a complex analysis of personal and national identity and a relentless critique of timeserving and compromise. The seemingly deterministic structure, however, cannot mask a great optimism in human potential, as the narrative reveals at certain moments when describing episodes in the Mexican Revolution and in the Spanish Civil War. While these two projects for freedom were thwarted, the novel seems to argue, what greater chances do we have in the sixties, once we have unmasked and revealed the old order of men like Artemio Cruz.

This optimism and an increasingly flamboyant and experimental style would mark his next two novels, *Cambio de piel* (*Change of Skin*, 1967) and *Zona sagrada* (*Sacred Place*, 1967), whether dealing with the horrors of the concentration camps in Nazi Germany, the very nature of evil in history, or the putative relationship between Mexico's best-known film diva María Félix and her son. Here is a teeming narrative imagination, equally at home with the structural anthropology of Lévi Strauss as with Mexican film melodrama or the carnival world of Fellini, mixing the genres, moving between "high" and popular culture, demanding a reader with the imagination and tenacity to play the game or participate in the "happening," to borrow an apposite term from a quintessential sixties art form.

Flamboyant or playful are words that can describe both Cortázar's and Fuentes's work in the sixties but are less appropriate to the novels of Mario Vargas Llosa, who produced three major novels in the sixties, *La ciudad y los perros* (*Time of the Hero*, 1963), *La casa verde* (*The Green House*, 1966), and *Conversación en La Catedral* (*Conversation in the Cathedral*, 1969). Together they seek an answer to the question posed at the beginning of *Conversación*: "At what precise moment had Peru screwed itself over?"

At this time, Vargas Llosa was the most tenacious socialist of Boom writers, and in his socialist period, which lasted until the early to mid-seventies, he saw literature, in Efraín Kristal's analysis, as a political phenomenon because a literary work was an *unconscious* expression of a writer's dissatisfaction with capitalism.[21] But it was at times of social upheaval that the writer's "demons," his largely unconscious obsessions, would be most active, and the writer, like a "vulture" would feed on the rotting carcass of society. Certainly the military teachers at Vargas Llosa's school in Lima, the Leoncio Prado, recognized the full force of these "demons" when they burned a thousand copies of his first novel, *La ciudad y los perros*, in the school parade ground for having defamed them and Peru. In these three novels, as Kristal argues pertinently, "his literary works were informed by a view that Peruvian society was too corrupt to be reformed. He fashioned a literary world where social respectability is a mask for corruption, where rebellious-ness is crushed by institutions that defend the established order, and where failure is a precondition to morality because success is not possible without co-optation."[22]

These novels use aspects of Vargas Llosa's autobiography as starting points or structural elements – the school in *La ciudad*, childhood memories of the desert town of Piura and a later trip to the Amazon jungle in *La casa*, and life as a student under the Odría dictatorship in Peru in the fifties in *Conversación* – but the fictions transform these autobiographical traces into rich and complex narratives.[23] Faulkner is the most quoted model here, especially techniques sometimes referred to by Vargas Llosa as "cajas chinas" (Chinese boxes) or "vasos comunicantes" (communicating vessels): stories within stories and juxtaposed narratives. It was Faulkner's particular genius, for Vargas Llosa, to tell ferocious stories of violence, greed, and unrestrained instincts in formally innovative ways. Faulkner was the first writer he read with pen and paper in hand in order to decipher the structural complexities of the narrative, and he would tell stories of similar ferocity about brutal military schools, the exploitation of indigenous peoples in the Amazon, or the social structures of dictatorship with similar formal complexity. Different incidents in time and space are superimposed, sometimes within a single sentence; many narrative voices compete for attention, in the third and first persons; previously unknown and withheld facts set up new readings; and the readers make their way through a structural labyrinth, gradually becoming aware, like the narrator in *Conversación*, of the brutality and corruption of the social order. This situation is offered no redemption within the narratives as even idealists are corrupted or marginalized: only radical change in society could usher in a new order. However formally complex, the novels have a great narrative energy: Vargas Llosa would always be a great storyteller.

His world was always that of the "realist" novel, the modern novel out of Flaubert and Faulkner. In this he shared the critical realist interests revealed in the early novels of Gabriel García Márquez, though he would remark in his studies of that writer, that from the publication of the novel *La mala hora* (*In Evil Hour*) and the stories of *Los funerales de la Mamá Grande* (*Big Mama's Funeral*), both of 1962, García Márquez's fictions began to be centered around a space, Macondo, and would use narrative voices that showed no surprise at the introduction of "magic" or the extraordinary. These are the seeds of *Cien años de soledad* (1967), the novel that many critics see as the central moment of the Boom. In his recent autobiography, García Márquez constantly refers to the world of his childhood, in Aracataca, a remote northern Caribbean coastal town of Colombia, and his life with his grandparents: his grandmother, whose storytelling introduced him to the narratives of rural popular culture, and his grandfather, a former Liberal soldier, whose stories were full of recent history, civil wars, and the stifling power of North American capital in the region. These memories and modes of narration would become part of the texture of *Cien años*, helping in particular the discovery of a storytelling voice that could weave the natural and the supernatural, the mundane and the marvelous, into a seamless whole.

Cien años is analyzed in detail elsewhere in this volume, so here we need briefly to summarize its historical moment. The novel has been labeled as "magical realist" and it became so popular wordwide that the term almost became synonymous with Latin American narrative. A useful definition of magical realism is offered in William Rowe and Vivian Schelling's work on Latin American popular culture, which points out that from the 1950s, certain writers like Rulfo, Asturias, and García Márquez wrote about native and popular cultures as valid forms of knowledge rather than as folklore, contrasting Western forms of rationalism and progress with other, "premodern," "magical" ways of seeing and thinking.[24] Magical realism, in these terms, is the creative tension caused by the juxtaposition of the avant-garde and the non-modern, Western thought and popular beliefs, Borges and García Márquez's grandmother. *Cien años* finds a voice to express these concerns shared by other writers of the sixties, to narrate afresh the experience of modernity, the problems of underdevelopment, the nature of heterogeneous cultures, the tension between the written word – the novel as a "European" form – and orality. It also expresses the hope that the new generation both inside the novel and outside it – the character who finally deciphers the enigmatic parchments, the "real" history of Macondo, Aureliano Babilonia, has a close friend called Gabriel – can do away with the solitude and inhumanity of one hundred years, or more, of Latin American history.

These were the writers who most clearly expressed the mood of the sixties and whose work found a new, expanded, readership in Latin America and then throughout the world. Carlos Fuentes and others also sought to add the Chilean José Donoso to the list of Boom writers – Fuentes was very supportive of Donoso's writing from the mid-sixties in particular – and, as the next chapter argues, Donoso's *El obsceno pájaro de la noche* (*The Obscene Bird of the Night*, 1970) took the novel form to the limits of experimentalism with the chaotic, nightmarish memories and impressions of a demented or schizoid narrator. But he joined the "group" just at the moment when any sense of abiding harmony would be shattered. The Boom has also been associated fundamentally with writing from Spanish America, although, as we have seen, narrative experimentalism in Brazil, in particular in the work of Guimarães Rosa, was as radical and innovative as anything seen in Spanish America. If the Boom was as much about audiences abroad as with readership at home, then the Brazilian writer to have the greatest impact, in particular in English translation, was Jorge Amado (1912–2001). His early work – the most notable being the epic proletarian novel *Terras do sem fim* (*The Violent Land*, 1943) – concentrated on the worker struggles in the cocoa-growing region of Minas Gerais. From the late fifties, however, his portrayal of regional popular culture became more relaxed and exuberant, focusing in particular on strong and voluptuous women characters who rebel against the values of bourgeois society. *Gabriela, cravo e canela* (*Gabriela, Clove and Cinammon*, 1959) and *Dona Flor e seus dois maridos* (*Dona Flor and Her Two Husbands*, 1966) are two examples of the most popular titles that would only later be criticized by some as mere erotic sex romps of a male fantasist. The mass appeal in 1976 of the film version of *Dona Flor* and its heroine Sonia Braga would further establish his reputation in Brazil.

The Boom promoted certain male writers. Widespread recognition outside Brazil, for example, of the work of one of Brazil's most innovative writers, Clarice Lispector (1920–77), who wrote extraordinary short stories, *Laços de família* (*Family Ties*, 1960) and *A legião extrangeira* (*The Foreign Legion*, 1964) and two existential novels, *A maça no escuro* (*An Apple in the Dark*, 1961) and *A paixão segundo G. H.* (*The Passion According to G. H.*, 1964) would not occur until the 1980s, with the translation of most of her work and her "Colonial" recognition by the major French feminist Hélène Cixous, who based her theory of *écriture feminine* on writers such as Lispector. The Boom in women's writing was a feature of a later period, dating in particular from the publication of Isabel Allende's (b. 1942) rewriting of García Márquez's male Boom novel in her *La casa de los espíritus* (*The House of the Spirits*, 1982).

Boom and bust?

If we talk of the end of the Boom, we should be clear as to what ended. By the end of the decade, Latin American fiction had an established readership at home and abroad and this would increase in subsequent decades, with many other writers enjoying some of the success of the initial group of four. The writers who have been the protagonists of this chapter continued to write, in many different styles, and all established a considerable body of work. With increasing fame and visibility, they also became international stars, but stars that continued an interest in politics and culture, albeit from changing ideological positions. Fuentes was an ambassador in the seventies and later, out of government office, he was a constant interlocutor of the Mexican and US political classes. García Márquez remained close to the Castro regime and to the troubled political situation in Colombia. Vargas Llosa ran for president of Peru in 1990.

Perhaps what came to an end was the optimism of the sixties and the utopian project that combined literary modernism with what Perry Anderson has called the "imaginative proximity of social revolution."[25] Marshall Berman has observed that in the seventies, with the stalling of economic growth and expansion, "modern societies abruptly lost their power to blow away their past. All through the 1960s, the question had been whether they should or shouldn't; now, in the 1970s, the answer was that they simply couldn't."[26] His remarks are true to an acute degree in Latin America. A wave of military dictatorships engulfed the Southern Cone. The 1964 coup in Brazil led to a more extreme dictatorship between 1968 and 1971. In Bolivia, General Hugo Banzer ruled with repressive severity between 1971 and 1978. In Uruguay, the military overthrew one of Latin America's most stable democracies in 1973. Later the same year the armed forces under General Pinochet ended Chile's three-year experiment of democratic revolutionary change. In Argentina, after the death of Perón in 1974, the country was torn by near civil war, a violence that was extended and systematized when the military took power in 1976. In Cuba the decade saw ideological austerity, a marked slowing down in the pace of artistic experimentation.

It was events in Cuba that would cause a rather public ideological parting of the ways. In the early seventies, a siege economy, the failure of the much vaunted 10 million ton sugar harvest, counterrevolutionary violence, and political isolation helped to form an embattled mentality on the island. In these circumstances, a poet, Heberto Padilla, was imprisoned and later subjected to a rather shameful show trial, in which he made an abject personal recantation. This infuriated a number of intellectuals, from Latin America, North America, and Europe, who wrote two open letters to the Cuban regime complaining about Padilla's shoddy treatment.[27] Fidel Castro replied in a furious manner, castigating bourgeois intellectuals who were the lackeys of imperialism and agents of the CIA, while the literary critic and poet Roberto Fernández Retamar wrote an aggressively polemical essay *Caliban*, which contrasted willfully nationalist Calibans standing up to Prospero's Colonial rule with Ariel-ist intellectuals and writers like Carlos Fuentes or critics like Emir Rodríguez Monegal whose critical brilliance masked a servility to their imperial masters.[28] *Caliban* was also, significantly, a manifesto for a kind of Latin American literature – testimonial literature, the function of the writer as a transmitter of social concerns – that clearly displaced individual creativity of the kind the Boom writers had celebrated. This gratuitous attack on Fuentes would distance him from the cultural policies of the island, if not from revolutionary politics in general. Vargas Llosa was also savaged by the regime at the time of the Padilla affair, and this probably helped to accelerate his reconsideration of revolutionary socialism as a panacea and the revolutionary function of literature. Cortázar and García Márquez defended the Cuban regime, and Cortázar's work, until his death in 1986, took on a more overtly political tone as in his somewhat politically naïve exploration of urban guerrillas in the novel *Libro de Manuel* (*A Manual for Manuel*, 1973).

The limits of the chimerical idea of a shared political or literary purpose were revealed in a polemic in 1968 and 1969 between Cortázar and the Peruvian writer José María Arguedas (1911–69). It had its origins in an article that Cortázar wrote for the magazine *Casa* in 1967, on the situation of the writer in Latin America. Cortázar talked of his commitment to socialism and of his discovery of Latin America through his voluntary exile in Paris. He included some pointed asides, attacking what he would term as "telluric" or "folkloric" nationalism, echoing the famous phrase by Jacques Vaché to André Breton that he had included as an epigraph to *Rayuela*: "rien ne vous tue un homme comme d'être obligé de represénter un pays." Arguedas, whose whole life and literary career had been spent vindicating indigenous cultures, felt attacked and slighted. As a response, he defended the "provincial" in literature as an attachment to the land and to popular values, the "flea-ridden" culture that he so admired, in contrast to the well-scrubbed, elegant, cosmopolitan "universalists" like Cortázar and Fuentes, who were in danger of losing, through their experimental novels, their connection to the real problems of the continent. This debate was never resolved since Arguedas was to kill himself on November 28, 1969, but it showed, in the starkness of its contrasts, fissures in that optimism and sense of unity that had defined the early Boom. Commenting on the polemic some twenty-five years after the event, Vargas Llosa argued that the polemic should "remind us that writers must be judged by what they write and not by anything else, because to try to introduce into literary analysis criteria like those of residence (or nation, political or religious affiliation, or race) can only lead to arbitrariness and to confusion."[29] Yet in the increasingly polarized world of the early seventies, it was precisely issues of commitment to nation, politics, and race that would come to dominate political and cultural debates. The moment of the Boom had come to an end.

NOTES

1. Vargas Llosa, *Making Waves*, trans. John King (New York: Farrar, Straus, and Giroux, 1996), p. 73.
2. Jean Franco, *The Decline and Fall of the Lettered City: Latin America in the Cold War* (Cambridge, Mass.: Harvard University Press, 2002). For an analysis of US cultural policies towards the arts in the sixties, see, J. King, *El Di Tella y el desarrollo cultural argentina en la década del sesenta* (Buenos Aires: Gaglianone, 1985) and Andrea Giunta, *Vanguardia, internacionalismo y política: arte argentino en los años sesenta* (Buenos Aires: Paidós, 2001).
3. Quoted in Valerie Fraser, *Building the New World: Studies in the Modern Architecture of Latin America, 1930–1960* (London: Verso, 2000), p. 244.
4. Angel Rama, "El boom en perspectiva," in Angel Rama (ed.), *Más allá del boom: literatura y mercado* (Mexico: Marcha, 1981), p. 98
5. Gabriel García Márquez, *Vivir para contarla* (Barcelona: Mondadori, 2002), pp. 137–38.
6. Ibid., pp. 277–79.
7. Tomás Eloy Martínez, interview with the author, Warwick, September 2000.
8. See "Erase una dictadura," *Cambio 16*, 183 (June 9, 1975): 78–84.
9. José Donoso, *Historia personal del boom* (Barcelona: Anagrama, 1971), p. 113.
10. Mario Vargas Llosa, "Primitives and Creators," *The Times Literary Supplement*, (November 14, 1968): 1287–88.
11. See in particular Chapter 5, "Into the Labyrinth: Ulysses in America," in Gerald Martin, *Journeys Through the Labyrinth: Latin American Fiction in the Twentieth Century* (London and New York: Verso, 1989), pp. 123–69.
12. See García Márquez, *Vivir*, p. 433 and Mario Vargas Llosa, *La verdad de las mentiras*, expanded edition (Madrid: Alfaguara, 2002), pp. 77–85.
13. "Carlos Fuentes: An Interview with John King," in J. King (ed.), *Modern Latin American Fiction: A Survey* (London: Faber and Faber, 1987), p. 140. For an analysis of Faulkner in Latin America, see Deborah N. Cohn, *History and Memory in the Two Souths: Recent Southern and Spanish American Fiction* (Nashville: Vanderbilt University Press, 1999).
14. Jorge Luis Borges, "The Argentine Writer and Tradition," in *Labyrinths* (Harmondsworth: Penguin, 1970), p. 218

15. "Julio Cortázar en la Universidad Central de Venezuela," *Escritura* 1 (January–June 1976): 162; Carlos Fuentes, *La nueva novela hispanoamericana* (Mexico City: Joaquin Mortiz, 1969), p. 26.

16. See Octavio Paz, "El arquero, la flecha y el blanco," *Vuelta* 117 (August 1986): 26–29. There is a biography of Borges that offers the much-needed subtle and detailed analysis of Borges and politics and Borges in history: see Edwin Williamson, *Borges: A Life* (London and New York: Viking, 2004).

17. See Charles Perrone, "João Guimarães Rosa: An Endless Passage," in King, *Modern Latin American Fiction*, p. 132.

18. Julio Cortázar, Chapter 109, *Rayuela* (Buenos Aires: Sudamericana 1963).

19. Cortázar's appreciation of Lezama is found in *La vuelta al día en ochenta mundos* (Mexico City: Siglo XXI, 1967), p. 533. His *boutade* on Ulysses is in *Life en español*, April 7, 1969.

20. Steven Boldy, *The Narrative of Carlos Fuentes: Family, Text, Nation* (Durham UK: University of Durham Press, 2002), p. 77.

21. Efraín Kristal, *Temptation of the Word: The Novels of Mario Vargas Llosa* (Nashville: Vanderbilt University Press, 1998), p. 13

22. Ibid., p. 30.

23. On autobiography see Mario Vargas Llosa, *El pez en el agua: Memorias* (Barcelona: Seix Barral, 1993) and *A Writer's Reality* (Syracuse University Press, 1991).

24. See William Rowe and Vivan Schelling, *Memory and Modernity: Popular Culture in Latin America* (London and New York: Verso, 1991).

25. Perry Anderson, "Modernity and Revolution," *New Left Review* 144 (March–April 1984): 96–113.

26. Marshell Berman, *All That is Solid Melts into Air: The Experience of Modernity* (New York: Verso, 1982), p. 332.

27. There are a number of accounts of the Padilla affair. See in particular *Index on Censorship* 1, 2 (1972): 65–134 and *Libre* 1 (September–November 1971): 95–145.

28. Roberto Fernández Retamar would return on several occasions to the topic of Caliban, revising some of his early opinions, but never quite apologizing to Fuentes. For a collection of his articles, see *Todo Calibán, Milenio*, 3 (November 1995).

29. See Mario Vargas Llosa, *La utopía arcaica: José María Arguedas y las ficciones del indigenismo* (Mexico: Fondo de Cultura Económica, 1996), p. 43.

FURTHER READING

Donoso, José, *Historia personal del 'boom,'* Barcelona: Seix Barral, 1972.

Franco, Jean, *The Decline and Fall of the Lettered City: Latin America in the Cold War*, Cambridge, Mass.: Harvard University Press, 2002.

Harss, Luis and Barbara Dohmann, *Into the Mainstream: Conversations with Latin American Writers*, New York: Harper and Row, 1967.

Martin, Gerald, *Journeys Through the Labyrinth. Latin American Fiction in the Twentieth Century*, London and New York: Verso, 1989.

Rama, Angel (ed.), *Más allá del boom: literatura y mercado*, Mexico City: Marcha, 1981.

Rodríguez Monegal, Emir, *El boom de la novela latinoamericana*, Caracas: Tiempo Nuevo, 1972.

Wilson, Jason, "Spanish American Narrative, 1920–1970," in John King (ed.), *The Cambridge Companion to Modern Latin American Culture*, Cambridge University Press, 2004, pp. 84–103.

4

PHILIP SWANSON

The Post-Boom novel

The New Novel in Latin America did not fade away with the end of the
Boom, and there has been a rich and varied pattern of literary production in
the region by both experienced and newer writers from the later 1960s up to
the beginning of the twenty-first century. However, a perceived critical clarity
about the nature of the Boom has not yet been matched by a similar sense of
clarity about what came after it. Though there have indeed been many lively
debates about the nature of the New Narrative and the Boom in Latin American fiction, there is now something approaching a broad consensus as to
their chronology and characteristics. Such a consensus is more elusive when
it comes to the rather more slippery category of the so-called Post-Boom, a
term that has come to be used to refer to developments from the late 1960s
and early 1970s onwards. Indeed, as late as 1990, a leading critic of the work
of Argentina's Manuel Puig (linked by many with the emergence of a Post-
Boom) was complaining of the way in which "critics were quick to produce a
new category . . . variously – and infelicitously – designated the '*petit*-Boom',
the 'Junior Boom', or even the 'post-Boom'."[1] However, the very cur-
rency of such terms does seem to indicate that some perceptible change of
sorts was underway from around 1970, even if it was difficult to define
clearly what that change really constituted. There are, for example, definite changes in material circumstances around this time which alert us to
the possibility of a shift in emphasis. A number of major novelists associated with the Boom noticeably develop in a somewhat different direction
during and after the seventies. And a cohort of new writers with a con-
spicuously different voice or agenda begin to publish around the turn of
these key decades. As time goes on, authors begin to articulate consciously
the sense of a break with the sixties, while a younger generation will emerge
who specifically define themselves in terms of a rupture or break with the
past (the "past" now being not the supposedly traditional realist and regionalist novel against which the Boom was seen as a climactic reaction, but as
something embodied in the canonized *nueva novela* of the Boom itself). But,

of course, thirty years is a long time (compared to the ten years often used to characterize the Boom): yet, at the beginning of the twenty-first century, critics are still talking about a Post-Boom phase in Latin American (principally Spanish American, though there are some commonalities with the situation in Brazil[2]) fiction. Surely such a lengthy period cannot elicit the same degree of critical consensus or coherence that has been identified in the Boom. This raises one of the problems of the notion of a Post-Boom. The term has true meaning only when it is used to refer, literary-historically speaking, to that which came after the Boom. But, of course, that could mean anything. The nature of the transition from Boom to Post-Boom is, in any case, as fuzzy as it is clear, and a very wide range of differing kinds of approaches to fiction have come to be encompassed under the latter umbrella term. As with the term postmodernism (with which the Post-Boom is sometimes, polemically, identified), which is both a marker of a break with modernism and of a reconfiguration of it, it is perhaps helpful to understand the Post-Boom not only as that which follows the Boom but also as a new attitude towards the experimental new novel associated with the Boom. The Post-Boom will then emerge as both a rejection of the New Narrative and as a new version of it, a sort of "new" new novel. Moreover, and in keeping with the idea of changing attitudes towards fictional phenomena, it must be remembered that the concept of a Post-Boom evolves during a period of commodification of the Latin American novel in the global market, the fetishization of certain types of Latin American writing by the universities or the academy in the USA and Europe, the rise of literary theory, the politicization of literary criticism, and the growth of cultural studies. Defining the Post-Boom thus becomes a matter of political choice as much as one of literary history, and its perception and use or manipulation as a term become as important as any sense of its underlying literary-historical validity. Any consideration of the Post-Boom, then, will have to tread a fine balance between explaining it as a reality or true phenomenon (in the sense that the Boom was), while maintaining an awareness of the fundamental fluidity and porosity of it as a category.

The idea of the existence of the Post-Boom depends on that of the demise of the Boom. In literary terms, as will be seen, this involves, very broadly speaking, the exhaustion of experimentalism and a return to an engagement with human reality. But the climate of change can be identified first in the extra-textual context of the material world outside of literary discourse. The end of the Boom is connected to two external phenomena or events. The first relates to the world of publishing. The New Novel may have been an evolving trend since the 1940s or earlier, but the Boom was really (as the word "boom" implies) a finite burst of commercial activity. For many, the

Spanish American Boom actually took place in Europe, and was particularly promoted by the Barcelona publishing house Seix Barral. With its canny combination of international novelists, conventions, and literary prizes, this publishing house sought to expand its market and is sometimes credited as being an engine of the Boom, particularly via its foundational discovery and publication of *La ciudad y los perros* (*The Time of the Hero*) and the award in 1962 of its highly prestigious Biblioteca Breve Prize to its author Mario Vargas Llosa – the first ever winner from outside Spain. Seix Barral also, in 1965, started up the series Nueva Narrativa Hispánica, reinforcing the sense of coherence, importance, and international identity of the new Spanish American narrative, now in some ways the voice of the Spanish-speaking world. However, by the end of the decade, there was a major split within Seix Barral and the key player, writer, publisher, and entrepreneur Carlos Barral, left to found Barral Editores in 1970 (though its Barral Prize fizzled out after only four years). The Biblioteca Breve Prize was suspended in 1970, and the novel which would have otherwise certainly been given the award in that year was Chilean José Donoso's *El obsceno pájaro de la noche* (*The Obscene Bird of Night*). However, *El obsceno pájaro de la noche* marks both the high point and the end of the Boom, in that it has been seen as representing the culmination of the process of complexity, fragmentation, tortuousness, and sheer difficulty that had come to be seen as synonymous with the Boom, but also as the extreme of experimentalism, the point of exhaustion and no return. In the words of one critic: "Con esta novela se cierra y se cumple un ciclo, más allá del cual no existe otra posibilidad expresiva . . . [L]a novela de Donoso es el broche que cierra una etapa, después de la cual sólo cabe cambiar de rumbo" ("With this novel a cycle is both completed and closed, beyond which no other possibility of expression exists . . . Donoso's novel snaps shut one stage, after which the only thing to do is change direction").[3] Donoso would himself later assert the need for a sharp change in direction and certainly saw the schism at Seix Barral as one indicator of the end of the Boom and as a factor in the halting of its promotion as a concept.[4]

Donoso also links the events at Seix Barral with a turning point in the Cuban Revolution (the so-called "caso Padilla"), the other main external matter pointing up the end of the Boom (Donoso, *Historia*, 89–90). The Cuban Revolution was actually an important factor in the Boom, though perhaps not always in the way some might expect. It is sometimes felt that the Cuban Revolution created a sense of political unity amongst Latin American writers, but this is true only in part – after all it is often noted that one of the main features of the New Narrative is the tendency to accent "universal" (so-called) existential skepticism despite the backdrop of specifically Latin American contexts.[5] Oddly enough, what the Cuban Revolution did for the New Novel was to make it fashionable and enhance its marketability, bringing Latin America to international public consciousness and creating an appetite for the consumption of Latin American texts. It probably also created a sense or illusion of community or solidarity amongst Latin American writers wishing to believe in the reality of a boom in the cultural projection of their region. However, the 1971 arrest and subsequent humiliation of the Cuban poet Heberto Padilla, on the grounds of being allegedly counterrevolutionary, led to a huge rift between Latin American writers and shattered the mirage of the unity of the Boom. Donoso again: "si en algo tuvo unidad casi completa el *boom* . . . fue en la fe primera en la causa de la revolución cubana; creo que la desilusión producida por el caso Padilla la desbarató, y desbarató la unidad del *boom*" ("if there was any sense in which there was complete unity in the Boom, . . . it was in the fundamental faith in the Cuban Revolution; I think that the disillusionment caused by the Padilla affair destroyed it, and destroyed the unity of the Boom itself" (Donoso, *Historia*, 46). It is obvious with hindsight that by the beginning of the 1970s a phase was drawing to a close. The Post-Boom, perhaps in an only gradually tangible way, was one of the signs of a reaction to this sense of an end of an era.

Of course, the idea of an "end of an era" is simply brought into sharper focus by the aforementioned external factors: the deeper reasons for it are internal, literary ones. The New Novel of the Boom was, to put it crudely, running out of steam by around 1970. The Boom as an idea was predicated on the notion of newness: the New Novel's appeal lay precisely in its shock value, the radical jolting and challenging of reader expectations grounded in traditional realism. Yet by 1970 features such as fantasy, multiple narrative voices, and structural fragmentation had become the norm, effectively *de rigueur* features of any fat new Spanish American novel aspiring to international recognition. A new orthodoxy had essentially been created, and it was inevitable that authors would react against it as writers had previously against realism. Donoso once more, commenting on his own fiction after 1970:

> Lo que me interesa . . . es hacer una batida contra la aceptada novela clásica: no la novela clásica antigua sino la contemporánea . . . Es decir la novela que bajo el disfraz de una libertad narrativa forja una serie de reglas de las cuales no es posible prescindir. Por ejemplo, todas las reglas terribles que me parece que usa Cortázar: *Rayuela* es un muestrario de reglas encubiertas que forjan toda una teoría de la novela: esta teoría pretende destruir la novela clásica pero forja otra novela clásica.

(What interests me . . . is to take a potshot at the accepted classical novel: not the old-style classical novel but the contemporary one . . . That is, the kind of novel which, operating under the disguise of narrative freedom, forges a whole series of rules which it is not possible to do without. For example, all those terrible rules which, it seems to me, that Cortázar uses: *Hopscotch* is a catalogue of covert rules that forge an entire theory of the novel: this theory seeks to destroy the classical novel but instead forges another kind of classical novel.)[6]

To maintain any sense of freshness or even effectiveness, the New Novel would therefore need to turn against what was beginning to seem a kind of rapidly fossilizing wilful narrative complexity or obscurity. This rebellion would take many forms, but would often basically boil down to some combination of: a return to some form of traditional structures, an embracing of, or engagement with, mass or popular culture, and an increased orientation towards social or political reality.

This happened in two broad ways. Firstly, via the emergence of a new group (sometimes, a little fancifully maybe, referred to as a new generation) of writers, the most notable of whom was probably Manuel Puig. Secondly, via a startling change in direction in the work of already established writers, most notably perhaps Donoso and Vargas Llosa. However, before moving on to consider these developments, it is important to note that the seeds of this change were already well and truly present within the Boom itself. The literary coherence of the Boom is questionable anyway. The so-called Big Four of Cortázar, Fuentes, García Márquez, and Vargas Llosa are as different as they are similar. Despite the use of fantasy and fragmentation as well as critical claims of existential uncertainty, all offer commentaries on Latin American politics and society. Vargas Llosa indeed is very much a realist whose aim is really to offer a more complex and therefore fuller picture of contemporary Peru – but a pretty clear one nonetheless. Moreover, García Márquez's *Cien años de soledad* (*One Hundred Years of Solitude*) – despite being considered by many as the culmination and the great novel of the Boom – has relatively little of the structural complexity of the other authors mentioned and a distinctly popular tone and content: published in 1967 it is really a pivotal work marking the transition from Boom to Post-Boom. It contains many of the features that some commentators would see as typical of the Boom: in particular a radical questioning of the nature of reality and literature's ability to describe it, coupled with a distinct whiff of metaphysical malaise or even pessimism. Yet if there is a lot of repetition of names and talk of circular time, the reader experiences events through a relatively easily digestible and largely linear narrative framework that deals with an ordinary rural culture in an often down-to-earth and perfectly entertaining way, and offers a fairly obvious sociopolitical reading of everyday Latin American reality. The novel, in other words, posits on the one hand a complex literary-intellectual problematization of the relationship between literature and reality; while on the other hand, it seeks to put forward a popular and in some ways authentically Latin American demystification of literature and reality. In a similar, if converse, way, Guillermo Cabrera Infante's *Tres tristes tigres* (*Three Trapped Tigers*), with its playful punning on pop culture, should be and often is linked clearly to the Post-Boom, yet was published two years before *Cien años de soledad* in 1965 and has much of the same tone and structural qualities as Cortázar's massively experimental Boom novel par excellence *Rayuela*. Political and apolitical at the same time, it is characterized by linguistic games, allusions to movies, and a love of nightlife, but is equally profoundly difficult and elusive. What *Cien años de soledad* and *Tres tristes tigres* illustrate is the fact that any shift to a Post-Boom is not as sudden or as radical as it might seem: as with most patterns of literary evolution, the process is a gradual, accretive, subtle one (and therefore, too, at the other end of the process, probably still ongoing as well).

Nonetheless, despite the preceding caveats, a marked sense of change was in the air by the late sixties and this owed much to the emergence of a string of new writers, the most prominent and successful of whom was Manuel Puig. Puig's *Boquitas pintadas* (*Heartbreak Tango*), which appeared in 1969, is the landmark text in the transition to the Post-Boom. In distinction to the supposed elitism of some Boom novels, Puig's novel was popular across certain perceived class and educational divides (though so, of course, was *Cien años de soledad*). It was about ordinary people, set in unglamorous small-town Argentina amongst the *cursi* or "vulgar" lower-middle classes. Moreover, its cultural allusions were specifically to mass and popular culture. Together with its companion piece of a year earlier, *La traición de Rita Hayworth* (*Betrayed by Rita Hayworth*), Puig's first works told their stories via reworkings of old Hollywood movies, romantic fiction, soap operas or *radionovelas*, and the slushy lyrics of popular songs such as tangos. Indeed the titles of the first two novels refer to a Hollywood star who came to prominence in the 1940s and a tango lyric. But if all this implies accessibility, the reality is a little more problematic. *Boquitas pintadas* was subtitled as a *folletín*, suggesting it would have the tone of a serial or melodrama: and to some extent it does. However, the narrative form is really an echo of the so-called autonomous narrative[7] of the Boom: instead of a third-person narrator, the plot is advanced via diary entries, letters, newspaper announcements, various listings, and even stream-of-consciousness passages. And if popular culture is to some degree embraced, its effects are also critiqued: the characters here are constructed in their tedious conformism by mass culture, while the fantasies such culture generates are doomed to failure – the first novel's title actually alludes to the treacherous nature of the Hollywood dream, and the second's hint of sex and glamour (it is a shortened form of "Boquitas pintadas de rojo carmesí" ["Lips painted with crimson red lipstick"]) gives way to "the unpalatable truth behind all illusions"[8] in the form of the epigraph to the second part, "Boquitas azules, violáceas, negras" ("Lips that are blue, purplish, black"). This same tension can be seen in Puig's most famous, and more explicitly political, novel, *El beso de la mujer araña* (*Kiss of the Spider Woman*, 1976). Once again, the text is structured around an interplay between, according to one's assessment of it, an awkward or productive exchange between bolero lyrics and the narration of B-movies on the one hand, and, on the other, a showy attempt at autonomous narrative based on dialogue, reports, footnotes, and stream-of-consciousness. The problem is that the novel seems to recuperate and repudiate both popular mass culture and serious high-modernist narration. This links to its relationship to politics and human reality. The protagonists are two male prisoners sharing a cell, one there because of political activism, the other because of a homosexual liaison with a minor. The former is associated with "serious" culture, the latter with "popular" culture. As the unlikely pair come closer together, the idea develops that sexual repression is at the heart of all repression, and that the sexually repressed must become more politicized while the politically aware must become more sensitive to human limitations. Connected with this is a dual notion: firstly, the sense that mass culture conditions individuals to play out their social roles in a way that fundamentally represses them; while, secondly, it provides an escape or liberation as well as real human insight and an outlet for emotion denied by the asceticism of certain brands of political commitment. At one stage, the cellmates argue over a romantic thriller which turns out to be a Nazi propaganda film: the difficulty is that while the film is an obvious example of manipulation through popular culture, the narrative itself is hugely enjoyable and completely interchangeable (if the affiliations of the heroes and villains were simply altered) with a more standard movie, this suggesting in part that film and narrative are no more than that and can never hope to capture reality. It seems that this is a Post-Boom novel seeking to achieve a more direct engagement with sociopolitical reality, while problematizing the relationship between fiction and reality à la Boom. In this sense, the Post-Boom is as much the new face of the New Novel of the Boom as it is its replacement.

This feeling of change and continuity is underlined by the fact that the other key marker of the transition to a Post-Boom is the transformation in the work of established writers who made their name in association with

the Boom. The turn to the popular is striking: Vargas Llosa turns his hand
to farce and soap opera; Donoso adopts the style of erotica, mysteries, and
transparent realism; Fuentes writes a tongue-in-cheek spy thriller, *La cabeza
de la hidra* (*The Hydra Head*, 1978); García Márquez produces a kind of
detective novel in *Crónica de una muerte anunciada* (*Chronicle of a Death
Foretold*, 1981) and later a nostalgic sentimental romance in *El amor en
los tiempos del cólera* (*Love in the Time of Cholera*, 1985). Vargas Llosa
and Donoso are perhaps the best examples. The Peruvian's *Pantaleón y las
visitadoras* (*Captain Pantoja and the Special Service*, 1973) is a sexual com-
edy, which uses the structures of autonomous narrative in a much more
accessible way. Equally entertaining (and an international hit) was his *La tía
Julia y el escribidor* (*Aunt Julia and the Scriptwriter*) from 1977. In a style
reminiscent of Puig, Vargas Llosa tells an autobiographical coming-of-age
story in counterpoint to accounts of an increasingly bizarre series of radio
soap operas. If anything, though, despite a clear level of social satire, there is a
diminution here in the political content of his work or at least in the strength
of political engagement. Moreover, both the military and the "people" are
mocked in the earlier text, while the later one charts the autobiographical
rise to authority of the mature serious author against the background of the
breakdown and eventual undoing of his former senior colleague, the writer
of popular potboiler radio serials. The formal conversion to the popular is
not matched, then, and may be even countered by content that might be
taken as the embodiment of a position of elitism. Donoso is more explicit
about overcoming the perceived elitism of the Boom, despite his earlier aspi-
ration to and eventual attachment to it. He sees the New Novel as "un
callejón sin salida" ("a blind alley") and asks (in 1982): "¿No ha llegado
un momento de ruptura para la novela latinoamericana contemporánea, de
cambio, para renacer de las cenizas de tantas y tantas novelas totalizado-
ras, agobiantes de significado, ahogantes de experimentos, que se imprimen
todos los días . . .?" ("Hasn't there come a moment of rupture for the contemporary Latin American novel, of change, so that it can be reborn from
the ashes of so, so many totalizing novels, oppressive with meaning, suffocating with experimentation, that are printed every day . . .?").[9] His *Casa de
campo* (*A House in the Country*, 1978) openly eschews the idea, so dear to
practitioners of and commentators on the New Novel, of the "disappearance
of the author" (similar to "autonomous narrative"), and instead adopts a
style which foregrounds and lays bare the workings of a narratorial-cum-
authorial figure, who declares at one stage that: "en la hipócrita no-ficción de
las ficciones en que el autor pretende eliminarse siguiendo reglas preestable-
cidas por otras novelas, o buscando fórmulas narrativas novedosas . . . , veo
un odioso puritanismo que estoy seguro que mis lectores no encontrarán en

mi escritura" ("in that hypocritical nonfiction of those fictions in which the author seeks to remove himself by following pre-existing rules established by other novels, or by trying to find fancy new narrative formulae . . . , I see an odious kind of puritanism which I am sure my readers will not find in my writing").[10] On top of this, the novel is a pretty transparent political allegory on the Allende government and the Pinochet military coup in Chile in the 1970s. Yet the new technique of the deliberate foregrounding of authorial machinations actually draws attention to the fictionality of the text and in so doing (apart from problematizing the political application of the allegory) emphasizes what was really the central contention of the New Novel of the Boom: that reality cannot be faithfully captured by literature. Donoso is thus a perfect illustration of the Post-Boom as being not simply a rejection of the Boom, but also a fresh reformulation of some of its core tenets. And this is what much of his fiction of the seventies and eighties does. For instance, *La misteriosa desaparición de la marquesita de Loria* ("The mysterious disappearance of the Marquise of Loria," 1980) subverts literature and reality from within, by seducing the reader into the easy comfort of a popular narrative style (with elements of, amongst other things, documentary, detective mystery, soft-porn) only to pull the rug out from under his or her feet by undermining the apparent pattern of narrative progress and leaving us with an inexplicable and unsettling mystery: the formal opposite of the attempted shock tactics of the seemingly chaotic *El obsceno pájaro de la noche*, then, achieves an exactly similar effect. The very interplay between Boom and Post-Boom is played out formally too in a semi-autobiographical tale that is actually about the phenomenon of the New Novel: *El jardín de al lado* (*The Garden Next Door*, 1981). What seems a straightforward realist account of frustrated male author Julio Méndez's attempt to write the Chilean *Rayuela* and gain access to the hallowed ranks of the Boom authors is thoroughly overturned by a startling final chapter in which the narrator reveals herself to be the seemingly feeble wife of Julio. Literary representation ends up being the opposite of what we thought it was and realist principles are undermined by a new narrative style based on the manipulation rather than outright destruction of realism. *El jardín de al lado*, a satire of the publishing scene for Spanish American writers, trumpets the death of the New Novel at the very same time that it renovates it: it is both a break with the past and the elaboration of an intimate connection to it.

The tension between Boom and Post-Boom noted above has led one of the key commentators on both phenomena to think in terms of a transitional phase. In Shaw's reading of, for example, Puig, the Argentine writer, with his mixture of skepticism and political engagement, is essentially a transitional figure.[11] However, the idea of a "transition" implies the existence of a clear

Post-Boom proper. Shaw seems to identify this Post-Boom proper with "a renewal of interest in referentiality . . . [,] reader friendliness, plot centeredness, the return to the here and now of Spanish America" (Shaw, *The Post-Boom*, 49). Hence Shaw's championing of Chile's Antonio Skármeta as one of the major embodiments of the values of the Post-Boom.[12] Skármeta certainly articulates in his essays a kind of manifesto for a Post-Boom, proposing a type of writing that is self-consciously in opposition to the Boom, anti-elitist, accessible, concerned with the everyday, socially committed, and generally positive.[13] He can also be seen as producing a series of novels that embody this type of writing – plot-centered and clearly structured works like: *Soñé que la nieve ardía* (*I Dreamt the Snow was Burning*, 1975) with its use of the mass cultural metaphor of soccer to explore a self-interested young man's growing and partly transformative relationship with ordinary mutually supportive working-class people; *La insurrección* (*The Insurrection*, 1982), a celebration of Sandinismo via an account of a revolt against the Somoza regime in Nicaragua; and *Ardiente paciencia* (*Burning Patience*, 1985), a story of love and poetry built partly around a postman's relationship with the great Chilean poet Pablo Neruda but used as a backdrop for an exploration of the overturning of a potentially joyous Allende era by the dark days of the Pinochet dictatorship.[14] Nonetheless, some may feel that Skármeta, if well known, is not quite as major (and therefore as representative) a figure as Shaw perhaps paints him. Moreover, the picture of the Post-Boom the Chilean proposes may not totally correspond to the reality, which is often a lot more ambiguous. Shaw himself effectively acknowledges this. He notes, for instance, the apparent existence of a very different kind of Post-Boom associated with writers like Cuba's Severo Sarduy and Mexico's Salvador Elizondo (Shaw, *The Post-Boom*, 49). Though there is a degree of change in their later work, both these writers are obsessed with language and textual self-referentiality – the opposite of a Post-Boom embodied in Skármeta and really an extreme version of the doubt about the relationship between fiction and external reality that characterized the New Novel linked with the Boom. Indeed a key influence here is Cuba's José Lezama Lima and his 1966 novel *Paradiso* (a work that can probably best be situated as adjacent to rather than part of the Boom), which is built around a near hermetic philosophy of poetics expressed in what is often described as a neo-baroque style. Sarduy is the more famous of the inheritors of Lezama Lima's barely penetrable version of the baroque. His best-known novels are *De donde son los cantantes* (*From Cuba with a Song*, 1967) and *Cobra* (1972). Neither has any real narrative in a conventional sense. In the first, the main characters (such as they are) seek their own meaning, but meaning is endlessly deferred; and plot (such as it is) is merely "dictated by phonetic associations or by the internal logic of language itself."[15] The mutational or seemingly free-associational structure is even more extreme in *Cobra*, where a transvestite stripper is male and female, dead and alive, wax doll and human, who moves with a bunch of bikers from Europe to India in order to join up with an oriental deity. Sarduy, a student of Roland Barthes, is clearly putting into novelistic practice some of the theoretical precepts of structuralism and post-structuralism where "writing" is merely a string of signifiers in a state of flight, with no ultimate meaning behind them, and is therefore no more than the very act of writing ("el acto de escribir"[16]) itself. The sexual dimension of *Cobra* underlines this idea: the erotic here is a ludic game which, like language, is perceived as wonderfully and lavishly wasteful and ultimately non-productive in its limitless pursuit of pleasure.[17] Although in its non-utilitarian playfulness *Cobra* explicitly rejects the Boom and has been described as "a work of the anti-Boom,"[18] it has obvious connections with it too: nobody could deny, for example, the ludic quality of, say, Cortázar in the 1960s – Sarduy's work is (in part at least) just a radical extension of that ludic dimension into a more complete and absolute rupturing of the notion of writing as a generator of meaning. In other words, Sarduy represents a refocusing or repositioning of some of the ideas behind the New Novel of the Boom as much as he represents its rejection or destruction. This is an important point. The notion of a transition may be slightly misleading. If Skármeta represents a kind of Post-Boom proper, this implicitly takes the meaning of the term "Post-" to refer to that which is in oppositon to and comes after the Boom. But perhaps a more fundamental meaning of the term "Post-" is to posit simply a new attitude to, or relationship with, that which is being followed or superseded. There has been much debate about the connections or differences between the Post-Boom and concepts such as postmodernism or postcolonialism (see Shaw, *The Post-Boom*). In fact the relationship between the Boom and Post-Boom could be seen usefully to echo that between modernism and postmodernism in the sense that the latter is not simply a rejection of the former but merely a new approach to it (just as postcolonialism is a new way of understanding, thinking about, and relating to colonialism rather than a plain assertion of its demise). In this sense, Sarduy and Puig, for instance, would be key figures of the Post-Boom rather than only transitional ones. This would help to resolve the tension in Shaw's argument between "the mainstream element in the Post-Boom [, which] is a tendency back to referentiality" and a Post-Boom that is "a continuum that runs from extreme documentality/testimoniality to patterns of writing in which referentiality is subordinated" (Shaw, *The Post-Boom*, 49, 50). The real value of the idea of a Post-Boom, then, is not merely to describe the new more referentially orientated writing that has emerged after the Boom, but to illustrate and explain the very interaction with the Boom which led to a dynamic of change that began in and around 1970.

Having said all of the above, the idea of some kind of mainstream Post-Boom based on social referentiality is given an appearance of solidity by other developments between the 1970s and the 1990s. Two such developments are the emergence of – as they are called – *testimonio* and the New Historical Novel, both of which reinforce the impression of a greater emphasis on the direct presentation of social reality. *Testimonio* or testimonial writing is a kind of autobiography told by another (usually more educated and narratorially gifted) person. The Mexican Elena Poniatowska did much to make *testimonio* fashionable in certain circles, but the most famous example of the genre is *Me llamo Rigoberta Menchú y así me nació la conciencia* (*I Rigoberta Menchú, an Indian Woman in Guatemala*, 1983). A harrowing account of the brutal treatment of a Guatemalan Indian community, the book gained eyewitness and campaigner Rigoberta Menchú the Nobel Peace Prize in 1992. A few years later, though, the North American anthropologist David Stoll's explosive exposé of alleged falsehoods and inconsistencies in Rigoberta's testimony, *Rigoberta Menchú and the Story of all Poor Guatemalans* (1998), brought into the open many debates about the authenticity of *testimonio*. Rigoberta's account was, of course, like other *testimonios* edited and presented by someone else (in this case, Venezuelan anthropologist Elisabeth Burgos-Debray). Thus, while *testimonio* gives voice to the ordinary or marginalized people, it risks setting up the same tensions between presentation and reality that characterized the earlier fiction it seemed to be a reaction against.[19] The New Historical Novel, posited by critic Seymour Menton in 1993,[20] represented another obvious attempt to recuperate reality (albeit here in a more literary way), particularly by revisiting certain protagonists of the colonial and independence periods. Abel Posse's *Los perros del paraíso* (*The Dogs of Paradise*) from Argentina in 1983 is a much-cited example. But Posse was born as far back as 1936 and other practitioners of the genre are Carpentier, Fuentes, and Vargas Llosa, who are equally linked to the Boom (and before). And Augusto Roa Bastos's massively difficult fictional autobiography of nineteenth-century Paraguayan absolute dictator Dr José Gaspar Rodríguez de Francia, *Yo el Supremo* (*I the Supreme*, 1974), in deconstructing historical discourse and generating a dynamic and open language, problematizes the very relationship between history and reality. In linking history to the unreliability of fiction, the New Historical Novel's worthwhile revisionism also harks back to a central idea of the New Novel of the Boom. In both genres, the connection to referentiality is strong, but still fundamentally problematic.

Of course, a very real problem is the intervention of academic or other "intellectual" discourse in the production of these generic terms. The temporal projection of the Post-Boom corresponds with a period of consolidation of the reputation of Latin American literature in Northern and Western universities and in the international literary establishment and market. Though it is true to say that Cuban intellectual Roberto Fernández Retamar's *Calibán* functioned as a manifesto which promoted the production and dissemination of testimonial novels, the idea of *testimonio* as an object of critical examination gained prominence in the 1980s and 1990s thanks to its embracing by the North American and then European academy.[21] The New Historical Novel is equally a critical category, as is the even more arbitrary "novel of exile" which is also sometimes associated with the Post-Boom.[22] *Testimonio*, for example, had been around for some time,[23] something which begs the question of whether its subsequent canonization by the academy in the later twentieth century provided fuel for those critics wishing to perceive a more socially- and reality-orientated Post-Boom. The 1970s onward also saw the politicization of academic discourse in literary studies in North American and UK universities. In this consciously ideologically charged atmosphere, it became tempting to see the drive towards political reality perceived in the Post-Boom as a response to the rise of terror, authoritarianism, and military dictatorship in Central America and the Southern Cone. Thus writers like Argentina's Luisa Valenzuela or Ricardo Piglia and Chile's Diamela Eltit came to be included in some accounts of the Post-Boom, even though their tortuous and sometimes barely penetrable style, if in many ways politically challenging, has little to do with a transparent brand of referentiality. Indeed entry to the international market (be that the literary market or the peculiar economy of the modern university) in some sense depended on a critical muddying of the waters between political referentiality and experimental play. At a time of a relative crisis of legitimacy in the humanities, the former was necessary to render the discipline "useful" or "relevant," while the latter helped to preserve the traditional guarantees of academic intellectual respectability. Thus the reliability of terms like the Post-Boom is a real problem. There is no doubt that the terrible political events of the seventies and eighties did foment political fiction, but the (often highly theorized and intellectualized) fiction so produced did not always necessarily fit the referential model à la Skármeta outlined earlier. Nor is it clear that these events were a material factor in the creation of the Post-Boom, which seems to have already been underway by the time of, say, the military dictatorships in Argentina and Chile, and seems in any case to have literary as much as political roots. It once again appears that the term Post-Boom is most useful to mark a moment or period of reaction and renewal in relation to the Boom itself, rather than to cover comprehensively the thirty or so years of literary production that have followed it.

One good illustration of the sorts of problem just discussed is the tendency to include the category of "women writers" (or, sometimes, "gay and lesbian writers") in the category of the Post-Boom, as if the emergence of such groups as literary phenomena were in some sense dependent on a literary rather than material shift in circumstances. In part, the choice to study such groupings is as much a manifestation of the history of universities and other institutions as it is one of literary history. Indeed our awareness of certain female, gay, or lesbian (or, of course, straight male) authors may have much to do with their promotion via the academy or its values and interests. The discomfort of some academic critics with the success of Isabel Allende (relative to the valorization of a writer like her – for many – more politically and intellectually acceptable fellow Chilean Eltit) is an interesting case. Allende is routinely included amongst lists of women of the Post-Boom, often in the company of writers with whom she has little in common. This has led to some ambiguities in her classification: in a 1997 encyclopedia of Latin American literature (long-awaited by professional Hispanists), she did not receive a proper entry of her own but was merely included in an entry for "Best-Sellers."[24] This was bizarre, since, she is clearly, in terms of her international success and impact, a much more important figure than someone like, say, Skármeta. This is an indication of the aforementioned awkwardness in some critics about recognizing the genuinely popular and accessible dimension of Post-Boom writing and hints at a lingering hankering after the intellectual complexity or even elitism of the Boom. The fact is that Allende is one of the best representatives of both main views of the Post-Boom discussed here: she embodies both, on the one hand, a relationship to and reorientation of the novel of the Boom, and, on the other, the trend towards readability, structural clarity, sociopolitical commentary, and relative optimism. Her *La casa de los espíritus* (*The House of the Spirits*, 1982), a key work of the Post-Boom, is an unmistakable reflection of modern Latin American history and, in particular, the modern history of Chile up to the awful aftermath of the Pinochet coup. But in directly reflecting that history, the novel also functions as a commentary on the evasive nature of the narrative of the Boom, in particular García Márquez's *Cien años de soledad*. It is arguable that the consistent use of fantasy and ambiguity in the Colombian's novel actually undermines its political effectiveness, and, while Allende has been criticized for mimicking *Cien años*, her novel is really a critical reworking of it. One character comments that "no era partidaria de repetir los nombres en la familia, porque eso siembra confusión en los cuadernos de anotar" ("she did not approve of the repetition of family names across the generations, because that would sow confusion in her notebooks")[25] – a thinly disguised poke at the potentially perplexing repetition of names in the García Márquez book. Moreover, the character's name is Clara (connoting clarity) and her notebooks, though not chronological, are not wilfully obscure like the manuscripts of García Márquez's Melquíades that they echo, and are (again unlike Melquíades' parchments) easily put in to order by a family member of a subsequent generation so that the facts are saved from the nebulous world of fantasy (Allende, *La casa*, 219). Indeed the entire structure of the novel could be seen to overturn its own early pattern of fantasy and replace it with a kind of harsh realism following the harrowing political realities of the coup: the spirits largely disappear and the novel builds up to a chapter entitled "La hora de la verdad" ("The moment of truth").[26] As was suggested earlier, García Márquez's seminal text may be a rather equivocal model for the Boom, but, nonetheless, Allende's novel perfectly demonstrates the idea of the Post-Boom as a rearticulation of the Boom while also exhibiting the trend towards greater referentiality that some associate with a Post-Boom proper.

Inevitably, all terms beginning with "Post-" are potentially problematic. In a sense, what has been suggested here is a spectrum of possible ways of understanding the Latin American Post-Boom ranging across: a moment of rupture with a perceived Boom aesthetic; a rejection of a Boom aesthetic; a new relationship with a Boom aesthetic, which is now retuned and revitalized; a tendency away from the textual ambiguity of the Boom and toward greater social referentiality, characterized perhaps by a transitional period leading eventually to a mainstream Post-Boom typified by a more straightforward engagement with reality; or as a long-running continuum covering a gamut of approaches from documentalism to non-referentiality. The problem with the last position is that it effectively reduces (or extends) the Post-Boom to refer to almost anything that has been published in Spanish America after the Boom. As a concept, then, its use is limited. Given the inevitable variety of types of fiction since the Boom, perhaps the term is most productively employed to refer to a type of fiction that is constituted by a sense of rupture with the Boom while remaining in some way connected to or in interaction with the Boom novel's underlying ideas. The point is that, even if the Boom was a finite material phenomenon, the idea of the Boom has still, at the beginning of the twenty-first century, not been supplanted by a Post-Boom proper.

It would be instructive to consider, for example, the recent phenomena of McOndo and the Crack generation. In 1996 the Chileans Alberto Fuguet and Sergio Gómez published a collection of works by Spanish American writers born after 1960. Entitled *McOndo*, the book – with its pun on the name of García Márquez's fantastical invention of the town of Macondo – is clearly a reaction against the weight of magical realism, a denomination which gained international prominence thanks to the success of the Boom and something Fuguet has described as "a sort of curse that has afflicted novelists, filmmakers and tour guides all over the Americas."[27] There is still, in other words, a sense that "young" Latin American writers still feel over-shadowed by the Boom and still feel a need to respond to it or challenge it. In the specific case of the McOndo writers, the perception that the new Latin America is a world of McDonald's, Mac computers, and condos pro-vokes a trend away from the exploration of national identities towards a new "pop" conception of the local saturated by North American influence and the processes of globalization – what Fuguet in another pun (on the name of the cross-borders NAFTA agreement) calls FTAA – a new Free Trade Area of the Americas sensibility. This seems essentially a refinement of a certain Post-Boom ethos of the seventies and eighties updated to a contemporary context.

An illustrative example of such an ethos is Peruvian Jaime Bayly's *La noche es virgen* ("Virgin is the night"). Bayly was a contributor to the *McOndo* book and his aforementioned novel won Spain's Herralde Prize after its pub-lication in 1997. The novel is essentially a pop cultural version of the stock Peruvian theme of *Lima la horrible* ("Lima the horrible").[28] The capital is presented as a sweaty, stinking, teeming cesspool, but mainly via the world of rock venues, sleazy clubs, drugs, booze, and illicit sex. The main charac-ter is Gabriel Barrios, a middle-class gay/bisexual and cocaine addict, and much of the novel charts the fun- and frustration-filled excesses of his sexual and narcotic adventures. However, the power of the text really comes from Gabriel's frenetically paced first-person narrative, which captures wonder-fully not only his own camp sensibility but also the feel of the cocky urban slang of the streets and clubs of Lima at the end of the twentieth century. But the exuberance of the drug-fuelled discourse is not necessarily matched by the content, which is ultimately rather dark. Gabriel's drug habit is in many ways an embarrassing form of escape: it marks him as apart from the bour-geois world from which he emanates (indicated in his run-ins with his own conservative mother and that of his would-be lover Mariano), yet is also a way of avoiding facing up to or coming to balanced terms with his identity. His sexuality remains, in essence, closeted and his self-expression therefore limited, as he does not want to risk any threat to his comfortable upper-class lifestyle as a TV show host and son of a well-to-do family. Indeed his sense of alienation is expressed via a rather self-damaging snobbery toward lower social and racial classes, including "los brownies" (nonwhites) as he color-fully but pejoratively refers to them. Though he valorizes Miami, to where he frequently repairs on shopping trips, there is a sense that pop-culture consumerism leaves him dissatisfied and tied to a Lima that is ultimately Third World and dismal. The novel ends with him alone at night on the capital's dingy streets, swallowing bitter cocaine tears and concluding that: "no puedo seguir siendo gay y coquero en lima. me estoy matando. lima me está matando" ("i can't carry on being gay and a cokehead in lima. i'm killing myself. lima is killing me").[29] For all that the extravagance, youthful energy, and aggressive contemporariness of Bayly's narrative projects a counter-Boom project, the traditional theme of Lima's apparent vibrancy actually being a stultifying microcosm of chaos and limitation links the novel to the past and, in some ways, does not progress us much beyond a 1969 Boom novel like Vargas Llosa's *Conversación en La Catedral* (*Conversation in The Cathedral*), which has, in the end, a remarkably similar tone.

The link between this born-after-1960 generation and the Boom is underlined by Fuentes's characterization (in yet another pun) of such new writers as eventually forming part of a "Boomerang" generation. The self-styled Mexican "generación del Crack," associated principally with writers Jorge Volpi and Ignacio Padilla, uses for its sobriquet a pun that echoes the term Boom while suggesting a break with it (and indeed they seem to favour a more "intelligent" style of writing – which could be seen as a return to the Boom as much as anything). What has been most commented on about their most successful novels – respectively *En busca de Klingsor* (*In Search of Klingsor*, 1999) and *Amphitryon* (*Shadow without a Name*, 2000) – is their setting, in part, in the non-American environment of Nazi Europe and their basis in European intellectualism. This may suggest a break, but Europeanism was precisely a criticism of the novel of the Boom. Unsurprisingly, in one interview Volpi is identified with a desire for differentiation from "la etiqueta Boom" (the Boom label), while citing some of his principal influences as "Carlos Fuentes, Vargas Llosa, los escritores del 'Boom', Borges, etc."[30] A reading of a novel like *En busca de Klingsor* (winner of the 1999 Biblioteca Breve Prize) would give the impression that what Volpi is actually reacting against is a perceived "light" strain in the later New Narrative that has come to be associated with a Post-Boom. This superb work is worthy of comparison with novels by successful middle- to high-brow professional writers from Britain, other European countries, and North America like, say, Michael Frayn, Stephen L. Carter, or even Umberto Eco. The novel, which is both intellectually challenging yet thrillingly suspenseful, is built around modern science; in particular around the theory of relativity, quantum physics, and the quest to build the atomic bomb. Taking us through the lives and theories of Einstein, Gödel, Heisenberg, Schrödinger, and Bohr (among others), the story deals with the American physicist Francis Bacon's military mission in postwar Germany to identify a mysterious figure code-named Klingsor who was thought to be Hitler's leading advisor on the atomic bomb. Apart from the Spanish language and a certain explanatory tendency in the exposition of European history, there is little to suggest a specifically Latin American perspective here. If anything, the tone is reminiscent of the alleged universalist skepticism of Borges. This is built into the plot itself, whose resolution remains enigmatic despite the superficial illusion of closure, and is carried into the many theoretical reflections that pepper the text. The role of science, for example, is investigated in a way that prompts questions on the nature of truth and the human tendency to construct artificial patterns of order. And, in a typically Borgesian twist, Klingsor himself, the unseen manipulator pulling the strings in the shadows, is surely identifiable with God, the manufacturing of belief and the questionable impulse behind creativity and the quest for meaning: one character asks if Klingsor "no era más que una abstracción de nuestras mentes, una proyección desorbitada de nuestra incertidumbre, un modo de colmar nuestro vacío" ("just some kind of mental abstraction of ours, a wild projection of our uncertainty, a way to fill our void"), while Bacon speculates that Klingsor may be no more than "una manera de justificar su investigación, asumiendo riesgos inexistentes e inventándose su propia tarea" ("a means of justifying his investigation, in which he was assuming non-existent risks and inventing his own task as he went along").[31] There is also, in the wartime and postwar context, a counterbalancing discourse of history, free will, and the morality of choice (echoes of Fuentes here, another Boom figure). However, as with Borges, the ultimate sense is that ideas (in their myriad variants) are used not so much in their own right as philosophy but rather as primarily the material for the fabrication of a rich and teasingly satisfying literary experience. Though without the artificial structural pyrotechnics of some Boom novels, the serious yet playful, complex yet compelling, quality of their eminently marketable professional fictions makes the likes of Volpi and Padilla, if anything, the true heirs of the Boom.

In conclusion, then, it seems that the notion of a Post-Boom proper must be taken with caution. The Post-Boom clearly does mark some kind of rupture, but, like postmodernism, it is above all a state of mind: a state of mind in which a sense of newness is conceived in terms of the past as well as the present and the future.[32]

NOTES

1. Pamela Bacarisse, "Manuel Puig: *Boquitas pintadas*," in Philip Swanson (ed.), *Landmarks in Modern Latin American Fiction* (London and New York: Routledge, 1990), p. 207.

2. Though the term "Latin American" is used throughout this essay, the emphasis here is on fiction written in Spanish. Given its different literary history, Brazil is often not included directly in categories such as Boom or Post-Boom. However, there are parallel developments, in particular with regard to a certain crisis of faith in modernism provoked by military dictatorship and the ensuing economic crisis in the 1980s. Brazilian fiction after 1970 remains heterogeneous, but there can be identified trends such as the re-emergence of a realist aesthetic, the growth of a perceived postmodern skepticism, and the rise of women writers. Two notable figures who could be considered as related to the Post-Boom are Rubem Fonseca, whose novels sometimes exploit the detective genre, and Silviano Santiago, best known for his boundary-breaking gay-themed and New York-based novel *Stella Manhattan* (1985).

3. José Promis Ojeda, "La desintegración del orden en la novela de José Donoso," in Antonio Cornejo Polar (ed.), *José Donoso. La destrucción de un mundo* (Buenos Aires: Fernando García Cambeiro, 1975), p. 203. All translations mine.

4. José Donoso, *Historia personal del "Boom"* (Barcelona: Seix Barral, 1983), pp. 89–90. Henceforth "Donoso, *Historia*."

5. See Donald L. Shaw, *Nueva narrativa hispanoamericana* (Cátedra: Madrid, 1992).

6. Interview with Z. Nelly Martínez, *Hispamérica* 21 (1978): 53.

7. Associated with the idea of the disappearance of the author, autonomous narrative (a term identified particularly with Vargas Llosa in the sixties) sought to create the impression of a self-propelled kind of writing with no guiding narrator figure, thus prompting the reader to play a more active role in constructing or reconstructing the text.

8. Bacarisse, "Manuel Puig," p. 211.

9. José Donoso, "Dos mundos americanos," *El Mercurio (Artes y Letras)* (November 14, 1982), p. 1.

10. José Donoso, *Casa de campo* (Barcelona: Seix Barral, 1980), p. 54.

11. Donald L. Shaw, *The Post-Boom in Spanish American Fiction* (Albany, NY: State University of New York Press, 1998), p. 37. Henceforth "Shaw, *The Post-Boom*."

12. See Shaw, *The Post-Boom* and Donald Shaw, *Antonio Skármeta and the Post Boom* (Hanover, NH: Ediciones del Norte, 1994). Shaw's accounts are amongst the most thorough and detailed on the Post-Boom available.

13. See Chapter 1 of Shaw, *The Post-Boom*. Skármeta's essays are referred to on p. 7 and provide a complementary perspective to the comments already discussed of a practitioner such as Donoso, who was formerly associated with the Boom.

14. More famous than the novel itself is the film based on it, *Il postino* (1995), directed by Michael Radford.

15. Ronald Schwartz, *Nomads, Exiles and Emigrés: The Rebirth of the Latin American Narrative, 1960–80* (Metuchen, NJ and London: Scarecrow Press, 1980), p. 99.

16. Interview with Emir Rodríguez Monegal, *Mundo Nuevo* 2 (1966): 25.

17. See, for example, Severo Sarduy, "El barroco y el neobarrocco," in César Fernando Moreno (ed.), *América latina en su literatura* (Mexico: Siglo XXI, 1972), p. 182.

18. Severo Sarduy, *Cobra* (Buenos Aires: Sudamericana, 1972), p. 66; Roberto González Echevarría, "Plain Song: Sarduy's *Cobra*," *Contemporary Literature* 28, 4 (1987): 437–59.

19. For an excellent account of such a tension in Poniatowska's *Hasta no verte Jesús mío* (*Until We Meet Again*, 1969), see Lucille Kerr, *Reclaiming the Author: Figures and Fictions from Spanish America* (Durham, NC and London: Duke University Press, 1992). Two excellent works on *testimonio* are: G. Gugelberger, *The Real Thing: Testimonial Discourses and Latin America* (Durham, NC and London: Duke University Press, 1996) and Elzbieta Sklodowska, *Testimonio hispanoamericano: historia, teoría, poética* (New York: Peter Lang, 1991).

20. Seymour Menton, *Latin America's New Historical Novel* (Austin: University of Texas Press, 1993).

21. It might also be contended that the selective adoption and promotion of certain Latin American intellectuals like Fernández Retamar (such as, for instance, Néstor García Canclini, Nelly Richard, and Beatriz Sarlo) is, as much as anything else, a reflection of trends within the North American and European academy. *Calibán* is a 1971 essay which acts as a northerly South American antidote to José Enrique Rodó's seminal southern cone work, *Ariel* (1900). Applying a consciously Third World perspective based on the experience of miscegenation, Fernández Retamar challenges Rodó's Latin Americanist interpretation of *The Tempest*'s Ariel and Caliban by identifying Latin America with Caliban as a means of exposing the mechanisms of colonialism and using them for the purposes of autochthonous empowerment.

22. See Shaw, *The Post-Boom*, e.g. p. 79.

23. *Testimonio* was effectively in existence during the Boom of the 1960s, one key work being Miguel Barnet's *Biografía de un cimarrón* (*Diary of a Runaway Slave*, 1966).

24. Verity Smith (ed.), *Encyclopedia of Latin American Literature* (Chicago and London: Fitzroy Dearborn, 1997).

25. Isabel Allende, *La casa de los espíritus* (Barcelona: Plaza y Janés, 1985), p. 233.

26. The account given here is somewhat simplified. For a more nuanced version of this reading of Allende's novel and for more on the Latin American novel after the Boom, see Philip Swanson, *The New Novel in Latin America: Politics and Popular Culture After the Boom* (Manchester and New York: Manchester University Press, 1995).

27. Alberto Fuguet, "Magical Neoliberalism," *Foreign Policy* (July–August, 2001).

28. The phrase has its origins in Sebastián Salazar Bondy's 1964 essay *Lima la horrible*, which presents Lima in terms of a society that has never escaped the negative legacy of its Colonial past.

29. Jaime Bayly, *La noche es virgen* (Barcelona: Anagrama, 1997).

30. Anna Solana and Mercedes Serna, "Jorge Volpi: 'La novela es una forma de explorar el mundo'," *Babab* 4 (September 2000). It is important to stress, incidentally, that Volpi's novels are by no means all set in Europe.

31. Jorge Volpi, *En busca de Klingsor* (Barcelona: Seix Barral, 2002), pp. 336, 153.

32. Other selected novelists not mentioned here include: associated with the Post-Boom (though for differing reasons) – Argentina's Mempo Giardinelli and Sylvia Molloy; Cuba's Reinaldo Arenas; Mexico's Carmen Boullosa, Laura Esquivel,

Angeles Mastretta, and Gustavo Sainz; Puerto Rico's Rosario Ferré and Luis Rafael Sánchez; associated with the McOndo and Crack "generations" – Bolivia's Edmundo Paz Soldán; Colombia's Santiago Gamboa; Mexico's Eloy Urroz.

FURTHER READING

Franco, Jean, *The Decline and Fall of the Lettered City*, Cambridge, Mass.: Harvard University Press, 2002.

Martin, Gerald, "Spanish American narrative since 1970," in John King (ed.), *The Cambridge Companion to Modern Latin American Culture*, Cambridge, UK and New York: Cambridge University Press, 2004, pp. 105–18.

Schwartz, Ronald, *Nomads, Exiles and Emigrés: The Rebirth of the Latin American Narrative, 1960–80*, Metuchen, NJ and London: Scarecrow Press, 1980.

Shaw, Donald L., *Nueva narrativa hispanoamericana*, Cátedra: Madrid, 1992.

   The Post-Boom in Spanish American Fiction, Albany, NY: State University of New York Press, 1998.

   Antonio Skármeta and the Post Boom, Hanover, NH: Ediciones del Norte, 1994.

Sklodowska, Ezbieta, *La parodia en la nueva novela hispanoamericana*, Amsterdam: John Benjamins, 1991.

Swanson, Philip (ed.), *Landmarks in Modern Latin American Fiction*, London and New York: Routledge, 1990.

Swanson, Philip, *The New Novel in Latin America: Politics and Popular Culture after the Boom*, New York: St. Martin's Press, 1995.

Williams, Raymond Leslie, *The Postmodern Novel in Latin America: Politics, Culture and the Crisis of Truth*, New York: St. Martin's Press, 1995.

2
HETEROGENEITY

5

PIERS ARMSTRONG

The Brazilian novel

The development of the Brazilian novel is inseparable from ethnic and geographic considerations. The Brazilian nation grew from the interaction and miscegenation of European, indigenous, and African populations in five distinct regions according to an enduring paradigm which has informed political and cultural discussions: the Northeast, originally a plantation society like the US "South," and a privileged storehouse of living traditions; the socioeconomically dominant Southeast, including the states of Rio and São Paulo and Minas Gerais; the predominantly indigenous North (essentially, the Amazon basin); the South, where settlement was principally European; and the frontier lands of the Center-West, less populated and relatively peripheral to national power. After Brazilian independence from Portugal in 1822, Rio de Janeiro quickly developed a European-style bourgeois cultural life, including numerous newspapers, in which most nineteenth-century novels were initially published in serial.

Joaquim Manuel de Macedo's *A moreninha* ("The little brunette," 1844) was perhaps the first successful novel in Brazil and inaugurates a recurrent nineteenth-century theme: a romantic relationship between idealistic young people in spite of cruelties of social fortune. The first notable work of realism focusing on the urban lower-middle class is Manuel Antônio de Almeida's *Memórias de um sargento de milícias* ("Memoirs of a constable," 1854), which presents a series of picaresque but touching scenes, and evokes the transformation of a town into a city with suggestive nostalgia. Romantic and realist modes both flourished through the late nineteenth century and often overlapped within works. The Romantic could even merge into naturalism, as in Bernardo Guimarães's *O seminarista* ("The seminarian," 1872), published before his better-known and distinctly Romantic novel, *A escrava Isaura* ("The slave-girl, Isaura," 1875), the melodrama of a virtuous light-skinned slave.[1]

With the consolidation of the Brazilian Empire the need for an autonomous cultural ideology was answered in "Indianism," a national version of

Romanticism casting indigenes as noble savages in chivalric adventures. The towering Romantic visionary was the novelist José de Alencar (1829–77), who articulated an optimistic vision of Brazil predicated on miscegenation and the establishment of Luso-Brazilian civilization. His best-known literary creation is Iracema (an anagram of "America"), the native virgin priestess and heroine of the eponymous novel of 1865. Enamored of the Portuguese Martim (from the Latin for the god of war), she bears him a child. She thus sacrifices the indigenous purity symbolized by her once chaste religious devotion. While still nursing Moacir ("child of pain"), Iracema dies, and the Portuguese father returns to the Atlantic, along with his son, the first *mestiço* (mixed-race person, usually Amerindian and European), the first "American." While power is firmly in Portuguese hands, the poetic glory of the novel is Iracema's. The artistic force of Alencar's language derives from his grandiloquent phrasal rhythms and a distinct vocabulary drawing on Amerindian languages to describe the flora and fauna of his settings. Alencar's invention of a Romantic national mythology also informs his regionalist novels which depict the sagas of various frontier Brazilians, affording his numerous readers – whom he was paternally inclined to address directly in his prefaces – a sort of museum of Brazilian natural and social history in words.

In sharp contrast, Joaquim Maria Machado de Assis (1839–1908), a mulatto of modest origins whose whole life was spent in Rio, portrayed the Victorian milieu in which most of his readers lived – urban, bourgeois, and Euro-Brazilian. After publishing several drawing room novels, still considered Romantic, he changed the course of Brazilian literature with the publication in 1880 of *Memórias póstumas de Brás Cubas* (*The Posthumous Memoirs of Bras Cubas*). The novel's protagonist is, upon death, transported on the back of a hippopotamus, backwards in time through the spectacle of the ages, with Pandora as cicerone. He then recounts his long and vapid bourgeois existence before his death. Perhaps liberated by Sterne's *Tristram Shandy* and his "train of discourse" model, rather than a hero or even a philosophy Machado's central protagonist is discourse itself and the successive association of disparate ideas. His sharp concision and morbid fascination with the slow drip of time is tempered by humor and irony. In his works are the seeds of many seminal ideas usually associated with later European modernism and even the postmodern.

Machado's narratives tend to camouflage passionate propositions and radical implications in apparently ordinary situations, uneventful outcomes, and prosaic phrasing. Great critics, from different generations, and diverse aesthetic and political ideologies, have successively interpreted his ironic eccentricity and attempted to diagnose its psychological or sociological underpinnings. Some attacked his disengagement from race issues as alienation. A later critical vanguard changed tack by emphasizing the distinction between the shrewd author and his unreliable narrators, his subtle subversion of Victorian patriarchy and empathy for female characters. In his own time Machado was recognized as the preeminent literary intelligence of the age and was the founding president of Brazil's Academy of Letters (1896).

By the end of the nineteenth century, Brazilian letters had much reduced the lag with which it followed Parisian modes. Several sophisticated "impressionist" novels appeared, notably, *O ateneu* ("The private school," 1888) by Raul Pompéia, a *carioca* (a person from Rio). While Rio was the literary capital, many writers hailed from regional provinces, whose mores they described. *O mulato* (1881), by Aluísio Azevedo (1857–1913) exposed racial intolerance in the northern state of Maranhão. Another historically precocious work, Adolfo Caminha's *Bom crioulo* (*The Black Man and the Cabin Boy*, 1895), thematizes and openly addresses interracial homosexual relations. Naturalism was particularly important to Euro-Brazilian intellectuals because of its promise to address racial issues with a "scientific" cachet. A brilliant novel of 1890, Azevedo's *O cortiço* (*A Brazilian Tenement*), portrays the dynamic of urban consolidation in a spectacle of feisty characters. Through two Portuguese immigrants, one a poor but ferociously ambitious capitalist (João Romão), the other a strong silent type (Gerônimo), the narrative charts inevitable paths of social ascent and descent. Gerônimo's New World degeneration is predicated on a *mulata* femme fatale (Rita Baiana). The interactions between the different types are scripted according to the putative psycho-social character of their respective groups, and yet vividly evoked. The text's resolution of utter conventionality of social stereotypes with poetic rhetoric moves freely beyond the ostensible frame of naturalism to admit Romantic and humorously realist elements.

In the 1890s, Brazilian historiography and literary practices began to engage with new approaches to Brazilian culture and society under the aegis of positivism. Literary critic and folklorist Sílvio Romero (1851–1914) charted a course away from simplistic racial stereotypes and toward a more productive assessment of Brazilian cultural and ethnic diversity, underscoring the significance of blacks and *mestiços* in Brazilian national identity. *Os sertões* (*Rebellion in the Backlands*, 1902), a book-length, multidisciplinary disquisition by military engineer and news reporter Euclides da Cunha (1866–1909), explores the material and symbolic conflicts between state troops and a millenarian Catholic folk community in the *sertão* (the dry interior of the Northeast). While his scientific models and methods have been superceded, Da Cunha's oratorical prose was supremely eloquent and insightful.

Da Cunha heralds a rich Brazilian tradition of essayists which anticipates today's "cultural studies," by using interdisciplinary approaches and drawing on creative expression as much as "hard" scientific data. The interface between socio-anthropology and literature is expressed in considerable crossover criticism and also in fiction written by social scientists. One example is the novel *Maíra* (1976), by Darcy Ribeiro (1922–97), an eminent anthropologist, politician and, like Da Cunha, a member of the Brazilian Academy of Letters. The novel evokes indigenous belief systems (Maíra is a sun-god), material conditions, and social values, and exposes the process of cultural and demographic annihilation consequent to contact with whites.

The most famous and influential essayist has been the anthropologist Gilberto Freyre (1900–1987), from the Northeastern state of Pernambuco. Freyre outlined the trajectory of the colonizer as "Luso-Tropical man" arguing, in the seminal text *Casa grande e senzala* (*The Masters and the Slaves*, 1933), that the Northeastern plantation was the foundation of a national culture, of which miscegenation was the key trait. For Freyre, the Brazilian soul derived primarily from the intimate and symbolic intercourse between slave-masters and their slave-mistresses and the diplomatic social strategies of their mulatto offspring. The reading of this interaction as predicated on mutual seduction rather than violence is fundamental to a pervasive view according to which Brazil is blessed by a unique multiethnic harmony and creativity.

While Freyrean views have generally prevailed, most particularly in the middle decades of the century, the ongoing counterarguments from various perspectives (including Ribeiro's radical revision of European colonization and of capitalism) reveal how much racio-cultural issues remain unresolved in the intellectual landscape which shadows the composition of socially conscientious fiction.

A Euro-centric *belle époque* in urban Brazilian society and letters lingered through the second decade of the twentieth century, financed by a slowly stagnating coffee-based economy complemented by rubber and cacao booms in distant provinces. A vital and rather solitary dissenter to the illusory status quo was the *carioca* (Rio) writer Lima Barreto (1881–1922). His single major novel, *Triste fim de Policarpo Quaresma* ("The sad end of Policarpo Quaresma," 1915), shares Azevedo's verve for characters with a social piquancy but, instead of accepting the period's naturalist orthodoxy, relies on a strongly intuitive critical sense and attains a more original vein of realism. *Policarpo Quaresma* presents fascinating peripheral social sketches – scenes of suburban Rio, and figures like a virtuoso of incipient Brazilian popular musical genres, as well as a Yankee Protestant preacher. Convinced that national wealth derives from agriculture, Barreto's idealist protagonist concludes that his comfortable government post in the city is of little service to the realization of a great and immanent national destiny. He thus resigns and sets off to make a living as a farmer. The results are predictably disastrous as his ingenuous good faith encounters debasing economic and social realities. Deploying the quixotic protagonist as a foil, the novel indicts the urban Brazilian elite, including its political leaders, as a parasitic enclave.

Avant-garde modernism arrived officially in Brazil in 1922, in São Paulo, with a week-long program literally called the *Semana de Arte Moderna* (the Week of Modern Art). While more noted for his iconoclastic poems and "Cannibalist Manifesto", one of the Semana's leaders, Oswald de Andrade, wrote brilliant experimental modernist novels, the best known being *Memórias sentimentais de João Miramar* ("The sentimental memoirs of João Miramar," 1924) and *Serafim Ponte-Grande* (*Seraphim Grosse Pointe*, 1933). His technical innovation is surprisingly methodical, particularly in the transposition of cubist perspective to narrative form. His 1922 novel, *Alma*, in which scene-cuts replace chapters, adapts montage techniques emerging in the American cinema of the period; the narrative repeatedly switches between simultaneous scenes, shifts viewpoints within a single scene, and underscores time-ellipsis. Oswald's novels capture the postwar modernist sense of intoxication while offering acute observations of provincial life in São Paulo (city and state). The novels' ironic social satire and psychological sophistication, including the author's self-parody, are fascinating, though often oblique or impenetrable because of stylistic and referential idiosyncrasies.

The iconic novel of 1920s modernism is *Macunaíma* (1928), by another seminal modernist, Mário de Andrade (1893–1945; friend but no relation to Oswald). The eponymous hero of *Macunaíma*, a black Amazonian Indian who eats spaghetti in São Paulo, was intended as a composite of quintessential Brazilian traits deriving from distinct national substrata. Macunaíma's amoral opportunism, sensuality, and a ludic compulsion are conjoined in the motif of *brincar* (to play or to make love). Upon his voluntary death, Macunaíma transforms into a constellation. Macunaíma has been assimilated into the Brazilian psyche like no other literary character as an emblematic national figure. But the author had no pretension to icon-status as he wrote the work experimentally over a few short weeks, drawing freely on (or "cannibalizing") ethnographic sources. Mário called *Macunaíma* a "rhapsody," implying a musicality in the association of ideas and the unconventionality of the narrative structure. While the episodic plot does have a unified story line, each chapter may be considered a separate exercise in style and as addressing a different external issue.

Despite its iconoclastic bravado, the Brazilian modernist movement was enthusiastically nationalist. From the late 1920s and into the 1930s, different wings matured and embraced various political movements. While the Catholic nationalists courted fascism, others, including Oswald de Andrade, embraced communism. In 1933 Oswald financed the publication of *Parque industrial* ("Industrial park"), a novel by his then wife, Patrícia Galvão (also called Pagu; 1907–62), an important political agitator and cultural activist. The novel, set in a rapidly industrializing São Paulo and covering the period from inception of the Republic through World War I, is simultaneously feminist, Marxist, and stylistically innovative, deploying Oswaldian narrative tropes but also contrasting a range of sociolects in its varied cast of class-representative women.

In the modernist capital, São Paulo, the movement accompanied international trends. Domestically, however, the cosmopolitan, Euro-Brazilian *paulistas* often acted as cultural colonizers, evoking less-developed regions in exotic terms. A second modernist phase, in the 1930s, was dominated by realist novelists from the Northeast, who undertook a more culturally authentic and socially responsible artistic representation. The most important were Raquel de Queiroz, Graciliano Ramos, Jorge Amado, and José Lins do Rego.

In the case of the first three, their early work has an air of the documentary and bears comparison to Steinbeck. The theses of the novels are generally progressive rather than revolutionary, though each was a member of the Communist Party at some point. For the first time in the Brazilian novel, the protagonists are intended as representative "subalterns" (i.e. from groups traditionally disempowered and excluded from expression through the dynamics of power relations of race, class, and gender, etc.); their subjective worldview is the psychological target of the narrative, while their material problems drive the plot. Emblematic of this emergence of vernacular narrative voices is *O quinze* ("The great drought," 1930), by Raquel de Queiroz (1910–2003), which describes the blight of drought and the consequent cycles of internal migration which mark the *sertão*.

José Lins do Rego's sugar cycle of novels, set in Pernambuco, is a perfect literary complement to Freyre's evocation of plantation life. Rego (1901–57) describes with great psychological sensitivity the sexual initiation of the boy-master with the colored women of the plantation, and his consequent moral corruption, in *Menino de engenho* (*Plantation Boy*, 1931). Rego also produced a number of very well-constructed novels covering different Northeastern locales and tending to a progressively stronger focus on individual subjectivity.

The greatest writer of this group was probably Graciliano Ramos (1892–1953), older than the others and experienced in the endemic corruption of Northeast politics (he had been mayor of a small backlands town). Politically committed and ambivalently Communist, he aspired to a progressive transformation of Brazilian society. Like Da Cunha, his social sense of the *sertão* derived from a determinist viewpoint somewhat at odds with his empathy for his subaltern subjects. As determinedly honest a writer as Camus, the obligation to authenticity and harsh scrutiny of the visceral impulses of his novels prevailed over the political theories he embraced. His most influential work is *Vidas secas* (*Barren Lives*, 1938), a series of sparely written scenes in the life of the family of a landless cowhand. Ramos bears comparison to the Mexican Juan Rulfo. They both shared a determination to achieve a radical economy of language, an intolerance for the false pretensions of leaders, and a vital concern with the experiences of the disenfranchised, which are nevertheless portrayed with little sentimentalism. The narrator-protagonist of Graciliano's *São Bernardo* (1934), a peon who fights his way to *fazendeiro* (squire-farmer) status, is so unpleasantly tough that his wife dies of despair. As he recounts his harsh life, the wasteland of his corrupt existence is partly redeemed by his relative honesty.

The Northeastern novelists were a dominant influence nationally, but analogous currents developed elsewhere. Érico Veríssimo (1905–75) portrayed the historical saga of his native *gaúcho* region (in the extreme south, bordering Uruguay) in the monumental trilogy *O tempo e o vento* (*Time and the Wind*, 1949–61). A technically accomplished and thematically varied writer, though stylistically conventional, Veríssimo is still very widely read.

A less conventional novelist who wrote in Rio was the Minas Gerais native Lúcio Cardoso (1913–68). This brilliant writer moved beyond the regionalist tendencies of his early novels to explore an inner voice critically attuned to conflict and contradiction, partly because of unresolved tensions between his own Catholicism and homosexuality. His psychologically charged novels include *A luz no sub-solo* ("Light in the cellar," 1936) and the better-known *Crônica da Casa Assassinada* ("Chronicle of a murdered house," 1959). Through Cardoso, Brazilian literature links to a dominant European mid-century theme – existential angst and the myriad complexities of bourgeois guilt.

Clarice Lispector (1925–77), a young friend to Cardoso, was also precocious, from her first novel, *Perto do coração selvagem* (*Near to the Wild Heart*, 1944) written at age nineteen. Her work evolved organically and with great consistency. Lispector ranks internationally as a preeminent novelist of twentieth-century existentialism and female experience. Her novels probe the mental processing of sensations of thought, perception, and emotion in a continuous flow of insight rather than plot. Lispector exploited synesthesia and other techniques to suggest an uncanny atmosphere even when describing the most ordinary of phenomena. Minimizing external action, the narrator proceeds as a diviner of the inner realm, on a quest in which introspection and scrutiny of unsuspected realities supercede conventional apprehension.

Lispector spent time in Europe as the spouse of a diplomat, and read widely. However, she resisted intellectualization, and the underlying optimism, childlike wonder, and even humor of her protagonists and authorial voice suggest an authentic Brazilian cultural presence. While class and other social indices do inflect the terms of interpersonal relations she depicted – in a particularly sharp way in her last short novel and swan song, *A hora da estrela* (*The Hour of the Star*, 1977) – the aim of the narrative experience is not to explicitly condemn old structures or propose changes, but rather to trace present, subjective realities. Lispector's eminently feminine writing practice greatly influenced Brazilian writers, male and female.

João Guimarães Rosa (1908–67), the other great prose writer of what is sometimes called the third phase of modernism, or the "Generation of 1945," was from rural Minas Gerais, a large land-locked state in the Southeast, with varying climates and terrains. Rosa was a country doctor and then a diplomat in Europe, but always an aficionado of the backlands where he tirelessly gathered names of flora and fauna, as well as narrative fragments from campfire tales. His prose style is a pastiche of oral syntactic rhythms and rural vocabulary, into which are woven many neologisms which read as folk colloquialisms. Similarly couched in backlands idiom are narrative themes and threads deriving from Rosa's encyclopedic readings in world literature.

Guimarães Rosa's only novel, *Grande sertão: veredas* (*The Devil to Pay in the Backlands*, 1956), was acclaimed as a revolution in Brazilian letters. For all its challenging complexities, the underlying theme of the novel is story-telling. An old farmer by the name of Riobaldo narrates his life from modest childhood into manhood, when he became the leader of a large band of armed men, struggling against a rival group in lands so remote that legal authorities are absent and communities separated by uncharted land. While the lovingly described natural topographic features of the backlands are clearly identifiable, the human data, such as the precise historical moment or the real names of towns, are blurred, suggesting a mythical world. The psychological intrigue hinges on Riobaldo's relationship with his handsome but shy best friend Diadorim, who, after his death in a battle, is discovered to be a woman. This motif of transformation, also present in a series of tests faced by the protagonist, endows the narrative with an aspect of chivalric romance. A deeper structural intrigue derives from the circumstance governing the act of storytelling: the old man addresses a silent interlocutor, an educated city man, recently encountered serendipitously. Riobaldo's constantly reiterated search for validation of his experiences belies his own faith. He both makes claims to, and casts doubts on, a Faustian pact sealed with the devil in order to ensure the success of his adventures. The novel affirms the power of unreliable memory and of storytelling against certainties and absolute truths. It ends on a note of inconclusion and with the symbol for infinity: "Sei de mim? Cumpro (. . .) O diabo não há! É o que eu digo, se for . . . Existe é homem humano. Travessia" (568; "Do I know myself? I do my part. (. . .) There is no devil! That's what I say, if it . . . What exists is man, the human. Passage").[2]

Rosa and Lispector constitute a cosmopolitan, mid-century plateau in Brazilian fiction. Both have been widely studied, but Rosa has had few followers given his difficult blend of rural motifs and eclectic literary themes. Despite the gulf between their thematic and stylistic agendas, both these writers aspired to a universalism and esthetic virtuosity which transcended immediate public concerns as well as the realist novel's engagement with broad socio-historic portraiture. Unlike most of their counterparts in the Spanish American *Boom*, the leading Brazilians did not take public political positions or write critical essays on social or historical matters. Diplomacy, the preferred professional path of many leading writers of this period, conveniently demanded neutrality or discretion, which was indirectly compensated in their development of magical or alternate verbal realms.

Within an influential sector of the Brazilian literary elite, aestheticism evolved into formalism. Most critics consider *Avalovara*, published in 1973 by Osman Lins (1924–78), to be the culminating novel in this movement. Lins's highly regarded earlier work, set in the interior of his home state of Pernambuco, was overtly realist and focused on middle-class characters beset with existential issues. *O visitante* ("The visitor," 1955) deals with the interactions of a circle of frustrated teachers, while *O fiel e a pedra* ("The faithful and the stone," 1961) is a contemporary family saga adapted directly from real events. The later novel also transposes themes and structures from Virgil's *Aeneid*, marking Lins's move toward more symbolic modes. From the mid-1960s, Lins became increasingly engaged with issues of form. *Avalovara* presents the loves of a protagonist, Abel, for three women who correspond to the principal settings of the novel (Recife, São Paulo, and Paris). The title, a neologism (suggesting "bird," "love," "praise," "egg," and more), denotes a bird made of birds, flying indoors above the lovers. The architecture of the novel is its most striking feature. Eight narrations are intercalated, deriving from the eight different letters in the Latin palindrome "Sator arepo tenet opera rotas" ("The planter carefully plies his plough in the furrows"). Prior to the text, the reader encounters the phrase as follows: the five words are written five times, one letter in each of the twenty-five squares of a 5 × 5 grid;

over the grid a spiral is drawn, moving from the center in tight but broadening circles, to the outer edge of the grid and beyond. The text alternates between the narratives, guided by the movement of the spiral through the grid: where the spiral strikes a given letter marks the point for a new chapter within the corresponding narrative line. In this novel's complex symbolism the grid is intended, among other things, to represent the female, and the spiral the male, while their conjunction is both a sensual and artistic sublimation. Generally, critics concur that the novel's thematic meditations are as compelling as its formal achievements.

The mathematical self-consciousness and stylistic abstraction of *Avalovara* are emblematic of Brazilian assimilation of French postwar formalist radicalism from the *nouveau roman* to *Tel Quel*. Some of the best writers of the next generation, such as Nélida Piñon (b. 1936), initially favored experimental narrative modes palatable primarily to intellectual readers. Piñon's novel *Fundador* ("Founder," 1969) uses retrospection from the future, mirror-reflections between characters, and other counter-realist devices to evoke the views of European discoverers of the Americas, moving through a labyrinth of classical, medieval, and Renaissance motifs. Piñon later moved toward more conventional narrative forms. Perhaps her best received work is *A república dos sonhos* (*The Republic of Dreams*, 1984), which traces several generations of Spanish immigrants in Brazil. The trajectories of Lins and Piñon together mark a general pattern of intensifying approximation to the French formalist vanguard followed by a contrary movement, a declining investment in technical radicalism and a resumption of more traditional realist approaches to society, history, and psychological drama.

The path away from and back to relatively conventional realist fiction that was followed by the intellectual elite constitutes a separate trajectory from the long tradition of more popular writers who always wrote with a broader audience in mind. The most important twentieth-century writer of this ilk is Jorge Amado (1902–2001), active from the 1930s until the 1990s, with seminal works until the early 1970s. Amado's early work describes cocoa workers in the south of his state of Bahia and urban workers in Salvador, its capital. His flair for picturesque adventure is enhanced by real empathy for his subaltern characters and deep knowledge of diverse popular cultural practices. The angry young black hero of his *Jubiabá* (1935) is unprecedented in Brazilian literature. *Capitães da areia* (*Captains of the Sands*, 1937) describes the lives of homeless children, mostly black, who sleep on the beach under boats – another first. Though Amado, whose work became steadily more sensual and humorously vulgar, was disdained as a populist by an influential sector of the intelligentsia, the courage and importance of this thematic novelty is undeniable.

The eponymous heroine of Amado's *Gabriela* (1958) is a fitting female complement to Macunaíma in the limited gallery of literary personae assimilated into the popular conscious. The novel portrays the transformation of a cocoa-boom town from a macho frontier jungle to an outpost of bourgeois civility. The protagonist is not Gabriela, but Nacib, an Arab immigrant restaurateur, whose gradual success confirms the bountiful opportunities of the Americas. His muse, Gabriela, is an angelic nymph, a sexually liberated moral innocent. A *mulata*, her skin is of the cinnamon color of the Amerindians; in her hair she suggestively wears a vivid carnation, like Gauguin's Polynesians. The maturing union of Nacib and Gabriela rewrites *Iracema* in the image of the twentieth century: the Old World travels to the New World in the person of an adaptable burgher rather than a conquistador. He succeeds through harmonious assimilation, learning from a native woman whose own transformation in overcoming stigmas of gender, class, and race, is the more important.

Amado parodies intellectuals and the spectacle of the pedagogical culture industry in his most experimental novel, *Tenda dos milagres* (*Tent of Miracles*, 1969). His protagonist is Pedro Archanjo (Archangel), an organic intellectual of the early twentieth century and high priest of his own theory of miscegenation as a panacea to the oppressive hierarchies of Brazilian society and government. In the post-realist spirit of the Boom novel, two narratives are intercalated; the second, set in the present, describes the discovery of Archanjo-as-intellectual by an American Nobel Prizewinning anthropologist and lampoons the disingenuous and yet sycophant embrace of the famous scientist by the Bahian intelligentsia and press. While the contemporary plot's derision of the modern culture industry appears apolitical, the Archanjo story affords an historical camouflage for a critique of the military dictatorship (1964–85).

Critical aversion to Amado should be historically contextualized. Amado's resilient optimism rings truer today than it did in 1969, the year the regime entered its most brutal phase of repression. During this traumatic period, the Freyrean sense of a unifying sociocultural national covenant eroded greatly as opposition was crushed through executions, torture, and exile. The brutal political context of the late 1960s and early 1970s meant real change for all. But given the resilience of Brazil's pacific self-image, the reality of the rupture was often psychologically deferred or diverted. While there were various small guerrilla initiatives, mass resistance was generally nonexistent. Nor did the situation precipitate unified movements from major groups of writers, as in Spanish America.

That said, the Brazilian protest novel does exist. Its leading exponent was Antônio Callado (1917–97; a *carioca*). The ambivalent nature of the genre is well represented by his two best-known novels. *Quarup* (1967; the title uses an Amerindian word for popular assembly), derives from a reporter's notebook – Callado's own field-notes while a traveling journalist. The novel moves around Brazil, from the Amazon to the Northeast, around the time of the military coup of 1964, depicting the practical dramas of workers, indigenes, and other subalterns in the face of government authority. Callado's *Bar Don Juan* (1971) turns the tables on urban Southeastern intellectuals and liberals engaging in or toying with revolutionary dissidence. As the title suggests, the work is skeptical, if not of progressive politics then of the human motivation it depends on.[3]

Through the 1970s and beyond, several major novelists exploited fantasy to satirize the regime. Ignácio Loyola Brandão (b. 1936) transposed Orwell in barren, totalitarian tomorrow worlds in *Zero* (published first in Italy in 1974) and *Não verás país nenhum* (*And Still the Earth: An Archival Narration*, 1981). The Amazonian novelist, Márcio Souza (b. 1946), ridiculed the trajectories of local *caciques* (political bosses), notably in *Galvez, imperador do acre* (*The Emperor of the Amazon*, 1976), in which he allegorically re-arranges the "stranger-than-fiction" history of frontier revolutionaries. His *A ordem do dia* (*The Order of the Day*, 1983) lampoons official propaganda by attributing "disappearances" (murders committed by the regime) to extraterrestrials in a flying saucer.

From the early 1970s, there is a trend to innovative psychological realism focused on the urban Southeast and South, which probes the personal and social spheres as distinct but intermeshing planes. The 1973 novel *As meninas* (*The Girl in the Photograph*), by Lygia Fagundes Telles (b. 1923), is an outstanding example. Its protagonists are socially representative but contemporary and beyond the traditional repertoire: one is the ideologically militant daughter of an Afro-Bahian woman and an immigrant who was a Nazi; another is a poor white girl disposed to modern hedonistic self-destruction. The third friend is bourgeois, protected but altruistic. The book maps race, class, and gender as foundational influences but also probes personal autonomy and responsibility. Telles's stories are layered on her familiarity with European psychoanalytic and Marxist feminist theory, complemented by a drive to distinguish the specifics of the Brazilian social dynamic, notably in relation to female fertility, motherhood, and Marianism (not as a theological point but as a social constraint which labels a woman either as "Madonna" or "whore").

Moacyr Scliar, a prolific writer of children's literature, novels, short stories, and critical essays on medical science and Judaism, often uses a magical realist approach to social commentary, as in his novel *O centauro no jardim* (*The Centaur in the Garden*, 1980), in which the protagonist's condition as a centaur symbolizes his intermediary position between the Jewish culture of his European immigrant parents and assimilation into a broader Brazilian cultural paradigm dominated by Christian discourse but also inflected with Animist tendencies.

In the works of Ivan Ângelo (b. 1936), a *mineiro* (from Minas Gerais), what seems a narrow focus on a specific group – intellectual professionals of Belo Horizonte (the state capital) – is allegorical of middle-class society nationally. *A festa* (*The Celebration*, 1976) explores the juxtaposition of 1970s liberal consciousness, political authoritarianism, and individual corruption. Ângelo's exposé of the unconsciously reactionary impulses of a hedonistic middle class with a progressive self-image is exemplary of a conceptual sophistication which emerged relatively quickly in Brazilian literature under the stresses of the dictatorship, well before the period of redemocratization. A later work by Ângelo, *A face horrível* ("The horrible side," 1986), compares the character of specific generations of modern Brazilian society but complements this socio-documentary aspect with scrutiny of perverse aspects in long-term amorous relationships. The horrid face of love is revealed at one extreme of the silent oscillation between *eros* and *thanatos*, where ego makes a lover, resentful of the very act of loving, strike out destructively against his or her partner.

Perhaps the most admired contemporary writer exploring the deeper recesses of love, both amorous and familial, is the *paulista*, Raduan Nassar (b. 1935). The narrator of his first novel, *Lavoura arcaica*, ("Archaic planting," 1975), the son of a family which emigrated from the Eastern Mediterranean to Brazil, works through evocative memories to fathom his own hidden identity and that of his family. The intellectual caressing of remembrance recalls Proust. Instead of a deliberately isolated rumination, however, the narrator draws on a simulation of interlocution, fudging the boundaries between dialogue, soliloquy, and what the protagonist retrospectively feels should have been or was said. The sense of temporal and spatial concentration is complemented by the narrow social range, which barely moves beyond immediate family members. The subjective past becomes vividly present in a flowing, poetry-in-prose style of a remarkably assured phrasal rhythm and replete with rich, earthy metaphors. While the narrative traces the difficulty of articulating filial rebellion, the moral viewpoint has strong biblical overtones.

The main narrator of Nassar's novela, *Um copo de cólera* ("A cup of cholera," 1978) is emphatically male and recounts the visit of a girlfriend which begins with high lovemaking and ends in a terrible fight. The final portion of the text is a contradictory account of the visit, narrated by the woman, which undermines the reliability of his extensive assertions. His discourse is consistent, however, with the symbolic implications of narrative motifs external to the lovers themselves, in the figures of the secondary characters, an old rural couple who breed rabbits including an aged stud whose ongoing potency is marvelous to them. For all the warring testimony of the lead characters, this animal fertility stands as a motif in tandem with their amorous coupling. The male lover's philosophical divagations invoke a telluric spiritual recuperation of self, against modern consumer culture and intellectualism. This thesis was apparently supported by the author, who, having produced two books which are considered unsurpassed in recent literature, gave up writing and dedicated himself to chicken-farming.

Nassar's cultural conservatism and concern with the land is an exception in the landscape of contemporary Brazilian literature, which is dominated by writers who underscore the erotic, often accompanied by crime, in pointedly urban settings. The most well-known is Rubem Fonseca (b. 1925), a Rio-based *mineiro*, a prolific short-story writer and an occasional but strong novelist. In his *A grande arte* (*High Art*, 1983), the cutting and clinical intelligence of the first-person protagonist-narrator, a lawyer dabbling as a detective, mixes lugubrious sensuality with abundant spleen, and complex, event-driven plots with personal and universal reflections, oscillating constantly between noir motifs and eclectic cultural banter.

The erotic hunting and gathering of the protagonists of Fonseca and other male authors is well complemented in the contemporary scene by women writers. Like Fonseca, Patrícia Melo (b. 1962; a *paulista*) pushes the erotic envelope hard enough that the thriller becomes its terminal envelope, notably in *O matador* (*The Killer*, 1994). *Os seios de Pandora* ("Pandora's breasts," 1998) by Sonia Coutinho (b. 1939), presents two single professional women, who, like the author, live in Rio but are from a small town, to which one returns and is killed. Though cast in the amateur detective frame, the thriller element is used as a device to draw the reader into social ruminations which explore the constraints on women in Brazilian patriarchy.

Expression of the sensibilities and social dilemmas of homosexuals developed in Brazil in concert with the gay movement internationally. A leading writer in exploring homoerotic themes was the *gaúcho* (Southern) writer Caio Fernando Abreu (1948–96). The author later integrated consciousness of AIDS both as a personal condition and as a broad cultural phase, seeing the disease as allegorical to global ecological deterioration. His novel *Onde andará Dulce Veiga?* (*Whatever Happened to Dulce Veiga?: A B-novel*, 1990) is set in a degenerating, socially diseased São Paulo, emblematic of national civil society.

All of these writers feature violence and abuse with erotic interaction.[4] Nassar's poetic and philosophical transcendence through the erotic is thus relatively unusual. Another relative exception is the tremendously admired Sergio Sant'Anna (b. 1941; *carioca*), whose narratives (often novelas) are meticulous in both overall architecture and clarity of phrasing. His 1997 novel, *Um crime delicado* ("A delicate crime"), characteristically presents as protagonist and narrator a theater critic, who frequently diverges into complex critiques on art which are then weaved back into the plot – an amorous entanglement with a crippled art-model and a subsequent sex scandal. In the vein of nineteenth-century French realism, Sant'Anna tempers social observation of human nature with estheticist poise and ethical detachment. Eros and Parnassus are truly central rather than serving allegorically to talk about the contemporary Brazilian condition.

Generally, however, Brazilian fiction after the coup reflects the state of permanent crisis, political, social, and economic, to which the country has become hostage, and to which there is no clear answer. As Brazil emerged from the military regime, economic distress and social violence compounded. Hopes that deep social problems would dissipate with the substitution of democracy for dictatorship proved naïve, as press freedom led to greater exposure of corruption, suggesting an endemic dysfunction.

The 1980s and 1990s work of the *gaúcho* novelist João Gilberto Noll (b. 1946) reflects the sense in middle-class Brazilian society of constant existential deferral – a generic postmodern angst exacerbated by local conditions which suggest a more urgent and radical deterioration. Noll's perambulatory protagonists are in constant motion without destination, wandering from one banal or painful incident to another in an anonymous urban landscape. The ensuing Beckett-like absurdity is unrelieved by any positive counter symbol. Noll's anti-poetry alternates from a baroque "stream-of-consciousness" which merges into a sort of "stream-of-experience" in *A fúria do corpo* ("Body rage," 1981) to a laconic minimalism, as in *Hotel Atlântico* (1989). The anonymous protagonist of the earlier work, aspiring to existential liberation from conventional social reality by concentration on the sexual act (literally, "being his penis"), wanders around a precarious Rio where every turn promises a new degeneration, however pointless. His will to sublimation is shared with his lover, a prostitute. He tries prostitution only to be robbed by the police; the two then dream of a child but are frustrated again. The protagonist of the later work is an actor, who leaves Rio on a completely random journey southwards, getting his leg amputated without explanation, before losing his hearing and sight. The first-person narration merely consolidates the protagonist's insularity from meaningful relations, while the spiritual darkness is periodically counterpointed by forlorn sexual encounters.

A novel which stands at the cusp between the dictatorship and the *abertura* (the "opening," or return to democracy) and seeks to reflect, both retrospectively and prospectively, on their cultural implications is *Stella Manhattan* (1985) by Silviano Santiago (b. 1936), another Rio-based *mineiro*. A fictional exposé of Brazilian gays in New York during the dictatorship, the novel ridicules the regime in the form of a military attaché and torturer with a masochistic bent, who conciliates conventional marriage with promiscuous homosexuality, and urbane conversation with repression. The novel patently avoids building plot on a preconceived theory, as it travels from the satire of an external discourse (cultural fascism) to the exploration of individual identities which are neither guilty nor heroic. What begins as a *roman-à-clef* evolves into self-conscious narrative performance. In an interlude which is apparently arbitrary in terms of the rest of the story, "the narrator" substantiates and pontificates on disparate personal and abstract themes. This exposure effects an eroticization of the act of writing and dramatizes both writing and reading. Transgressive resistance to the subjugation of individual expression by gender and power codes (as in camp "acting up") is paralleled by the narrative's sabotage of the reader's conventional inclination to engage in entertainment reading. The deliberate lack of seamlessness preserves signifying tensions indefinitely, as if to impede closure and, beyond the text, to prevent dispatching the regime's iniquities to the realm of tales about a bygone era.[5]

This highly intellectual approach stands in complete contrast to the populist path of Jorge Amado as an empathic ally to subalterns, seeking genuine inspiration in them in order to represent popular reality. The choice between such stances has been an issue for various middle-class Euro-Brazilian writers conscious of the cultural gulf between the upper classes and the masses. The work of fellow Bahian, João Ubaldo Ribeiro (b. 1941), is significant in this respect. He burst onto the literary scene in 1971 with *Sargento Getúlio*, whose narrator and protagonist, named after the dictator, Getúlio Vargas, is the quintessentially violent, amoral, and anti-intellectual foot soldier of a repressive regime. The entire piece is an interior monologue, a stylistic tour de force in foul, sadistic language. It is a remarkable exposé of abusive alienation, and an interesting bottom-up parallel to the dictator novels of the Spanish American Boom. Ubaldo's voluminous 1984 novel, *Viva o povo brasileiro (An Invincible Memory)*, which recounts the history of Brazilian independence from the Bahian perspective, takes the opposite approach. By their populous presence, though they suffer undemocratic regimes and social injustice, the colorful and good-humored cast of this meandering, panoramic fresco constitutes a democracy, a popular *Comédie Humaine*.

Ubaldo's foray into populist history was complemented in the 1990s by other recuperations of history, some retrospectively imagining the lives of the anonymous poor, others recreating the socio-historic context of famous figures, such as *Boca do inferno* (*Bay of All Saints and Every Conceivable Sin*, 1989) by Ana Miranda (b. 1951 in the Northeast, an adopted *paulista*) about the brilliant libertine poet of baroque Bahia, Gregório de Matos, as well as her *Dias e dias* ("Days and days," 2002), about the Romantic Indianist poet, Antônio Gonçalves Dias, as seen by a distant female admirer. This sort of creative historicism in fiction, which involves recuperating or reinventing speech patterns and other ambient details, is symptomatic of a sophisticated post-dictatorship re-imagining of the national past.

Subaltern voices speaking for themselves, meanwhile, or simply writers not from the Euro-Brazilian middle class, remain radically underrepresented. A cluster of Afro-Brazilian, mostly women writers, published through their São Paulo-based joint-project, *Grupo Quilombhoje* (from *quilombo*, "runaway slave community" + *hoje*, "today"). Dissenting from the entrenched Brazilian resistance to the North American insistence on the racial divide and its injustices, their work constitutes a self-consciously subaltern presence on the literary scene. Preferred genres have generally been verse and short fiction rather than the novel. In 2003, the Rio-based *mineira* Conceição Evaristo (b. 1946), a long-time *Quilombhoje* contributor, published the novel *Ponciá Vicêncio*, a loose *Bildungsroman* which evokes the memories of an Afro-Brazilian woman through the different stages of her life, her impressions of significant family members, and their impressions of her. While sustaining an implicit critical racial conscience, the narrative is highly personal and concerned with subjective gender and identity issues.[6]

A new breed of subaltern literary articulation emerged in the long novel, *Cidade de Deus* ("City of God," 1997) by Paulo Lins (b. 1958). The book portrays the drug wars, interminable violent robberies, sexual brutality, and general jungle-law of the eponymous *favela* (slum community) of Rio, where Lins, an Afro-Brazilian, grew up. Originally a poet, he gathered material for the novel while employed as the research assistant of an ethnographer. The narrative flows between overlapping subsets of characters, who represent a range of individual psychologies and constitutive groups in terms of gender, racial adscription, and regional origin. The ethno-regional variation includes the traditional local black population and immigrants from the interior of the Northeast (predominantly *mestiços* of Amerindian and European blood). Lifestyle profiles range from Pentecostal and evangelical fundamentalists to youths who emulate the more cosmopolitan hedonism associated with Rio's privileged beach-side suburbs. The tremendous contemporary impact of the novel is indissociable from the fact that the viciousness it depicts, which previously was forcibly constrained to the urban periphery, has gradually penetrated downtown Rio and other large cities.

Erotic sensuality, often colored by violence, is perhaps the most conspicuous feature of Brazilian literature of the late twentieth century. The erotic is explored for individual discovery but has also been widely deployed in social allegories of abusive power relations which pertain at the interpersonal as much as at the political level. Through the ongoing deterioration of the civil sphere, the middle classes, central to both the literary market and democratization, have recognized the complex implications of the social gulf between Brazil and its preferred analog, Europe and the USA – a difference often obfuscated by the esthetic and intellectual sophistication of Brazilian artists. Many of the best novels written during and after the military dictatorship evince existentially rich perspectives which question both traditional hierarchies and conventional mythologies of Brazilian identity. More than by any single theme, contemporary Brazilian literature is marked by an increasing diversity of methods, styles, and interests.

NOTES

1. See note on translations on p. xii.
2. João Guimarães Rosa, *Grande sertão: veredas*, 2nd edn. (Rio de Janeiro: José Olympio, 1958). Translation mine.
3. Nancy Baden's *The Muffled Cries: The Writer and Literature in Authoritarian Brazil, 1964–1985* (Lanham, Md.: University Press of America, 1999), provides a wide-ranging overview of the political changes on the literary scene during the dictatorship. Dissent within the Brazilian progressive Left is covered in Heloisa Buarque de Hollanda and Carlos Alberto Pereira's *Patrulhas Ideológicas, Marca Reg.: Arte e Engajamento em Debate* (São Paulo: Brasiliense, 1980). A seminal contrarian essay is Roberto Schwarz's "Culture and Politics in Brazil: 1964–1969," in his *Misplaced Ideas: Essays on Brazilian Culture*, ed. John Gledson (London: Verso, 1992): pp. 126–59.
4. The question of perversions of erotic practice as an expression of abusive power relations in an authoritarian society, in literature from the mid-1970s through to the *abertura* (re-democratization) in 1985, is explored in Rodolfo Franconi's *Erotismo e Poder na Ficção Brasileira Contemporânea* (São Paulo: Annablume, 1997).
5. Santiago's seminal essays on Brazilian identity and international dependence, "Latin American Discourse: The Space In-Between" and "Universality in Spite of Dependence," are in his translated anthology, *The Space In-between: Essays on Latin American Culture* (Durham: Duke University Press, 2001): pp. 25–38 and pp. 53–63.

6. See the bilingual anthology edited by *Quilombhoje* poet Miriam Alves with translator Carolyn Richardson Durham, *Enfim – Nós: Escritoras Negras Brasileiras Contemporâneas (Finally – Us: Contemporary Black Brazilian Women Writers)* (Colorado Springs, Colo.: Three Continents Press, 1995).

FURTHER READING

Arenas, Fernando, "Subjectivities and Homoerotic Desire in Contemporary Brazilian Fiction: The Nation of Caio Fernando Abreu," in Fernando Arenas, *Utopias of Otherness*, Minneapolis: Minnesota University Press, 2003, pp. 42–65.

Buarque de Hollanda, Heloísa, "Parking in a Tow-Away Zone: Women's Literary Studies in Brazil," *Brasil: Revista de Literatura Brasileira (Brazil: A Journal of Brazilian Literature)*, 6, 4 (1991): 6–19.

Cândido, Antônio, *Formação da literatura brasileira: momentos decisivos* (1836–1880), São Paulo: Martins, 1959, Vol. II.

On Literature and Society, Princeton University Press, 1995.

Coutinho, Eduardo and Angela Bezerra de Castro (eds.), *José Lins do Rego: Coletânea*, Rio: Civilização Brasileira; João Pessoa: FUNESC, 1991 (Series "Coleção fortuna crítica," Vol. 7).

Coutinho, Eduardo de Faria, *The Synthesis Novel in Latin America: A Study on João Guimarães Rosa's* Grande Sertão: Veredas, Chapel Hill: UNC Dept. of Romance Languages, 1991.

Ellison, Fred, *Brazil's New Novel: Four Northeastern Masters: José Lins do Rego, Jorge Amado, Graciliano Ramos, Rachel de Queiroz*, Berkeley and Los Angeles: University of California Press, 1954.

Fitz, Earl, *Clarice Lispector*, Boston: Twayne, 1985.

Machado de Assis, Boston: Twayne, 1989.

Foster, David William, "Adolfo Caminha's *Bom-Crioulo*: A Founding Text of Brazilian Gay Literature," *Chasqui: Revista de Literatura Latinoamericana* 17, 2 (November, 1988): 13–22.

Haberly, David, *Three Sad Races: Racial Identity and National Consciousness in Brazilian Literature*, Cambridge University Press, 1983.

Jackson, Kenneth David, "Rediscovering the Rediscoverers, João Miramar and Serafim Ponte Grande," *Texas Quarterly* (Fall 1976): 162–73.

Johnson, Randal, "Brazilian Narrative," in John King (ed.), *The Cambridge Companion to Modern Latin American Culture*, Cambridge University Press, 2004, pp. 119–35.

Johnson, Randal (ed.), *Tropical Paths: Essays on Modern Brazilian Literature*, New York: Garland, 1993.

Nunes, Benedito, "The Literary Historiography of Brazil," in Roberto González Echevarría and Enrique Pupo-Walker (eds.), *The Cambridge History of Latin American Literature*, Vol. III: *Brazil: Bibliography*, Cambridge University Press, 1996; pp. 11–46.

Oliveira, Solange and Judith Still (eds.), *Brazilian Feminisms*, University of Nottingham, 1999.

Peixoto, Marta, *Passionate Fictions: Gender, Narrative and Violence in Clarice Lispector*, Minneapolis: University of Minnesota Press, 1994.

Quinlan, Susan Canty, "Cross-dressing: Silviano Santiago's Fictional Performances," in Susan Canty Quinlan and Fernando Arenas (eds.), *Lusosex: Gender and Sexuality in the Portuguese-Speaking World*, Minneapolis: University of Minnesota Press, 2002, pp. 208–32.

Schwarz, Roberto, *A Master on the Periphery of Capitalism: Machado de Assis*, trans. John Gledson, Durham: Duke University Press, 2001.

Süssekind, Flora, *Tal Brasil, qual romance? Uma ideologia estética e sua história. O naturalismo*, Rio de Janeiro: Achiamé, 1984.

Valente, Luiz Fernando, "Fiction as History: The Case of Joao Ubaldo Ribeiro," *Latin American Research Review* 28, 1 (1993): 41–60.

Vincent, Jon, *João Guimarães Rosa*, Boston: Twayne, 1978.

Wasserman, Renata, *Exotic Nations: Literature and Cultural Identity in the United States and Brazil, 1830–1930*, Cornell University Press, 1994.

Williams, Claire and Cláudia Pazos Alonso (eds.), *Closer to the Wild Heart: Essays on Clarice Lispector*, Oxford: Legenda, European Humanities Research Centre, 2002.

Young, Theodore R., *O questionamento da história em O tempo e o vento de Érico Veríssimo*, Lajeado: Fates Editora, 1997.

6

WILLIAM LUIS

The Caribbean novel

The Caribbean is defined by its geographic location and its many islands, of which Cuba, Puerto Rico, Hispaniola, which the Dominican Republic and Haiti share, and Jamaica are the largest. The Caribbean, whose name is derived from the Carib Amerindians, was the first point of contact between the Old and New Worlds. During his first voyage, Columbus made landfall in Hispaniola and Cuba, and in his second, in Puerto Rico. As the first and last points of contact between the Old and New Worlds, the Caribbean became a privileged area of transit and cultural exchange between Europe, America, Africa, and Asia.

The Caribbean revealed a different kind of wealth, not of gold and silver, but of fertile lands for planting and harvesting sugarcane, and producing sugar. In fact, this area would be defined by the plantation and sugar-mill systems described so masterfully by Antonio Benítez Rojo and Manuel Moreno Fraginals, respectively. Sugar is labor intensive and, with the advent of slavery, West Coast Africans were robbed from their lands and taken in large numbers to Santo Domingo (Haiti) and Cuba, but also to other islands. If other European powers like Great Britain, France, and Holland challenged Spain for supremacy in the Caribbean, the Spanish Crown was able to set the foundation for the development of culture in Cuba, Puerto Rico, and the Dominican Republic.

The origin of the Caribbean novel in Cuba, Puerto Rico, and the Dominican Republic is associated with the early nineteenth-century movements for independence in Spanish America, and the need to forge a national identity. However, these Caribbean countries obtained their independence many decades after those in Spanish America had gained their freedom from Spain, and with some important differences: the Dominican Republic received its sovereignty in 1844, not from Spain but from Haiti; Cuba and Puerto Rico became independent from Spain, but not until the Spanish American War of 1898. Though Cuba developed into a republic in 1902, Puerto Rico became a Free Associated State of the United States. Despite distinct political beginnings, the Spanish Caribbean of the nineteenth century was a crucial moment for the development of a national consciousness, and the novel records the unique historical circumstances unfolding in each country.

Cuban literature in general, and the novel in particular, can be traced to Domingo del Monte and his literary circle, where this critic shared his vast library with writer friends. He encouraged them to abandon Romanticism and accept realism, and write about slavery, thereby incorporating blacks and slaves into early Cuban literature. Del Monte requested that the slave poet Juan Francisco Manzano write his *Autobiografía* (1835, published in Spanish in 1937), arguably the first narrative to document life on the island.

Cecilia Valdés, o La Loma del Ángel (*Cecilia Valdes, or Angel's Hill*), Cuba's national novel, was also begun under Del Monte's tutelage. Cirilo Villaverde, one of the most prolific writers of the century, wrote a short story "Cecilia Valdés" and a first volume under the same name, in 1839. But the definitive version was not available until 1882, not in Cuba but in New York, where Villaverde lived after he escaped from jail in 1848, for conspiring against the Spanish government. Though the short story was included as an early chapter, the first and last versions of the novel are different. The early one documents the triangular relationship among the characters, the definitive one does the same but frames it during Gen. Dionisio Vives' government, from 1812–32, records the suffering of blacks, and condemns slavery. More than any other novel of the nineteenth century, *Cecilia Valdés* captures accurately a period that defines the development of Cuban culture, based on the tensions associated with the harvesting of sugar and coffee, and the interaction between whites and blacks. The novel speaks to the coming together of the races, but also their separation, and how they influenced what later would be known as Cuban culture.

There was another literature forged outside of the Del Monte literary salon. In Spain, Gertrudis Gómez de Avellaneda wrote *Sab* (1841), about slavery and the sacrifices the slave protagonist makes to help his mistress marry. Gómez de Avellaneda was one of the first women to write literature, and she profited from Romanticism and the liberal reforms associated with the Spanish Constitution of 1812, which called for the elimination of slavery. The other was the Condesa de Merlín, Santa Cruz y Montalvo, who wrote about her experiences in Cuba from her residence in Paris.

In Cuba there were other themes and works published in the same period. Ramón de Palma y Romay originated *indigenismo* or what later became *ciboneyismo*, which sought inspiration in the life and customs of the Amerindians. He wrote *Matanza y el Yumurí* (1837), about the tragic love between Ornofay and the princess Guarina. In this tradition, Gómez de Avellaneda wrote *Guatimozín* (1846) and *El cacique de Turmeque* ("The chief of Turmeque," 1860), about the Amerindian past. But Palma was also interested in *costumbrismo* or customs and researched *El cólera en La Habana* ("Cholera in Havana," 1838), about this infestation in the capital city in 1833, and *La pascua en San Marcos* ("Easter in San Marcos," 1838), a controversial novel critical of gambling and the upper classes.

The early literature had a lasting effect on writers in Cuba and the antislavery theme continued well into the contemporary period. Antonio Zambrana wrote *El negro Francisco* ("The black Francisco," 1873), a rewriting of *Francisco*, and it was published not in Cuba, where slavery continued to be a viable institution until 1886, but in Santiago de Chile, his temporary home. Francisco Calcagno was critical of certain Spanish administrators and slavery, and wrote *Los crímenes de Concha* ("Concha's crimes," written in 1863, published 1887); *Romualdo, uno de tanto* ("Romualdo, one among many," 1881), and *Aponte* (1885), which refers to the leader of the Aponte Conspiracy of 1812 to liberate Cuba and emancipate slaves. The black journalist and politician Martín Morúa Delgado did not consider Villaverde's novel to be credible and his *Sofía* (1891) is a rewriting of *Cecilia Valdés. La familia Unzúazu* ("The Unzúazu family," 1901), is about independence and slavery.

Unlike Cuban literature, the Puerto Rican novel does not emerge out of a coherent movement, but from individuals, and the European literary currents that played a decisive role in the development of this genre. In comparison to Cuba, Puerto Rico played a small role in Spain's economy. Though societal contradictions and reform movements were not as well developed as those of the larger sister island, Puerto Ricans joined Cubans in New York in fighting Spanish colonialism. Early instances of the novel include Eugenio María de Hostos's *La peregrinación de Bayoán* ("Bayoán's pilgrimage," 1863), inspired by the patriot's own travels, the Amerindian past, and the current colonization process. The novel is organized around the patriotic and romantic aspirations of Bayoán, a young man whose love relationship can be read as an allegory of Hostos's political ideals: Bayoán (who represents Puerto Rico) is intent on fulfilling his patriotic obligations and on marrying Marién (who represents Cuba) with the blessing of her father Guarionex (who represents the island of Hispaniola). Indeed, the novel has been properly read as a call for a Caribbean confederation that would unite Puerto Rico, Cuba, and the Dominican Republic. Though the novel was first published in Madrid, in 1863, it was confiscated and was not available to a larger public until its second printing in Chile.

There are other writers who promoted this early genre, like Manuel Corchado y Juarbe, who wrote *Historias de ultratumba* ("Stories from beyond the grave," 1872), about the author's spiritualism and contact with the dead; and Salvador Brau, who authored naturalist novels, *La pecadora* ("The sinner," 1887), which takes place in the countryside, and *Lejanías* ("Distance," 1912) an action novel about maritime activities and escapes to nearby islands. But Manuel Alonso's *El gíbaro* ("Hillbilly," 1882) is generally accepted as the first major work. It describes scenes taken from the lives of peasants, symbols of Puerto Rican identity, especially after they migrate to the United States; he also wrote a sequel to the novel seven years later. More in the Romantic tradition is Alejandro Tapia y Rivera, whose works include *La leyenda del cacique* ("The chief's tale," 1852) and *La leyenda de los veinte años* ("The twenty-year tale," 1874). He also authored novels that revealed his interest in the Orient, such as *Enardo y Rosael* (*Enardo and Rosael: An Allegorical Novel*, 1880) and *Póstumo el transmigrado* ("Posthumous the transmigrated one," 1882).

The novel in Puerto Rico comes into fruition with Manuel Zeno Gandía, who captures with care life on the island. Zeno Gandía abandons the Romanticism of his early works and accepts naturalism with works he subtitles "Crónica de un mundo enfermo" ("Chronicles of a sick world"). *Garduña* (1896) takes place in a sugar mill and describes the protagonist's destruction of the characters. It marks a transition in society, from those who inherit land to those who will do what is necessary to obtain it. His best-known work, *La charca* (*The Pond*, 1894), is about coffee and coffee farms in Puerto Rico, but also about human decomposition: rape, robbery, murder, and suicide. *El negocio* ("The business deal," 1922), which reconstructs life in Ponce, on the southwestern part of the island, documents political injustices. *Redentores* ("Redeemers," 1925) is about the US presence on the island. It narrates how the new masters of the country help the opportunistic Puerto Rican Aureo Sol become the first governor of Puerto Rico, but also how Madelón, the North American woman, wants to save him from betraying his people. Zeno Gandía also wrote an inconclusive novel *Nueva York*, which outlines Puerto Rican migration to the mainland.

The Dominican Republic obtained its independence from Haiti in 1844. Although Dominicans are of African descent, their own national heritage does not dwell on African traditions, which they tend to associate with the culture of their Haitian neighbors. The early works do not confront an African reality, preferring to reject it. Instead, they embrace an idealized Amerindian past. From this tradition emerges the country's most important work, Manuel de Jesús Galván's *Enriquillo* (1877, 1882). The novel traces the nation's identity to the time when the island was a Spanish colony, as it describes the love between the Amerindian Enriquillo and Mencía, daughter of an Amerindian and a Spanish conquistador. A Christian, Enriquillo is forced to fight against the Spaniards to stop their abuses against his family, including an attempted rape of his own wife. The novel shows that the protagonist is more Christian than the Spaniards and, like the Cuban antislavery novels, the reader sympathizes with someone of a different race and culture.

Other works of this period were written in a different literary style, without abandoning an interest in history. For example, Francisco G. Billini's *Engracia y Antoñita* (1892) is a novel of customs that describes the environment as well as the triangular relationship between the two women and a man. But Billini also incorporates history into his work, as did Tulio Manuel Cestero, one of the more prolific writers of this period. Concerned with native and modernist portrayals, he also wrote about historical themes, as represented in *La sangre* ("Blood," 1914), as did Federico García Godoy in *Rufinito* (1908), *Alma dominicana* ("Dominican soul," 1911), and *Guanuma* (1914), novels that document and reconsider the past.

In the twentieth century, and after the founding of the Cuban Republic, two themes became popular among novelists: the decay of Cuban society and slavery. Writers who developed the first theme reflected the mood of the time. The founding of the Republic did not represent the change everyone expected; the decadence of the past continued into the present. From this period two writers stand out. Miguel del Carrión combines psychology with naturalism and is critical of false religion in *El milagro* ("The miracle," 1903). He explores the feminine psyche, women's rights and issues in *Las honradas* ("The dignified ones," 1917), *Las impuras* ("The impure ones," 1919), and the unfinished *La esfinge* ("The sphinx," 1961). Carlos Loveira distinguishes himself as a student of societal problems and attacks marital infidelity and the critics who also engage in the same practice in *Los inmorales* ("The immorals," 1919), and corruption that accompanied independence in *Generales y doctores* ("Generals and doctors," 1920). *Juan Criollo* (1927) is his most ambitious work and it narrates the negative influences of the period, as the society moved from colony to independence, and republic.

The theme of blacks and slavery is continued by Lino Novás Calvo, who earned his reputation as a short-story writer. He wrote *El negrero* ("The slave trader," 1933), which has not received the attention it deserves. It documents slavery and the slave trade, and the life of Pedro Blanco, one of the most notorious yet successful slave traders of the nineteenth century. The theme of slavery during this period serves to explain the past, but also describes the present. José Antonio Ramos's *Caniquí* (1936), about nineteenth-century slavery, can be read alongside the Machado dictatorship, which came to an end in 1933.

Alejo Carpentier, José Lezama Lima, and Guillermo Cabrera Infante are the three most important Cuban writers of the twentieth century and are among the best of Latin American literature. Like other writers of his generation, Carpentier also wrote about blacks. His early works reflect an interest in Afro-Cuban culture and religion, as seen in the writings of the anthropologist Fernando Ortiz, and the Afro-Cuban poetic movement, but whose origin can be traced to the nineteenth-century antislavery novel. Africa and black culture were dominant elements in European vanguard movements and Cubans looked to their culture for a more meaningful and authentic expression. Carpentier's *Ecue Yamba-Ó!* ("Lord be praised," 1933) describes Afro-Cuban rites, religions, and secret societies of its African population. His next novel, *El reino de este mundo* (*The Kingdom of This World*, 1949) is also about blacks, not in Cuba, but in the neighboring country of Haiti. His 1943 visit to that first black republic helped him formulate his ideas about marvelous (magical) realism in America, which he includes in the prologue to his novel. In this work, he records transitions in Haitian history, from Mackandal's slave rebellion to the Boyer government. The novel juxtaposes Western history and voodoo, or African religions. Mackandal, Boukman, and Ti Noel use voodoo to defeat the slave masters, but also the black Henri Christophe, and the Mulatto Republicans; the last two abandoned their African roots and accepted a European form of culture and government.

Carpentier also wrote about other concerns and his two other novels of this first period have little to do with blacks. *El acoso* (*Manhunt*, 1954) describes the end of the Machado dictatorship, when the protagonist is hunted for betraying his political allies. As with *El reino de este mundo*, *Los pasos perdidos* (*The Lost Steps*, 1953) reflects upon a search of the foundation of America, a theme developed by other major writers of the period. The setting is the South American jungle, and the protagonist, alienated from contemporary society, travels to the past, to an origin before time and writing, which he visits, but to which he cannot return.

Carpentier, who lived in Venezuela during the period of Castro's armed insurrection, returns to the island and embraces the revolution. His *El siglo de las luces* (*Explosion in a Cathedral*, 1962) is celebrated as a novel of the new society. However, Roberto González Echevarría has shown that upon his return, Carpentier carried back with him a completed manuscript of the novel. Like the revolution, Carpentier refers to tyranny and change. The French guillotine enforces broken promises. The cycles of liberation and oppression, already present in *El reino de este mundo*, are applied to a different historical context. The novel's ending describes another change, the uprising against the Napoleonic forces.

El recurso del método (*Reasons of State*, 1974) belongs to the Latin American dictator novel. It presents a composite picture of many ruthless leaders of the region and narrates the similarities and differences between the dictator and a rebel student. *Concierto barroco* (*Concierto Barroco*, 1974) inverts the conquest of America, when a Mexican and his servant travel to Europe. The novel underscores America's contribution to Western music. *La consagración de la primavera* ("The rites of spring," 1978) is Carpentier's only novel to describe events in the revolution, which he does only at the end, as he calls attention to events related to the Spanish Civil War and the Batista dictatorship. Spring, in the title, implies change and rebirth, and also refers to Stravinsky's ballet score, thus mixing literature and music, which he had done in *La música en Cuba* (*Music in Cuba*) and other earlier works. Carpentier's last novel, *El arpa y la sombra* (*The Harp and the Shadow*, 1979), alludes to music, and to Christopher Columbus's proposed canonization, and his lesser saintly attributes.

José Lezama Lima is another towering figure of Latin American literature. Known as a major poet and editor of literary journals, he is also the author of the novel *Paradiso* (*Paradiso*, 1966) which earned him the reputation of the Proust of Latin America. It is a *Bildungsroman* and narrates the life of José Cemí, who is guided by his classmates Ricardo Fronesis and Eugenio Foción, and later by Oppiano Licario. The novel is rich in symbolism from various cultures, including Christian, Oriental, Greek, and Nordic mythologies. *Paradiso* met with resistance from government officials because of a chapter that contains explicit homosexual descriptions, a behavior they associated with Western capitalism. It was rumored that Castro himself read the novel and ordered its distribution. His posthumously published *Oppiano Licario* (1977) – named after a character who appears in *Paradiso* – has not had the same impact as the earlier master work. Lezama lived an internal exile of sorts and died in Cuba in 1976.

Guillermo Cabrera Infante is one of the few writers to equal Carpentier and Lezama in literary stature. Cabrera Infante became dissatisfied with the revolution and has lived in London since 1966. With *Tres tristes tigres* (*Three Trapped Tigers*, 1967), Cabrera Infante, along with Julio Cortázar, Carlos Fuentes, Mario Vargas Llosa, and Gabriel García Márquez, became one of the writers of the Latin American Boom novel. *Tres tristes tigres* showcases Havana. The novel is presented as one of the acts of the famed Tropicana nightclub and underscores the nightlife, prior to the revolution, as Silvestre and Arsenio, and a host of other characters, intermingle. Its structure is experimental and includes a black page representing a shot, a blank one revealing hidden truths, the recordings of Bustrófedo, different versions of a short story, and sections describing La Estrella, a black singer. Havana, Cuban speech, and puns are also characters in the novel.

La Habana para un Infante difunto (*Infante's Inferno*, 1979) is semi-autobiographical and narrates the protagonist's sexual exploits, from his early encounters with Julieta to his conquest of Margarita, while still married to his wife. Cabrera Infante was particularly fond of the two mentioned novels and he compiled the chapters on La Estrella, of the first, and those of Margarita, of the second, along with a "Metafinal," a story of Estrella's death, and published them under the title *Ella cantaba boleros* ("She sang songs of love" 1996). Cabrera Infante wrote other works, including *Holy Smoke* (1985), in English, about the history of the cigar and popular culture.

The most important event of the century is Castro's rise to power in 1959. For better or worse, it is the single most significant event in the Spanish Caribbean, and perhaps in all of Latin America. The Cuban Revolution transformed society, culture, and literature. It divides Cuban culture between the present and the past, between writers who support the new government and those who oppose it and seek exile. Like the Latin American novel of the Boom, Cuba experienced its own literary explosion, thus bringing literature and culture to the attention of a world audience. Events related to Castro's threat to export communism and the Cuban Missile Crisis made Cuba and Latin America preferred areas of study, and inspired the creation of Latin American Studies programs throughout US institutions. Literature was no longer viewed as a national or regional enterprise, but as a weapon against Western imperialism. In his *Prose Fiction of the Cuban Revolution*, Seymour Menton divides this literature into four stages and periods: The Struggle against Tyranny (1959–60), Exorcism and Existentialism (1961–65), Epos, Experimentation, and Escapism (1966–70), and The Ideological Novel (1971–73). Although there are some works that do not fit into these periods, Menton's study continues to be the most exhaustive on the subject.

The early stages of the revolution are associated with enthusiasm and support for the government, and members of the July 26 Movement, which brought Castro to power, promoted literature and the novel. Carlos Franqui's newspaper *Revolución*, and Guillermo Cabrera Infante's literary supplement *Lunes de Revolución* opened their pages to established and young writers alike. When Castro announced the revolution's communist intent in April 1961, he eliminated all opposition, including *Lunes*. Instead, he favored literary organizations that controlled the interpretation of literary production. The Union of Writers and Artists of Cuba (UNEAC), and Casa de las Américas, the latter created to break the literary and cultural blockade imposed by the United States, were the two most influential institutions that promoted literature.

Writers who supported the revolution and wrote about contemporary events in the new society did so from an ideological perspective. However, there were some writers who were successful in problematizing life in the new society. Edmundo Desnoes's *Memorias del subdesarrollo (Inconsolable*

Memories, 1965) best captures a period of conflict, experienced by a well-to-do businessman who decides to stay in Cuba; it narrates how the revolutionary process affected him directly. More in line with the government's ideology is Manuel Cofiño's *La última mujer y el próximo combate* ("The last woman and the next combat"), winner of the 1971 Casa de las Américas Prize, whose protagonist sacrifices his marriage for the revolution and is successful in his profession to help peasants. Since writing their works, Desnoes abandoned the island for the United States in 1979, and Cofiño remained and died in his native Cuba in 1986.

The testimonial novel is a more successful sub-genre promoted by Cuban literature. It is based on interviews with an informant, usually someone marginal to society, and whose story has not been recorded or for which there is little information. The writer edits the interviews and writes the book. However, it is difficult to remain totally objective, and the editing process coincides with the writer's interpretation of events. While there were many works that highlighted the revolutionary process, Miguel Barnet's *Biografía de un cimarrón* (*The Autobiography of a Runway Slave*, 1966) was the first work to publicize the testimonial novel. He interviews Esteban Montejo, a 106-year-old Afro-Cuban, who escaped from slavery. The work narrates his life throughout three different periods in Cuban history: slavery, emancipation, and the republic. Though the interviews also deal with events in the revolution, these have been edited from the final text. Barnet varies this style and interviews a number of women for his *Canción de Rachel* (*Rachel's Song*, 1969), about a Cuban vedette, who is a reflection of the Machado period. He has also published *Gallego* (1981), *La vida real* ("The real life," 1986), and *Oficio de ángel* ("Angel's trade," 1989), which have not received the same recognition as his earlier works. There is one other testimonial work that should be recognized. Daisy Rubiera Castillo's *Reyita, sensillamente* (*Reyita: The Life of a Black Cuban Woman in the Twentieth Century*, 1997) is based on interviews with the writer's mother. Reyita, who claims to have been born with the Republic, describes her life during this period in Cuban history. Reyita narrates life from the unique point of view of a black woman, who was even discriminated against by her own mother. With the hope of sparing her children the prejudice she experienced, Reyita marries someone white but later realizes that her supposed husband never married her. The testimonial novel has also played a role in providing an outlet for marginal subjects in Latin American literature.

Cuba's Special Period, created by the fall of the Soviet bloc, marks the latest stage in the island's economic and cultural production. Pedro Juan Gutiérrez is conceivably the best and most prolific writer of his generation. He writes in a harsh language that is matched only by the crumbling situation in his country. Not unlike the antislavery novel, which undermined the Spanish colonial authorities, *Trilogía sucia* (*Dirty Havana Trilogy*, 1998) is born of the country's current conditions, of scarcity, deprivation, and decay. The situation gives birth to a character, who appears to be the author's alter ego, cares about nothing, and for whom sex is perhaps the most important escape. Everything is in a constant state of decomposition. Even the famed Superman, a Havana black known for the size of his penis, who makes an appearance in *Godfather II*, urinates from a small rubber hose. *El rey de La Habana* ("King of Havana," 1999), *Animal tropical* ("Tropical animal," 2000), and his collection of stories *El insaciable hombre araña* ("The insatiable spiderman," 2002) follow a theme already seen in *Trilogía sucia*, and mix reality with decadence, frustration, and sex.

Many of Cuba's best writers have left the country. One of the early writers to do so was Severo Sarduy. In the revolution, he obtained a scholarship to study art criticism in Europe. Sarduy stayed in Paris, joined the Tel Quel group, and became the Latin American series editor of Editions du Seuil, though he officially never broke with the revolution. Sarduy incorporates techniques associated with the *nouveau roman* into his works. His first novel *Gestos* ("Gestures," 1963) describes life during the Batista dictatorship and captures with imaginative flare the activities of a black woman, who by day washes clothing and by night is a terrorist. In *De donde son los cantantes* (*From Cuba with a Song*, 1967) Sarduy affirms that Cuban culture is Spanish, African, and Chinese, as his characters represent. With *Cobra* (*Cobra*, 1972) Sarduy transcends Cuban culture and his protagonist, a transvestite, and searches for meaning and identity in other parts of the world. *Maitreya* (*Maitreya*, 1978) takes the search to Asia and seeks it in Buddhism but returns to Cuba and the United States. *Colibrí* ("Hummingbird," 1984) takes place in the Latin American jungle, in a homosexual brothel, where the protagonist works as a dancer and wrestler. He escapes persecution only to return and impose upon others the same condition he suffers. Sarduy's last work was *Cocuyo* ("Cocoon," 1990), which he published before his untimely death in 1992.

Of those writers who became novelists after the revolution, Reinaldo Arenas was the most active and best known. As officials of the government insisted, he wrote about events in the new society. However, he did not glorify them but was critical of the Castro government. His first novel, *Celestino antes del alba* ("Celestino before dawn," 1967), received a first mention in a national competition, yet this was the only work he published in Cuba. *El mundo alucinante* (*Hallucinations*, 1968) and *El palacio de las blanquísimas mofestas* (*Palace of the White Skunks*, 1980) were smuggled out of the country and published first in French. Arenas became disillusioned with the Cuban government, which persecuted him for his sexual preference. He escaped detention and went into hiding, fleeing the island during the Mariel Boat Lift in 1980. In the United States he continued to write and denounce the Castro government until he died from AIDS in December of 1990.

Arenas's international standing can be attributed to *El mundo alucinante*, awarded *Le Monde*'s First Prize for foreign novels. The novel narrates the life of the seventeenth-century Fray Servando Teresa de Mier and uses his *Memoirs* as a subtext. It describes his travels and experiences, including his polemical sermon about the origins of the Virgin of Guadalupe that caused his downfall, and struggles for Mexican independence both at home and abroad. He writes not to reconstruct history, but to subvert it and uncover its multiple facets.

Arenas wrote and published most of his works in the United States. They include *Otra vez el mar* (*Farewell to the Sea*, 1982), which he had begun in Cuba; *La loma del Ángel* (*Graveyard of the Angels*, 1987), another rewriting of *Cecilia Valdés*; and *El portero* (*The Doorman*, 1989), about life in New York. *Adios a mamá*, *El asalto* ("Goodbye mother," 1995, "The assault," 1990) and *El color del verano* ("The color of summer," 1991) were published posthumously. But the most important work of his exile period was his autobiography, *Antes que anochezca* (*Before Night Falls*, 1992), a scathing denunciation of the Castro government, written on his death bed. Arenas provides the reader with his version of events about his life and uses homosexuality as a weapon against Castro's supporters, as he accuses police and government officials of engaging in similar acts.

In the Special Period, René Prieto has seen an acute interest in erotic literature. This is the case with Pedro Juan Gutiérrez, but also with women exile authors who write against the male dominant culture. Zoé Valdés, who resides in France, writes about Havana before and during the revolution, with the same humor and sexual descriptions already seen in the works of Cabrera Infante. In fact, she writes in a crude and sexually explicit language, thus revealing the female position in sexual aggression. *La nada cotidiana* (*Yocandra in the Paradise of Nada*, 1997) is about the protagonist's unequivocal sexual exploits under a crumbling communist government and society; *Café nostalgia* ("Nostalgia cafe," 1998) refers to friends who reconstruct their everyday difficult lives in Cuba via the telephone and Internet; *Te di la vida entera* ("I gave you all I had, 2000), whose subtext is pre-revolutionary Cuban music, moves from the nostalgic Havana before the revolution, to the start of the revolution, and to the present city under collapse and decay, as marked by the three visits of Cuca Martínez's boyfriend Uan Pérez.

Mayra Montero, a Cuban by birth, has made her home in Puerto Rico. Like Valdés, Montero writes erotic literature with flair but places her characters in a rich Caribbean setting. In *La última noche que pasé contigo* (*The Last Night I Spent With You*, 1991), Celia and Fernando embark on a voyage through the Caribbean to spark a relationship that will unfold in ways that neither of them could have anticipated. *Tú, la oscuridad* (*You, Darkness*, 1995) takes place in Haiti as herpetologist Víctor Grigg looks for the almost extinct "blood frog." The story alternates between the researcher and his Haitian guide, Thierry Adrien, who describes the magic of his country's culture, which includes his father's hunt for zombies. Their lives become intertwined and their search is interrupted by the political events that force President Bertrand Aristide from power. *Del rojo de su sombra* (*The Red of His Shadow*, 1992) highlights voodoo as Simil Bolosse, Zul, and other Haitians migrate to the Dominican Republic in search of work in the sugarcane fields. Once lovers, Zul, a voodoo priestess, and Simil, a voodoo priest backed by Duvalier's "tonton macutes," become enemies and Simil threatens to kill her if she does not join forces with him. *Como un mensaje tuyo* (*The Messenger*, 1998) continues to insist on Caribbean cultural mixture, when Aida Petriena Cheng, a Cuban mulatto woman of Chinese descent, narrates Caruso's 1920 trip to Havana and his relationship with her, and gives him a daughter. *Púrpura profunda* (*Deep Purple*, 2000) is based on Agustín Cabán's recollections of his male and female lovers and their relationship to music, and especially the Antiguan mulatto Virginia Tuten.

Cubans were influenced by events in the republic and the revolution, but Puerto Ricans responded to their relationship with the United States. Some authors made attempts to write a modernist novel that focused on the esthetics. However, an increasing number studied life on the island, which included addressing Puerto Rico's political situation. More recent writers document the mass displacement of Puerto Ricans to New York. If the Cuban Revolution marked the life of every Cuban writer, the US control of the island did the same for Puerto Rican authors.

In the decade of the thirties, Enrique Laguerre emerges as the most important Puerto Rican novelist of the period. His works cover many decades and reflect the concerns of the moment in which he writes. He indulges in sociological and psychological descriptions in his best-known novel *La llamarada* ("The flare-up," 1935), about the sugarcane industry. *Solar Montoya* (1941) studies another crop, coffee, and describes the protagonist's attempt to preserve the plantations. *La resaca* ("Undertow," 1949) looks at colonial life during the last quarter of the century, at a moment in which Puerto Ricans were discussing their political status, and *Los dedos de la mano* ("Fingers on the hand," 1951) is a psychological novel. In his later years, Laguerre becomes more experimental with form and ideas, as seen in *La ceiba en el tiesto* ("The bombax in the flowerpot," 1956), *El laberinto* (*The*

Labyrinth, 1959), which touches upon the themes of emigration and New York, and also in *El fuego y su aire* ("The fire and its air," 1970). His last novel, *Los amos benévolos* ("Benevolent masters," 1977), is a commentary on exploitation and greed on the island.

The large migration of Puerto Ricans to the United States influenced Puerto Rican culture and the novel. Writers of the Generation of the Forties began to document this unprecedented period, caused, to a large extent, by Operation Bootstrap in the late forties and fifties, the US attempt to industrialize the island, making it a model of development for the rest of Latin America. Unfortunately, it also upset the island's economy, sending large numbers of peasants looking for jobs to the capital city, and from San Juan to New York City. José Luis González was among the first narrators to capture this process in his short stories, and he also wrote *Paisa* (1950), about the migratory process and the difficulties Puerto Ricans experienced in the United States.

Better known for his collection of short stories *Spiks*, Pedro Juan Soto wrote *Usmaíl* (1959), about the US presence in Puerto Rico, reflected in the troubled child of a black Puerto Rican and a white US officer. In *Ardiente suelo, fría estación* ("Hot land, cold season," 1961), he narrates a different problem experienced by New York Puerto Ricans who return to the island, having to contend with being foreigners in their own land. In *El francotirador* ("The sniper," 1969), he addresses another issue facing Puerto Ricans on the island, the presence of Cuban exiles. He narrates the life of an exile writer in the odd chapters, and a counterrevolutionary in the even, representing aspects of the same person. Soto died in 2003. Of a more experimental nature, and closer to the novel of the Boom period, is Emilio Díaz Valcárcel's *Figuraciones en el mes de marzo* (*Schemes in the Month of March*, 1972), portraying a fragmented view of reality, as the protagonist in Spain defends himself against remnants of the empire. But like other writers of the period, Díaz Valcárcel also wrote about his countrymen on the continent. In *Harlem todos los días* (*Schemes in the Month of March*, 1987) he studies the lives of both oppressor and oppressed, and in *Mi mamá me ama* ("My mother loves me," 1981) he does the same on the island.

The Puerto Rican novel reached a new level of expression with Luis Rafael Sánchez, whose *La guaracha del macho Camacho* (*Macho Camacho's Beat*, 1976) became an instant success. Sánchez skillfully mixes techniques associated with the Boom writers and social commentary of the island's political status. Written in Puerto Rican speech, the novel unfolds during an afternoon rush hour, as the characters, while listening to the Guaracha, are affected, in one form or another, by the same traffic jam. *La importancia de llamarse Daniel Santos* ("The importance of being Daniel Santos," 1988) demystifies the image of the popular Puerto Rican singer. Though it was received with less enthusiasm, this novel demonstrates that Puerto Rico is not insular, but that the country's symbols are present throughout Latin America and the United States.

Of the next generations of Puerto Rican novelists, Edgardo Rodríguez Juliá has become the conscience of the Puerto Rican nation. The themes he describes range from the eighteenth century to the present, from *Renuncia del héroe Baltazar* (*The Renunciation*, 1974) to *Una noche con Iris Chacón* ("A night with Iris Chacón," 1986). Puerto Rican identity is not a fixed concept, rather it is subject to a rigorous analysis. With his impressive research, he dismantles images of Puerto Rican history, politics, society, and popular culture. He writes in a style that also questions the boundaries between fiction and essay. In this particular vein is *El entierro de Cortijo* ("Cortijo's burial," 1983), about the wake and burial of Rafael Cortijo, Puerto Rico's famed black percussionist of the popular Bomba and Plena music. In the first part, the protagonist journalist, a white outsider from a well-to-do family, ventures into the sinister Villa Palmera neighborhood. In the second, he is drawn into the event, thus changing his status from observer to participant. He is caught in the chaos of the event, which unites him with his black and poor countrymen, and this mixture, and music, define Puerto Rican identity.

Puerto Rican women writers constitute a significant group of new writers. In their works, these authors interpret Puerto Rican political and cultural events from a feminist perspective. They narrate events from a point of view not previously available from other writers and attempt to correct the society's perception of women. Certainly, these authors have been influenced by the Women's Movement in the United States. Of this group, Rosario Ferré has been most active. *Maldito amor* (*Sweet Diamond Dust*, 1986) is divided into four stories, from colonialism to modern-day imperialism, each outlining a historical period, interpreted from a woman's perspective. Ferré has also inserted herself into the most recent literary current, Latino writings in the United States, which refers mainly to authors born or raised in the United States, who write in English. Though she considers herself a Puerto Rican and Spanish American writer, Ferré's *The House on the Lagoon* (1995) was written in English, and some critics are now promoting her as a Latino writer. The novel constructs Puerto Rican society and identity. Isabel Monfort writes the history of her and her husband's family. Quintín discovers the manuscript, corrects his wife's recollections, and provides his interpretation of events. Ferré confronts the sexual, racial, and political aspects of Puerto Rican culture. Though whites occupy the main house, the black servants are its foundation. The destruction of the house and the survivors' escape to the United States represent a metaphorical answer to the Puerto Rican dilemma. *Eccentric Neighborhoods* (1998), Ferré's second novel also written in English, continues to highlight Puerto Rico's elite families, whose fortune and fate are tied to the island's history and culture. The narrator Elvira Vernet describes in rich detail the Rivas de Santillana family, whose money comes from sugar, and the Vernets, whose fortune is in cement. The most exciting female writer is Ana Lydia Vega, who is better known for her short stories and chronicles. Of these, *Encancaranublado y otros cuentos de naufragio* ("Encancaranublado and other stories of a shipwreck," 1983) and *Esperando a Loló y otros delirios generacionales* ("Waiting for Loló and other generational insanities," 1994) should be mentioned.

The twentieth-century Dominican novel reflects the political conditions of the country, motivated mainly by three events: the US occupation of the country, from 1916 to 1924, the Trujillo Dictatorship, from 1930 to 1961, and the US invasion in 1965. Examples of the first are Rafael Damirón's *La cacica* ("The woman chief," 1944) and Ramón Marrero Aristy's *Over* (1939), which use the criollista techniques of the times and depicts US companies and their exploitation of Dominicans.

Traditions of the countryside are best represented in the works of the nation's greatest known short-story writer, Juan Bosch, who lived and wrote most of his works in exile. His novel, *La mañosa* ("The clever woman," 1936), was the most popular of its time. A blend of costumbrism and modernism, the novel takes place in the rural sector and narrates the conflicts among the different classes. The coming together of Haitians and Dominicans is present in Julio González Herrera's *Trementina, clerén y bongó* ("Turpentine, booze, and drums," 1943), one of the few works to recognize the neighboring country and its culture.

Trujillo's fall allowed writers to revisit this period; fear had prevented established and beginning authors from questioning the government. The example of Andrés Francisco Requena was well publicized. Trujillo's henchmen assassinated him in New York for having written *Cementerio sin cruces* ("Cemetery without crosses," 1949), a denunciation of the Trujillo dictatorship. Freddy Prestol Castillo's *El masacre se pasa a pie* ("Walking across the massacre river," 1973) revisits the 1937 Trujillo massacre of Haitians living on the Dominican border. Critical of the US invasion is Aída Cartagena Portalatín's *Escalera para Electra* ("Ladder for Electra," 1970).

In the contemporary period, writers are incorporating the experimental techniques associated with the Latin American novel of the Boom period. Marcio Veloz Maggiolo's novels are a notable example. Also known for his short stories, his novels include *El prófugo* ("The fugitive," 1963), *De abril en adelante* ("From April onwards," 1975), and *La biografía difusa de Sombra Castañeda* ("The difused biography of Sombra Castañeda," 1980), which refer to the Trujillo dictatorship. Virgilio Díaz Grullón's *Los algarrobos también sueñan* ("The carob trees also dream," 1976) belongs to the same tradition.

Other novels have been welcomed by a general audience. Pedro Vergés's *Sólo cenizas hallarás: (bolero)* ("You will find only ashes [love songs]," 1980) is an experimental novel that describes the aftermath of Trujillo's downfall; and Viriato Sención's *Los que falsificaron la letra de Dios* (*They Forged the Signature of God*, 1992), recipient of the National Novel Prize, uncovers the complicity between the church and the Trujillo dictatorship. Unlike other Dominican writers, Sención lives in the United States. Even the famed Mario Vargas Llosa was compelled to write about the dictator. His *La fiesta del Chivo* (*The Feast of the Goat*, 2000) describes Trujillo's seduction of young girls and the day of the assassination. However, in his *Bienvenida y la noche (Crónicas de Montecristi)* ("Bienvenida and the night" 1994), Manuel Rueda narrates Trujillo's marriage to his wife but also highlights his appetite for boys. Mixing autobiography and chronicles, Rueda also reconstructs the Trujillo years.

There is a recent literary phenomenon that is receiving much-deserved attention. This one pertains to a Caribbean literature written in English in the United States, one that Ferré has also embraced. Among its many other exponents one could cite Oscar Hijuelos, Cristina García, Piri Thomas, and Julia Alvarez. Many of these authors are the sons and daughters of recent immigrants and exiles and were born or raised in the United States. They write a literature that brings together the culture of the parents and that of their adopted country. Cuban, Puerto Rican, and Dominican literatures exist in their country of provenance, but with the increased migration and exile of Caribbean people, the novels are also written abroad, in Spanish but also in English, as their descendents living in the United States come of age.

FURTHER READING

Álvarez Borland, Isabel, *Cuban-American Literature of Exile: From Person to Persona*, Charlottesville: University of Virginia Press, 1998.

Arnold, James (ed.), *A History of Literature in the Caribbean*, Amsterdam: John Benjamins, 1994.

Balaguer, Joaquín, *Historia de la literatura dominicana*, Ciudad Trujillo: Editorial Librería Dominicana, 1958.

Benítez Rojo, Antonio, *The Repeating Island: The Caribbean and the Postmodern Perspective*, trans. James Marannis, Durham, NC: Duke University Press, 1992.

Berroa, Rei (ed.), *La literatura dominicana siglo veinte*, special issue of *Revista Iberoamericana* 54, 142 (1988).

Bueno, Salvador, *Historia de la literatura cubana*, Havana: Editorial Nacional de Cuba, 1963.

Callaloo 23, 3 (2000). Special issue on Dominican Republic, Literature and Culture, edited by Lizabeth Paravisini-Bebert and Consuelo López-Springfield.

Candelier Bruno, Rosario, *Tendencias de la novela dominicana*, Santiago, D. R.: Departamento de Publicaciones de la Pontificia Universidad Católica Madre y Maestra, 1988.

Gómez Tejera, Carmen, *La novela en Puerto Rico*, Río Piedras: Universidad de Puerto Rico, 1947.

González Echevarría, Roberto, *Alejo Carpentier: The Pilgrim at Home*, Ithaca, NY: Cornell University Press, 1977.

La ruta de Severo Sarduy, Hanover, NH: Ediciones del Norte, 1987.

Henríquez Ureña, Max, *Panorama histórico de la literatura dominicana*, Santo Domingo: Colección Pensamiento Dominicano, 1966.

Hillman, Richard S. and Thomas J. D'Agostino, *Understanding the Contemporary Caribbean*, Boulder, Colo.: Lynne Rienner Publishers, 2003.

Luis, William, *Literary Bondage: Slavery in Cuban Narrative*, Austin: University of Texas Press, 1990.

Dance Between Two Cultures: Latino Caribbean Literature Written in the United States, Nashville: Vanderbilt University Press, 1997.

(ed.), *Modern Latin American Fiction Writers, First Series*, Detroit: Gale Research, 1992.

with Ann González (eds.), *Modern Latin American Fiction Writers*, Second Series, Detroit: Gale Research, 1994.

Manrique Cabrera, Francisco, *Historia de la literatura puertorriqueña*, San Juan: Editorial Cultural, 1971.

Méndez Rodenas, Adriana, *Gender and Nationalism in Colonial Cuba: The Travels of Santa Cruz Y Montalvo, Condesa de Merlin*, Nashville: Vanderbilt University Press, 1998.

Menton, Seymour, *Prose Fiction of the Cuban Revolution*, Austin: University of Texas Press, 1976.

Moreno Fraginals, Manuel. *El ingenio: complejo económico social cubano del azúcar*, 3 vols., Havana: Editorial de Ciencias Sociales, 1978.

Prieto, René, "Tropos tropicales: contrapunteo de la frutabomba y el plátano en *Te di la vida entera* y *Trilogía sucia de La Habana*," in Anke Birkenmaier and Roberto González Echevarría, *Cuba: Un siglo de literatura (1902–2002)*, Madrid: Editorial Colibrí, 2003.

Santí, Enrico Mario, *Bienes del siglo: sobre cultura cubana*, Mexico: Fondo de Cultura Económica, 2002.

Sommer, Doris, *One Master for Another: Populism as Patriarchal Rhetoric in Dominican Novels*, Lanham, Md.: University Press of America, 1983.

7

ISMAEL MÁRQUEZ

The Andean novel

The South American subcontinent is a region of marked differences and contrasts not only in its history and geography, but also as the result of the interaction of its many cultures, races, ethnicities, languages, religions, customs, and traditions throughout the ages. A topographically fragmented space, the area and its inhabitants are defined and conditioned by major physical environments and systems that encompass impenetrable jungles in the Amazon basin extending over large areas of Peru and Brazil, to some of the most arid regions in the world, such as the Atacama Desert in northern Chile. The dominant and most notable geographical feature of this land is, however, the Andes, a mountain range that boasts some of the highest peaks in the world, running along a general North–South direction parallel to the Pacific Ocean, and occupying significant portions of Venezuela, Colombia, Ecuador, Peru, Bolivia, to the southernmost tip of Chile and Argentina.

In this essay we will examine the development of the novel in Andean countries and the crucial effect that their native Indian populations, history, and cultures have had on the genre. It must be noted, however, that this approach can be best be applied to countries whose populations consist of a majority of Indians, as is the case of Peru, Ecuador, and Bolivia. Though the natural habitat of the Andean Indians has for centuries centered around agrarian communities, starting in the 1950s, major segments of those populations have gravitated towards urban centers for economic, political, and social reasons. This demographic phenomenon had a powerful effect on the novel.

In order to examine the centrality of the Indian in the novel of Andean countries, it is necessary to define certain literary categories: *indianismo*, *indigenismo*, *indígena*, and *neoindigenismo*. The term *indianismo* refers to the Romantic literary production of the nineteenth century written about the Indian and is characterized by its exoticism, the lack of a political agenda vindicating indigenous values, and a sense of nostalgia for the grandeur of the ancient civilizations. The wars of independence from Spain brought about a desire among Latin American intellectuals, writers, and artists to define a new vision of the American continent and its peoples. In their quest to forge a new Latin American identity, different from the heritage of Spain, novelists and poets depicted the magnificent geography and natural beauty of the continent, as well as the customs of its inhabitants. Such is the case of the Ecuadorian Juan León Mera's *Cumandá* (1878), a novel filled with picturesque details of indigenous customs.

The second category, *indigenismo*, developed as a movement of vast ideological and aesthetic projections early in the twentieth century; its influence was felt in Peru, Bolivia, and Ecuador, and as far as Mexico and Guatemala. Essentially, *indigenismo* seeks to reassert the cultural values of the indigenous peoples of the Americas, vindicate their social and economic interests, and reveal their authentic being and reality. *Indigenismo* is a movement that encompasses different fields of intellectual activity: social, political, economic, philosophical, and artistic, while *indigenista* literature is the literary expression of such movement. In his *Siete ensayos de interpretación de la realidad peruana* (*Seven Interpretive Essays on Peruvian Reality*, 1928), José Carlos Mariátegui (1894–1930), the first Latin American Marxist thinker, coined the term *indigenismo* as a literary category, and yet he argued that *indigenista* literature cannot portray a true picture of the Indian. Mariátegui claims that a true indigenous literature (*indígena*, as contrasted to *indigenista*) would come, when Indians themselves would produce it.[1] Written for and by an emerging middle class, *indigenista* literature, produced in an urban environment, deals with themes about the Indian as a referential element but does not allow the Indian to express himself; on the contrary, it speaks for the Indian. Moreover, Mariátegui points out, readers of such literature do not include Indians.

According to Mariátegui, any attempt to address the so called "problem of the Indian" in social, ethnic, religious, ethical, educational, political, or juridical terms would be destined to fail. For Mariátegui, the problem was strictly economic, and its solution could only be found in socialism. Mariátegui's ideas on *indigenismo* have, over a period of time, been expanded and nuanced. Contemporary critics such as Antonio Cornejo Polar, Ángel Rama, and Ariel Dorfman, and writers such as José María Arguedas, propose that economic vindication of the Indian would be inadequate and insufficient unless non-Western autochthonous Indian cultures are fully vindicated.

Cornejo Polar, Peru's leading literary theorist of *indigenismo*, has related the sociocultural division between a subaltern Indian culture and an hegemonic Western culture to what he calls the "heterogeneous" nature of *indigenista* literature.[2] Heterogeneous literatures are characterized by the plurality of the sociocultural sectors that participate in the process of literary production. Cornejo Polar concludes that this perspective illuminates the essential elements of *indigenismo*: its conflictive heterogeneity that results from a literary system that places in asymmetrical relationship two different and opposite sociocultural universes, one of which is indigenous, while the other is located in the most modern and Western sector of society.

The Western nature of the process of literary production of *indigenismo* is underscored by several factors: the choice of a written rather than an oral form which is more germane to indigenous cultures; the choice of Spanish rather than Quechua or Aymara as its linguistic means of expression; and, indeed, the fact that the novel, a European genre, is its main textual form. *Indigenista* literature evolves according to the vicissitudes of the Western literary tradition and its movements, such as Romanticism, modernism, realism, and naturalism.

The heterogeneity of *indigenista* literature is not limited to cultural encounters, ethnic conflicts, or regional duality. It is, in fact, the result of the effects of a disintegrated society: on the one side, there is an underdeveloped urban society, dependent upon a capitalist structure, in which the modern bourgeoisie and the middle and lower classes clash; on the other hand, an agrarian society consisting of pre-capitalist landowners and *campesinos* subject to an archaic colonial system that preserves feudal or semi-feudal practices. This dual economic infrastructure informs the heterogenous nature of *indigenismo*: the emerging middle class, the class that produces *indigenismo*, is part of the vast anti-oligarchic movement that emerged during the 1920s and 1930s and that denounced capitalism as incompatible with the traditional socioeconomic structures of the Andean region.

There is a critical consensus that *indigenista* literature exhibits a number of distinctive features: a tone of social protest aimed at undoing immediate evils; the imposition of ideology on plot and character; a black and white construction of good and evil; little stylistic preoccupation; little or no character development; superficial description of folklore and customs. Referring to the most representative *indigenista* novels, Ariel Dorfman maintains that their principal intent is to portray oppression. The world depicted in these social novels is static and often pessimistic; when the Indians finally opt to rebel, it is an instinctive impulse, a last effort to prevent being stripped of the last piece of land they have left.[3]

The transition from *indigenismo* to *neoindigenismo* begins in the decade of the 1950s with the publication of the Peruvian José María Arguedas's *Los ríos profundos* (*Deep Rivers*, 1958) and represents an organic transformation of *indigenismo*, but not its demise. Cornejo Polar has identified three essential elements of *neoindigenista* literature: (1) the use of magical realism to reveal the mythical dimension of the indigenous world;

(2) the intensification of lyricism as a category integrated into the narrative; and (3) the expansion and improvement of narrative techniques through a process of experimentation.[4] While *indigenismo* was informed by the basic contradiction between the indigenous communities and the landowners allied with the state, *neoindigenismo* deals with more intangible problems, existential conflicts, and the human condition.[5] *Neoindigenista* literature rediscovers and revalues the intrinsic features of the indigenous socioeconomic system and, at the same time, it is enriched by the contributions received from the mestizo culture, thus forging a new mestizo Andean discourse that informs new national identities.

The Peruvian novel

The development of the Peruvian novel begins effectively when Narciso Aréstegui (1826–69) publishes *El Padre Horán* ("Father Horán") in 1848. Though deficient in narrative technique, this novel initiates a trend of political and social criticism that would characterize the genre for years to come. Aréstegui targets the corrupt practices of the Church, abusive Andean landowners, and government officials, themes that will prepare the ground for Clorinda Matto de Turner's *Aves sin nido* (*Birds without a Nest*, 1889), and for subsequent *indigenista* fiction. For the first time in Peruvian fiction, Matto de Turner (1859–1909) attacks directly the institutionalized exploitation of Andean Indians by the religious, judicial, and governmental officials, and calls for a program of national public education as the primary solution to the predicaments of the indigenous peoples.

Matto de Turner's portrayal of the Andean people, however, is external and stereotypical and represents the Indian as an individual dispossessed of any vestiges of cultural or ethnic identity. All the same, *Aves sin nido* is the first significant effort to bring to light the appalling condition of the Peruvian Indian in a novel. It will be up to a later generation of writers who steered away from Romantic sentimentalism and Modernist exoticism to place the plight of the Indian in its proper economic and cultural context. Born in the political and ideological turmoil of the second decade of the twentieth century, *indigenista* narrative, exemplified in the works of Enrique López Albújar (1872–1966), Ciro Alegría (1909–67), and José María Arguedas (1911–69), would have a lasting effect in future Peruvian fiction.

The political and intellectual upheaval of the twenties, marked by the Russian and Mexican Revolutions, provided fertile ground for the emergence of left-wing political movements and José Carlos Mariátegui, founder of the Socialist Party of Peru, offered his vision for the emancipation of Indian communities from their endemic oppression by feudalism. In 1928, two dissimilar works appeared that marked the coming of age of Peru's modern novel: *Matalaché* by López Albújar and *La casa de cartón* ("The cardboard house") by Martín Adán. Set in the latter part of the colonial period, *Matalaché* is a historical novel denouncing the institution of slavery. By analyzing the tensions in a colonial society in its struggle for independence, the novel condemns the failure of independence in social and human terms. Influenced by Proust and Joyce, Adán's *La casa de cartón* is clearly avant-guarde, with no discernible plot, and consists of a series of vignettes evoking the author's adolescence. The novel is a forerunner of the process of experimentation of the new narrative fiction in the fifties and sixties. In the meantime, however, Peruvian fiction would maintain its traditional realist mold. Social protest would be the mainstay of contemporary fiction, where the harsh conditions of the poor, rural and urban, would become the dominant themes of a number of authors who found an audience in a small, though literate middle class.

The political factionalism of the first two decades of the twentieth century in Latin America, and particularly in Peru, caused an intense campaign on behalf of indigenous populations. *Indigenismo* succeeded in producing important novels about the economic exploitation of the Indian, denouncing the dominant society that kept them in bondage, including César Falcón's *El pueblo sin Dios* ("A town without God," 1923), and César Vallejo's *El tungsteno* (*Tungsten*, 1931). Considerably more radical than *Aves sin nido*, from a political standpoint, these novels still characterize the Indian superficially. While uncompromising in their condemnation of institutionalized economic injustice, Falcón and Vallejo relegate Indians to a secondary position placing them in the wider spectrum of generalized class struggle, rather than exploring their racial and cultural situation. The resulting portrayal of Indians thus tends to be merely external and stereotypical; where Falcón's Indians are powerless victims of an abusive system, Vallejo's are romanticized images of primitive communalism.

The publication in 1941 of *Yawar fiesta* (*Yahuar Fiesta*) by José María Arguedas and *El mundo es ancho y ajeno* (*Broad and Alien is the World*) by Ciro Alegría marks a milestone in Peruvian *indigenista* literature. Though different in their literary discourse, in their vision of the Andean world, and the place of the Indian in Peruvian society, the novels share a common place that foreshadows a thematic coincidence with future *indigenista* fiction: the awareness of the urban milieu as a pervasive, negative influence. Furthermore, these fictional works illustrate a new cultural type: the individual with Andean roots who, transformed by his experience in the city, returns to his place of origin as an agent of an alternative modernity. Both novels are protests against the destruction of Indian societies by a feudal system, but they are also a vindication of Indian culture as a way of life that survived for centuries after the Spanish Conquest. Central to this way of life is a socioeconomic order based on the communal ownership of land and property. The community, then, rather than the individual, is the entity that holds society together, and its survival becomes the main purpose of its members. Organized according to ancestral practices, communal life revolves around the preservation of its cultural manifestations, such as language, religion, customs, and the relationship with the natural world, as well as its political organization based on a hierarchy privileging the elders. This is the Andean world that both Alegría and Arguedas use as a referent for the dramas that will unfold in the fiction of their respective novels, albeit colored by their personal ideologies and life experiences. Alegría's novel succeeds in arousing the reader's conscience to the plight of the Indian but tends to paint a pessimistic image of the indigenous peoples' ability to rebel against oppression, leaving the impression that there is no solution to their predicaments. A work comparable in scope to its European models of the past century, *El mundo es ancho y ajeno*, the first novel to represent the clash of cultures in Peru, is a classic of Latin American literature.

Following in the steps of Alegría, Arguedas, a trained anthropologist, continued to work towards perfecting the true representation of the Indian, and creating a special literary language that would reflect the oral qualities of Quechua. With the publication of *Los ríos profundos* (*Deep Rivers*, 1958), Arguedas initiates a new stage of development in *indigenista* fiction, now known as *neoindigenismo*. His *Todas las sangres* ("All bloods," 1964) is a fierce denunciation of the abuse of the Indian by mestizo landowners and the domination of coastal society over Andean culture. In his posthumous novel, *El zorro de arriba y el zorro de abajo* (*The Fox From up above and the Fox From down below*, 1971), Arguedas examines the socioeconomic and cultural dislocation of Andean peasants who migrated to the coastal town of Chimbote to work as fishermen and in foreign-owned industrial plants. *Los ríos profundos* is Arguedas's most important novel, in that it is arguably the most genuine representation of Andean culture in *indigenista* fiction; the novel is rich not only in the portrayal of Quechua folklore, music, and language, but in the careful treatment of the Indian magical-religious vision of the world. By incorporating Quechua oral syntax into a carefully crafted, written Spanish, Arguedas's linguistic innovations are a critical element in the representation of a more authentic and convincing image of the Indian. Narrated in the first person by a well-educated mature man, the novel is a recollection of the predicaments of the fourteen-year-old Ernesto as he struggles to cope with life in a religious boarding school in the Andean town of Abancay, where his father has left him. Generally viewed as autobiographical, the novel consists of a series of episodes in which Ernesto, who is white, and who has been brought up in an Indian rural community, suddenly finds himself in the alien and hostile environment of the school. There, he meets with rampant violence and oppression, an endemic condition resulting from ethnic, cultural, and racial differences, which in turn give way to sexual debasement and repression, psychological and physical abuse, all promoted and condoned by the school's administration. Overwhelmed by this suffocating and dehumanizing environment, Ernesto seeks refuge in the taverns where he can mingle with Indians and mestizos and where he can listen to *huaynos*, Andean songs that bring him spiritual solace and mitigate his nostalgia for a paradise lost. In his quest for a closer communion with nature, Ernesto appeals to the supernatural powers of the *zumbayllu*, a spinning top that can conjure up magical experiences and visions of the idyllic world for which he yearns. The violence that permeates the novel is but a reflection of the feudal nature of the society it depicts. This state of oppression, exacerbated by a powerful land-owning class supported by civil, military, and ecclesiastical authorities, gives way to a subversive reaction of unforeseen magnitude and consequences against the established order. At first a passive witness to unfolding events, Ernesto is caught up in the euphoria of the insurgents and participates enthusiastically in the ensuing riots. A second uprising, this time by peasants who flee to Abancay from an epidemic of the plague, succeeds when authorities accede to their demands. The novel highlights the conflict not only between two different social orders, but between two diverging views of the world. Ernesto's identification with the downtrodden is more than an expression of his social conscience, it represents his total embrace of Quechua cultural values with full confidence in its virtues and powers. The victory of the peasants reaffirms and vindicates his faith, and helps him resolve his conflictive feeling of identity. Taken as a whole, the novel offers a comprehensive view of Arguedas's vision of the Indian and its role in Peruvian society. His literary and ideological projects go hand in hand in portraying Andean culture as a self-sufficient alternate to Western culture. Furthermore, Arguedas uses the Spanish language and the novel itself, a genre identified with European cultural values, to subvert from within the hegemony of the dominant social classes. As such, *Los ríos profundos* remains the greatest *indigenista* novel of the Andean region.

The decade of the fifties witnessed the emergence of a predominantly urban fiction informed by the masses of Andean migrants to the urban centers of Peru. It documented socioeconomic changes taking place in society as a whole, giving a voice to the disenfranchised classes of Indians, mestizos, blacks, and to an urban proletariat. The Indian, thus, becomes part of an underclass, no longer shackled to feudal bondage, but the victim of new social maladies such as unemployment, political corruption, and racial discrimination. The implications of this demographic phenomenon stimulated the emergence of new cultural expressions, reflecting the marginality of a large segment of the country's population, an alienation that manifested itself in every aspect of creative activity. Writers such as Julio Ramón Ribeyro (1929–95) (*Los geniecillos dominicales* ["The Sunday rascals"], 1965), Enrique Congrains Martín (b. 1932) (*No una, sino muchas muertes* ["Not one, but many deaths"], 1957), and Oswaldo Reynoso (b. 1932) (*En octubre no hay milagros* ["There are no miracles in October"], 1965) produced a body of novels having as their central theme the failure of Lima as the center of social and economic upward mobility. Racial discrimination, unjust economic conditions, political violence, cultural disintegration, and personal alienation are the topics that permeate the fiction of this decade.

Another group, represented by Julián Huanay (1907–69), Eleodoro Vargas Vicuña (1924–96), and Carlos E. Zavaleta (b. 1928) continued to develop themes related to Andean social and cultural conflicts. Armed with innovative narrative techniques, these writers went beyond Arguedas's attempts to vindicate Indian culture. They dealt with problems arising from the economic disparity between the city and the countryside, and from the threat of domestic and international economic forces that would eventually displace the Indian from its rural environment. Novels such as Huanay's *El retoño* ("The young branch," 1950) and Zavaleta's *Los Ingar* ("The Ingars," 1955) are examples of a period that saw the modernization of Peruvian fiction without abandoning the traditional themes of social protest and the denunciation of corrupt and abusive political practices. Such innovations – particularly in the works of Vargas Vicuña – are evident in the narrative approach to the portrayal of rural life, in contrast with the traditional picturesque accounts of local customs, types, and folklore. There is in this fiction a concerted avoidance of most physical and temporal referents in favor of the projection of sequential images filtered through the conscience of the narrator.

The process of literary renovation initiated in the fifties culminated in the publication of *La ciudad y los perros* (*The Time of the Hero*, 1963) by Mario Vargas Llosa (b. 1936), a novel that received immediate international recognition and which paved the way for the author's meteoric career. One of the pillars of the "Boom" of Latin American fiction, Vargas Llosa now ranks as one of the leading novelists in the world. His vision is not of order or stability but of haunting complexity, manifested in a body of work that is the product of his lifelong rebellion against convention, and of his systematic exposure of Peru's corrupt moral social values bred in a history of militarism, violence, machismo, racial prejudice, ignorance, religious and political fanaticism, and disregard for the most basic human rights. Vargas Llosa's narrative has, except for a few instances, not dealt with Andean themes, but, in 1993, he published *Lituma en los Andes* (*Death in the Andes*), a controversial novel that received harsh criticism for his treatment of Andean culture. The novel is about the investigation of the disappearance of three men in a remote Andean location, conducted by police sergeant Lituma. During the investigation, Lituma, who is not of Andean origin, must sort out a number of possibilities, including murder by members of the Shining Path terrorist forces, to ritual human sacrifices and cannibalism perpetrated by local inhabitants in order to placate the mountain gods for the construction of a highway through their community. The suggestion that Andean people might resort to such barbarous practices upset many Peruvian intellectuals, who were offended by the terrible implications of social and cultural regression manifested in wanton, unjustified violence.

The seventies were marked by a search for new themes, new narrative spaces, and new fictional dimensions. The literary interest in the city as the center of significant social experience tends to diminish, and a renewed approach to Andean rural life gains strength in a movement that seeks to comprehend the totality of society. However, the return to rural themes no longer conforms to traditional *indigenista* molds: it exhibits new technical resources, more creative and rigorous uses of the language, and, more significantly, it displays conflictive interpretive views among authors facing the social and cultural context of the times. A vigorous *indigenista* canon began to emerge in the works of Manuel Scorza (1928–83), Marcos Yauri Montero (b. 1930), Edgardo Rivera Martínez (b. 1934) and, later, by a younger group that includes Hildebrando Pérez Huaranca (b. 1946), Oscar Colchado Lucio (b. 1947), Félix Huamán Cabrera, and Víctor Zavala Cataño. Also to be noted are Samuel Cárdich, Andrés Cloud, and Carlos Malpartida, all three from the Andean region of Huánuco. Scorza's cycle of five novels – the most notable being *Redoble por Rancas* (*Drums for Rancas*, 1977) – is *neoindigenista* because of their themes, ideology, and literary language. Social realist in character, but enriched with magical realism and Andean folklore and mythology, these novels record the historic events surrounding the struggles of Indian communities in the central Andes to defend their ancestral lands.

Peruvian narrative of the last three decades has developed around different trends from those that shaped the fiction of the sixties and seventies. Perhaps the most representative writer of this period is Alfredo Bryce Echenique (b. 1939). Though contemporary with Vargas Llosa, Bryce was not considered part of the "Boom," as he did not indulge in the experimentation with form that marked that period. Moreover, his works were at first dismissed because of their light autobiographical tone, intimate subjective themes, and an apparently apolitical stance, at a time when many Latin American writers wholeheartedly embraced the Cuban Revolution. Bryce's narrative distinguishing mark is his autobiographical oral tone, a trait that creates an intimate perspective, which, coupled with a rich sense of humor, give his work a warm sense of familiarity shared by the reader. Born into an aristocratic family in Lima, he gained international fame with *Un mundo para Julius* (*A World for Julius*, 1969), a novel that dissects Peru's decadent oligarchy. Set in the Lima of the fifties, the novel depicts Peruvian society through the experiences of Julius, a young boy belonging to an aristocratic family, and whose mother, a widow, has just remarried to a wealthy entrepreneur representing the new emerging class that will dominate the country. The move from the old colonial home, where Julius played in a carriage belonging to a Spanish viceroy, to his stepfather's modern house is symbolic of the changes affecting Peruvian socioeconomic structures. The novel is an indictment of a social class that is morally blind to the plight of the masses of disenfranchised and dispossessed that make up the majority of Peruvians. Isolated in their own sheltered world, the new aristocracy is shielded from the outside world by their servants, who for the most part are of Andean origin. Julius, ignored by his parents and siblings, suffers this same isolation but finds solace in the midst of the household servants who become his real family. Though he has no real consciousness of the nuances of the differences among social classes, Julius's precarious world is shattered when faced with the ugly reality that begins to unfold around him. The death of his sister and the discovery that his nanny has become a prostitute after being raped by his older brother are traumatic experiences that create perturbing moral questions as he enters adolescence. Written in the *Bildungsroman* tradition, *A World for Julius* is a postmodern urban novel that grips the conscience of the reader as it bares the secular injustices inherent to a society torn apart by racial and ethnic prejudices, and endemic injustice resulting from the abuse of power, social position, and wealth.

With the end of the military dictatorship in 1980, Peru embarked on a difficult road towards democratization, a process that was marred by violence, economic debacle, and the collapse of its social and political institutions. In spite of such fertile ground for moral indignation, Peruvian fiction did not attempt to offer ideological solutions, or to reexamine the historical roots of the country's problems. Instead, it raised more questions than it provided answers to the social ills that afflicted the country. Faced with one of the worst political and economic crises in the country's history, a period which witnessed the ravages of terrorism and unemployment, narrative fiction of the 1980s and of the early 1990s unfolded in a number of directions.

Contrary to the dictates in some literary circles that *indigenista* fiction was on the wane, it resurfaced with renewed vigor and quality. *Neoindigenista* narrative evolved into a highly lyrical form portraying a positive, even joyous, image of the complex process of *mestizaje*, an image different from Arguedas's somber view. Without doubt, the most successful writer of this group is Edgardo Rivera Martínez, whose novel, *País de Jauja* ("Country of Jauja," 1993), ranks among the most important Peruvian novels. The case of Rivera Martínez is almost unique in Peruvian letters. Long known as an accomplished stylist because of his outstanding collections of short stories and *nouvelas*, he remained in relative obscurity. *País de Jauja*, however, brought him immediate recognition and critical acclaim.

País de Jauja is set in the decade of the forties and spans several weeks of summer vacation for Claudio, an adolescent belonging to a well-educated, but economically struggling, middle-class family. During this happy but short time, Claudio's life will be affected by a series of events that will serve as a rite of passage to a higher level of intellectual and affective maturity, including the discovery of an incipient sexuality. Claudio's sentimental education will be enhanced by his mother who encourages his musical vocation and talent, and by his older brother who promotes his literary interests. Under his mother's guidance, he records the lyrics of Andean music, which he later transcribes to be played at the piano. Following his literary interests, Claudio is fascinated by the epic events and characters of Homer's *Iliad* but, with the same enthusiasm, he is absorbed by Andean oral legends transmitted to him by an old housemaid. Thus, the boy who started the summer playing with his classmates reaches a degree of maturity with a full realization of his artistic vocation, but what is more important, of his multicultural heritage. Significant as Claudio's personal development is, it is the city of Jauja itself that is the real center of the novel, in that it serves as the symbiotic element promoting the intermingling of cultures in a true and positive process of *mestizaje*. Jauja, a utopian enclave in the Andes, is the mediating space between the reality of a modernity that irradiates from the capital city of Lima, and the remote highlands. There, the Apus – tutelary gods of the mountains – and the mythical Amarus – winged serpents inhabiting the sacred mountain lakes – still exert their powerful influence on the lives of its inhabitants. This paradisiacal place, where people from all over the world flock attracted by the curative power of its climate, is the ultimate symbol of the felicitous union of dissimilar cultural values that had secularly been considered incompatible. This is perhaps the most meritorious aspect, among many others, of this extraordinary novel. Rivera's second novel, *Libro del amor y las profecías* ("The book of love and prophesies," 1999), also located in the mythical Andean city of Jauja, where he was born and raised, confirmed Rivera Martínez's position as one of Peru's leading novelists. Following in the footsteps of Rivera Martínez, Laura Riesco's *Ximena de dos caminos* ("Ximena at the crossroads," 1994) is a novel that provides a new feminine view of Peru's complex society, by examining the conflictive relationship of Andean and coastal cultures. *La violencia del tiempo* ("The violence of time," 1992) by Miguel Gutiérrez is still another critical examination of *mestizaje* and its effect on Peruvian history and social development.

The Ecuadorian novel

The development of the novel in Ecuador follows essentially the same pattern as in other Andean countries. Its nineteenth-century classic is arguably *Cumandá o un drama entre salvajes* (*Cumanda*, 1879) by Juan León Mera (1832–94). Steeped in Romanticism, this *indianista* novel is a reflection of the author's sympathies for the Indian, but also of his identification with the theocratic ideology of the dictator Gabriel García Moreno. The Liberal Revolution of 1895 and the adoption of the Constitution of 1906 were milestones in Ecuadorian history; their anticlerical impulse affected every sector of society while stimulating artistic and literary creativity. A combative and progressive literature emerged that found its best expression in the novel. *A la costa* ("To the coast," 1904), by Luis A. Martínez (1869–1909), is the precursor of the social realism that would characterize narrative fiction during the decade of the thirties. A blending of historical novel and *Bildungsroman*, this novel became the model for future narrative, such as *Plata y bronce* ("Silver and Bronze," 1927) by Fernando Chávez (b. 1902), considered the first Ecuadorian *indigenista* novel.

As a result of the popular revolts in Guayaquil in 1922, the founding of the Socialist Party, and the military coup of 1925, the so-called "Guayaquil Group" was formed by Demetrio Aguilera Malta (1909–81), Joaquín Gallegos Lara (1909–47), and Enrique Gil Gilbert (1912–73) who, together, wrote *Los que se van* ("Those who go away," 1930), a collection of short stories that redefined Ecuadorian fiction. The most important novel of this period is without doubt *Huasipungo* (*The Villagers*, 1934) by Jorge Icaza (1906–78), one of the paradigmatic *indigenista* works of all times in Latin American letters. The novel portrays in the crudest terms the systematic exploitation of the Indian, relegating the victims to an almost subhuman condition. Icaza's career would extend until 1972, when he published *Atrapados* ("Trapped"), an autobiographical novel summarizing his public life. He had by then published *El chulla Romero y Flores* ("The worthless Romero y Flores," 1958), a novel dealing with the conflict of social and ethnic identity of mestizos, and other novels and short stories that confirmed him as Ecuador's leading *indigenista* writer.

The forties and fifties entailed a softening in the social struggle that characterized the previous decade; the middle class and the intellectuals of the time were subdued by governments representing the oligarchy on one hand, and populist charismatic leaders on the other, such as José María Velasco Ibarra, who would be elected president five times. The social problems of the times are best represented by two novels: Adalberto Ortiz's *Juyungo* (1943) and *El éxodo de Yangana* ("Yangana's exodus," 1949) by Angel Rojas. The first examines the problems of the segment of Ecuadorian population of African descent, while the second deals with the secular problem of Andean peoples exploited by the powerful oligarchy that controls the country.

The Ecuadorian novel achieves an unprecedented position in the sixties in the works of Pedro Jorge Vera (b. 1915), Miguel Donoso Pareja (b. 1931), and Alfredo Pareja Diezcanseco (b. 1908). Vera's *La semilla estéril* ("The sterile seed," 1962) is a study in racism and the usurpation of Andean communal property by foreign companies; Donoso Pareja's *Krelko* (1962) also deals with anti-imperialist sentiments. Pareja Diezcanseco, an essayist, novelist, and historian, gained a reputation for maintaining a consistent ethical position in his examination of Ecuadorian society in works such as *Los nuevos años* ("The new years," 1956–64) and *La manticora* ("The manticore," 1974), his most notable novel. The emergence, also in the sixties, of a group of talented novelists, such as Ivan Egüez (b. 1944), Jorge Dávila Vásquez (b. 1947), Eliécer Cárdenas (b. 1950), points towards a canonical revision that would lead to the concept of The New Novel of Ecuador, an idea that would mature during the seventies in works such as Jaime Galarza Zavala's *El festín del petróleo* ("The oil banquet," 1972) and, in 1976, Jorge E. Adoum's (b. 1923) masterpiece *Entre Marx y una mujer desnuda* (*Between Marx and a Naked Woman*), Egüez's *La Linares* ("The Linares woman"), and Vera's *El pueblo soy yo* ("I am the people"). Two notable novels mark the end of the seventies: Donoso Pareja's study in eroticism, *Día tras día* ("Day after day," 1976), and Cárdenas's *Polvo y ceniza* ("Dust and ashes," 1979), which deals with the deeds of the mythical bandit Naún Briones. A mixture of historical novel, autobiography, and social criticism, Adoum's novel is by far the most significant because of his use of the latest narrative techniques and deconstructionist literary theories in order to debunk literary discourse itself. The suggestive title of the novel reflects the paradox facing the main protagonist, Galo Gálvez, a writer who holds Marxist ideas but overtly behaves like the bourgeoisie. Galo's dilemma – that of the bourgeois intellectual with revolutionary ideals – lies in his effort to transform the social order of a corrupt capitalist society by attacking the passivity and lack of class conscience of the proletariat. The novel departs radically from the type of criticism commonly found in social realism and engages in a critical revision of history as it adopts modern narrative techniques such as internal monologues, stream of consciousness, visual aids, press clippings, graphics, dreams, fantastic experiences, and the effective use of humor and irony. Adoum's novel is similar to other Latin American novels of the period in their anti-imperialist discourse, directed mainly against the United States, and in their appeal to Latin Americans to search for an authentic national identity that would eventually lead to durable and meaningful social transformations.

Special consideration must also be given to Gustavo Alfredo Jacomé's *Por qué se fueron las garzas* ("Why did the herons leave?" 1979). Together with Mera's *Cumandá* and Icaza's *Huasipungo*, this novel highlights the condition of the Andean Indian but differs from the former in its representation of Indian reality, just as José María Arguedas in Peru would present an internal vision of the Indian in *Los ríos profundos*. Clearly within the *neoindigenista* movement, Jacomé's novel addresses the issue of Indian culture threatened by external socioeconomic forces, at the same time that the Indian himself needs to become integrated into occidental culture for economic survival. The result is a search for personal identity within the general context of ethnic conflict which has at its center the process of *mestizaje*.

The decade of the eighties sees the emergence of women writers, best represented byAlicia Yánez Cossío, whose novels, *Bruna, soroche y los tíos* ("Bruna, Soroche and the uncles," 1975), *Yo vendo unos ojos negros* ("I am selling black eyes," 1979), *Más allá de las islas* ("Beyond the islands," 1980), and *La cofradía del mullo de La Virgen Pipona* ("The brotherhood of the potbellied virgin's bead," 1985) give a poignant personal view of the position of women in Ecuadorian society. Urban life in Ecuador also becomes a center of literary attention, in novels such as Abdón Ubidia's *Ciudad de invierno* ("Winter city," 1984) and Alfonso Barrera Valverde's *Dos muertes en una vida* ("Two deaths in one life," 1980). The corrupt world of the landed Andean higher social classes is the object of satire and derision in Carlos de la Torre Reyes's novel, . . . *Y los dioses se volvieron hombres* (". . . And the gods became men," 1981). In *El devastado jardín del paraíso* ("The devastated garden of paradise," 1990), Alejandro Moreano ventures into the deadly world of armed insurgency by dwelling on the demise of the revolutionary myth during the sixties. Following Adoum's formalistic model, Javier Ponce's (b. 1948) *El insomnio de Nazario Mieles* ("Nazario Mieles's insomnia," 1990) is a psychological tour de force through the mind of the protagonists, under the setting of the rubber plantations in the jungle.

The novel of the nineties in Ecuador corresponds to the literary period generally known as the "Post-Boom," a period in which experimentation with language and narrative techniques ceases to be the narrative focal point to give way to the portrayal of personal feelings and interrelationships, in a world dominated by popular culture and mass media. Though there is a considerable number of novels written during the decade, perhaps the best and most representative are: *El Cristo feo* ("The ugly Christ," 1995) and *Aprendiendo a morir* (1998, "Learning to die") by Alicia Yánez Cossío, *El viajero de Praga* ("The traveler from Prague," 1996) by Javier Vásconez, *Una silla para Dios* ("A chair for God," 1996) by Eliécer Cárdenas, *Destino Estambul* ("Destination Istambul," 1998) by Jaime Marchán, and *En busca del Paraíso* ("In search of paradise," 1999) by Iván Cárdenas Mizo. Notwithstanding that the theme of the condition of the Andean Indian had lost the influence it once had, Marcelo Robayo brings it again to the fore-front in *Rojo es el poncho del chirote* ("Red is the Chirote's poncho," 1991). Influenced by the Peruvian Ciro Alegría and the Mexican Juan Rulfo, and availing itself of magical realism and innovative narrative techniques, the novel documents the destruction of the Andean town of Chuquimarca by *gamonales* who seek to usurp community lands.

The Bolivian novel

The Bolivian novel is marked by social, cultural, and historical contexts that define in large measure its thematic and formal development, as well as its ideological tendencies. Bolivia's geographic isolation during colonial times, exacerbated by the loss of territories and access to the Pacific Ocean in 1879, has traditionally been given as a major cause for the late development of its novel. Other factors affecting both the quantity as well as the quality of Bolivian fiction are the political factionalism that defined the country since the creation of the Republic, its parochialism, and the use of the novel almost exclusively as the means to denounce social inequities.

The advent of Romanticism in Latin America coincides with Bolivia's independence from Spain in 1825, a movement best represented by Vicente Ballivián's (1816–91) sentimental novel, *Recreos Juveniles* ("Youthful pas-times," 1834). However, it was not until late in the nineteenth and the begin-ning of the twentieth century – the high point of Spanish American mod-ernism – that prose fiction in Bolivia reached some degree of maturity in the works of Ricardo Jaimes Freyre, Nataniel Aguirre, and Alcides Arguedas. Though Jaimes Freyre is best known for his poetry and historical short nar-rative, Aguirre's novel, *Juan de la Rosa* (1885), is an example of the search for literary expressions different from canonic traditions. The novel's style foreshadows what will be a distinguishing feature of Latin America fiction of the twentieth century: the experimentation with narrative structure and the loss of stature of the author as an active subject of the discourse, and the ascendancy of the narrator as the focal point of the novel. However, technical and structural innovations are not the only important qualities of this novel. Aguirre's narrator, though not the protagonist of the novel, symbolically fixes his attention on the last soldier of the Independence Wars, while assigning the true protagonist role in the struggle to the people of Cochabamba.

During this time, Bolivia's economy followed the pattern imposed during colonial times, with mining and agriculture as the main sources of wealth in a semi-feudal system. Independence from Spain did not alter the power of *latifundismo*, the system of landownership by a minuscule minority of landowners, nor the continued subjugation of large masses of Andean peasants. The plight of the Andean Indian in his struggle against the white oppressor is best represented by Alcides Arguedas (1879–1946), who, by blending historiographic and sociological points of view, produced a number of novels that had a powerful impact at the time. Soon after the publication of his first novel, *Psagua* (1903), an attempt at recreating an obscure historical event, Arguedas wrote *Wara Wara* (1904), a novel which would later be revised and expanded to become *Raza de bronce* ("Race of bronze," 1919), his best work, and paradigmatic of Spanish American *indigenista* narrative. *Raza de bronce* is a devastating denunciation of the condition of the Indian, exploited by the *gamonales*, feudal lords who had total control over the the land and lives of its inhabitants. Immersed in realism, the novel also describes in crude detail the extremely harsh natural environment of the Andean *altiplano* in which Indian peasants barely subsist. A severe critic and keen observer of Bolivian society, Arguedas also ventured into the portrayal of urban life in his *Vida criolla* ("Creole life," 1905), a novel that develops some of the themes of his *Pueblo enfermo* ("Sick nation," 1909), a controversial sociological treatise in which he reflects on the Bolivian national character and its tradition of subservience, and blames the condition of the country on the alleged genetic incapacity of Indians to cope with modern social and economic forces. Arguedas's contradictory position – on the one hand denouncing the exploitation of Indians and, on the other, attributing the backwardness of Bolivia to the Indian – drew harsh critical reaction from many sectors that coincided in condemning the extreme stance he had taken in his bitter appraisal of Bolivian society. Though his dictates were often exaggerated and incomplete representations of facts, Arguedas followed the precedent of members of the Spanish "Generation of 98," who also had written scathing essays on the maladies affecting Spain at the end of the century. Be that as it may, Arguedas's writings had the effect of stimulating critical reflection in his country by highlighting the complexity of Bolivia's social and racial elements.

Since colonial times, mining has been one of the most, if not the most, important economic activities of Bolivia. The "novel of the mines" examines the condition of Indian peasants who migrate to become miners, a historical condition with deep socioeconomic implications that continues to affect Bolivian society. It is not surprising, then, that it would be the focus of literary attention in novels that tend to reflect the ideological position of their authors, from the positivist point of view of Jaime Mendoza, the first "mining novelist," in *En las tierras de Potosí* ("In and around Potosí," 1911) to Roberto Leitón's Marxist stance in *Los eternos vagabundos* ("The eternal vagabonds," 1939). Though different in their approaches to a common theme, both authors coincide in their denunciation of the exploitation of the Indian miner, in a close relationship between fiction and the sociopolitical reality that it intends to portray. An early example of this recurring theme is *Metal del diablo* ("The devil's metal," 1946) by Augusto Céspedes, who also examines the failures of Bolivian political history in novels such as *El dictador suicida* ("The dictator commits suicide," 1956) and *El presidente colgado* ("The president who was hanged," 1966). The most important novel within this theme is *El precio del estaño* ("The price of tin," 1960/1980) by Néstor Taboada Terán, a novel in which he recounts the massacre of striking miners at the Catavi mine in 1967 at the hands of the army. A more recent development in the treatment of the subject of the mines is René Poppe's *La Khola* (1978), a *nouvelle* where the narrative focus shifts from the exterior of the mine to the underground, a more "real" world for the miner.

The Chaco War (1932–35) between Bolivia and Paraguay became the central theme of a number of novels that reflected the horror of the conflict and the devastating effect it had on the nation as a whole, but especially on the combatants, who were primarily Quechua and Aymara Indians. Some of the most important titles are: *La tragedia del altiplano* ("The tragedy of the highlands," 1934) by Tristán Marof, *Prisionero de guerra* ("Prisoner of war," 1936) by Augusto Guzmán, *Sangre de mestizos* ("Mestizo blood," 1936) by Augusto Céspedes, *La punta de los 4 degollados* ("The group of the four beheaded," 1946) by Roberto Leitón.

Just as important a milestone as the Chaco War was the revolution of 1952, a momentous event that sought to change the nature of Bolivian socioeconomic structures through the nationalization of the mines and the agrarian reform that confiscated land from the *gamonales* to be distributed among the peasants. However, the revolution did not become a central subject of narrative fiction. The few works that were published dealing with the revolution did not produce discernible positive social changes, as they simply reiterated the critical position of well-established Bolivian writers towards endemic and institutionalized injustice, particularly affecting the Andean Indians, but also city dwellers, and the inhabitants of the tropical lowlands. The most influential of this group of writers are Jesús Lara and Néstor Taboada Terán, who became implacable critics of the revolution in its failure to bring justice to the Indian. Lara's *Surumi* (1943) and *Yanakuna* (1952), and Taboada Terán's *Indios en rebelión* ("Indians rebelling," 1968) are indictments of the continued abuse perpetrated on the Indian and the inability and lack of interest of the government in solving this secular problem. The most important novels situated in the period after the agrarian reform are Lara's *Yawarninchij* (1959), *Sinchicay* (1962), and *Llalliypacha* (1965). The relative lack of significant Bolivian narrative fiction after the 1952 revolution can be attributed to the crisis affecting the country resulting from the failure in attaining a modicum of social justice. A novel that reflects this sentiment is *El valle del cuarto menguante* ("The valley of the last quarter moon," 1975).

From this state of Bolivian fiction emerge two writers who set the standard for future generations by establishing a new direction in thematic and narrative approaches: Oscar Cerruto (1912–81) and Marcelo Quiroga Santa Cruz (1931–80). In 1957, they published *Cerco de penumbras* ("Fence of shadows"), a collection of short stories, and *Los deshabitados* ("The vacant"), a novel, respectively. Both works, but especially the latter, examine the theme of personal and social failure, and the resulting alienation derived from meaningless lives. *Los deshabitados* paved the way for a new generation of novelists who would concentrate on the absurdity of life, and on rebellion, as conditions dominating Bolivian society. Among these, Renato Prada Oropeza's *Los fundadores del alba* ("The founders of dawn," 1969) was the most significant in that it introduced the theme of the transition from dejection and frustration to armed insurrection by organized guerrillas, as represented in *Larga hora: la vigilia* ("Long hour: the vigil," 1979). The trend started by Oropeza in examining the human and social motivations for the guerrillas reaches a high point in Julio de la Vega's novel, *Matías, el apostol suplente* ("Matthias, the substitute Apostle," 1971), in the form of a diary, in which he compares the fate of the guerrillas after the assassination of "Che" Guevara by government troops, and the development of the Christian Church after the death of Jesus.

An important current trend in Bolivian fiction is the growing emphasis on the city, especially La Paz, both as a physical referent and as narrative subject. As contrasted with contemporary Peruvian narrative that examines the city as a social melting pot resulting from Andean migrations, its Bolivian counterpart does not, in a significant way, deal with this phenomenon. Among the most notable examples of the novel of the city are Arturo

Von Toscano's *Sombra del exilio* ("Shadow of exile," 1971) and *Morder el silencio* ("Biting silence," 1980), which mostly focus on individual lives alienated by urban society's indifference.

In the analysis of the development of the novel in a region as vast and complex as the Andes, one single fact becomes evident: the enormous diversity of human and environmental experiences that inform the many peoples and cultures occupying these countries, experiences that have had a direct and lasting effect on their literatures. Consequently, the task of bringing together such dissimilar realities under the common denominator of the Andean novel becomes almost impossible to achieve. And yet it is still a relevant task, for one thing is certain: the novel has been and will continue to be the main and most effective means of literary expression representing Andean reality.

NOTES

1. José Carlos Mariátegui, *Siete ensayos de interpretación de la realidad peruana* (Lima: Bibioteca Amauta, 21st edn, 1972), p. 335.
2. Antonio Cornejo Polar, *Escribir en el aire: ensayo sobre la heterogeneidad sociocultural en las literaturas andinas* (Lima: Editorial Horizonte, 1994), pp. 11–24.
3. Ariel Dorfman, *Imaginación y violencia en América* (Santiago: Editorial Universitaria, 1970) p. 9.
4. Antonio Cornejo Polar, *La novela peruana: siete estudios* (Lima: Horizonte, 1977), p. 58.
5. Miguel Gutiérrez, *Los Andes en la novela peruana actual* (Lima: Editorial San Marcos, 1999), p. 67.

FURTHER READING

Cáceres Romero, Adolfo, *Nueva historia de la literatura boliviana*, La Paz, Bolivia: Editorial Los Amigos del Libro, 1987.
Carillo, Francisco, *Clorinda Matto de Turner y su indigenismo literario*, Lima: Ediciones de la Biblioteca Universitaria, 1967.
Chica, Jimmy Jorge, *La novela ecuatoriana contemporánea de 1970–1985 y su marginación*, New York: Peter Lang, 1995.
Cornejo Polar, Antonio, *Literatura y sociedad en el Perú: la novela indigenista*, Lima: Lasontay, 1980.
  La novela peruana: siete estudios, Lima: Horizonte, 1977.
  Los universos narrativos de José María Arguedas, Lima: Editorial Horizonte, 1972.
Guzmán, Augusto, *La novela en Bolivia 1847–1954*, La Paz: Juventud, 1955.
Higgins, James, *A History of Peruvian Literature*, Liverpool: Francis Cairns, 1987.
Kristal, Efraín, *The Andes Viewed from the City: Literary and Political Discourse on the Indian in Peru (1848–1930)*, New York: Peter Lang, 1987.
Rodríguez-Luis, Julio. *Hermenéutica y praxis del indigenismo: la novela indigenista de Clorinda Matto a José María Arguedas*, Mexico: Fondo de Cultura Económica, 1980.

Rojas, Angel F. *La novela ecuatoriana*, Mexico and Buenos Aires: Fondo de Cultura Económica, 1948.

Sacoto, Antonio, *La novela ecuatoriana, 1970–2000*, Quito: Ministerio de Educación y Cultura, Sistema Nacional de Bibliotecas, 2000.

Salmón, Josefa, *El espejo indígena: El discurso indigenista en Bolivia, 1900–1956*, La Paz: Plural Editores, 1997.

Vargas Llosa, Mario, *José María Arguedas y las ficciones del indigenismo*, Mexico: Fondo de Cultura Económica, 1996.

Wiethüchter, Blanca (ed.), *Hacia una historia crítica de la literatura en Bolivia*, Vols. I and II, La Paz: PIED, 2002.

Wishnia, Kenneth, J. A., *Twentieth Century Ecuadorian Narrative: New Readings in the Context of the Americas*, Lewisburg: Bucknell University Press, 1999.

8

ROY C. BOLAND OSEGUEDA

The Central American novel

The Central American novel can be traced back to José Milla (1822–82), one of Guatemala's most revered and popular writers to this day. His novels *La hija del Adelantado* ("Governor's daughter," 1866), *Los Nazarenos* ("The Nazarenes," 1867), and *El Visitador* ("The Inspector," 1867) are historical romances set in the colonial era. In novels whose plots involve political intrigue, the travails of love and some fantastic elements, Milla endeavors to portray authentic Guatemalan speech, manners, and popular types.[1] One of his notable achievements is the creation of a stock character named Juan Chapín (Juan the Guatemalan), the fictional hero of *Un viaje al otro mundo* (1874), a book of semi-fictional memoirs and quixotic adventures. In contrast to the engaging Juan Chapín, the figure of a vain, scatterbrained compatriot, the laughing stock of Paris, is the creation of Hermógenes Alvarado (1845–1929) in *Las aventuras del gran Morajúa y los apuros de un francés* (1896), considered the first novel written in El Salvador.

The Central American novel paralleled developments in the rest of Latin America, although it usually lagged behind in the latest styles and techniques. In the last thirty years of the nineteenth century historical and sentimental novels were the favorite modes. Nicaragua's first novel, *Amor y Constancia* ("Love and perseverance," 1878) by José Dolores Gámez, would today be labeled a pulp-romance, while Panama's first novel, *La verdad triunfante* ("The triumphant truth," 1879) by Gil Colunje (1831–99), is also a sentimental tale. In Costa Rica the novelistic tradition began a few years later with Manuel Argüello, who experimented with short historical novels in *Margarita, Elisa Delimar*, and *La trinchera* ("The trench," 1900). In Guatemala, Agustín Mencos Franco published *Don Juan Núñez García* (1898), a historical novel inspired by Walter Scott and Alexandre Dumas which recounts the rebellion by the Tzenal Indians in Chiapas at the beginning of the eighteenth century.

The early practitioners of the Central American novel were influenced by trends and styles by writers, mostly foreign, consecrated in the metropolitan centers of Latin America. A case in point is the best-known novel by the Guatemalan Fernando Pineda, *Luis, memorias de un amigo* ("The memoirs of a friend," 1878), a self-conscious local version of Jorge Isaacs's *María* (1867), the most influential Latin American novel of its time. Ramón A. Salazar (1852–1914) wrote *Conflictos* ("Conflicts," 1898), which bears the imprint of Balzac, Dickens, and Galdós in its portrayal of contemporary Guatemalan society. The influence of Galdos's *Doña Perfecta* (1876) is particularly evident in the conflict between liberals and conservatives, embodied in the doomed relationship between María Luisa, the devout, God-fearing heroine, and Hernando, a progressive, free-thinking engineer. The redoubtable, aristocratic matriarch, Doña Manuela de Villacreces, recalls the tryrannical Doña Perfecta. The powerful influence of the Catholic Church and the prudishness of the local oligarchies meant that full-blooded naturalism never gained a foothold in Central America. That being said, in Guatemala, Enrique Martínez Sobral (1875–1950) made a brave if ponderous attempt to apply Zola's literary principles to local reality. In a series of novels published between 1899 and 1902, *Los de Peralta* ("The ones from Peralta"), *Humo* ("Smoke"), *Su matrimonio* ("Their marriage"), *Alcohol* ("Alcohol"), and *Inútil combate* ("Useless combat"), Martínez Sobral examined the basest aspects of Guatemalan society, including adultery, domestic violence, incest, drunkenness, and prostitution. Another novel worthy of special mention is *Angelina* (1898), a fine historical romance by Honduran Carlos F. Gutiérrez (1861–99) that combines themes of love, death, violence, mystery, madness, and horror with touches of undisguised eroticism, unusual for its time.

The nascent novelistic tradition in Central America was curtailed by the flowering of the poetic school known as *modernismo*, identified with Rubén Darío (1867–1916).[2] While poetry thrived, the novel languished, as illustrated by the fact that between 1896 and 1925 only about twenty-five novels were published in El Salvador. Darío himself published one novel, *Emelina* (1887), and left at least three others unfinished, *Caín, El oro de Mallorca* ("The gold of Mallorca"), and *En la isla de oro* ("The island of gold"). Although Darío's novelistic prose resounds with flashes of *modernista* brilliance, it is of greater biographical than literary interest.

Guatemala produced the outstanding *modernista* novelist in Enrique Gómez Carrillo (1873–1927), an expatriate who lived in France from the age of seventeen until his death. Between 1894 and 1899 Gómez Carrillo wrote a trio of novels – *Del amor, del dolor y del vicio, Bohemia sentimental*, and *Maravillas* – which he linked under the collective title of *Tres novelas inmorales*. The poetic descriptions and exotic settings frame an overriding theme: love in its more decadent manifestations, from heterosexual lust to lesbian prostitution and incest. In spite of his apparent concentration on carnality, Gómez Carrillo ultimately favors art and spirit over sensuality. Indeed, in his most famous novel, *El evangelio del amor* (1922), set in licentious Byzantium of the fourteenth century, he suggests that true fulfillment may be found only in divine love.

Another Guatemalan of the period, Máximo Sotto-Hal (1871–1944), is best remembered for *El problema* ("The difficulty," 1899), the first anti-imperialistic novel. Like Rubén Darío, in his celebrated poem "A Roosevelt," Sotto-Hall kept faith with his *modernista* aesthetic while embracing an overt political stance. *El problema* is set in an imaginary Nicaragua in 1928 where English has become the national language, Protestantism has replaced Catholicism, "gringo" values hold sway, and the whole region is about to be annexed by the USA. Many other novelists would soon follow Sotto-Hal's lead in denouncing US territorial ambitions. Another Guatemalan *modernista*, Rafael Arévalo Martínez (1884–1971), published *Una vida* (1914), *Manuel Aldano* (1922), and *La Oficina de Paz de Orolandia* ("The office of the peace in Orolandia," 1925),³ a trilogy in which the author lambasts "Yanquilandia" with a mixture of controlled passion and anguish, while at the same time criticizing the Latin race for its lethargic and opportunistic response to the imperialistic ambitions of the United States. *La Oficina de Paz in Orolandia*, one of the funniest books ever written by a Central American, uses mockery as a weapon of social and political satire.

A small coterie of *modernistas* delved into the supernatural. One of the most daring incursions into this area was *El vampiro* ("The *vampire*," 1910), by Honduran Froylán Turcios (1872–1943). Inspired by Bram Stoker's *Dracula* (1897), *El vampiro* combines a Gothic atmosphere of foreboding and dread with grandiloquent disquisitions to tell a tragic story of love between two adolescent cousins, Rogerio and Luz. Set in the former colonial capital of La Antigua, a place resounding with ancestral Mayan echoes, the vampire figure is a Catholic priest who kills Rogerio's father and sets out to devour Luz, the incarnation of chaste love. Shrouded in shadows and signposted with supernatural elements, the novel strikes a chillingly realistic note when the vampire priest uses the confessional to sexually abuse Luz when she is still a child. The association of the priesthood with evil is found in another famously anticlerical novel, *Alba América* ("Alba, or the American daybreak," 1920), by the Guatemalan César Brañas (1900–76), in which a perverted priest forces himself upon the eponymous heroine (depicted as an ideal feminine model for the New World).

Disenchantment with Catholicism and disgust with the political situation in their countries led some writers to seek answers in alternative religions and philosophies. Perhaps the most celebrated case in Central America is that of Salvadorean Salvador Salazar Arrué (1899–1975), who wrote under the pseudonym of Salarrué. A confirmed theosophist, Salarrué uses this esoteric philosophy to give form and meaning to *El Cristo Negro* ("The black Christ," 1926). In the novel, Uraco, a dark-skinned friar in colonial Guatemala, embarks on a campaign of good by doing evil, using un-Christian means (fornication, violence, theft, murder, and sacrilege) to fulfill his messianic aims. Ultimately Uraco's crimes lead to his crucifixion by the Inquisition. In death he gains a measure of ironic triumph when his corpse is used as the model for the statue of the Black Christ of Esquipulas, the patron of Central America.

Costumbrismo, antiimperialismo, criollismo, and indigenismo

As the star of *modernismo* waxed and waned, the Central American novel explored a number of interrelated modes which, for heuristic purposes, could be labeled as *costumbrismo* (relating to the folkloric representation of customs and manners), *antiimperialismo* (attacking US hegemonic ambitions), *criollismo* (focusing on various aspects of national and/or regional reality), and *indigenismo* (defending Indian rights and culture). Whereas the plots and arguments of these novels can stir the heart of even the most cynical reader, their styles and techniques can be rudimentary. A Manichean vision – good versus evil, justice against injustice, man against nature, urban vices opposed to rural virtue – can also strike the modern reader as unsophisticated. In spite of such reservations, it is thanks to this kind of writing that the novel gradually came of age in Central America.

One of the earliest exponents of *costumbrismo* was Costa Rica's Joaquín García Monge (1881–1958). His first novel, *El moto* ("The orphan," 1900), written when he was only nineteen, is considered a classic in his homeland. A tale of thwarted love between a peasant lad and the local strongman's daughter, this novel's folksy realism features the typical language of the Costa Rican countryside, utilized to describe the landscape and customs of the *campesino* (peasant). Monge also published *Las hijas del campo* ("Daughters of the countryside," 1900), a denser novel which moves fluently from rural to urban settings and combines folklore with social criticism. Costa Rica produced another master of *costumbrismo* in Manuel González Zeledón (1864–1936). Publishing under the name of Magón, he quickly became the nation's most popular author with a prolific series of pen-portraits of nineteenth-century society. In his only novel, *La propia* (1911), a tragic tale of sex, betrayal, and murder in the Costa Rican coffee plantations, Magón dissects the psychology of *machismo* with uncanny insight.

Other Central American novelists focused upon their national realities with varying degrees of depth, range, and acuity, often utilizing regional dialects to give their fictions a sense of authenticity. In *El primo* ("The cousin," 1905), Costa Rican Genaro Cardona (1863–1930) portrays the bourgeois decadence of San José. In *En una silla de ruedas* ("In a wheelchair," 1916), Cardona's compatriot Carmen Lyra (1888–1949) incorporates a strong dose of sentimentalism in a portrayal of national customs and manners through the eyes of a paralyzed artist. In El Salvador, Alberto Masferrer (1868–1932) condemns the mores of a hypocritical society which keeps women in thrall in *Una vida en el cine* ("A life in the cinema," 1922), a novel based on a series of intense conversations between a man and a woman in the darkness of a cinema. Another Salvadorean, José María Peralta (1873–1944), delighted his country's small reading public with *Doctor Gonorreitigorrea* (with an obvious pun on gonorrhoea), a populist satire of the nation's bourgeoisie enthralled with foreign goods of consumption.

A harsher, overtly political outlook informed the work of many Central American novelists who responded to the historical events shaking the region. The Mexican Revolution (1910–20) opened many eyes to the oppression of the masses and the liberating potential of the armed struggle. The consequences of the self-interested intervention of the USA in Panama in 1903, followed by the invasion and subsequent occupation of Nicaragua by marines between 1912 and 1933, fanned opposition to the political and economic ambitions of the "Colossus of the North." In 1932, in El Salvador, there was a wholesale slaughter of political dissidents and landless Indians, known as "La Matanza" ("The great slaughter"), on the orders of the dictator Maximiliano Martínez. In Guatemala the brutal dictatorship of Manuel Estrada Cabrera (1898–1920) was followed by the fascistic regime of Jorge Ubico (1931–44), and after a brief springtime of political reform under Presidents Arévalo and Arbenz (1945–54), a military regime came to power with the backing of the CIA.

In Nicaragua, where the legendary César Augusto Sandino was still leading a war of liberation against the occupying US forces, Hernán Robleto wrote *Sangre en el trópico* ("Blood in the tropics," 1930), a classic of anti-imperialist literature. Robleto, who fought alongside Sandino, uses personal experiences to recount a saga of revolutionary heroism. His novel may be regarded as a precursor of the testimonial writing that would become popular in Nicaragua, El Salvador, and Guatemala fifty years later. In *Sangre en el trópico*, a group of twenty-two students leave Mexico on a ramshackle boat, "La Carmelita," to join Sandino's struggle to expel the marines from their homeland. The novel contains a raw power in its depiction of the collective courage of the young rebels in the face of overwhelming odds, from rain-soaked, mosquito-infested jungles and swamps to US military force. *Sangre en el trópico* pioneered another theme that was to become a staple of anti-imperialist literature: the vicious exploitation of peasant labor in plantations, mines, and factories flying the American flag in Nicaraguan territory.

Perhaps no single image conveys as powerfully the mixture of fear and loathing with which Central American novelists viewed the USA as that used by Honduran Marco Antonio Rosa (1899–1983) in *Eva Crucificada* (1951): a repulsive worm devouring a white rose. A novel that captures and transmits the barbarity of plantation life without unduly sacrificing literary quality is *Mamita Yunai* ("Mummy Yunai," 1941), by Costa Rican Carlos Luis Fallas (1909–66). A former "linero" (plantation worker) turned union organizer and communist politician, Fallas depicts the plantation as a Dantesque hellhole. The capitalist "gringos" and the local bosses are shameless, while peons of Indian blood are portrayed as abject caricatures of their once fierce and noble ancestors. The deepest pathos is reserved for the black peons, depicted as members of a race forgotten by history. Following the expectations of socialist realism, the protagonist enjoins the poor and the oppressed of Central America to link arms with their brothers in the USA in the struggle for liberation.

An anti-imperialist message lies at the heart of two other finely wrought novels, *Puerto Limón* (1950) by Costa Rican Joaquín Gutiérrez (b. 1918), and *Luna verde* (1951) by the Panamanian Joaquín Beleño (b. 1922). *Puerto Limón* focuses on the historic banana workers' strike of 1934 in Cost Rica. With considerable skill, the narrative fuses the collective struggle with a personal saga as it traces the development of Silvano, a black peon, from an insecure adolescent to a mature and confident man. *Luna verde* constitutes a lament for Panama, whose Indian, black and Hispanic legacies have been harmed by US capitalism. Written as a diary, it depicts the sordid chase for the dollar that degrades Panamanians of the Canal Zone, irrespective of class, gender, or race.

No Central American novelist had the talent to combine literature and anti-imperialism so persuasively as Miguel Angel Asturias in his trilogy: *Viento fuerte* (*Strong Wind*, 1949), *El papa verde* (*The Green Pope*, 1954), and *Los ojos enterrados* (*The Eyes of the Interred*, 1960). Connected by plots and characters, these novels recount with restrained fury the ruthless strategies employed by US capitalists to establish and perpetuate an economic empire in both the Atlantic and Pacific coasts of Central America. The defiance of local planters and the formation of cooperatives, allied to the courage and idealism of determined individuals, stand in opposition to a Chicago-based mafia, aided and abetted by a cohort of corrupt politicians and military thugs. Land seizures, the razing of entire villages, murder, blackmail, bribery, and cover-ups by the press comprise the backdrop against which Geo Maker

Thompson turns himself into a secular, money-hungry "pope" controlling a vast tropical empire. For the evolution of the Central (and Latin) American novel, the manner in which Asturias tells his anti-imperialist story is as important as the story itself. Long, winding, rhythmical sentences are offset by onomatopeic words and phrases, while temporal jumps, the intermittent change of linguistic registers, monologues, dialogues, and metaphors that range from the most primitive to the most sophisticated, maintain the reader's engagement. Overall, this trilogy comprises a daring verbal experiment that fulfills the novelist's ambition to write a "tropical opera."

Another important dimension to the Central American novel was *criollismo*, which purported to capture the essential spirit and nature of the region. *Criollismo*'s central preoccupation, as with many other Latin America regional novels, was the conflict between civilization and barbarism as embodied in the opposition between tradition and modernity, rural values and metropolitan mores. In many cases nature is portrayed as a primeval force that dominates the lives of the protagonists. From a long catalog of regional Guatemalan novelists two stand out: Carlos Wyld Ospina (1891–1956) and Flavio Herrera (b. 1895). In his best and last novel, *La gringa*, Wyld Espina transfers the plot of Rómulo Gallegos's *Doña Bárbara* (1929), from the plains of Venezuela to the tropical coast of Guatemala. "La Gringa" is presented as a new breed of woman, the symbol of an emerging modern Guatemala which will fight hard to find its rightful place in the world. She is also an oligarch who runs her two coffee plantations with ruthless efficiency and contempt for the indigenous peoples who work for her. Ultimately, *La gringa* is a celebration of the ideal of civilization represented by an educated gentry willing to follow the example of the USA, and a repudiation of barbarism, which is identified with the Indians, whose "depressing melancholy" has held back progress in Guatemala.[4] By contrast, Flavio Herrera's most famous novel, *El tigre* (The tiger," 1932), conveys the savagery of life in the tropics while inverting the dichotomy of civilization and barbarism. Scenes of rape, murder, and other kinds of unbridled violence portray supposedly educated, westernized men and women as "degenerates." In a Darwinian struggle between moral values and base instincts, civilization proves no match for barbarism.

In *El tunco* ("The hog," 1933), Honduran Arturo Mejía Nieto (1901–72) uses fifty years of revolutionary warfare as a backdrop to his take on civilization and barbarism: Hondurans, and by extension Central Americans, are by nature wild, primitive, and uncivilized, but these genetic traits express an unshakeable desire for freedom and liberty incomprehensible to Europeans and North Americans. Another engagement with the theme of barbarism is found in *Pedro Arnáez* (1924) by Costa Rican José María Cañas (b. 1904).

The narrative traces the protagonist's epiphanic journey from the coast to the jungle to San José to Mexico and finally to El Salvador, where the massacre of 1932 is taken as evidence that violence is an irremediable condition in Central America. Pessimism is also prevalent in *Entre la selva de neón* ("In the neon jungle," 1956), by Salvadorean Rolando Vásquez (1903–72). Whereas the principal action of most *criollista* novels occurs in rural areas (the jungle, the plains, provincial towns), *Entre la selva de neón* is set in the Mexican capital, a magnet for thousands of displaced Central Americans before World War II. A melodrama of crime, violence, deceit, tragedy, and death, this novel conveys the pessimistic message that a blighted star governs the destiny of Central Americans. By contrast, *Amanecer* (1953), by Honduran Ramón Amaya Amador (1916–66), delivers what may be described as a Central Americanist clarion call. The Guatemalan capital is depicted as "la ciudad corazón" ("the urban heart"), whose exemplary courage in rising up against the tyranny of the dictator Jorge Ubico will lead to the recovery of freedom in the region. What lends pathos to this message is the appeal by a Honduran for the restoration of "aquella lejana Federación de Centroamérica" ("that distant Central American Federation") under the aegis of Guatemala, the largest country in the isthmus, and one whose territorial ambitions were for many years viewed with suspicion by its neighbors.

No Central American novel with an urban setting can compare with the emotional power and stylistic flair of Miguel Angel Asturias's *El señor presidente* (1946). Composed in Paris between 1922 and 1932, it is a denunciation of the dictatorship of General Estrada Cabrera in Guatemala (1898–1920), and a call to arms against the dehumanizing militarism that had thrown a pall over Central America since independence. Set in an archetypal city, it anticipates "magical realism" in the way it fuses fantasy and reality to project a totalizing vision. From the very first page the use of incantatory language turns the act of reading into a surreal experience, as if the story were being narrated by an ancient Mayan shaman. At times the novel reads as if it were a grotesque fairy tale, as when the trees of a forest surrounding the presidential palace metamorphose into anthropomorphic ears eavesdropping on the dictator's enemies. *El señor presidente* is a tour de force that reinforces Central America's *mestizo* identity, Western and Amerindian, Christian and pagan.

The role of indigenous culture in forging a Central American identity was crucial in the first half of the twentieth century. Struggling against exoticism, *indigenista* novelists endeavored to express Indian language, feelings, and ideas as part of the universal human condition, while raising the reader's consciousness regarding the plight of the native populations since the Conquest.[5] In Panama a historical focus was preferred, as in *La India dormida* ("The sleeping indian girl," 1936) by Julio B. Sosa (b. 1910). While perhaps overly sentimental in its depiction of the relationship between Flor del Aire, an Indian of the Guaymí tribe, and a conquistador named Rogel de Loria, this novel makes the edifying suggestion that true love has no racial or cultural boundaries. Another Panamanian historical saga, *Vasco Núñez de Balboa* (1934), by Octavio Méndez Pereira (1870–1954) portrays the discovery of the Pacific Ocean as a heroic enterprise for which Indian chiefs deserve as much credit as the Spanish hero. *Isnaya* (1939), by the Honduran Emilio Murillo (1902–86), stands out for being the first account of the fierce resistance waged against the conquistadores by the legendary Lempira, who is portrayed as a precursor to Sandino in Nicaragua and Zapata in Mexico. The title refers to an Indian princess who retains her feminine dignity and charm even as she is transformed into a defiant Central American Amazon warrior.

One of the most sophisticated exponents of *indigenismo* was Guatemalan Mario Monteforte Toledo (b. 1911). His celebrated novel, *Entre la piedra y la cruz* (*Between the Stone and the Sword*, 1948), focuses upon the existential dilemma of Lu/Pedro Matzar, a man caught between a millenary indigenous culture and a "ladino" (Hispanicized) culture that can trace its roots only to the "cross" (the death of Christ). By an adroit use of an invisible, indirect, third-person narrator the reader experiences the dilemma of an Indian growing up and making his way in a "ladino" society.

For many *indigenismo* in Central America is synonymous with *Hombres de maíz* (*Men of Maize*, 1949), by Miguel Angel Asturias. From a literary perspective, *Hombres de maíz* is a contemporary *mise-en-scène* of Mayan and Aztec cosmogony as inscribed in such texts as the *Popohl Vuh* and *Chilam Balam*. These pre-Hispanic sources inspire its ritualistic, liturgical character, as becomes evident in the first page, when the hero, Gaspar Ilom, is "sung" into existence by ancestral elders. As the story unfolds over six subtly integrated sections, the animism, superstition, and magic of the ancient sacred texts breathe life into the novel: men become deer and coyotes, curses are enacted, the devil appears in the form of a serpent, prophecies are fulfilled, and a son pays for the sins of the father by his banishment to the skies. The novel's mythical elements underscore the pathos of Amerindian history since the Conquest, as the technologically superior Spanish conquerors and their "ladino" descendants have attempted to reduce the "maize people" to the status of the "chucho" (mongrel dog).

As Gerard Martin has demonstrated, *Hombres de maíz* is a dense and visionary novel with numerous layers of significance.[6] In a universal sense the story of the "maize people" is an allegory of the transition of humanity from a tribal stage based upon family ties to the development of a society based upon class and capitalist modes of production. In this regard, the novel draws on Marxist assumptions. On the other hand, a broad anthropological explanation sheds light on the apparently chaotic structure of *Hombres de maíz*, characterized by chronological discontinuities, the reappearance of characters the reader has presumed dead, the juxtaposition of unrelated words, phrases, images, and metaphors, and abrupt transitions from a concrete, visible world of objective reality to an irrational, invisible dimension of myth and magic. The act of reading this novel has been compared to chasing startled rabbits darting across a page![7] In fact, Asturias utilizes this apparent anarchy to represent the "Savage Mind" of tribal societies as described by Claude Lévi-Strauss. Since they lived in harmony with nature, pre-Columbian societies viewed life as a spontaneous, violent, creative flux of contradictory ideas, feelings, and emotions, and they related equally to the physical and spiritual worlds. In its dazzling manipulation of language, style, and technique *Hombre de maíz* is groundbreaking. Asturias was, deservedly, the first Latin American novelist to be awarded the Nobel Prize for literature.

Experimentalism, testimony and the Boom

Asturias was not the only Central American striving to expand the boundaries of the novel before the "Boom." Panamanian Rogelio Sinán (1904–94) published *Plenilunio* (1947), in which metafiction, reader involvement, multiple perspectives, the unconscious, and psychoanalysis all come into play. The novel tells the story of Elena Cunha, the daughter of a prostitute, whose confessions alternate with those of other characters to project the existential anguish of living and dying in the maelstrom of Panama. In Costa Rica, Yolanda Oreamuno (1916–56) introduced a similar level of experimentation in *La ruta de su evasión* (*The Route of His Escape*, 1949). This complex, fragmented narrative consists of a painful interior monologue about death, violence, and suicide, with a forceful criticism of patriarchal society. Another outstanding experimentalist was Costa Rican Carmen Naranjo (b. 1931), whose masterpiece, *Diario de una multitud* ("Diary of a multitude"), was composed in the 1960s but not published until 1974. This polyphonic narrative echoes the existential frustrations of Western culture with a multitude of alienated voices crying out in anguish at whomsoever may be listening.

   A mode of non-fictional, documentary narrative known as *testimonio* (testimony) characterized the last half of the twentieth century, particularly in Guatemala, Nicaragua, and El Salvador, the three republics that endured the immediate traumas of revolution, post-revolution, or civil war. The principal feature of testimonial writing is that the narrators are also participants who feel an urgent need to "bear witness" to their time and place and history. *Miguel Mármol* (1970), by the Salvadorean poet-revolutionary Roque Dalton (1935–1975), uses an interview with a communist survivor of the massacre that followed the 1932 uprising to interpret the history of his embattled country. In *La montaña es algo más que una inmensa estepa verde* (*Fire From the Mountain: The Making of a Sandinista*, 1982), Nicaraguan Omar Cabezas recounts with gusto and irony the coming-of-age of a young city slicker training to become a guerrilla in the inhospitable jungle. In the classic of the genre, *Me llamo Rigoberta Menchú, y así me nació la conciencia* (*My Name is Rigoberta Menchú: An Indian Woman in Guatemala*, 1983), a young Maya-Quiché activist recounts her personal story, which is conflated with the collective story of her community, via a narrative mediated by a professional anthropologist.

The writers of these *testimonios* borrowed techniques and devices from narrative fiction, such as the imaginative reconstruction of events, the selective use of memory, flashbacks, humor, irony, and pathos. Such "literariness" certainly makes these works more readable, but some have raised doubts about their reliability – are they in fact the "truth" or are they fictional elaborations of the truth? Is *Miguel Mármol* a "novelized testimony"? Is *La montaña es algo más que una estepa verde* an "autobiographical novel"? Does *Me llamo Rigoberta Menchú* fictionalize personal and historical truths in order to dramatize its political message?[8]

If some *testimonios* may have been mediated by modes of narrative fiction, many novels were certainly influenced by the gestures and impulses of the *testimonio* genre. Indeed, Central American novelists, to this day, continue to write "testimonial fiction," privileging the voices of the subaltern: the proletariat, the peasant, the guerrilla, the Indian, the Black, or the victims of *machismo*. The first major testimonial novel was *Cenizas de Izalco* (*Ashes of Izalco* 1966), written by Salvadorean-Nicaraguan Claribel Alegría (b. 1924) in collaboration with her husband, Darwin Flakoll, a US citizen. Set in Santa Ana and Izalco, in western El Salvador, the novel utilizes interior monologues, diary entries, folk tales, Amerindian myths, and a rich network of references to Western literature and art to "bear witness" to "La Matanza" of 1932. Alegría looks back at this defining moment of the past to understand the present. In this regard it is no exaggeration to say that the best testimonial novels in Central America represent the equivalent of the "Boom" in the rest of Latin America.

In *Pobrecito poeta que era yo* ("The poor little poet that I was," 1976), Roque Dalton composed a stylistic and verbal extravaganza combining prose, poetry, song, reportage, dialogue and even a manual on how to become a successful revolutionary. The dilemma enshrined in this testimonial novel is typically Sartrean: how can a revolutionary exchange a rifle for a pen when ruthless colonels and fat, bloated oligarchs are sucking the blood out of his country? The answer provided by Dalton is sad but prophetic: "The best writers are the dead ones." In *Los compañeros* (*The Comrades*, 1976), a disenchanted Marxist, Guatemalan Marco Antonio Flores, unburdens himself with a scathing satire at the expense of his erstwhile comrades whose revolutionary commitments were superficial. The dashed hopes of a revolutionary are narrated in a series of testimonial monologues bristling with profanity, graphic sexuality, bitter humor, and wordplay.

In *El tiempo principia en Xibalbá* (*Time Begins in Xibalbá*, 1972), Luis de Lión (1939–84) uses a choral narrative voice to portray a "miserable little Indian village" inhabited by Spanish-speaking Mayas who are "joyfully sad." The significance of this existential oxymoron lies in the dual aspect of indigenous existence. While physical life is a daily drudgery of discrimination and exploitation, relief is afforded by a magical, mischievous spirit. In the novel sexuality is a symbolic weapon of political vengeance deployed by the indigenous peoples of Mayan descent. Such defiance cost the writer dearly, as in 1984 he was "disappeared" by the military dictatorship.

Published as the Sandinistas were sweeping triumphantly but painfully toward Managua, *¿Te dio miedo la sangre?* (*To Bury our Fathers: A Novel of Nicaragua*, 1977), by Sergio Ramírez, combines the testimonial focus of a political activist with the narrative skills of an accomplished novelist. Composed of six narrative strands that move back and forth between 1932 and 1961 to portray the history of Nicaragua, the novel resounds with the voices of people from every level of society to ask the rhetorical question: "What is the destiny of Nicaragua?" The answer, is in the hands of the FSLN (the Sandinista Front for National Liberation), which was founded in the year that the novel's action ends. A Rabelaisian ribaldry suffuses the novel, which ultimately may be read as joke at the expense of Somoza, the fat, bloated dictator ready for the slaughter. The joke is implicit in a literal translation of the Spanish title, *¿Te dio miedo la sangre?* ("Did the blood scare you?"), the second part of a popular Nicaraguan saying, which begins with another question: *"¿Mató chancho tu madre?"* ("Did your mother kill a pig?"). The question is answered in the first chapter, which describes the funeral of another "pig," Guatemalan dictator Carlos Castillo Armas, who was assassinated in 1957. In this way, the novel begins with the prophecy of a bloody end to the Somoza dictatorship and the triumph of the Sandinista Revolution.

Towards the end of his term as vice-president of the Sandinista government (1985–90), Ramírez wrote *Castigo divino* ("Divine punishment," 1989). Behind the complex façade of a "whodunit" set in his native León in 1933, this novel contains the prophetic warning that the Sandinistas will face electoral punishment if they betray the ideals of the revolution. After this prophecy came true and his own subsequent rupture with other Sandinista leaders, Ramírez wrote *Baile de máscaras* ("Masked ball," 1995) and *Margarita, está linda la mar* ("Margarita, the sea is beautiful," 1999), which express metaphorically and allegorically his growing disenchantment with the most negative aspects of post-revolutionary Sandinism (lies, theft, propaganda, nepotism, and a desperate lust for power). In *Adiós muchachos: una memoria de la revolución sandinista* ("Goodbye friends: a memoir of the Sandinista Revolution," 1999), Ramírez has produced a moving testimony to his disillusionment with the failure of the Sandinistas to fulfill the goals of the revolution.

The region's most consistent testimonial novelist is El Salvador's Manlio Argueta (b. 1935).[9] His first novel, *El valle de las hamacas* ("The valley of the hammocks," 1970), resounds with stylistic pyrotechnics. Infused with a spirit of nausea and bad faith, it depicts El Salvador as "el culo del mundo" ("the rear-end of the world") in desperate need of redemption. *Caperucita en la zona roja* (*Little Red Riding Hood in the Red Light District*, 1977), a cryptic collage of monologues, conversations, speeches, sermons, songs, and fables, is a homage to Roque Dalton. *Un día en la vida* (*One Day of Life*, 1980) speaks directly to the reader through the voices of the *campesinos* (peasants), the subaltern community in a country despoiled since independence by an oligarchical network of "fourteen families" and their imperialistic allies. In *Cuzcatlán donde bate la mar del sur* (*Cuzcatlán, Where the Southern Sea Beats*, 1986), Argueta applies previous devices and motifs to narrate a syncopated history of Cuzcatlán, the indigenous name for El Salvador. The novel is also a stirring homage to the women of El Salvador, depicted as a source of hope.

The testimonial impulse continued to beat strongly, particularly in Nicaragua, Guatemala, and El Salvador, in the 1980s and 1990s. However, responding to the ethos of postmodernism and to the example of the Latin American "Post-Boom," Central American novelists became more inventive, playful, allusive, and erotic. A case in point is the Nicaraguan Gioconda Belli (b. 1948), who brings a feminine/feminist optic to bear upon Nicaraguan history in *La mujer habitada* (*The Inhabited Woman*, 1988). Based upon her own experiences as an FMLN rebel in the 1970s, Belli fuses the political and literary dimensions of testimonial fiction while embodying another duality: that of Nicaragua's Indian and mestizo heritages. Lavinia, a Sandinista freedom-fighter, is "inhabited" literally and magically by Itzá, an Indian princess who died five centuries earlier fighting against the conquista-dores. Lavinia/Itzá is depicted as a beautiful, sensual creature who delights in her body and is fully aware of its power over men. The novel's unabashed eroticism constitutes a triumphant affirmation of female sexual liberation, which is equated with political freedom.

A talented group of Guatemalan novelists experimented with various guises of testimony in the 1980s, among them Roberto Morales (b. 1947), Dante Liano (b. 1949), Arturo Arias (b. 1950), Méndez Vides (b. 1956), and the older Edwin Cifuentes (b. 1926).[10] Of the four, Arturo Arias has made the greatest impact with *El jaguar en llamas* ("The jaguar in flames," 1989), one of the most imaginative exercises in intertextuality in Central American literature. Mikhail Bahktin's notion of carnival explodes within the novel's pages as humor is exploited to compose a "contrahistoria" ("alternative history") of Guatemala from 1492, when the Moors, Jews, and gypsies were expelled from Spain, to the mid-1980s, when the URNG (Guatemalan National Revolutionary Union) was waging guerrilla warfare against a US-backed military regime. The novel is an indictment of imperialism and an affirmation of Guatemala's shared heritage of Amerindian and Western cultures. The narrative is playfully woven together from a multiplicity of sources that range from the *Rabinal Achí* and the *Popohl Vuh*, through the *Satyricon* and the legends of King Arthur and the Round Table, to Cervantes, Flaubert, James Joyce, and Miguel Angel Asturias. Popular culture enters the scene via Superman (alias Clark Kent) and a Broadway musical in which a chorus line of scantily clad girls disguised as tigers performs the story recounted in *El jaguar en llamas*.

The diversity of the contemporary Central American novel

While testimonial fiction flowered in the Central American zones of conflict (Guatemala, Nicaragua, and El Salvador), in the other three republics not directly involved in civil war or revolution a heterogeneous band of novelists experimented with a variety of themes and techniques. This diversity is epitomized by three Honduran novels: *El corneta* ("The bugler," 1980), by Roberto Castillo (b. 1952); *Una función con móbiles y tentetiesos* ("A performance with mobile toys and roly-polys," 1980), by Marcos Carías (b. 1938); and *Rey del albor. Madrugada* ("King of the light. Daybreak," 1993), by Julio Escoto (b. 1946). *El corneta*, a popular success in Honduras, is a short novel with an episodic plot narrated in clear, uncomplicated language. It is a picaresque tale about the travels and adventures of Tito, a Guatemalan "everyman" whose strategy for survival is to accept whatever life has to offer with equanimity and good humor. On the surface, *El corneta* seems to enshrine a "turn-the-other-cheek" morality. However, this ostensible message is subverted through Tito's son, a worker in a nail factory in Tegucigalpa, who emerges as a rebellious Christ figure who will fight to extricate the nails from his father's cross.

There could not be a greater contrast with the straightforward narrative of *El corneta* than the complexities of *Una función con móbiles y tentetiesos*. The curious title conveys the novel's equivocal character. Like a series of "móbiles" (mobiles) it creates the illusion of movement, but like a "tentetiesos" (collapsible toy) the novel seems to fall down under its own weight. At the end of this multidiscursive disquisition, the reader is drawn to the title of the first chapter: "No pasa nada" ("Nothing happens"). Indeed, the novel seems to be a hugely inflated joke, a carnival of voices talking past each other, with no apparent plot, character, or setting. Dimly in the background, the reader does perceive Tegucigalpa, a phantom city of disembodied actors staging the performance ("función") mentioned in the title – a performance without meaning that reflects the alienation of life in a modern Central American city.

Escoto's *Rey del albor. Madrugada* is an engaging novel packed with plots, subplots, characters, and episodes drawn from every period and layer of Honduran history. It is a brilliant illustration of "The New Central American Novel," a narrative trend that has become popular in the region since testimonial fiction began to wane in the 1990s.[11] Combining the serious intent and the sophisticated structure of a highly "literary" text with colorful ingredients borrowed from popular culture, the narrative looks to the past of Honduras from the vantage point of 1989. Escoto does not hide the fact he is constructing his own private version of the history of Honduras and willfully transforms well-known dates and events. Indeed, the relation between fact and fiction constitutes the novel's central concern. At the outset the reader learns that the president of Honduras has commissioned a historian from Cornell University to rewrite the nation's history by omitting all negative references to the USA. Whereas Escoto is working with the lies of fiction to tell a personal truth, the president embodies the tendentious lies of partisan historians.[12]

Gloria Guardia (b. 1940), Panama's outstanding novelist of the last twenty five years, gained regional attention with *El último juego* ("The last game," 1977). Using a guerrilla assault on a VIP's residence as a pretext, the novel calls attention to the country's problematic relations with the USA from the "sell out" of the Panama Canal in 1903 to the upsurge of nationalist fervor under Colonel Omar Torrijos in the late 1960s and early 1970s. Through the anguished stream-of-consciousness of Tito Garrido, the male protagonist whose mistress has been killed in the guerrilla assault, the novel also explores the issue of gender relations. The story moves seamlessly back and forth between the first- and third-person narrators, the latter's apparent objectivity utilized to deflate both the political and phallic pretensions of the powerful males who govern Panama. In the end, the fate of the two-timing Tito Garrido exposes the fraudulent character of the Panamanian patriarchy.

The question of identity has been a major concern in Costa Rica, where women novelists continue to figure prominently. *Asalto al paraíso* ("Assault on paradise," 1992), by Tatiana Lobo (b. 1939), draws on historical events and characters to project a tantalizing vision of what the future could have been had the Spaniards dared to establish an egalitarian *mestizaje* (fusion) with the Indian population. Set in the former colonial capital of Cartago and in the Talamanca mountains between 1700 and 1710, this "New Historical Novel" offers a revisionist account of the biggest Indian uprising in Costa Rica, when Pa-brú Presbere led the Boruca people in unequal combat against the Spaniards, with "flying arrows" opposed to "the burning vomit of rifle-fire." A parallel story narrates the adventures and hardships of Pedralbrán, a fugitive from the Inquisition who seeks refuge in Costa Rica, where he falls in love with la Muda, a deaf and dumb Boruca, his conduit to the magical harmony of the Amerindian world.

Costa Rican readers have responded with unusual fervor to *La loca de Gandoca* ("The madwoman of Gandoca," 1993), an "eco-novel" by Anacristina Rossi (b. 1952). Suffused with a pantheistic spirit, this novel is a denunciation of the depredation of the country's Atlantic coast by a conspiracy of local and foreign interests. The female protagonist identifies with the threatened trees of the forest, and embraces death as return to the "moist, tender earth" from which humanity is molded. *La loca de Gandoca* posits that the future of Costa Rica may well depend upon a new breed of woman whose body is a natural extension of the nation's ecological heritage. In *Limón Blues* (2002), another novel intended to raise her Costa Rican readers' consciousness, Rossi writes from the perspective of a sensitive white woman to imaginatively reconstruct the life and times of Marcus Garvey and his movement in support of Caribbean blacks. The novel succeeds in conveying the magic of "old" Puerto Limón, with its linguistic medley of Spanish, English, and ancestral African tongues, its animistic traditions and its messianic rituals, while in the background the reader hears the haunting melodies that sing of a culture threatened with extinction.

An insider's perspective of the black experience in Costa Rica is found in the novels of Quince Duncan (b. 1940). In *Kimbo* (1990), also set in Puerto Limón, the protagonist traces his roots back to Jamaica three generations ago, in the process raising issues of self, racism, sexism, identity, and the manipulation of the truth by a society too prejudiced – or afraid – to confront its demons. In Panama, on the other hand, the black community has found a stirring voice in Guillermo Wilson (alias Cubena). His outstanding novel is *Los nietos de Felicidad Dolores* ("The grandchildren of Felicidad Dolores," 1991), a dense historical narrative of the black diaspora with mythic overtones.

The most recent development in the Central American novel has been the product of new diaspora: the massive emigration to the USA from a region convulsed by poverty, oppression, and war. There are novelists who live and work in the USA but continue to publish in their native countries. A writer in this category is the promising Salvadorean Jacinta Escudos (b. 1961), whose daring first novel, *El desencanto* ("The disenchantment," 2000), tells the story of an elusive search for love. There are also novelists who have emigrated to the USA but who publish in Spanish in their adopted country. A prominent writer in this category is Salvadorean Mario Bencastro (b. 1949), who, in *Odisea del Norte* ("Odyssey to the North" 1998), explores the experiences of Salvadoreans and other Central Americans who have made the hazardous journey to the "promised land." Finally, there are novelists who live in the USA, and publish in English, such as Guatemalan Francisco Goldman (b. 1955). In *The Long Night of the White Chickens* (1992), an impressive first novel that combines at least three different strands of fiction – murder mystery, romance, and political intrigue – Goldman shocks the reader with a tale about international adoption agencies and the sale of babies and human organs to wealthy US clients.

The Central American novel may be short in history, but it is surprisingly rich in tradition and increasingly diverse in themes, styles, and techniques. Although it is not by any means univocal, as a corpus it does speak persuasively of the common experiences of six republics that have been consigned to the margins by the larger, more influential, cultural centers in the Spanish-speaking world. This marginalization is epitomized by the notion that "Central America is a novel without novelists."[13] Thus, with the conspicuous exception of Miguel Angel Asturias, no Central American novelist is included in the literary canon of Latin America. Whether published in Spain, Mexico, Chile, Argentina, the USA, or Great Britain, general books on Latin American literature or Spanish American fiction seldom contain more than two or three Central American names.[14] That being said, the range and quality of the Central American novel certainly deserves more readers and greater critical attention.

NOTES

1. See Seymour Menton, *Historia crítica de la novela guatemalteca* (Guatemala, Editorial Universitaria, 1960), pp. 21–50. Menton's book is indispensable for the student of Guatemalan literature.

2. For a concise overview of *modernismo*, see Stephen Hart, *A Companion to Spanish-American Literature* (London: Tamesis, 1999), pp. 76–81.
3. An introduction to this important novelist is found in María A. Salgado, *Rafael Arévalo Martínez* (New York: Twayne, 1979).
4. Arturo Arias offers a searching analysis of *La gringa* in *La identidad de la palabra: narrativa guatemalteca a la luz del siglo XX* (Guatemala: Editorial Artemis and Edinter, 1998), pp. 41–61.
5. For a definition and discussion of this concept, see Peter Standish, "Indigenism," in Verity Smith (ed.), *Encyclopedia of Latin American Literature* (London and Chicago: Fitzroy Dearborn, 1997), pp. 440–41.
6. Gerald Martin's magisterial treatment of this novel is found in "Hombres de maíz," Edición crítica (Paris, Mexico: Editions Klinsiek/Fondo de cultura Económica, 1981), pp. xxi-ccxxliv and 241–441.
7. Ariel Dorfman, *Imaginación y violencia en América* (Santiago de Chile: Editorial Universitaria, 1970), p. 69.
8. For the controversy surrounding *testimonio*, and particularly *Me llamo Rigoberta Menchú*, see Marc Zimmerman, "Rigoberta Menchú, David Stoll, Subaltern Narrative and Testimonial Truth: A Personal Testimony," *Antípodas 13/14* (2000/2001): 119–42.
9. A review of Manlio Argueta as a testimonial novelist is found in Roy C. Boland, "La evolución novelística de Manlio Argueta desde *El valle de las hamacas* hasta *Cuscatlán donde bate la mar del sur*," *Antípodas 10* (1998): 111–18.
10. Arturo Arias includes interesting sections on Dante Liano, MéndezVides and himself in *Identidad de la palabra*, pp. 173–234.
11. A description of the "New Central American Historical Novel" is found in Werner Mackenbach, "La nueva novela histórica en Nicaragua y Centroamérica," in ISTMO (http://www.denison.edu/istmo/vtnt/artículos/novela.html).
12. For a provocative discussion of the difference between "truth" in fiction and history, see Mario Vargas Llosa, *Fiction: The Power of Lies* (Melbourne: La Trobe University, 1993).
13. Quoted by Linda Craft in "Latin American Novel. Central America," in *Encyclopedia of the Novel*, ed. Paul Schellinger (London: Fitzroy Dearborn, 1998), p. 730.
14. For instance, one of the best recent general books, Stephen Hart's *A Companion to Spanish-American Literature*, deals only with Miguel Angel Asturias.

FURTHER READING

Acevedo, Ramón Luis, "La nueva novela histórica en Guatemala y Honduras," *Letras de Guatemala* 18–19 (1998): 3–17.
Arias, Arturo, *Gestos ceremoniales: narrativa centroamericana, 1960–1990*, Guatemala: Artemis and Edinter, 1998.
La identidad de la palabra. Narrativa guatemalteca a la luz del siglo XX, Guatemala: Artemis and Edinter, 1998.
Arellano, Jorge Eduardo, *Literatura centroamericana. Diccionario de autores centroamericanos. Fuentes para su estudio*, Managua: Fundación Vidas, 2003.
Panorama de la literatura nicaragüense, Managua: Editorial Nueva Nicaragua, 1986.

Barbas-Rhoden, Laura, *Writing Women in Central America: Gender and the Fiction-alization of History*, Ohio University Press, 2003.

Collard, Patrick and Rida De Maeseneer (eds.), *Murales, figuras, fronteras: narrativa e historia en el Caribe y Centroamérica*, Frankfurt: Iberoamericana Vervuert, 2003.

Gallegos Valdés, Luis. *Panorama de la literatura Salvadoreña*, San Salvador: UCA, 1987.

Lorand de Olzagasti, Adelaida. *El Indio en la narrativa guatemalteca*, San Juan: Editorial Universitaria, 1968.

Menton, Seymour, *Historia crítica de la novela guatemalteca*, Guatemala: Editorial Universitaria, 1960.

  Caminata por la narrativa latinoamericana, Mexico City: Fondo de Cultura Económica, 2002.

Prieto, René, *Miguel Angel Asturias's Archaeology of Return*, Cambridge University Press, 1993.

Rodríguez Rosales, Isolda, *Una década en la narrativa nicaragüense y otros ensayos*, Managua: Centro nicaragüense de escritores, 1999.

Ramírez, Sergio, *La narrativa centroamericana*, San Salvador: Editorial Universitaria, 1969.

3

GENDER AND SEXUALITY

9

CATHERINE DAVIES

Gender studies

Gender studies is not synonymous with women's studies, feminist criticism, or queer theory though it may encompass all of these. Gender refers to the social and symbolic relations of perceived sexual differences. In literary studies it provides a concept, a category of analysis, that enables us to think about how and why the terms "man" and "woman," and the differences between them, have been produced historically through language. Gendered readings of Latin American novels, therefore, will focus on the constructions of masculinities and femininities in specific texts, the aim being to explore how this category of identification predicated on sexual difference is inscribed discursively in a particular time and place and how it comes to function as a principle of social organization and representation. Such a reading will also involve being alert to textual renditions of sexualities (sexual desires and behaviors) and questioning the heterosexual norm. Inevitably, power is a key issue here; what gendered readings hope to expose is the interplay of gender and social control, the fallacy of the self-contained autonomous individual (predicated on the masculine universal subject set up only by virtue of what it is not), and the exclusion of those identified (by themselves or others) as women or transgendered subjects. Gendered readings should be subversive in that they historicize the gender relations informing the cultural constructions of collective identities and thus unmask and challenge resulting power relations. Attention to the significance of gender has resulted in a sea change in the way the Latin American novel is perceived, interpreted, valued, and produced.

Studies of gender formation and the performance of gender roles in the Latin American novel have concentrated primarily on representations of women and the female body. Studies of masculinity have been more piecemeal and have tended to privilege gay writing and certain geographical locations (Cuba, Argentina). While a large corpus of criticism, mainly psychoanalytical, is available on the work of gay novelists, the sociological and psychosexual significance of other masculinities should also be examined, particularly hegemonic masculinity. This might explain the preponderance in fiction of certain types of behavior, values (religious, militaristic, family) and assignments of gender roles, particularly in the work of novelists where masculinity is of crucial concern (for example, Echeverría, Güiraldes, Onetti, and Vargas Llosa). These questions will be discussed more fully in the next chapter. This chapter will focus on feminist or woman-centered approaches to the Latin American novel.

Feminist criticism

Since the late 1970s, emphasis on researching women's contribution to print culture has resulted in a radical revision of the commonly accepted version of the development of the Latin American novel. The issue addressed is the exclusion of women novelists from critical history, from the literary traditions with which they engage but from which are often excluded. In this view, a literary tradition is an area of political and intellectual contention. One of the first tasks for feminist criticism is to recover the lost, forgotten, or deliberately suppressed practice of Latin American women's prose writing from colonial times to the present. Another is to critically reassess the works of acknowledged women novelists, often considered second-rate, in the light of new woman-centered priorities. A third is to encourage today's women to write and publish their novels, often put aside for many years, and to promote these works in Latin America and elsewhere. This concerted effort of over twenty-five years has born fruit: these days, novels written by women and feminist literary criticism is a growth industry. Yet standard histories of the Latin American novel still consist almost entirely of novels written by men. A comprehensive reassessment of the development of the novel and a readjustment of the canon itself is still on the agenda.

No less important is the general reevaluation of Latin American novels from a feminist critical approach. Attention may be paid, for example, to the way novels invent women and men and, more importantly, how gender categories are discursively constructed and interrogated in particular contexts. This has led to new interpretations of even the most celebrated novels. The Latin American novel was often considered (selected and critically assessed) in relation to its impact on or response to political issues involving class and race. Once gender politics is brought into the equation a different picture emerges; a novel which may seem radically subversive from a class point of view might be deeply conservative with respect to gender. No one can deny, for example, that Mario Vargas Llosa's La ciudad y los perros (The Time of the Hero, 1963) demolishes any trace of credibility the Peruvian military may have had in the 1960s. It is a subversive novel and was for that reason burned publicly by the cadet training academy it condemned. From a feminist point of view, however, it is a conservative novel: women characters hardly appear and when they do they fall squarely into the categories of domesticated wife or whore. On the other hand, from a gender studies perspective this is one of the most interesting novels of the "Boom" because it deals not only with the military and male bonding per se but the social construction of male subjectivity, from the level of the individual psyche, through the family, to all civil society, on the basis of violence, deception, and the subjection of women. Masculinity is shown to be predicated on the rejection of so-called feminine attributes such as emotion and caring (associated in the novel with homosexuality when expressed among men). Even so, the women characters are portrayed as little more than caricatures who collude with hegemonic masculinity, to the extent that the original cause of the misery depicted in the novel, the trigger for male violence, is the inconstancy of Teresa, the colorless woman at the center of the plot.

Feminist critical attention has shifted in recent years to nineteenth-century culture and society in order to trace the historical processes that resulted in the consolidation of gender roles and the subordination of women and in post-independence Latin America. This is a welcome development as the nineteenth-century Latin American novel has been relatively neglected. There are few studies of even the most celebrated male novelists of the day, such as Jorge Isaacs, Cirilo Villaverde, or Federico Gamboa (a notable exception is Sommer, 1991). Not surprisingly, women novelists, if mentioned at all, were given short shrift. Recent research, however, has revealed that the incidence of nineteenth-century women novelists in Latin America is respectably high. Some of them (Soledad Acosta de Samper in Colombia, Juana Manuela Gorriti in Argentina) are better known than others (Eduarda Mansilla in Argentina, Mercedes Cabello de Carbonera in Peru), while the work of some women novelists remains virtually unknown (Juana Manso in Argentina, Maria Firmina dos Reis in Brazil). A parallel development has been the recovery of early Mexican American women novelists (for example Maria Antonia Ruiz de Burton, in California, and Leonor Villegas de Magnón, in Texas) by specialists in Chicano literature.

Feminist studies of twentieth-century women novelists have tended to follow in similar directions: to recover forgotten authors and their works (Ofelia Rodríguez Acosta in Cuba, Josefina Vicens in Mexico, Rachel de Queiroz in Brazil); to reassess the novels of recognized authors from a feminist or woman-centered perspective (the novels of María Luisa Bombal and Rosario Castellanos in Chile and Mexico respectively), and, in addition, to promote the novels of women authors today by dedicating serious critical attention to their work (Luisa Futoransky, Ana María Shúa, and Angélica

Gorodischer in Argentina). There is now a long list of twentieth-century Latin American women novelists (especially in Mexico and Argentina) whose works are meeting with increasing critical success: Angeles Mastretta (Mexico), Rosario Ferré (Puerto Rico), Cristina Peri Rossi (Uruguay), Margo Glanz (Mexico), and Patricia Galvão (Brazil). Sadly, not all these authors were recognized during their lifetimes. It was not until 1987 that Diana Marting's *Women Writers of Spanish America* brought together short articles on over fifty Spanish American women writers. Since then there has been an explosion of criticism studying these authors.

Re-righting criticism, rereading texts

Gender awareness challenges received criticism, often leading to new readings of a novel. A good example is Peruvian Clorinda Matto de Turner's end-of-century controversial bestseller *Aves sin nido* (1889), trans. Miss J. G. Hudson[1] and published with the title *Birds without a Nest: A Story of Indian Life and Priestly Oppression in Peru* in London in 1904. Until recently, *Aves* was credited as being the first indigenous novel of Peru, and it was probably the first Latin American novel written by a woman translated into English, selected no doubt on account of its attack on the Catholic priesthood. Yet it seldom received serious critical analysis. The other two novels of Matto's trilogy, *Indole* ("Disposition," 1892) and *Herencia* ("Heredity," 1895) have been largely forgotten. *Aves* was the fictional version of a particular political discourse associated with the Peruvian industrial elite captained by Manuel González Prada. The fortunes of the novel and the author were caught up in the often violent shifts of political power and attracted harsh criticism from González Prada's opponents.[2] Matto suffered on account of her political views; her home was ransacked in 1895 and all her work lost; the publication of *Aves* resulted in her excommunication from the Catholic Church; and she spent her final years in exile in Argentina. What strikes us today is the especially virulent, sexist, nature of the attacks waged against Matto, targeting not her writings as such but that the novelist was a woman. In 1910, a year after her death, Ventura García Calderón, a respected author in his own right, referred to her as: "the literary seamstress, genius of vulgarity, who patched up domestic prose in letters, novels – novels like those written by each and every English governess – until death broke the spool of thread and stopped the machine."[3] *Aves* was deliberately ignored until the 1920s, when political power shifted once again, but by then it was deemed irrelevant to a Marxist class analysis of Peru's indigenous problem. José Carlos Mariátegui's seminal *Siete ensayos de interpretación de la realidad peruana* (1927) fails to mention Matto or her novels. In 1980 the highly influential Peruvian intellectual

Antonio Cornejo Polar, pursuing a similar line as Mariátegui, criticized Matto for her "incapacity to imagine collective solutions" to Indian oppression, not only in *Aves* but also in its "dull continuation," *Herencia*.[4] He takes issue with her for not providing in-depth social and economic analysis and for privileging instead a moral approach to the problem which, in his view, results in a profound contradiction: the Indian is morally good, but in order to progress must reject his identity. For Cornejo Polar *Aves* fails in that it presents a merely liberal bourgeois solution. The upshot is that even Matto's role in promoting *indigenismo* is denied; Cornejo Polar states that *indigenismo* did not begin until the 1920s. Cornejo Polar's analysis is perfectly legitimate in its own terms, but it is gender-blind. It fails to see that the concern of Matto's three novels is not only the indigenous population of Peru but the redemptive power of Peruvian women across class and race: women of the city and the country, the coast and the sierra, the married and the single, the wealthy and the working class, the indigenous, mestizo, and white. Only from this perspective do the three novels present a coherent argument as a trilogy. *Indole*, the first in the story, attacks the Catholic Church for its manipulation of women through confession and sexual abuse: a priest rapes Indian women and attempts to seduce a wealthy woman through blackmail. In *Herencia*, the last novel in the trilogy, the focus is not on women in rural communities (as in *Aves*) but in the class-divided city. In all three novels, upright women (irrespective of class or race) represent the moral redemption of the nation at a time of institutional corruption and political strife in the public sphere. This reading is immediately apparent when gender (rather than class and race) is privileged as a category of analysis. Further gendered readings of this novel are discussed below. Matto herself was a feminist, as attested by her contributions to two important journals, of which she was editor-in-chief, *El Perú Ilustrado* (Lima) and *El Búcaro Americano* (Buenos Aires), and by her founding in 1892 of "La Equitativa," a feminist press staffed only by women set up to publish contemporary women's writings in Latin America.

Some feminist criticism aims to uncover a continuous tradition of women's writing in Latin America existing parallel to and in dialogue with the literary mainstream authored by men. It is debatable whether women's novels should be considered as a separate group in a category of their own (as in this chapter) or included alongside male-authored novels in the chronological and generic categories (the regional, Boom, Andean novel, etc.) of which the literary histories of Latin America habitually consist. The latter is the more radical option and involves a major reassessment of the canon, entailing not only the incorporation of women novelists but questioning the very premises on which that selection was made in the first place. But it is also the case that to identify gender-specific characteristics common to novels written by women, traces perhaps of a woman writer's experiences or perspective resulting from a particular form of socialization according to gender, the novels need to be studied together. Both options are political moves to identify and counteract patterns of oppression.

Redressing selection

It is hardly credible that many histories of Latin American literature fail to mention, let alone study, the novels written by women between the 1930s and the 1960s. Many of these vanguard or "new" novels, often published long after they were written, are gems of the genre, ground-breaking in their narrative techniques and clear precursors of the magical realism of the 1960s. Centering on female characters they draw attention to language as a complex signifying process through which subjectivity is tentatively inscribed; memory, imagination, intimate experience, and perception are rendered in poetic prose that avoids linear and representational forms. Most notable is Elena Garro's masterpiece, *Los recuerdos del porvenir* (*Recollections of Things to Come*, 1963). Set in 1920s Mexico, in Iguala, the town of the author's childhood, it tells the stories of the two mistresses of General Rosas who is occupying the southern town to quash the anti-revolutionary Cristero rebellion. In the first part of the novel the radiantly beautiful Julia is whisked off magically by a stranger, and in the second part Isabel, one of the rebels' sisters who has changed sides, is turned to stone. The backdrop is the violence and poverty of rural Mexico. But Garro's novel is distinguished above all by its inventive representation of time, which revolves in cycles or ceases entirely, presenting a version of mythic perfection, associated with indigenous culture, and contrasting with the flow of chronological time that captures the bloody process of Mexican history. This technical virtuosity, resulting in the creation of powerful though passive female characters, also characterizes the two avant-garde novels of Chilean María Luisa Bombal, *La última niebla* (*The House of Mist*, 1935) and *La amortajada* (*The Shrouded Woman*, 1938). Like Garro, Bombal deconstructs reality as we know it, challenging realism, so that dream and consciousness merge in an atmospheric, lyrical, subjective vision of the world. For the women protagonists of Bombal's novels, life is death and death is liberation. *La amortajada*, for example, is narrated by a dead woman who is nevertheless fully aware of everything around her. Her memories, shaped by intuition and sensitivity, are woven into a self-reflective narrative in which she passes from the world of the living to that of the dead. She remembers above all her love–hate relationship with the man who attempted to annul her sense of self, her unfulfilled desires, and a longing for freedom which can only be articulated as such as she exits life.

Woman-centered experimental fiction or anti-novels were important in Argentina (Norah Lange), Venezuela (Teresa de la Parra), and Brazil (Nélida Piñón). Teresa de la Parra's *Ifigenia: diario de una señorita que escribió porque se fastidiaba* (*Iphigenia: the Diary of a Young Lady who Wrote Because She Was Bored*, 1924), a poetic account of the attempts of a woman to find herself through self-reflection, was followed by the delightful *Las memorias de Mamá Blanca* (*Mamá Blanca's Souvenirs*, 1929), the fictional memoirs of a girl growing up on a rural estate under the rod of a tyrannical father from whom she eventually breaks free. The genre was developed to new depths of subjective exploration and stylistic innovation in the work of Brazilian novelist Clarice Lispector, who published her first novel *Perto do coraçao selvagem* (*Near to the Wild Heart*) in 1944. Lispector's obsession with inner states, pieced together in broken, abstract language, underlines (like Bombal) the impossibility of coherent communication in life. Her masterpiece, *A paixão segundo G.H.* (*The Passion According to G.H.*, 1964), in which the female protagonist G.H. engages in a conversation with an unidentified interlocutor and absorbs the other into the self by devouring a cockroach, was famously marked out as a model of *écriture féminine* by French feminist Hélène Cixous. Lispector's last novel, *A hora da estrela* (*The Hour of the Star*, 1977), written while she was dying, secured her an international following. Beautifully translated into English by Giovanni Pontiero and made into a film by Suzana Amaral (1986), this is the story of the hopelessly ignorant and inept Macabéa who wants to be a film star and is finally run over by a yellow Mercedes, killed by her boyfriend. Throughout the novel Macabéa, like the reader, tries to make sense of an uncomprehending and incomprehensible world. Again, poetic prose deconstructs the conventionally familiar, breaking down the barriers of gendered identities and narrative voices, making space for contradiction, meaninglessness, and silence and, like Garro and Bombal, privileging the semiotic. Lispector's novels were published in the period of the Boom and Post-Boom. Does she belong to either? In many ways this question is irrelevant, as her novels seem to be in dialogue with a woman's literary tradition which has, as we shall see, different priorities.

Rethinking traditions

If the Latin American novel written by women is studied as a literary tradition in its own right, what kind of conclusions may be reached? A brief discussion of this question follows, with reference to a representative selection of novels written by women from the 1840s until today. These novels are all very different and may be classified as sentimental, indigenous, avant-garde, neo-avant-garde, Boom, semi-autobiographical, and so on, but a number of gender-related common features do emerge. They all situate the action of the novel within the family and the domestic space, and they all bring to their readers' attention important, often controversial, social and economic issues. Such social concern might be for the slave (*Sab*), the Andean Indians (*Aves sin nido*), or the Mayan Indians (*Balún Canán*), or for all those oppressed by the Church, the military, and the state, particularly women (the novels of Poniatowska, Valenzuela, Esquivel, Allende, and Eltit). Even in the anti-novel *Jardín*, which also centers on the family and the domestic space, there is a deep concern for a woman's self-fulfillment in life. Most importantly, all these novels address such issues from a woman's point of view.

Sab (1841) by Cuban Gertrudis Gómez de Avellaneda is a feminist abolitionist novel and, as far as we know, the first of its kind published in the Spanish-speaking world; the only other antislavery novel written by a woman in Spanish (though less radical) was Juana Manso's *La Familia del comendador* ("The commander's family," 1854). There were many published by women in English and French. Gómez de Avellaneda was born in Cuba, a Spanish colony until 1898. It was only due to the fact that she and her family moved to Spain that she was able to publish the novel, in liberal Madrid, in 1841. The novel is set on a Cuban sugar estate owned by the distinguished Creole "de B" family. The family's mulatto slave, Sab, loves his white owner, Carlota, but his love is not reciprocated. Instead she makes a disastrous marriage to an Englishman who only wants her money. By the end of the novel all the characters are dead, except Carlota and her husband, who leave Cuba for Europe. The novel includes strong criticism of slavery, racial prejudice, and the subjection of women. As might be expected by its date of composition (1830s) this is a Romantic, sentimental romance, but the love story may be understood in terms of important economic considerations which center on a series of transactions, one of which is the exchange of Carlota herself (as a commodity) in marriage, and the transfer of Cuban wealth and property to capitalist speculators. The novel raises these key economic and political concerns from a moral perspective within the framework of the domestic sphere. The family "de B" represents colonial Cuba in the process of being sold off to Anglo-American commercial interests. All the characters are grouped into families: the "de B" family which includes Sab (Carlota's illegitimate cousin – the incest motif is important); the Otway family; and a third family comprising Sab's adoptive *mestizo* mother and brother. The space inscribed in the novel, then, is the traditional family circle of the white Cuban elite and other associated family dwellings: the beautiful country house, garden, and estate of the oligarchy; the town house of the foreign commercial classes, and the peasant shack. The old order, the Cuban rural home, is destroyed by modernity represented by global commerce. Its destruction symbolizes the demise of Cuba; there is no place for the younger generation, including the mulatto Sab, who might have represented a new Cuba founded on traditional family values and social justice.

This was a radical novel and could not have been published in slave-holding Cuba. Copies shipped to Cuba were confiscated and sent back to Cadiz. The novel did not make an impact or find a space in either the Cuban or Spanish literary canons. When Gómez de Avellaneda later became famous, as a poet and dramatist, she omitted the novel from her complete works and it was largely forgotten for over a hundred years and not translated into English until 1993. At the other end of the century, as we have seen, Matto's *Aves sin nido*, though widely read, was censored in a similar way. *Aves* is a realist, not a Romantic, novel informed by positivism, and whereas in *Sab* there is ambiguity as to the merits of commerce and progress, in *Aves* there is no doubt as to the desirability of modernity, associated here with the professional urban middle classes. Like *Sab*, the novel is set mainly in the countryside, in a small Andean town named Kíllac. Again, most of the action takes place in the domestic sphere: in the house belonging to newcomers, the progressive Marín family, the protagonists of the novel; in the luxurious home of governor Pancorbo, representing the corrupt old order, and in the Indian huts. The novel attacks and ridicules the rural oligarchy, the Church, the Judiciary, and the State, which are shown to be absolutely corrupt and evil. The victims of the novel are the Indians who are manipulated, abused, and brutalized by the white men in power. Like *Sab*, the plot centers on the fear of incest in the family. The two young lovers, Manuel and Marcela, want to marry but cannot because they share the same father: the local bishop. Matto's main target is the enforced celibacy of priests and the rampant sexual abuse of defenseless women representing, ultimately, corruption at all levels of civil society. The family, once again, stands for the nation as a whole. The middle-class family and their adopted Indian daughters cannot remain in the sierra and must return to Lima to survive. In the final chapters, fol-lowing the family's journey to the city, the setting switches from Kíllac to a train compartment and a modern hotel. The train, whose driver is North American, is derailed as it crosses a weak Peruvian bridge. But thanks to his ingenuity everyone survives and they are soon on their way. Modernity, driven by foreign investment, is shown to be risky when exported to Peru but absolutely necessary for progress in that it leads the enlightened away from the rural backwaters to the progressive urban coast. This urban/rural polarity is reinforced by a gender polarity between women and men. All the women are good irrespective of race and class; they embody the moral fiber of the nation. Like *Sab*, then, the novel emphasizes the centrality of domestic politics and morality in the national political economy.

Balún Canán (*The Nine Guardians*) published by Mexican author Rosario Castellanos in 1957, seventy years after *Aves*, also condemns the exploitation of the Indians, in this case the Maya-Quiché of Chiapas in southern Mexico. It is set, like *Sab*, in the "big house" of the landowners, the Argüello family, during the 1930s Tzeltal rebellion. This is a semi-autobiographical novel, referring to events occurring within the Castellanos household when Rosario was a child. The traditional Mexican family is shown to be not only dysfunctional (the tyrannical patriarch, César, bullies his wife and their two children, the anonymous girl-narrator and her brother) but also the seedbed of authoritarian rule in society at large. The gender discrimination and sexual abuse practiced by the white male oligarchy in the domestic space is extrapolated to all sectors of society leading to rigid social stratification, widespread racism, and class exploitation of both Indians and poorer whites. César's wife colludes with this regime and in her turn oppresses the children's Mayan *nana*, who also remains nameless. From the point of view of feminist criticism the most interesting parts of the novel are the two-thirds that are set in the home narrated from a young girl's first-person point of view; the central chapters revert to a more conventional realist perspective and the field of action extends to the ranch and other outdoor locations. Thus a clear distinction is set up between a more historical and purportedly objective account of events, and how these affect and are perceived subjectively by a girl socialized into subordination. As the daughter grows up she realizes the extent to which her family exploit the Indians. The strong bonds that tie her to the *nana* place her in the impossible position of wishing to identify across race and class with her non-biological indigenous mother. Unlike *Sab*, which never describes the inside of the slave quarters, *Balún Canán* includes scenes set in the Indians' miserable space where, it is confirmed, Indian women – dominated by white men and women and Indian men – are substantially more oppressed than the white women in the "big house"; the most badly treated character in the novel is the wife of the Indian Felipe. Although the outcome of the novel is pessimistic, woman-centered bonding is presented as a possible future solution to the intractable social problems of Mexico. As in *Aves*, the Catholic Church and its nefarious manipulation of women is a target of censure while progressive reform is associated with the city and the enlightened middle classes.

From the 1950s until the mid-1970s *Balún Canán*, although relatively successful, was considered, like *Aves*, another second-rate *indigenista* novel written by a woman. Castellanos herself was dissatisfied with the result and wrote a later version in a more conventional realist style, *Oficio de tinieblas* (1962). Thanks to several incisive studies, however (primarily by women critics), Balún Canán is now acclaimed as a profoundly subversive feminist-indigenous novel informed by Castellanos's feminist ideas expressed explicitly in her doctoral thesis on women's culture and in her short fiction, notably *Album de familia* (1971).

Another largely neglected Mexican novel, set this time in Mexico City in the 1940s, is *La "Flor de Lis"* (1988) by journalist Elena Poniatowska, better known for documentary novels and testimonios, such as *Hasta no verte, Jesús mío* (*Until We Meet Again*, 1969) and *La noche del Tlatelolco* (*Massacre in Mexico*, 1968). *La "Flor de Lis,"* like *Balún Canán*, is semi-autobiographical and related mainly in the first person through the eyes of a young girl, Mariana, who attempts to understand the world around her. The novel's setting is, again, the "big house," located not in rural Mexico but in the wealthy French quarter of the capital. Mariana's family, an offshoot of the French-Polish aristocracy, is representative of the *haute bourgeoisie* living in splendid elitist isolation. But the family is just as dysfunctional as the family in *Balún Canán*, not on account of a domineering father of the family (who, in this case, is weak and indecisive) but due to an aloof mother and an unscrupulous father of the Church. The main target of criticism therefore, as in Matto's and Castellanos's novels, is once again, the Catholic Church. *La "Flor de Lis"* shows how this corrupt institution manipulates and oppresses rich women highlighting especially the sexual transgressions of the clergy; the villain of the novel is Padre Teufel (meaning devil in German). Like her counterpart in *Balún Canán*, as Mariana grows up she becomes increasingly aware of the hypocrisy and social injustice perpetuated by the class to which she belongs but is powerless to effect change. *La "Flor de Lis"* and *Balún Canán* are Mexican novels of *concienciación* that trace a growing feminist critical awareness grounded in personal experience; in fact, both authors went on to address social injustice later in life and took active parts in social reform. Reminiscent of the avant-garde novels mentioned previously, *La "Flor de Lis"* is written in an idiosyncratic style, comprising disconnected fragments of hauntingly evocative poetic prose. Yet it has still not been translated into English and is seldom studied in literary histories of the Latin America novel.

Jardín (1951) by Cuban author Dulce María Loynaz was also largely ignored, for some forty years, perhaps because Loynaz, like Poniatowska, was identified with the white elite or because her novel also displays stylistic experimentation (the novel was finished in 1933). In addition *Jardín* does not raise any obvious social problems, other than the utter dereliction of an individual woman. None of these factors would have made it acceptable to the post-revolutionary Cuban literary establishment, but its neglect elsewhere is nevertheless surprising. This is a poetic Gothic novel located, as expected, in a "big house" and its garden. Like La "Flor de Lis" and Balún Canán, it is semi-autobiographical narrated in the first person from a young woman's point of view. The house, modeled on one Loynaz knew as a child, is situated in the elegant Vedado district of Havana with a huge wild garden running down to the sea. The strange, psychological plot involves a girl, but it is difficult to explain what happens exactly. The protagonist belongs to a family, although their existence is only vaguely felt in the novel – there are no tyrannical parents or exploited servants. Usually alone in the house or the garden, in dialogue with the past and the future, the garden, perceived as a living, threatening presence throughout her life, finally devours or strangles her. It is as if she were suffocated by her very family roots. On one level Jardín is a love story, culminating in an encounter with a ghost from the past. But in the middle section the protagonist leaves the self-imposed confines of domestic space and travels round the world with a sea captain. The episode is rendered as a short flirtation with modernity, a temporary escape from self-absorption. Inevitably, however, the ghost pulls her back to the garden. There is no escape from this menacing male presence which possesses her and to which she is fatefully attracted. It functions as the male other which absorbs the female self, obviating the development of female subjectivity. While in other novels of the period written by men, such as Rivera's La vorágine (The Vortex, 1924) and Gallegos's Doña Bárbara (1929) in which the characters, male and female, are devoured by the vast South American landscapes, the jungle and the plains, in Jardín it is an overgrown garden, jungle-like but bounded, that functions in the same way. Jardín has not yet been translated into English and it is only since Loynaz was awarded the Cervantes Prize for literature in 1992 (at the age of ninety) that her works, including Jardín, have been published in modern editions which are now finding a place in the Cuban literary canon. There are clear links between this novel, with its interrogation of inner states, psychological and existential processes, and those mentioned previously by Garro, Bombal, and Lispector. Together they represent the carefully crafted writerly novel continued, as we shall see, in the work of Luisa Valenzuela and Diamela Eltit among others.

Moving to the contemporary scene, many recently published novels by women share the characteristics noted so far. Laura Esquivel's Como agua para chocolate (Like Water for Chocolate, 1989), adapted to film in 1993 by Alfonso Arau (to whom she was married), is a Mexican bestseller. Set in the "big house," on a ranch in revolutionary Mexico, it centers on a traditional landowning family in which the youngest daughter, Tita, is expected to remain single to look after her mother. She rebels when she falls in love, and thus begins a love story which follows the formula of sentimental romance. For this reason, unlike Castellanos's and Poniatowska's novels, *Como agua para chocolate* is light-hearted, humorous, and deliciously ironic. It is lifted out of its violent historical context by episodes of hyperbolic magical realism and immerses the reader in the world of women, using food and cookery, literally and metaphorically, as an unspoken form of communication in a censored environment. Tita uses the gender role forced on her against itself, to subvert the old order from within. In the end, though, like Bombal's heroines, her self-fulfillment is only possible in death. Isabel Allende's first novel, *Casa de los espíritus* (*The House of the Spirits*, 1982), as the title indicates, was set in a Chilean "big house," the home of authoritarian patriarch Esteban Trueba, who, like César Argüello before him, attempts to control the women of his domestic fiefdom. But here the women resist and forge an alternative way of being by rejecting the values associated with the masculinity Trueba upholds. Their nonconformism in the domestic space spreads out to encompass the police state. *Casa de los espíritus* clearly continues in the woman-centered novel tradition discussed above: it is set in the home, focuses on the lives of women, raises controversial social and political questions, and is told by the female protagonist. However, a shift in this pattern may be detected from the mid-1980s.

In Allende's second novel, *De amor y de sombra* (*Of Love and Shadows*, 1984), the domestic space is left behind. The heroine's house and family are important, but more significant are her trips on a motorbike with her boyfriend, to the countryside, to the caves of Lonquén where she discovers the bodies of the "disappeared" killed by the military. The protagonist, Irene (signifying "peace"), is no longer constrained by the family. She is a professional journalist, controls her life, and is politically involved. This pattern, where the strong female heroine carves out a space for herself, and hence for the novel, is developed in *Hija de la fortuna* (*Daughter of Fortune*, 1999). Allende, who now lives in the United States, is without doubt the most successful bestselling woman novelist writing in Spanish of all time. She is a celebrity and a millionaire. Bookshops all over the world display copies of her novels. *Hija de la fortuna*, published in Barcelona by Plaza y Janés, was translated into Danish, Portuguese, French, Dutch, German, and Italian. *Casa de los espíritus* was translated to many languages including Czech, Farsi, Finnish, Hebrew, Hungarian, Japanese, Norwegian, and Turkish. *Hija de la fortuna* is featured on the Internet, with links to reviews, discussion questions, and an interview with the author. This is the face of twenty-first century globalization: the publishing industry advertises a novel as a commodity for purchase, consumption and, once used, for

disposal. To be profitable, Plaza y Janés, at the time one of the two most powerful publishing houses in Spain (the other being Planeta), needed to market
multinationally, targeting Mexico, Chile, and of course the USA. *Hija de la
fortuna*, an adventure story appealing to Chilean, English, and US readers
(especially Hispanics and Chinese-Americans in California), fits this commercial bill. Moreover, its strong feminist protagonists appeal to women across
the world. The most striking aspect of this novel is that the female protagonist Eliza does not remain at home but travels across the Americas, from
Chile to California. In a way, her traveling mirrors the international public
space increasingly occupied by several Latin American women novelists. The
phenomenon is recent, post-1980, and parallels the development of gender
studies and feminist criticism. These novels, upbeat sentimental romance for
the modern woman, clearly create and meet popular demand. The formula is
successful: a blend of love and politics from a woman's perspective coupled
with semi-exoticism and easy reading.

The novels of Diamela Eltit, Allende's Chilean contemporary, could
not be more different. These are challenging, experimental works for an
elitist public, yet Eltit is also a bestselling author. Unlike Allende, Eltit
did not leave Chile during the horrific Pinochet regime. Her first novel,
Lumpérica (E. *Luminata*, 1983), written in powerfully surreal poetic prose,
sold 7,500 copies, and its second and third editions were published by
Planeta. *Lumpérica* radically breaks with the parameters noted above in
relation to novels written by women. There is an anonymous female protagonist, but she has no home, house, or family. She is placed instead, alone and
at night, in a park, a kind of wasteland or concentration camp where she is
observed by spectral figures and an illuminated advertisement. The family
patriarch has been replaced by an all-powerful "big-brother" whose ubiquitous presence is felt at all times. Unlike Allende's characters, this woman does
not travel. Instead she is trapped and, apparently, tortured; her words are
incoherent. There is no clear plot. Eltit and *Lumpérica* are closely associated
with the Chilean neo-avant-garde, and there are many points of comparison
with the novels of Garro, Loynaz, Bombal, and Lispector mentioned above
which inscribe not only the socialization of women into gender roles but also
articulate the emergence of frustrated female subjectivity through stream-
of-consciousness and other disruptive techniques privileging psychological
insight. These novels interrogate the very concepts "man" and "woman,"
separating the biological body from consciousness, and communicating the
violence that the imposition of gendered identities produces in the human
psyche. In Eltit's *El Cuarto Mundo* (*The Fourth World*, 1988), for example,
the narrators are a boy with a girl's name, María Chipia, and his twin sister.
The novel is set in a dysfunctional family and the boy never manages to

develop a sense of who he is. But Eltit probes even further; a large portion of the novel takes place not in the family as such but inside the mother's womb. The unborn boy narrates these parts too; he is a speaking embryo – in fact, he speaks even before he is conceived.

In Argentina, Luisa Valenzuela pursued a similar narrative strategy during the "Dirty War." Her multilayered anti-novels explore the power of language to engender identities and impose social control. The experimental prose of *El gato eficaz* ("The Efficient Cat," 1972), connecting women to cats and language, was intensified in the overtly political novel *Cola de lagartija* (*The Lizard's Tail*, 1983). This novel ridicules a former government minister (under Isabel Perón in the mid-1970s) who is shown to be so full of his own self-importance that he literally implodes. Related by the fictionalized Valenzuela, the novel intertwines myth and history, memory, imagination, and social commentary in highly inventive language, demonstrating that avant-garde techniques can be as politically subversive as realism.

It could be said that the two Chilean authors, Allende and Eltit, represent the extreme polarities of women's novel writing in Latin America today: popular/historical romance on the one hand, and neo-avant-garde exper-imentation on the other. Together they provide a two-pronged attack on patrocentric political oppression, especially that of the violent military state. Cultural critic Jean Franco shows how bestsellers employ romance (either "art romance" or the popular romance of the Mills and Boon/Harlequin variety), while neo-avant-garde novels reject the manipulative techniques of romance, according to which women achieve power by means of seduc-tion and guilt: romance "reproduces the seduction of commodity culture under neo-liberalism."[5] Market values and concepts such as "nation" and "community" may be challenged only by repoliticizing the esthetic. What needs to be exposed is the way gender is implicated in social control, how power and rights intersect with masculinity and femininity. For Franco, the women writers of the neo-avant-garde position themselves at the limits of the gender system, so that their work fragments rational narrative into the language of the marginalized, "women, the mad, the outcast, or the child."[6] Franco, quoting Chilean cultural theorist Nelly Richard, refers to this as the "refractory aesthetic."

Yet the Latin American bestsellers, like the sentimental novels before them, are not entirely collusive: they are also powerful texts which move readers on social and political issues. One of the most distinctive sub-genres in Latin American women's novel writing is the political love story. As this brief overview has shown, Allende's novels are the latest versions of a long Latin American sentimental-romance tradition: romance set in a political context to gain readers and raise awareness. Women writers in nineteenth-century

Latin America employed this strategy to encourage readers to empathize with the marginalized: the slave, the Indian, the poor. They too challenged public-centered liberal thought by giving voice to those excluded from the nation-state. The shift from sentimental romance to bestseller over 150 years mirrors the process of modernization in Latin America from the emergence of a market economy to global capitalism. But to what extent can the novel-commodity undercut the global market it sustains? Unlike the early novels, today's bestsellers are themselves a central component of the global market economy, and even if they partially subvert this system's social organization of sexual difference by questioning gender roles, unless they adopt disruptive techniques they do not get to grips with the more crucial concern, the psychosexual constitution of the gendered subject through language.

NOTES

1. "La inteligente escritora educacionista Miss Hudson," Clorinda Matto de Turner, *Viaje de recreo: España, Francia, Inglaterra, Italia, Suiza, Alemania* (F. Sempere: Valencia, 1909), p. 109.
2. Efraín Kristal, *The Andes Viewed from the City: Literary and Political Discourse on the Indian in Peru 1848–1930* (New York: Peter Lang, 1987), pp. 93–126.
3. Ibid., p. 160.
4. Antonio Cornejo Polar, *Literatura y Sociedad en el Perú. La novela indigenista* (Lima: Lasontay, 1980), p. 39. This view was repeated in the "Foreword" to John H. R. Polt's translation of the novel, *Torn From the Nest* (Oxford: Oxford University Press, 1998), p. xxxix.
5. Jean Franco, "Afterword: From Romance to Refractory Aesthetic," in Anny Brooksbank Jones and Catherine Davies (eds.), *Latin American Women's Writing* (Oxford: Oxford University Press, 1996), p. 228.
6. Ibid., p. 236.

FURTHER READING

Bassnett, Susan (ed.), *Knives and Angels: Women Writers in Latin America*. London and New Jersey: Zed, 1990.
Biron, Rebecca, *Murder and Masculinity: Violent Fictions of Twentieth-Century Latin America*, Nashville: Vanderbilt University Press, 2001.
Brooksbank Jones, Anny and Catherine Davies (eds.), *Latin American Women's Writing: Feminist Readings in Crisis and Theory*, Oxford: Oxford University Press, 1996.
Castillo, Debra, *Talking Back: Toward a Latin American Feminist Criticism*, Ithaca: Cornell University Press, 1992.
Davies, Catherine, *A Place in the Sun?: Women Writers in Twentieth-Century Cuba*. London and New Jersey: Zed, 1997.
Forastelli, Fabrizio and Ximena Triquell (eds.), *Las marcas del género: configuraciones de la diferencia en la cultura*, Córdoba, Argentina: Universidad Nacional de Córdoba, 1999.

Franco, Jean, *Plotting Women: Gender and Authority in Mexico: 1650–1970*, New York: Columbia University Press, 1989.

Guerra Cunningham, Lucia, *Splintering Darkness: Latin American Women Writers in Search of Themselves*, Pittsburgh: Latin American Literary Review Press, 1990.

Kaminsky, Amy, *Reading the Body Politic: Feminist Criticism and Latin American Women Writers*, Minneapolis: University of Minnesota Press, 1993.

Kantaris, E. G., *The Subversive Psyche: Contemporary Women's Narrative from Argentina and Uruguay*, Oxford: Oxford University Press, 1996.

Marting, Diane E., *The Sexual Woman in Latin American Literature: Dangerous Desires*, Miami: University Press of Florida, 2001.

(ed.) *Women Writers of Spanish America: An Annotated Bio-Bibliographical Guide*. Westport, Conn.: Greenwood Press, 1987.

(ed.), *Escritoras de Hispanoamérica: Una guía bio-bibliográfica*, Mexico City: Siglo XXI, 1990.

Masiello, Francine, *Between Civilization and Barbarism: Women, Nation and Literary Culture in Modern Argentina*, Lincoln and London: University of Nebraska Press, 1992.

Medeiros-Lichem, Maria Teresa, *Reading the Feminine Voice in Latin American Women's Fiction from Teresa de la Parra to Elena Poniatowska and Luisa Valenzuela*, New York: Peter Lang, 2002.

Mercado, Tununa, *In a State of Memory (Latin American Women Writers)*, trans. Peter Kahn, intr. Jean Franco, Lincoln and London: University Press of Nebraska, 2001.

Quinlan, Susan C., *The Feminine Voice in Contemporary Brazilian Narrative*, New York: Peter Lang, 1991.

Sommer, Doris, *Foundational Fictions: The National Romances of Latin America*, Berkeley and Los Angeles: University of California Press, 1991.

Vidal, Hernán, *Cultural and Historical Grounding for Hispanic and Luzo-Brazilian Feminist Literary Criticism*, Minneapolis: Institute for the Study of Ideologies and Literature, 1989.

10

DANIEL BALDERSTON AND JOSÉ MARISTANY

The lesbian and gay novel
in Latin America

Literary tradition can be defined in terms of a select corpus of texts that have held meaning for readers and critics. In the case of a homoerotic tradition, it is worth reflecting on whether what is at stake is the mention of gay, lesbian, bisexual, or transgender practices in literature, whether the sexuality of the authors is central, whether the works are judged "authentic" (which for many signifies the presence of positive images), whether they express an esthetics that is in some sense "queer," whether they have some political content that ties them to programs of sexual liberation, and whether they are worth thinking about as works of literature. These questions are not even parallel to one another in terms of the semantic fields or epistemologies they invoke, so the difficulties of defining a tradition are obvious. Taking them one by one, then:

(1) Is it sufficient for there to be gay and lesbian "themes" in a novel to claim it for such a tradition? Works as diverse as Mario Vargas Llosa's *Los cachorros* (*The Cubs*, 1967), *Conversación en la Catedral* (*Conversation in the Cathedral*, 1969), and *Historia de Mayta* (*The Real Life of Alejandro Mayta*, 1984), Julio Cortázar's *Los premios* (*The Winners*, 1960) and Leonardo Padura's *Máscaras* ("Masks," 1996) have gay male characters, and Aluísio Azevedo's *O cortiço* (*A Brazilian Tenement*, 1890), Juan Carlos Onetti's *Dejemos hablar al viento* (*Let the Wind Speak*, 1979), and Rosario Castellanos's *Album de familia* ("Family album," 1971) have lesbian characters, but it is our contention that this is not sufficient to define these works as part of a Latin American homoerotic tradition, at least in the terms that we will be setting out here. Although these works are certainly fertile ground for queer readings, there has not been a sustained tradition of critical readings of them in terms of their representation of lesbian and gay lives, and they have not been claimed for a homoerotic tradition in the same way that, say, José Donoso's *El lugar sin límites* (*Hell Has No Limits*, 1966), Manuel Puig's *La traición de Rita Hayworth* (*Betrayed by Rita Hayworth*, 1968), or Sylvia Molloy's *En breve cárcel* (*Certificate of Absence*, 1981) have. We

therefore respectfully disagree with David William Foster who, in a series of important collections on gay and lesbian writing in Latin America, sees the presence of such "themes" as crucial to the definition of a corpus. While it is true that there are numerous works by Vargas Llosa that treat these themes, something about that treatment has repelled a gay and lesbian readership. *Historia de Mayta*, for instance, posits Mayta's sexuality, at least until the last chapter of the novel, as a dirty secret, fascinating in a voyeuristic sense, and it is allied with Mayta's revolutionary practice in an ambivalent way; the narrator is perhaps slightly more sympathetic to Mayta's sexual quandary than to his political beliefs, but ultimately the novel functions as a damning critique of Mayta, at least in his politics. In contrast, a novel in which the gender (and perhaps sexual) identity of one of the main characters is a secret for most of the text, João Guimarães Rosa's *Grande sertão: veredas* (*The Devil to Pay in the Backlands*, 1956) narrates this sexual and gender ambiguity in a sympathetic way that brings the reader in.

Another way of saying this is that some of the works mentioned above have gay male and lesbian characters whose identities are fixed, and who therefore are usually relegated to secondary roles, whereas the works that have often been read as providing a seductive or mobile view of homoerotic desire (and this would include such characters as Donoso's Manuela in *El lugar sin límites*, Puig's Molina in *El beso de la mujer araña* (*Kiss of the Spider Woman*), and Guimarães Rosa's Diadorim (in *Grande sertão*) resist this fixity. This clarifies the problem in Cortázar, Onetti, and Vargas Llosa: the gay characters in their work are objects of fascination for the protagonists, but are not the protagonists themselves. E. M. Forster's distinction (in *Aspects of the Novel*) between "flat" and "round" characters is helpful here, since the protagonists or narrators of these novels define themselves (in their psychological complexity) by contrast to the stock background characters, even when these are as important for the works as the lesbian Frieda is for Onetti in *Dejemos hablar al viento* or the tortured homosexual revolutionary Mayta is for Vargas Llosa. That is to say, the "marginal" characters serve to shore up the "normative" quality of the main characters; homosexuality, as happened in the history of psychology in the nineteenth century, begets heterosexuality.

(2) Is the sexuality of the author key to the delineation of a lesbian and gay literary tradition? If not, why not? The problem here is multiple. There are authors about whose sexuality we know quite a lot (e.g. Virgilio Piñera), whose work rarely concerns gay and lesbian "themes," and authors about whose sexuality we know little (e.g. Carlos Montenegro or João Guimarães Rosa), whose works are rich in these themes. For reading *El lugar sin límites* it seems less important to know whether or not Donoso had homosexual

experiences (although he did), and certainly not whether he was the transvestite madam of a provincial Chilean brothel, than with analyzing the ways in which his portrayal of the sexuality of La Manuela is complex and absolutely central to the narrative. For whatever biographical reason, Donoso in his literary work focuses on marginal characters whose marginality is very revealing of the society in which they live (this would be true also in a very different sense of *El obsceno pájaro de la noche* [*The Obscene Bird of Night*, 1970]), and his work "queers" Chilean society and family relations even when its main theme is not sexuality.

It is also worth remarking here on the importance of narrative works that tell of a sexuality that is different from the author's. Cristina Peri Rossi is not a heterosexual man, nor is Sylvia Molloy a gay Argentine-American man, nor is Manuel Puig a lesbian, yet their respective *Solitario de amor* (*Solitaire of Love*, 1999), *El común olvido* ("Common oblivion," 2002), and *Pubis angelical* (*Pubis Angelical*, 1996) foreground these varieties of sexual experience.

(3) In feminist literary criticism it has been posited that there is such a thing as "écriture feminine," with important theorists like Hélène Cixous insisting that there is an essence, a sensibility that informs women's writing. (Many feminist critics disagree, however.) Could such a thing as gay, lesbian, or queer writing exist? If so, what would characterize it?

Some critics of gay male writing have seen camp as an esthetics, even a tradition, that informs a significant body of texts. Certainly in Latin America one can find a camp esthetics in such writers as Manuel Puig, Severo Sarduy, and Luis Zapata. And certainly Sylvia Molloy's *En breve cárcel* works with familiar motifs of "écriture feminine" such as interiority, closed spaces, and a mixing of experience, desire, and memory. Such examples do not exhaust the range of gay and lesbian writing, however. A "queer" esthetics, which is much more difficult to define, seems to play with gender categories in a freer way.

(4) Is there a need for a gay and lesbian literary work to have some political dimension, to appeal to an "imagined community"? It could be argued that works after 1970 or so treat gay, lesbian, bisexual, and transgender identities in a rather different way from works before that time, and that the social and political context is crucial in defining that difference. In that sense there is a difference between, say, Puig's *El beso de la mujer araña* (1976) and D'Halmar's *Pasión y muerte del cura Deusto* ("The passion and death of Father Deusto," 1924), or between Senel Paz's *El lobo, el bosque y el hombre nuevo* (*Strawberry and Chocolate*, 1991) and Lezama's *Paradiso* (*Paradiso*, 1966), or between Sylvia Molloy's *En breve cárcel* (1981) and Ofelia Rodríguez Acosta's *La vida manda* ("Life commands," 1929).

The possibility of appealing to a collective identity known to the readership is very different in 1990 from what it was in 1924 or even in 1966. The movements of women's liberation and of lesbian and gay liberation that begin in Latin America in the 1970s created new collective subjects, and related liberation struggles of different kinds to one another. The interesting thing about many of the literary works that can be claimed for a homoerotic tradition from the 1970s to the present is precisely that they do not work with categories of sexual identity alone or in isolation; questions of gender, race, class, ethnicity, and religious identity are often intertwined with the affirmation of gay, lesbian, bisexual, and transgender identities, and these many categories of identity are subjected to radical critique. A work like the Mexican-Peruvian novelist Mario Bellatín's *Salón de belleza* ("Beauty parlor," 1999) says as much about poverty, access to public institutions of health care, and the market for transvestite prostitutes as it does about AIDS, and the power of the text turns on its radical critique of gender identity.

We should also emphasize the relation between this literary corpus and lesbian and gay movements in Latin America. These movements, beginning in the early 1970s, echoed liberationist ideas that came from the United States after the Stonewall rebellion of 1969 and also the rather different formulation of liberationist ideas that came from Europe (Hocquenghem and Melli), especially the French "homosexual liberation front," whose name was echoed in the names of liberation groups in Argentina, Mexico, and Brazil. Manuel Puig's interest in liberationist practices is obvious in the footnotes to *El beso de la mujer araña*, and certainly one cannot read the works of Darcy Penteado, João Silvério Trevisan, Aguinaldo Silva, and Caio Fernando Abreu without taking into account the presence of gay liberationist ideas that were bravely asserted during the Brazilian military dictatorship. Similarly, the richness of gay and lesbian literature in Mexico (Zapata, Blanco, Monsiváis, Calva) is tied to the robust quality of the liberationist groups from 1975 on, and certainly a survey of lesbian culture in Mexico today cannot ignore the political dimension of the work of Jesusa Rodríguez and Liliana Felipe.

In what follows we will reflect on a variety of literary works that form parts of a lesbian and gay tradition in the Latin American novel; we will refer to more gay male than lesbian examples because they are more numerous. We will group these novels loosely in three stages, not because there is any rigid periodization (in fact, there is considerable overlap among the stages) but to make sense of the configuration of "theme," authorship, readership, and community, a configuration that changes with the emergence of gay and lesbian collective identities. We define these stages as:

1) the gay and lesbian as other, set in scenes dominated by discourses of the nation, science and law, often viewed through the lens of the "decadence" of a social class or as social or psychological pathology,

2) the estheticizing of homosexuality, with the homosexual posited as heir of the humanist tradition (Wilde and Gide), and the emergence of a homosexual subject without overt consciousness of community, and

3) the emergence of a lesbian and gay political subject concerned with the creation of a community and acting as an agent of social change, and the widening of definitions of queer subjects to include bisexuals, transgender people, transsexuals and even a queering of heterosexuality.

Important critical work has been done in the last few years to recuperate a series of literary texts that were somehow isolated in their moment and in their national tradition but that now, in retrospect, can be linked together. The earliest work of this kind that has drawn attention is Raúl Pompéia's O Ateneu ("The Athenaeum"), a *Bildungsroman* published in 1888 that describes a variety of perversions, including male homosexuality, to attack the false aristocratic culture of the late Brazilian empire; selections from this work were included by Winston Leyland in *My Deep Dark Pain Is Love* (1983), the second anthology of Latin American gay writing published by Gay Sunshine Press.[1] Another key early text is Adolfo Caminha's 1895 novel *Bom Crioulo* ("Bom Crioulo: the black man and the cabin boy") which describes the love between a black ex-slave and a much younger white cabin boy, a love that begins on shipboard and ends tragically on a street in Rio de Janeiro. Like *O Ateneu*, the Caminha novel is critical of the decadence of the old aristocracy in Brazil and uses homosexuality (as well as race) to describe social conflict that the new Brazil needs to overcome. What is different about *Bom Crioulo* is that the love between the two protagonists constitutes the center of the narrative intrigue and that a whole "sex gender system" (including anxieties about male passivity and female activity) is invoked. Caminha, like his contemporary Aluísio Azevedo, is inspired by Zola's naturalism, which proposes to cast a clinical eye on the ills of a society; the narrative voice, while sympathetic to the characters, is ultimately concerned with a national pathology. In addition, the relation between Aleixo and Amaro rehearses familiar tropes of heterosexuality (particularly in its insistence on Aleixo's "passivity"), though oddly the subsequent relations between Aleixo and Carolina (a "heterosexual" relationship) turns these stereotypes on end by making Carolina an aggressive, even a butch, character.

In Spanish America the works that have drawn most attention are from a slightly later period, from 1910 to 1940. Besides the long short story

"El hombre que parecía un caballo" ("The man who looked like a horse"), written by the Guatemalan Rafael Arévalo Martínez about the Colombian poet Porfirio Barba Jacob in 1915, a crucial work is Augusto D'Halmar's *Pasión y muerte del cura Deusto*, a novel that the Chilean sets in Seville. As Sylvia Molloy has argued in a recent article,[2] the exoticism of the Andalusian milieu serves not only to free the Basque priest's sensuality but also to provide a safe distance for the Latin American reader to imagine a different, even a "Mediterranean," sexuality, embodied in D'Halmar's novel in the gypsy altar boy, part of a world that the Basque priest finds exotic and enticing. Like Anna Karenina, he will die a suicide, killed by the train that is carrying his beloved to Madrid.

There are also several Cuban works from this period that are of interest: Alfonso Hernández Catá's *El ángel de Sodoma* ("The angel of Sodom," 1928), Ofelia Rodríguez Acosta's *La vida manda* (1929), and Carlos Montenegro's *Hombres sin mujer* ("Men without women," 1935). The Hernández Catá novel tells of the "difference" of José-María Vélez-Gomarra, the male protagonist (who ends a suicide, like Father Deusto), a melancholic victim of family expectations who falls into a chaste love for a male trapeze artist; the preface to the novel by the Spanish physician and essayist Gregorio Marañón emphasizes the pathological aspects of the world revealed by the novelist and asserts that social progress needs to take such pathologies seriously. Rodríguez Acosta's *La vida manda* purports to be about the subjugation of women in marriage and patriarchy but, interestingly, includes a Platonic lesbian subplot that seems to offer other possibilities before being closed off by the homosexual panic of one of the female protagonists. Montenegro's *Hombres sin mujer*, set in a Cuban prison like the one where Montenegro spent several years, concerns a black prisoner, Pascasio, and a white one, Andresito Pinel, whose love is tested by the warden's interest in Andresito. The warden punishes Pascasio to get him out of the way, and when Andresito, concerned about Pascasio, gives in to the warden, he sets in motion Pascasio's jealousy which will end with Andresito being murdered by Pascasio. Rodríguez Acosta and Montenegro include homosexual plots as part of a larger concern with oppression in Cuban society; important recent analyses of these works have been written by Nina Menéndez and Emilio Bejel.

In a second stage, we see the emergence of the gay and lesbian as esthetic objects, and of a complex coding of a minority gay and lesbian culture. The example par excellence of this stage is José Lezama Lima's *Paradiso* (1966), in which there is a defense of a homoerotic tradition in Western culture as part of a bohemian esthetic and of the invention of a spiritualized poetic tradition. José Cemí, the protagonist of Lezama's novel (based clearly on elements of Lezama's early life and the history of his family, as has been explored in the criticism), joins a group of radical esthetes at the university, which includes his two closest friends, Foción and Fronesis. In the famous ninth chapter there is a neo-Platonic dialogue on the importance of gay love (which Lezama considers part of an "hipertelia de la inmortalidad," something like Wordsworth's "intimations of immortality"), which complements a series of sexual discoveries in the eighth chapter. Of the three friends only Foción is defined as a gay character, and he (like the heroes of many of the earlier novels we have discussed) ends up committing suicide, a nihilist act forced at least in part by his unconsummated love for Fronesis; nevertheless, the dialogue in the ninth chapter is echoed in many later works of Cuban (and more broadly of Latin American) literature. What is of interest here is not to claim *Paradiso* as totally, or even mostly, a gay novel; it is instead the way in which the "type" of the gay esthete is transformative of the whole world of the novel, and informs Cemí's development even if his maturing does not seem to have a homosexual identity as its teleology. Literary vocation, and the spiritualizing lessons of poetry, are bound up for Lezama with the homoerotic, however these may inform lived experience. Lezama's dense neo-baroque prose would also prove highly influential on many later writers, and for some would seem to condense a "gay" or "queer" style in Latin America: see, for instance, later works of Sarduy, Senel Paz, and Pedro de Jesús, among others.

A complementary example of a gay esthetics is Lúcio Cardoso's final literary work *Crônica da casa assassinada* ("Chronicle of an assassinated home," 1959). A novel of existential anguish and bourgeois decadence, centered on a series of diaries including that of a gay character, *Crônica* is a complex novel in which the homoerotic elements are part of the estheticizing of loss and nostalgia. Celebrated by recent critics such as Mário Carelli and Severino Albuquerque (the latter also noting tantalizing connections between the works of Cardoso and that of his close friend Clarice Lispector, the most important woman writer in modern Brazil), Cardoso views sexual difference as a component of the struggle for artistic creativity; in this sense he queers the Brazilian literary tradition of the mid-twentieth century.

Other works that could be connected with this estheticizing of gay experience are Virgilio Piñera's *La carne de René* (*René's Flesh*, 1952) and many of the works of Manuel Mujica Láinez. Piñera's work includes a homoerotic sensuality (heroically resisted by René, the protagonist) as part of a "religion of the flesh," a sharp (and sometimes campy) parody of Catholicism with its plethora of martyrs; José Quiroga has argued that the scene of the "softening of René's flesh" is the most erotic in Cuban literature. Mujica Láinez, who in his public life cultivated a dandy image, even dressing in imitation of Marcel Proust (captured in a photograph in Herbert Craig's book *Marcel Proust and Spanish American Literature*), was Argentina's ultimate esthete, writing in flowery language about the mysteries of artistic creation. His fiction often includes implicit homoerotic impulses and situations, though these are somewhat obscured by a focus on tormented characters who exemplify the decadence of a local aristocracy. Gay characters in Mujica Láinez are sensitive flowers of these aristocracies, strongly attached to European (especially French) culture; their desires are sublimated through cultural allusion. Another writer who deserves mention in this regard is José Bianco, whose two novellas, *Sombras suele vestir* (*Shadow Play*, 1941) and *Las ratas* (*The Rats*, 1943), and much later novel *La pérdida del reino* ("The loss of the Kingdom," 1972) are powerful examples of the esthetics of homoeroticism, though this is never made explicit. (Some of these elements are also present in the short stories of Bianco's friend Silvina Ocampo.) In Bianco's *Las ratas* the powerful scene that precedes the murder of the half-brother by the narrator includes an intensely erotic description of the half-brother's nude body; the murder bestows a mysterious power on the narrator, as if he had taken in some of the dead man's erotic aura. A younger writer with ties to Mujica Láinez, who wrote a biography of Mujica, a collective biography of the *Sur* group, and a memoir of childhood in northern Argentina, Oscar Hermes Villordo was famous in the period of the Argentine transition to democracy for his rather crude gay novel *La brasa en la mano* ("The ember in the hand," 1983), a celebration of furtive encounters in a repressed Buenos Aires. Another writer who uses homosexuality to evoke a world of conflict and decadence is Mauricio Wacquez, particularly in *Frente a un hombre armado: cacerías de 1848* ("In front of an armed man: hunts of 1848," 1981).

Severo Sarduy wrote his fiction after his exile from Cuba in 1960, especially after he became part of Roland Barthes's circle in Paris. Already in his second novel, *De donde son los cantantes* (*From Cuba with a Song*, 1967), there is a camp self-consciousness about the portrayal of gender, with biologically female characters acting the part of drag queens. His best-known novel *Cobra* (*Cobra*, 1972) is largely set in an Amsterdam peopled by transvestites, motorcycle gang members, and a variety of fetishists. In this novel Sarduy writes: "La escritura es el arte de la elipsis" (Writing is the art of ellipsis); his novel includes divagations on fashion, Buddhism, Forster's *The Passage to India*, and invented rituals, while evoking a mysterious sex change experienced by the protagonist. Sarduy's much later novel *Pájaros de la playa* ("Beach birds," 1993) is an allegory about AIDS presented once again through a spiritualizing language and a densely strange atmosphere; its influence can be felt later in Mario Bellatín's *Salón de belleza*.

Perhaps the richest of the texts of our second stage is José Donoso's 1966 novel *El lugar sin límites*, the account of the life and death of La Manuela, the transvestite co-owner of a bordello in a small town in Chile (perhaps the first novel that centers on questions of transgender). Narrated partly in interior monologues by La Manuela (who alternates masculine and feminine pronouns when speaking of him/herself), it recalls his arrival in Estación El Olivo as the young dancer who has been contracted to entertain the male population of the town in the company of several prostitutes including one known as La Japonesa Grande. The novel includes an extraordinary chapter in which La Manuela evokes the scene by which he became co-owner of the house of prostitution (sharing it with La Japonesa Grande) by winning a bet in which the owner of the town and the surrounding hacienda challenges him to make love to La Japonesa; she becomes pregnant and years later (after her death) the co-owner of the house is now La Manuela's frigid daughter La Japonesita (who is ashamed of her cross-dressing father). The plot turns on the sexual obsession with La Japonesita and La Manuela on the part of Pancho, a local truckdriver who is probably the illegitimate son of the local landowner; the novel ends in an orgy of homophobic violence. Many of Donoso's other works include scenes of sexual dissonance, from the hilarious bestiality of the *La misteriosa desaparición de la marquesita de Loria* ("The mysterious disappearance of the Marquise of Loria," 1980) to the bizarre scenes of blood transfusion in *El obsceno pájaro de la noche* to the sexual obsession with the androgynous figure in *El jardín de al lado* (*The Garden Next Door*, 1981). The center of many of Donoso's novels is a sexually attractive and ambiguous figure about whom there is woven a web of intrigue; this figure is isolated from the community but its life revolves around him or her.

In Manuel Puig's first novel, *La traición de Rita Hayworth*, this estheticizing of the homosexual continues to some extent, with the *Bildungsroman* format that narrates Toto's coming to artistic consciousness through daily excursions to the small town cinema with his mother, troubled relations with the macho bullies at school, and a conflictive relationship with his homophobic and anti-artistic father. Some of these elements are also present in his next two novels, *Boquitas pintadas* (*Heartbreak Tango*, 1969) and *The Buenos Aires Affair* (*The Buenos Aires Affair*, 1973). We consider, however, *El beso de la mujer araña* (1976) as the founding text of a post-Stonewall gay literature in Latin America. Explicitly focused on the political maturing of a gay man, Molina, and of the changing perspective of an imprisoned revolutionary, Valentín Arregui, who comes to see the place of sexual oppression in the society he is struggling to change, Puig's novel depends for its force on identity categories that it ultimately questions. As in Puig's earlier work, there is not a unifying narrative voice in *El beso*, which consists mostly of the dialogues between Molina and Valentín; in turn, these conversations are largely concerned with the narration, usually by Molina, of a series of films. Gender and sexuality are staged and analyzed in the two characters' conversations as they come to understand the other's worldview and to modify their own. The analytical undercurrent of the conversations is underscored in a series of footnotes in which Puig grapples with theories of sexuality and their relations to theories of social change; the synthesis of psychoanalytic and liberationist ideas on sexual oppression serves in counterpoint to elucidate the changes in the two characters in the prison cell. Elements of camp and melodrama are used to heighten the urgent search for a new and inclusive community. As Puig argues (in drag, in the final footnote), sexual liberation is part of a larger social transformation.[3] The novel exemplifies the connections made among struggles for liberation in the New Left and uniquely dramatizes those struggles in the prisonhouse dialogue. Puig's novel is arguably the first in which a gay character is given the status of a political subject, and in which the struggle for a new society explicitly includes a vision of the place of gay people in that society.

Sylvia Molloy's *En breve cárcel* (1981) is another landmark in the Latin American novel. An unnamed woman waits in an apartment and writes; she reflects on her past love for Vera and weaves in her present love for Renata; the writing and the incidents of the advancing story inform each other. An interior story, sometimes rather claustrophobic in its extreme interiority, Molloy's novel nevertheless tells of momentous incidents in the life of her protagonist. The lesbian context of the novel is central to the story, even as the protagonist explores the meaning of her relationships with her dead father and aunt, with her mother, with her sister. Minimalist, dense, intensely moving, *En breve cárcel* is the most important lesbian novel in Latin American literature to date.

Luis Zapata's *Las aventuras, desventuras y sueños de Adonis García, el vampiro de la colonia Roma* (*Adonis García: A Picaresque Novel*, 1979), while not the first Mexican novel that focused on a gay male character,[4] was the first one that was a popular success precisely because of its use of this theme in a new picaresque novel of marginal life in Mexico City, one of the great mega-cities of contemporary Latin America. Using the device of an interview with a male hustler, the Adonis of the title (a device linked to the testimonial genres of the time and to the new urban novel of Gustavo Sainz and others) tells the story of his sexual life. The silent interlocutor (who stands in for the reader and perhaps for the author) takes a voyeuristic interest in García's life but is also a potential victim of García's mischievous view of society, where the prostitute's clients only seemingly dictate the terms of the encounter, and where the hustler/narrator takes pleasure in the sexual commerce of which he forms part. It is this focus on the narrator's sexual pleasure that contrasts with earlier narratives of prostitution which so often cast the prostitute as victim, and are usually narrated from a dominant male perspective. García in contrast "feminizes" his clients, sometimes portraying them with gentle ridicule, and reveals that despite their economically dominant positions in society they often prefer to take a passive role in their relations with the hustler. At the same time, the hustler here clearly defines himself as a gay subject who is led into this "trade" not only by economic necessity but also by desire.

Zapata's later fiction explores other dimensions of gay life in Mexico, including the relation of gay men to their families (*Melodrama*, 1983), transsexual identities (*La hermana secreta de Angélica María*, "The secret sister of Angélica María," 1989), and extreme sexual obsession that verges on madness (*En jirones*, "In shreds," 1985). Zapata's contemporary José Rafael Calva also explores a wide variety of sexual experience including sadomasochism (*El jinete azul*, "The blue horseman," 1985) and gay male pregnancy (*Utopía gay*, 1983). Two important Mexican novels of lesbian life are Sara Levi Calderón's *Dos mujeres* (*The Two Mujeres*, 1990) and Rosamaría Roffiel's *Amora* (1989). *Dos mujeres* is concerned with the relationship between Genovesa, a painter, and Valeria, a writer, who defy the social expectations of their gender and class; it also explores the outsider status of Jewish lesbians in a mostly Catholic country, and the protagonists finally choose to migrate to the United States in search of a more accepting community. *Amora* is concerned with lesbian participants in several feminist groups who end up forming an alternative family; less concerned with the lesbian couple than Levi Calderón's novel, it is also more deeply concerned with the place of lesbian communities in the Mexican feminist movement. Deborah Shaw has questioned the literary value of both books, which she argues are rather simplistic in their portrayal of their main characters.[5]

Perhaps most famous at the moment because of his self-promoting myth as a gay Cuban martyr in the posthumous memoirs *Antes que anochezca* (English translation and subsequent film version by Julian Schnabel both entitled *Before Night Falls*, 1992), Reinaldo Arenas wrote a series of novels (which supposedly form a "Pentagony") that narrate aspects of the homosexual condition in a patriarchal Cuba before and after the revolution of 1959. The first novel, *Celestino antes del alba* (*Singing from the Well*, 1967), tells of the boy poet's coming of age in rural Cuba where he writes poems on trees and is brutalized by his male relatives; *Otra vez el mar* (*Farewell from the Sea: A Novel of Cuba*, 1982) is an anguished account of sexual obsession in the repressive atmosphere of the revolution; *El color del verano* (*The Color of Summer*, or *The New Garden of Earthly Delights*, 1991) narrates in fictional form some of the episodes of persecution and imprisonment that are also narrated in *Antes que anochezca*. The humorous novel *El mundo alucinante* (*Hallucinations: Being an Account of the Life and Adventures of*

Friar Servando Teresa de Mier) includes extravagant sexual scenes amidst religious and political persecution in the period of the Mexican struggle for independence.

Other gay novelists of note in recent years include the Puerto Rican Angel Lozada for *La patografía* ("Patography," 1998), the late Colombian writer Fernando Molano Vargas for *Un beso de Dick* ("A kiss from Dick," 1992), Colombian novelist Alonso Sánchez Baute for *Al diablo la maldita primavera* ("To hell with damned spring," 2003), and the Argentine journalist and novelist Osvaldo Bazán (*La más maravillosa música, una historia de amor peronista*, "The most beautiful music, a Peronist love-story," 2002). Brazilian writers of note who have written novels on gay themes are João Silvério Trevisan (*Vagas notícias de Melinha Marchiotti* ["Vague news of Melinha Marchiotti"], 1984 and *O livro do avesso* ["The book of the inversion"], 1992), Caio Fernando Abreu (numerous short stories, as well as the novella "O marinheiro" ["The sailor," 1983] and the novel *Morangos mofados* ["Spoiled strawberries," 1982]), João Gilberto Noll (*Bandoleiros*, 1988 and several subsequent novels), and Jean-Claude Bernardet (*Aquele rapaz*, "That boy," 1990). A novel that powerfully evokes the persecution of gay men in the Inquisition and the Cuban Revolution is Antonio José Ponte's *Contrabando de sombras* ("Smuggled shadows," 2002). Several other younger Cuban writers who have focused on gay and lesbian experience are Pedro de Jesús López Acosta (in his short stories *Cuentos frígidos* [Literally, "Frigid tales," but translated in English under the original Spanish title], but also in his novel *Sibilas en Mercaderes* ("Sibyl of Mercaderes," 1999), Jorge Angel Pérez in *El paseante Cándido* ("Strolling Candide," 2000), Ena Lucía Portela in *El pájaro: pincel y tinta china* ("The bird: paintbrush and Indian ink," 1999) and *La sombra del caminante* ("The shadow of the walker," 2001), and Abilio Estévez in *Tuyo es el reino* (*Thine Is the Kingdom*, 1997) and *Los palacios distantes* ("The distant palaces," 2002).

Although his work is extremely slight in volume, Senel Paz is known as the author of *El lobo, el bosque y el hombre nuevo* (*Strawberry and Chocolate*, 1991), later used by the Cuban director Tomás Gutiérrez Alea as the inspiration for the film *Fresa y chocolate* (and some later editions of the novella use *Fresa y chocolate* as their title instead of the rather clumsy original title). In Paz's novel, Diego, the gay character, has as his model the Lezamian dandy and explicitly reenacts scenes from *Paradiso* in his attempted seduction of the young communist David. Like Bazán's *La más maravillosa música* ("The most marvellous music," 2002) and Pedro Lemebel's *Tengo miedo torero* (*My Tender Matador*, 2001), the plot is derived from Puig's *El beso de la mujer araña* in that it focuses on a dialogue between a revolutionary and a homosexual. Filled with references to Cuban and international gay culture, the novella narrates the gay character's love of and alienation from Cuba, the revolutionary utopia that he ends up leaving. The novella is narrated by the young revolutionary David who evokes the memory of his now exiled friend as a fictional plea for reconciliation and tolerance. Paz's novella marks an attempt by a member of the post-revolutionary generation of writers to pay homage to crucial figures in Cuban culture (including Lezama) and to forge a reconciliation with Cuban gays (inside and outside of the island) who had been rejected by a homophobic revolutionary culture.

Silviano Santiago, best known outside Brazil as a literary and cultural critic, has published two novels, *Em liberdade* ("In liberty," 1982, a continuation of Graciliano Ramos's prison memoirs of 1953) and *Stella Manhattan* (1985, translated into English in 1994). The latter novel is focused on the life in New York City of a young gay Brazilian, Eduardo da Costa e Silva, who is working at the Brazilian consulate after his family decides that his life at home is scandalous. In New York he is a protégé of Coronel Valdevinos Vianna, an old friend of his father's who despite an ostensibly proper married life has a nocturnal double life as the leatherclad Black Widow (a Viúva Negra). Eduardo's explorations of life in Manhattan are fraught with danger, as he encounters a maniacal professor of Brazilian literature and a series of Brazilian graduate students who are linked to urban guerrilla groups in Brazil. Eduardo's death in jail covers for one of Vianna's nocturnal escapades; the novel ends with a sickening letter of condolence from Vianna and his wife to Eduardo's parents. Eduardo's explorations of gay life, and his imaginative doubling as the Stella Manhattan of the title, end tragically (as in earlier melodramas), though Santiago undoubtedly intends the tragedies to be viewed with a measure of camp humor.

Cristina Peri Rossi's most explicitly lesbian work is her early book of poetry *Evohé* (1971), and sexual obsession of every type is discussed in the essays of *Fantasías eróticas* (1991), but it is important to mention here the final chapter of *La nave de los locos* (*The Ship of Fools*, 1984) and the subsequent *Solitario de amor* (1988). *La nave de los locos*'s final chapter is a fantasized lesbian encounter between Marlene Dietrich and Mexican film star Dolores del Río (though Dietrich cultivated a lesbian persona, del Río did not, so the fantasized encounter is surprising). *Solitario de amor*, a tale of heterosexual obsession with a male narrator, has been read as a covert meditation on lesbian butch-femme relations, though Peri Rossi herself has refused to authorize this reading (for queer readings of her work see Martínez and Kaminsky). Another writer who has made an elliptical reference to lesbianism is María Moreno in her novel *El affair Skeffington* ("The Skeffington affair," 1992), the purported translation of materials by an English woman writer on the edge of the Bloomsbury group; Francine Masiello has discussed the significance of this novel in terms of the staging of a woman-centered literary tradition. Another writer who makes elliptical use of same-sex relations in a woman-centered world is the Colombian Albalucía Angel, particularly in *Estaba la pájara pinta sentada en el verde limón* ("The colored bird was sitting on a green lemon tree,"[6] 1975) and *Misiá señora* (1982).

Jaime Bayly, a Peruvian television personality and writer, became famous with the publication of *No se lo digas a nadie* (*Don't Tell Anyone*, 1994), a narrative focused on Joaquín, a gay *limeño* (details of whose life story are very close to Bayly's) who struggles to come to terms with his homosexuality in light of his tense relations with a womanizing, racist, and homophobic father and a devoutly Catholic mother who is part of the Opus Dei. Though the plotting is clumsy and the novel much too long, *No se lo digas a nadie* has won an audience with its attempts to capture a Lima vernacular, the experience of a yuppie youth culture, and its seeming frankness about the sexuality of the protagonist. At the same time, the novel is dedicated to Sandra, Bayly's wife, and the biographical note on the cover clarifies that Bayly is married and has a daughter: at least one could speak of a sales strategy that wants to have it both ways, with a photogenic and ostensibly straight author and a flamboyantly gay (and passive) protagonist. Bayly's subsequent career – he has published four more novels and a book of verse (one hesitates to call it poetry) – has continued to play on the angles that made *No se lo digas a nadie* famous (and eventually resulted in its transformation into a film), notably the tensions in the family (with parents, spouse, and daughters) brought about by the hero's unresolved sexual identity (or at least the unresolved relation between his public persona and his private identity or identities). Bayly himself is novelized as the narrator's love interest in Luis Corbacho's recent *Mi amado Mister B.* ("My beloved Mr. B.," 2004).

The great bulk of Fernando Vallejo's work is autobiographical, especially the massive series of *El río del tiempo* ("The river of time," 1983–95), as well as in his recent *El desbarrancadero* ("The derailer," 2000), and *La Rambla paralela* (2002). *La virgen de los sicarios* (*Our Lady of the Assassins*, 1997) is the most novelistic of his works; it narrates the return of the middle-aged narrator, Fernando, to his native Medellín, where he falls in love with a young hired gun, Alexis, and then (after Alexis's death) with another, Wílmar (who turns out to be Alexis's killer). The novel, adapted for the screen by the Franco-Colombian director Barbet Schroeder, is lyrical in its evocation of a lost love, even though that love turns out to be a killer who is shockingly indifferent to the narrator's esthetic and ethical concerns. A brilliant text that has been viewed as a celebration of man-boy love, as the supreme fiction of Colombia's violence, and as a diatribe against Nation and Church, *La virgen* (which unfortunately has been translated badly) is one of the most widely commented upon of recent Latin American novels.

Mario Bellatín, born in Mexico but raised in Peru, has recently emerged as one of Mexico's most powerful writers; his work has considered topics as varied as a blind poet, a young man afflicted by the loss of limbs from the drug thalidomide, a Japanese writer with an abnormally large nose, and various other marginalized figures. His finest work to date is *Salón de belleza* (1999), an allegorical novel about AIDS that bears some relation to Sarduy's final *Pájaros de la playa* (1993). *Salón de belleza* is narrated by a hair stylist who decorated his beauty shop with aquariums full of brilliantly colored fish, and who has another source of income when he goes out at night (with some of his fellow stylists) to work as a cross-dressing prostitute. The novel takes place after the narrator's co-workers have fallen sick from a mysterious and stigmatized illness that has forced their isolation from the world; it tells of the death of the fish in the aquariums and of the co-workers as the beauty shop is converted into a hospice, a place of death and dying. The intensity of the narrator's account is heightened as the reader comes to realize that the narrator also is afflicted with the mysterious disease and that the world of the beauty shop is coming to an end. A brief, intense, and apocalyptic novel, *Salón de belleza* is a beautiful evocation of a lost community, at the same time that the magical space of the beauty salon also is part of a network of solidarity and caring (a topic also discussed by the Chilean Pedro Lemebel in *Loco afán: crónicas de sidario* ["Mad pursuit: AIDS chronicles," 1996]).

In 2002 Sylvia Molloy published a second novel, *El común olvido*, twenty-one years after the publication of *En breve cárcel* (and as important we think to any history of the gay and lesbian novel as the earlier text was). It tells the story of Daniel, the gay male narrator, and his return to Buenos Aires to explore the reporting of the Oscar Wilde trials in Argentine newspapers of the 1890s. Spurred on by a more urgent personal need to explore the story of his late parents, *El común olvido* is notable for the ways in which the protagonist's contemporary story of life as an Argentine-American in New York is woven into the stories of his Anglo-American father (and the father's relatives that Daniel encounters on his return to Buenos Aires), of his mother's (lesbian?) friends, and of stories of gay life in Buenos Aires both past and present. A rich tapestry of lives, an interweaving of voices, *El común olvido* is an intense, mature work of exile and return, of the search for identity, of the construction of an "imagined community."

A notable feature of *El común olvido* is how it relates gay and lesbian lives in the past to the present, and how it shows the impact on contemporary communities of AIDS, exile, and globalization. In this regard it is typical of a variety of novels of the present moment, including Ponte's *Contrabando de sombras*, Bellatín's *Salón de belleza*, and the works of Pedro Lemebel: reflecting on how a community is forged in adversity, it shows how essential memory is to the invention of a tradition. There can be no doubt that at the time of this writing the homoerotic tradition in all its fullness (gay, lesbian, bisexual, transgender, and queer) is a powerful one in the Latin American novel.

NOTES

1. On these anthologies, see Balderston and Quiroga, "A Sinister, Beautiful Fairyland: Gay Sunshine Press Does Latin America," *Social Text* (Fall, 2003): 85–108.
2. Sylvia Molloy, "Of Queens and Castanets: *Hispanidad*, Orientalism, and Sexual Difference," in C. Patton and B. Sánchez-Eppler (eds.), *Queer Diasporas* (Durham, NC: Duke University Press, 2000), pp. 105–21.
3. See Balderston, "Sexuality and Revolution: On the footnotes to El beso de la Mujer arāna," in Matthew C. Gutmann (ed.), *Changing Men and Masculinities in Latin America* (Durham, NC: Duke University Press, 2003), pp. 216–32.
4. See Claudia Schaefer, *Danger Zones: Homosexuality, National Identity, and Mexican Culture* (Tucson: University of Arizona Press, 1996) for discussion of earlier novels, notably Manuel Barbachano Ponce's *El diario de José Toledo*, 1964.
5. Deborah Shaw, "Erotic or Political: Literary Representations of Mexican Lesbians," *Journal of Latin American Cultural Studies* 5, 1 (1996): 51–63.
6. The title of this novel corresponds to the first line of a children's song – well known in Columbia – about a colorful female bird. The song's innocent connotations are belied by Angel's depiction of patriarchal violence against women.

FURTHER READING

Albuquerque, Severino, "Fictions of the Impossible: Clarice Lispector, Lúcio Cardoso, and 'Impossibilidade,'" in S. C. Quinlan and F. Arenas (eds.), *Lusosex: Gender and Sexuality in the Portuguese-Speaking World*, Minneapolis: University of Minnesota Press, 2002, pp. 84–103.

Balderston, Daniel, "Sexuality and Revolution: On the Footnotes to *El beso de la mujer araña*," in Matthew C. Gutmann (ed.), *Changing Men and Masculinities in Latin America*, Durham: Duke University Press, 2003, pp. 216–32.

El deseo, enorme cicatriz luminosa: ensayos sobre homosexualidades latinoamericanos, Rosario: Beatriz Viterbo Editora, 2004.

Balderston, Daniel and José Quiroga, "A Sinister, Beautiful Fairyland: Gay Sunshine Press Does Latin America," *Social Text* (Fall 2003): 85–108.

Bejel, Emilio, *Gay Cuban Nation*, University of Chicago Press, 2001.

Craig, Herbert E., *Marcel Proust and Spanish America: From Critical Response to Narrative to Narrative Dialogue*, Lewisburg: Bucknell University Press, 2002.

Foster, David William, *Gay and Lesbian Themes in Latin American Writing*, Austin: University of Texas Press, 1991.

Sexual Textualities: Essays on Queer/ing Latin American Writing, Austin: University of Texas Press, 1997.

(ed.), *Latin American Writers on Gay and Lesbian Themes: A Bio-Critical Sourcebook*, Westport, Conn.: Greenwood Press, 1994.

Kaminsky, Amy K., *Reading the Body Politic: Feminist Criticism and Latin American Women Writers*, Minneapolis: University of Minnesota Press, 1993.

Leyland, Winston (ed.), *My Deep Dark Pain Is Love: A Collection of Latin American Gay Fiction*, San Francisco: Gay Sunshine Press, 1983.

Martínez, Elena M., *Lesbian Voices from Latin America*, New York: Garland Press, 1996.

Masiello, Francine, *The Art of Transition: Latin American Culture and Neoliberal Crisis*, Durham, NC: Duke University Press, 2001.

Menéndez, Nina, "*Garzonas y Feministas* in Cuban Women's Writing of the 1920s: *La vida manda* by Ofelia Rodríguez Acosta," in Daniel Balderston and Donna J. Guy (eds.), *Sex and Sexuality in Latin America*, New York University Press, 1997, pp. 174–89.

Molloy, Sylvia, "Of Queens and Castanets: *Hispanidad*, Orientalism, and Sexual Difference," in C. Patton and B. Sánchez-Eppler (eds.), *Queer Diasporas*, Durham, NC: Duke University Press, 2000, pp. 105–21.

Quiroga, José, *Tropics of Desire: Interventions from Queer Latino America*, New York University Press, 2000.

Schaefer, Claudia, *Danger Zones: Homosexuality, National Identity, and Mexican Culture*, Tucson: University of Arizona Press, 1996.

Shaw, Deborah, "Erotic or Political: Literary Representations of Mexican Lesbians," *Journal of Latin American Cultural Studies* 5, 1 (1996): 51–63.

Sifuentes-Jáuregui, Ben, "Gender Without Limits: Transvestism and Subjectivity in *El lugar sin límites*," in Daniel Balderston and Donna J. Guy (eds.), *Sex and Sexuality in Latin America*, New York University Press, 1997, pp. 44–61.

4

SIX NOVELS

11

MARTA PEIXOTO

Dom Casmurro by Machado de Assis

Dom Casmurro (1899), perhaps Brazil's most celebrated novel, has acquired in the century since its publication what must be the longest critical bibliography devoted to any single work of Brazilian fiction. Part of its attraction no doubt lies in the enigma concerning possible adultery and betrayal that many critics have found in its pages. In the distinct stages the interpretation of the novel has gone through, betrayal has been the key issue of debate. Readings can be seen to organize themselves around the different answers to the questions of exactly who betrays whom, why, and to what end.

The third of the five major novels that Machado de Assis published between 1881 and 1908, *Dom Casmurro* is a retrospective first-person memoir – fictional, of course – told by an unreliable narrator. His perspective colors all elements of the narrative, subordinating them to his viewpoint. We have only Bento's stubborn opinion of events and characters, which, however, his very text suggests may be different from what he makes them out to be. The "reality" the novel represents is radically subjectivized, nuanced, and complex, filtered by a problematic consciousness that ends up revealing perspectives other than the one he seems to intend. But while acknowledging this and other aspects of the novel that are in tune with modernism, we should also place it in the realist tradition where it also surely belongs. Recent critics, such as John Gledson and Roberto Schwarz, have argued persuasively for recognizing the novel's keen understanding of class privilege and class relations in Brazilian society of the Second Reign (under Emperor Pedro II 1840–89).

The key to interpreting *Dom Casmurro* lies with the narrator-protagonist and with our view of his designs and possible covert purposes. Bento Santiago is a comfortably retired old gentleman who lives on the outskirts of Rio de Janeiro at the turn of the century. Witty, urbane, the narrator discusses the process of writing on almost every page, indulging in the famous seemingly casual digressions that mark this novel's style and that only a careful reading reveals to be pertinent (in most cases) to the main narrative. Bento settles on composing his memoirs after considering other possible topics, including philosophy, politics, or history. But the aim of enlivening his quiet days ultimately seems better served by setting down his life story, a project, however, that soon appears driven by compelling forces of which he is not entirely aware.

For many years after the novel's publication Bento was seen as a reliable guide to the central plot (in more than one sense) that determined his life: his betrayal by his childhood sweetheart and later wife Capitu in a secret affair with his best friend Escobar. Owing to the uncanny similarity to Escobar of the son who for some years Bento thought to be his own, the betrayal in due time became evident and undeniable – undeniable for Bento, that is, and for readings that take him at his word. All the more detailed readings of the novel until 1960 fell into this category, agreeing with Bento that he was betrayed at the treacherous hands of those nearest and dearest to him. Capitu, in particular, came in for scathing appraisals as an avatar of female cunning and treachery, a blend of Eve and the serpent. But is Bento really trustworthy or is he, on the contrary, an unreliable narrator whose vision is affected or even produced by his jealousy?

It seems impossible to disagree with the current prevailing critical opinion that the novel offers an exceedingly well-crafted example of a first-person narrator who, while placing the blame for grave misdeeds on other characters, ends up incriminating himself. Most current readers agree that the novel does not leave open the question of adultery for readers to decide as they see fit but rather blocks the possibility of a final decision on this crucial issue, while nevertheless engaging urgently the question of moral judgment.

Readings that acknowledge the novel's indeterminacy, and that therefore must withhold moral condemnation of Capitu, have tended to pronounce the question of her guilt or innocence irrelevant. Silviano Santiago, for instance, in a seminal article, discusses the implications of the narrator's dubious rhetoric of verisimilitude, where what matters is a surface persuasiveness, and urges us to see Bento's moral substance as the only relevant subject of inquiry.[1] Capitu's possible betrayal is for this critic unknowable and beside the point. I would like to bring Capitu, perhaps the most famous character in Brazilian fiction, back into the picture, as some recent critics have done, in order to examine issues of gender and power in the world of the novel and see how they are constellated around the central question of betrayal. In particular, I want to investigate Capitu's irreducibly double character, for if the question of her betrayal is left open, she too is left as either adulteress or a faithful wife. She cannot be both, of course (or could she, at different moments?). This essay will examine the purpose and the artistic effect of this double construction within the framework of gender relations in the novel.

Dom Casmurro, as has been often noted, is composed of two intricately imbricated parts. Each features a promise that has a direct impact on Bento's sexuality, his reproductive capacity and sense of himself as a man. The first part, the longest (two-thirds of the novel) and happiest, contains a love story that begins on a never-to-be-forgotten afternoon of 1857 and hinges on a broken or cleverly bypassed promise. With nostalgic ardor, the narrator tells us – or rather shows us, for much of the novel is made up of effectively composed theatrical scenes – how he comes to realize at age fifteen that he has fallen in love with the girl next door, an attractive and self-possessed fourteen-year-old of quite modest means. The main stumbling block to their union is the promise that Bento's mother, Dona Glória, had made to God before his birth to dedicate this child to the priesthood if he were born alive. A wealthy widow, Bento's mother governs, in her husband's absence, a household that includes her brother and a middle-aged female cousin, both childless. This rather gloomy home, "a casa dos três viúvos" ("the house of the three widows"),[2] inauspicious for matters of reproduction and marital happiness, also includes an elderly bachelor, José Dias, a man without an independent livelihood who, in exchange for room and board, does errands for Dona Glória and looks after Bento. The only vestige of a functioning sexual union, with its traditional prerogative of power granted to the man, is the painted portrait on the wall of Bento's parents. In his female-dominated world, his mother holds the power and Bento himself is a most submissive son, his hopes of occupying a place like his father's shattered by the obligation of priesthood. The adult dependents in the household have little freedom of action or opinion, for to maintain their position they must always please Dona Glória or appear to do so.

In Capitu's home next door, the power also lies more with the women, the mother and daughter. The father, Pádua, is a civil servant, a comically portrayed, well-intentioned but foolish man. He becomes so distraught by the loss of a temporary position that brought him some prestige that he contemplates suicide and his worried wife pleads with Dona Glória to convince her husband to give up such a notion. In words that sum up the balance of male and female power in that household and perhaps also in the first part of the novel as a whole, Dona Glória tells him to be a man and a proper father, adding the startling suggestion that to do so, he should emulate his wife and daughter.

When Bento finally bows to his mother's will and begins his studies at the seminary – his schemes, with Capitu's help, to avoid that outcome having proved unsuccessful – he nevertheless retains a firm intention of leaving before ordination. At the seminary he forms close ties with Escobar, an ambitious young man from a provincial city, who intends in time to pursue his vocation in commerce. During Bento's absence, Capitu also finds her way into his mother's heart. Although Dona Glória's promise ostensibly blocks the marriage, the class difference between Bento and Capitu is an unspoken and parallel obstacle, unmistakably alluded to but never explicitly characterized as such. Capitu understands the total configuration of unfavorable circumstances and sets out to overcome them by winning Dona Glória's affection.

Escobar eventually comes up with the idea, more expedient than pious, that frees Bento from the priesthood. Dona Glória should pay for the studies of an orphan boy, he counsels, and in that way be instrumental in giving a priest to God. This self-indulgent interpretation – it's like paying a servant to keep one's own promise – could be considered a betrayal but nevertheless wins ready acceptance. Dona Glória's desire to see Bento and Capitu married had come to surpass her allegiance to her promise. This dubious manner of keeping faith with her promise is compensated by the perfect keeping of another pledge, Capitu and Bento's secret betrothal. Bento leaves the seminary and goes on to study law in São Paulo and in due time realizes his fondest wish of marrying Capitu, to the general satisfaction of all.

During this part of the novel, Capitu and Escobar collaborate with Bento in his secret plan to avoid the priesthood and marry Capitu. A necessary step is the breaking of Dona Glória's promise that drastically affected the love life of someone else (Bento himself). Is this perhaps a parallel to that later promise (the marriage vow), also perhaps broken by someone else (Capitu) and also drastically affecting Bento's life? Both in the case of the promise certainly broken (the religious one) and the one possibly so (the marriage vows), Escobar was and would be a key participant. The symmetries and oppositions in this novel are dazzling but fixed meanings impossible to establish. Although one can never know whether the second promise was broken, the first part of the novel carefully lays the groundwork for suspicion in that regard, for the narrative is shaped by Bento, who is himself the man who believes he was betrayed. While explicitly the narrator praises Capitu and Escobar for their qualities – self-possession, charm, the ability to plan things and carry out those plans – implicitly he foreshadows their later infidelity.

Capitu and Escobar have unquestioned ascendancy over young Bento, a dreamy, sensitive boy, full of ideas of questionable practicality, ideas "sem pernas e sem braços" (846; "without legs and without arms" [71]), reluctant to cross his mother or to assert himself. Many scenes show to advantage Capitu's clear-thinking mind as she figures out how they should proceed to overcome the obstacle of Dona Glória's promise. Capitu excels not only in logical thinking but also in tact and in the understanding of how best to engage the interests of others to further her own. She has the dependent's skill in manipulating the power of those who detain it. Capitu also excels in the ability to dissimulate. Early on in the novel, four similarly organized dramatic episodes show Capitu's cleverness and self-control as she and Bento conceal their intimacy from the adults who intrude upon them, interrupting handholding and kisses, the latter, it must be said, always initiated by Capitu. When adults walk in, she adroitly conceals by her easy words what Bento reveals by his abashed silence. The narrator claims to emphasize such episodes because of his envy of Capitu's poise, which contrasts with his younger self's confusion.

Although younger than Bento, she is not only taller but far more mature. In the few physical descriptions, her beauty is not idealized. With large, light-colored eyes, thin lips, a long nose and a broad jaw, she does not seem conventionally pretty. Bento's attraction to her is nevertheless overwhelming. Much has been made of Capitu's "eyes like the tide"; we might note that their power to pull Bento in, more than any property of the eyes themselves, reveals Bento's attraction, his sense that his will is no match for the force that draws him to her. The early episodes where Bento has attacks of intense though short-lived jealousy, always on flimsy pretexts and never directed at Escobar, seem motivated by Bento's insecurity and designed to keep Capitu's power in check.

Could it be, we might wonder, that her attraction to him is less overwhelming, leaving her social graces intact? Does she pursue the marriage mainly as a means to social ascent? Surreptitiously, as Bento tells us the happy story of his adolescent love, he hints at those underlying issues, only occasionally making them more explicit. The narrator also hints at Escobar's interest in Bento's wealth and in the precise amount of his mother's monthly income. Without making the criticism explicit, he also points to Escobar's deviousness in many passages, describing, for instance, Escobar's shifty eyes, hands, feet, and speech. As Capitu and Escobar aid young Bento in the initial plot that culminates in marriage, the presentation of their traits is such that it later serves as a basis for denunciation. A host of apparently insignificant facts, gestures, incidents, and comments end up forming an accusatory pattern, suggesting that Capitu and Escobar are calculating, deceptive, and perfectly capable of daring ideas.

In the last third of the novel the marriage slowly unravels. After Bento and Capitu establish their household, they continue a lively friendship with Escobar and his wife Sancha. When the child Bento and Capitu ardently desire finally arrives, they give the boy Escobar's first name, Ezequiel. The stability and happiness of their life does not, however, dissipate Bento's habitual jealousy, incited by the most commonplace events: Capitu's waiting at the window for him in the evening, her bare arms on elegant occasions, her momentary distraction during a conversation. What has changed drastically is Capitu's attitude towards Bento, now characterized by meek subservience: she waits inside the house, covers her arms when she wears an evening gown, and so forth. If social climbing was a key motive for her wish to marry Bento, she does not now seem unduly interested in finery or elegant society. The couple lead a quiet life and Capitu seems to conform her behavior to her husband's will. Indeed, after the marriage Bento takes hold of patriarchal power with a fierce determination that implies insecurity and, surprisingly, to Capitu's apparent satisfaction.

Where has her assertiveness gone? Where are her cleverness and daring ideas? If Capitu as a young girl held the dominant position in the couple by virtue of her strong personality and native intelligence, it would seem that women's constricted position in nineteenth-century society came to alter that situation. Her education, as was common for middle- and upper-class women at the time, did not go beyond a rudimentary level. By age fourteen she had finished her studies and expected to be married. The early chapter entitled "Capitu's curiosity," while implicitly pointing up Capitu's interest in the wealth that the objects in Bento's house denote, also shows her wanting to learn everything she can: Latin, English, lace-making, backgammon. She eyes longingly their old piano and the jewelry his mother wore in the portrait and asks for stories of Dona Glória's youth and of the elegant functions she attended. Is Capitu interested in enriching the rather basic menu of knowledge and lore her own family could afford for her? Is she taking measure of the benefits a match with Bento would provide? In any case, Bento's five years of law school in São Paulo widen his intellectual and other horizons, while Capitu spends that time sewing at his mother's side. The system of unequal education for the sexes plays its part, it seems, in reestablishing the traditional balance of power between the sexes, as it was designed to do.

Yet certain plot incidents in the last part of the novel prevent us from assuming too quickly that there's no hidden and far more assertive component to Capitu's behavior after she marries Bento. She has one avowed secret meeting with Escobar, who helped her exchange into pounds sterling (as a counter to inflation) the money she managed to save from her household allowance. In this plot incident, as in many others, at least two possible and strongly hinted at interpretations squarely contradict each other: perhaps she is having an affair with Escobar, perhaps she is not. That she had left-over money on her hands shows she was content to enjoy life in Bento's shadow, with no special interest in clothes or social display, prizes that her advantageous marriage could have brought her. But she did wish to salvage some financial independence for herself and the meeting with Escobar, unbeknownst to Bento until she herself confessed it, surely could have been one of many. But then why did she confess to it? And yet . . . and yet . . . Definitive conclusions are simply not possible.

Bento continues to be plagued by a kind of free floating jealousy. Yet it is only after Escobar's death by drowning while swimming in a rough sea that Bento comes to suspect him. As he observes Capitu's eyes staring at Escobar's dead body, a sudden, unwelcome revelation hits him like a lightning bolt. Had Escobar also dared to swim, like Bento himself, in the dangerous tides of Capitu's eyes? In its skillful weaving of the literal and the figurative ocean, the parallelism poses and highlights the question but does not answer it.

What makes Bento so sure he can arrive at an accurate interpretation of the way Capitu gazed at Escobar's dead body? Within Bento's narrative, words, acts, and looks frequently call up and frustrate interpretation, marking it as a dubious, subjective activity. In the first part of the novel especially, young Bento is often in the position of bewildered would-be interpreter or else plays the obfuscating role, eluding the interpretive efforts of his observers. And in the second part of the novel, a crucial incident stands out, where Bento asks himself how he can interpret the warm, inviting glances he receives from Escobar's wife Sancha on the eve of his friend's drowning. When Bento juxtaposes his memory of those looks with the widow's apparently genuine grief the next day, he concludes (perhaps too quickly) that Sancha's sexual advances were an illusion created by his own vanity. In the world of the novel, words, gestures, and actions are often no more than surfaces that hide contradictions: wandering desires, unstable thoughts, motives, and allegiances. In this context, Bento's interpretive jump from appearances to definite fact seems positively rash.

Although the impact of Bento's suspicion during Escobar's funeral fades somewhat, a second and graver incriminating circumstance, also involving appearances, comes to obsess him: he begins to notice an increasing resemblance of his son to his dead friend. Already before Escobar's death the matter of the resemblance had come up, then ascribed to the boy's much remarked upon fondness for imitating others. Later, Capitu comments (innocently or with feigned innocence?) on an odd expression she finds in Ezequiel's eyes, which she had only seen before in a friend of her father's and the late Escobar. Could the resemblance perhaps be due to mere chance, as she suggests? Bento also recalls an incident in which Sancha's father maintained that Capitu was the picture of his dead wife. The discourse of familial and extra-familial resemblances appears frequently in the novel, with its component of flattery, wishful thinking, desire to retain something of those who have died and, ultimately, its inescapable subjectivity. In any case, the possibility of a chance resemblance does not hold Bento's attention for long and he soon decides that the boy is not his son.

In desperation, Bento thinks of suicide by drinking poisoned coffee; and then, in a murderous impulse, thinks of forcing the mixture down the boy's throat, both of these remaining, as it turns out, ideas without legs and without arms, considered but not acted upon. But the revenge he settles on, brilliant and cruel, allows Bento to preserve appearances while inflicting punishment. Bento determines that Capitu and the boy will henceforth live in Switzerland: not France, not Italy, but in colder climes where they will presumably feel their exile more keenly. Bento travels to Europe regularly, also to preserve appearances, bringing back news of them as if they had just been together, but in fact he never visits them at all.

Part of the sense of depth that this novel creates has to do with the opening of disquieting vistas into the possibility that the surface of incidents or characters hides realities of a different kind. If Bento was gullible and cuckolded, as he contends he was, then Capitu was a faithless wife and Escobar a false friend. But if Bento was as obsessed and mistaken as Othello, then Capitu was most grievously wronged. The point is that Machado has structured his novel so that, beneath the cracks of the surface veneer, alternate realities appear that don't merely enrich that surface, but actually contradict it. If we read the novel in full awareness of the undecidable nature of certain questions regarding behavior, ethics, and interpretation that nevertheless are not trivial or inconsequential, we are left to contemplate a fictional world composed of irreducibly multiple personalities and events. Yet they are not all multiple in the same way.

Bento's various personalities are taken up sequentially and even go by different names: Bentinho the boy and young man; Bento the adult; and Dom Casmurro the disillusioned old man who is our narrator. Unlike some of Capitu's multiple guises, the various Bentos are not hypothetical but displayed as actualities in the narrative. First we have the timid and enamored youth, persuaded that the world revolves around him. Bento's second guise is darker, authoritarian, and impulsive and gets ever more somber as the novel progresses. By the time he accuses Capitu of having borne Escobar's child he displays a willful egotism that grants no rights to anyone else. He decides on the dissolution of his family and on the self-protective manner in which it will be accomplished, without wanting to hear anything Capitu might have to say. When Bento takes on his third guise as Dom Casmurro and our narrator, he regains some of the mildness of his youthful self: as narrator he is genial, nostalgic, engaging, appealing directly to readers of various kinds, taking us nonchalantly on seemingly unrelated digressions that only after further readings of the novel may reveal their second intentions.

Yet an attentive reading of Dom Casmurro's personality makes plain his continuing immaturity and self-centeredness. As early as the second chapter, the possibility arises that the driving force of the narration is not merely Bento's wish to amuse himself or to recreate fond memories but also to subdue the ghosts of those he betrayed. His patriarchal authoritarianism that wishes to exercise absolute command over matters he cannot control (the passage of time, the innermost thoughts and desires of Capitu, and yes, even her sexual behavior) has damaged not only others but himself. At the end of the novel he tells us that he decided to build a replica of his childhood home because he himself had the original torn down: it, too, he felt, had betrayed him. If he doesn't find in others – house, wife, or son – the exact image he believes it is their function to reflect back to him, then they betrayed him and must be demolished or banished.

It seems that even the female companions Bento finds after Capitu's departure are debased replicas of his adolescent sweetheart. The women who come to his house, where he remains as devoted to the past as a curator in a museum, would be prostitutes, as Schwarz has plausibly observed.[3] The girls, at fifteen or younger, are Capitu's age when his love for her began in earnest. They are also, presumably, like her of humble social extraction. Though repeatedly seeking out their company, Bento is ultimately removed from them by irreducible gaps and as uninterested in them as they are in his retrospective exhibition. They are substitutes, like the house, that do not and cannot satisfy him.

Even his text escapes him by not proving conclusively what he thinks it conclusively proves. Although the novel leaves as undecidable whether his jealousy and revenge were founded on an actual betrayal or upon a completely groundless obsession, the blame he merits ends up being a matter of degree. Bento jumps to the most damning conclusions, is uninterested in taking other perspectives into account, and is incapable of forgiveness, even when the supposed lover is dead and the supposed son is in need of a father. If we read the novel historically, Bento constitutes a damning portrait of common traits of the Brazilian elite and of masculine prerogatives at the end of the nineteenth century, condensed to the point of pathology.

Capitu is also multiple, but all our views of her are mediated by Bento's intense emotions. What we know from the portion of the novel where Capitu figures as an adolescent is that she possesses intelligence, tact, and firmness of purpose. What we don't know is the moral ground where these qualities are set in her adult personality. Does she use them merely for what could be a blameless, even laudable purpose, to marry her neighbor and thus better her own social condition? Or did she later also use those same qualities to betray her husband? In the second part of the novel, all we see on the surface is a dignified, submissive wife and a loving mother. Perhaps for this reason, critics who recognize Bento's objectionable qualities, even those who rightly recognize the undecidability of the adultery question, end up appearing to absolve Capitu, as if his shortcomings somehow guaranteed her innocence, for the married woman's submissive demeanor makes it difficult to keep in view her adolescent daring and what it could possibly foreshadow. But the question does remain: was her second guise as a meek wife merely a front that hid a third guise, the woman who betrayed him, as Bento himself believed? Misogynist myths of the essentially treacherous nature of women lurk in the background to make this version of Capitu readily acceptable to some readers. Bento himself is perhaps swayed by those myths. But misogyny aside, Bento's narrative makes it easy to imagine that she could have fallen in love with a man more enterprising, virile, and charming than her husband and decided to act on that passion. Escobar – ambitious, practical, competent – made his fortune in coffee trading without the help of inherited privilege or wealth and was finally able to afford a house practically next door to Bento's in a prestigious beach-front neighborhood. The narrative hints that Capitu and Escobar, because of their similarly enterprising personalities, would make a good match and certain physical traits they share (light-colored eyes and thin lips) underline their resemblance.

It is a disappointment to any reader first charmed by Capitu's assertiveness in the first part of the novel to see her recede into meek compliance in the second. In the crucial scene where Bento tells Capitu outright that he believes Ezequiel is not his son, she first indignantly asks for an explanation but quickly retreats into resignation. She does not dispute the resemblance of Ezequiel to Escobar, though she deems it accidental. Is Capitu maintaining a dignified demeanor under pressure and finally resigning herself to Bento's irrational jealousy, or is she adroitly preserving a façade of innocence when the deceit has been found out? Another crucial scene at the end of the novel also points to contradictory possibilities regarding Capitu's character: the return of Ezequiel from Europe as a young man, after Capitu's death (callously dismissed by Bento in a couple of sentences). Are the boy's friendly, well-adjusted personality and respectful fondness for Bento as his father evidence that Capitu had the maturity to accept the inevitable and to raise the boy, for his own good, without bitterness? Or, ever foresightful, did she have in mind preserving the path to his inheritance?

Bento, in any case, holds onto all the bitterness of the supposed betrayal. When the boy expresses an interest in traveling to the Middle East to study archeology, he provides the money, glad to be rid of him, and shows complete indifference when he hears news of the boy's death by typhoid fever. We could say that one of the novel's most egregious betrayals is that of Bento with regard to Ezequiel, the boy whom he first adored and later rejected completely, after calling the blood tie to himself into question.

The domestic world of the novel depicts the circumvention of patriarchal power (in its acceptations both as class and as masculine hegemony) and later its outright assertion. Its circumvention is aligned with enlightened democratic values, where inherited privileges can step aside to accommodate the affirmation and fulfillment of those without them and women may rule, if personal qualities or circumstances make it advisable. The later assertion of patriarchal power, willful and uncontested, also, however, describes its failure: Bento is left in the end without love or progeny, the literal end of a line. Ezequiel's untimely death contributed to this outcome although without it the possibly illegitimate son would establish the next Santiago generation, a fate Bento saw cut short with relief and one of the eventualities that the subjection of women in patriarchy is itself set up to prevent.

After Capitu's portrayal as a self-confident and charming adolescent able to bring about the outcome she desires largely by her own resourcefulness, her depiction bifurcates in the second part of the novel into two opposed and irreconcilable figures. The visible plot shows Capitu in utter compliance with the traditional subordinate role exacted by her husband, while the possible invisible plot that would result in an illegitimate son suggests a woman unwilling to allow laws and social conventions to place limits on her behavior. It would, of course, have been very easy for Machado to foreclose one of those images and leave Capitu either as submissive wife or as adulteress. In other major novels of his that also feature adultery or its threat, he has portrayed unambiguous female characters. Virgínia, for instance, the wealthy female protagonist of *Memórias póstumas de Brás Cubas* (*The Posthumous Memoirs of Brás Cubas*, 1880), lives out a contented life both as the guilt-free partner in an adulterous union and as a respected wife, until boredom released her from the former role and her husband's death from the latter. In *Quincas Borba*, Sofia, the beautiful woman who enjoys tempting the protagonist Rubião, went no further than that, with her husband's encouragement and for the higher purpose of securing Rubião's attachment to the couple and her husband's access to his wealth. In *Dom Casmurro* Machado refuses to settle with certainty whether Capitu's adult behavior is blameless or deceitful.

But unlike the vain and frivolous Virgínia and Sofia, Capitu is established as intelligent, serious, and mature. Even if, in the invisible and suggested plot, Capitu did betray her husband, we are led to imagine that she would have done so deliberately, rather than motivated by a passing whim or pressured by the desires of others. This doesn't excuse her and might increase the gravity of her supposed transgression, but she is shown as a woman in full command of her actions, and her motivations cannot be considered trivial. As a literary achievement, *Dom Casmurro* is Machado's most forceful examination of both an obsessive jealousy and of a possible adultery, as well as of the larger structures of patriarchy in which they take place and the multiple betrayals they engender. Moral implications are powerfully and richly delineated, despite the fact that the boundaries between actual reality and possible realities cannot be demarcated, or perhaps for that very reason.

According to the historian Emília Viotti da Costa, at the close of the nineteenth century in Brazil there was "a growing awareness of the oppressive conditions in which women lived and of the negative effects that their upbringing had on the family and society, as well as the recognition of the importance of women's education, and their access to some professions (medicine, law, dentistry, architecture)."[4] These achievements, due in part to the efforts of the protofeminists of the last several decades of the century, would open up more opportunities for many women in Brazil in the years to come, including suffrage in 1932. Perhaps Capitu's self-determining energy and irreducibly double guise responds to and engages with an awareness of shifting patterns of possibility for women. The unsettling changes on the horizon will soon alter the balance of gender-ascribed power. Her portrayal can be seen to capture, not women's inherent ambiguity or treachery or any such misogynist myth, but the anxiety produced by women's changing roles, increasing confidence and self-direction. Women, with Capitu as their representative, can be capable and determined. What guarantee do we have that female subjection will continue? What energies might their liberation release?

Female enterprise and the prerogatives of patriarchy both come to a bad end in the novel. The suprapersonal structures of male hegemony foreclose Capitu's assertiveness (or at least banish it from the realm of visible events) and end up casting her out entirely from her country and social milieu, forcing upon her a fate worse than widowhood. Whether or not Capitu betrays Bento, we see that historical circumstances are not yet such as to allow Capitu's independent spirit to flourish. Yet those same structures that allow for an elite man's unchecked power prove dangerous, in the cult of the past they foster and in their backward-looking insistence on absolute control. They too ultimately betray Bento by allowing him scope to frame his own doom.

NOTES

1. Silviano Santiago, "Retórica da verossimilhança," in his *Uma literatura nos trópicos* (São Paulo: Perspectiva, 1978), pp. 29–48.
2. J. M. Machado de Assis, *Dom Casmurro* in *Obra completa*, Vol. I (Rio de Janeiro: Aguilar, 1962), p. 813. Page references in the text refer to this edition. The translation is J. Gledson's, *Dom Casmurro* (Oxford: Oxford University Press, 1997), p. 13. Later references unless otherwise noted will be to this translation and followed by page number in the text.
3. Roberto Schwarz, "A poesia envenenada de *Dom Casmurro*," in his *Duas meninas* (São Paulo: Companhia das Letnas, 1997), p. 32.
4. Emilia Viotti da Costa, "Patriarchalism and the Myth of the Helpless Woman in the Nineteenth Century," in her *The Brazilian Empire: Myths and Histories* (Chapel Hill: University of North Carolina Press, 2000, revised edn), p. 264.

FURTHER READING

Baptista, Abel Barros, *Autobibliografia: solicitação do livro na ficção e na ficção de Machado de Assis*, Lisboa: Relógio D'Água Editores, 1998.
Barreto Filho, José, *Introdução a Machado de Assis*, Rio de Janeiro: Agir, 1947.
Caldwell, Helen, *The Brazilian Othello of Machado de Assis*, Berkeley and Los Angeles: University of California Press, 1960.
Dixon, Paul B., *Retired Dreams: Dom Casmurro, Myth and Modernity*, West Lafayette, Indiana: Purdue University Press, 1989.
Costa, Emilia Viotti da, "Patriarchalism and the Myth of the Helpless Woman in the Nineteenth Century," in her *The Brazilian Empire: Myths and Histories*, revised edn, Chapel Hill: University of North Carolina Press, 2000.
Gomes, Eugênio, *O enigma de Capitu*, Rio de Janeiro: José Olympio, 1967.
Gledson, John, *The Deceptive Realism of Machado de Assis*, Liverpool: Francis Cairns, 1984.
Graham, Richard (ed.), *Machado de Assis: Reflections on a Brazilian Master*, Austin: University of Texas Press, 1999.
Lisboa, Maria Manuel, *Machado de Assis and Feminism*, Lewiston/Queenston/ Lampeter: Edwin Mellen Press, 1996.
Santiago, Silviano, "Retórica da verossimilhança," in Silviano Santiago, *Uma literatura nos trópicos*, São Paulo: Perspectiva, 1978.
Schwarz, Roberto, "A poesia envenenada de *Dom Casmurro*," in Roberto Schwarz, *Duas meninas*, São Paulo: Companhia das Letras, 1997.
Stein, Ingrid, *Figuras femininas em Machado de Assis*, Rio de Janeiro: Paz e Terra, 1984.
Xavier, Therezinha Mucci, *A personagem feminina no romance de Machado de Assis*, Rio de Janeiro: Presença, 1986.

12

JASON WILSON

Pedro Páramo by Juan Rulfo

In 1955 Juan Rulfo published his sole novel, *Pedro Páramo*. It followed a collection of short stories, *El llano en llamas* (*The Burning Plain*), in 1953. Apart from a few more stories added to subsequent editions, some film-scripts, and a promised second novel that never fully appeared, to be titled *La cordillera*, that was the sum of Rulfo's fictional work. The story of how such a meager output could attain canonic status, both within Mexico and abroad through translation, is itself instructive for the novel was poorly reviewed when it first appeared, and took four years to sell the first 1,000 copies of a first edition of 2,000 copies.[1]

In a general way, Rulfo's rural fiction offers a mirror into which local and foreign readers can explore the complex identity of what it meant to be Mexican in the twentieth century. The plot of this inquiry into identity follows an abandoned son setting out to confront his father. This personal quest is framed in a fiction that recreates the shattering experiences of the so-called Mexican Revolution (1910–20), especially how the decade of violence and the consequent jostling for power initiated the massive migration from the countryside to the city. This social phenomenon of migration to the cities is not solely due to political upheavals, for it happened across all Latin America. In 1928 Mexico City (México D. F.) reached 1 million inhabitants. Today, the rough figure is somewhere between 18 and 23 million. Juan Rulfo (1918–86) was but one of these urban migrants in his move from the state of Jalisco to the capital Mexico City. The majority of his local Mexican readers would also have made the same move. So we have this curious pact between an urbanized writer, an urban reader, and rural texts, whose reticent characters would not be able to read what had been written about them, because they have remained behind, in the rural backwaters. Such displacement leaves a bitter taste, a kind of nostalgia for roots, within the framework of an urban experience of anonymity and loss.

Geography

Both the titles of Rulfo's stories and novel refer to landscape; the *llano* to plains, and *páramo* to bleak plateau, or wasteland. Immediately, we notice that the title of Rulfo's novel *Pedro Páramo*, supposedly the name of the cacique or local boss, is a surname based on a geographical feature that resists translation. Rulfo's novel has been translated twice into American English, first by Lysander Kemp in 1959, and then again by Margaret Sayers Peden in 1993, both retaining the title as *Pedro Páramo*.[2] So my first point is to underline that Rulfo's title is both a surname and a symbolic comment on the content, a wasteland. This symbolic allusion is made clear when we link Rulfo's fiction to T. S. Eliot's epoch-marking poem about urban anguish, *The Waste Land*, published in 1922, and translated into Mexican Spanish by Enrique Mungía, Jr. as *El páramo* in an avant-garde magazine in Mexico called *Contemporáneos* in 1930.[3] For example, reading this translation of Eliot in 1930 changed the Mexican poet and critic Octavio Paz's views on life, for this prose translation reinforced the geographic links between mental sterility, Mexican desert, and the loss of the religious and mythological imagination through the title "páramo."[4] We have no idea if Rulfo actually read this translation, but the overlap of titles between his novel and Eliot in translation is not a coincidence, for Rulfo also deals grippingly with the same losses that Eliot's poem did. For example, the second stanza of T. S. Eliot's opening section, "The Burial of the Dead" is rendered into prose alluding to "ese basurero rocalloso" ("stony rubbish") where "el sol late, el árbol muerto no da sombra, el grillo enmudece, y la peña no abriga rumor de aguas" ("... the sun beats / And the dead tree gives no shelter, the cricket no relief, / And the dry stone no sound of water ...") where the prose banishes the English rhythms, and sounds like a description of Rulfo's Jalisco.[5]

Rulfo once remarked that he always situated his fictional characters "geographically."[6] At a first level, then, Rulfo's fiction is vividly local to "la tierra caliente" of the mountainous state of Jalisco, with its farming "mestizo" peasants who lost their indigenous roots and culture with the Spanish conquest in the sixteenth century which robbed them of their past and a meaningful history. At the same time, these rural people have not been able to integrate themselves into the modern, progressive post-revolutionary Mexico. They are in-betweens in a no man's land, orphans of both past and future.

All Rulfo's characters, then, are tied to land both economically and spiritually. Those that can leave, do. Those that remain behind, outside society, suffer, for Rulfo inverts the great myth of progress. In his relentless short story "Es que somos muy pobres" ("It's that we are very poor"), the opening line summarizes this inversion of hope: "Aquí todo va de mal en peor"

("Here everything goes from bad to worse").[7] The story links a flooding river, the loss of a cow that was to be a dowry to save a young girl from the fate of her escaped older sisters (prostitution in towns), to the suggestion that puberty itself was an end not a beginning. For the flooded river, the dead cow, and the girl's breasts all contribute to her "perdición" (36; "perdition"), the story's last word.

The harsh landscape, the desert, the extremes of climate, the migration of people to the cities lead to the creation of ghost towns. Again, one of Rulfo's earlier short stories, "Luvina," links directly to *Pedro Páramo*. Note again the title, with its echoes of "luna," sterile moonscape, and the way Rulfo evokes this abandoned mountain village through its grey stones, where the Spanish "pedregoso" hints at "Pedro" and "piedra," so that the "Pedro" of the novel, a plain name, is another allusion to sterile stone. In Luvina there is nothing but white broken stones, a bitter wind, a few weeds like the "dulcamara" which are "smeared" to the land ("untadas a la tierra"), or the "chicalote" which soon dries out so that you can hear its branches scratching like knives (94). Comala in *Pedro Páramo* is also a ghost town, with empty streets, weeds growing out of windows and "bardas descarapeladas que enseñaban sus adobes revenidos" (46; "meager thatch revealing crumbling adobe" [42]).

Rulfo gives specific names to the landscape, the weeds, the birds, as if the landscape is active, alive, at war with its inhabitants, so that we can read landscape into soulscape, just as T. S. Eliot did in his *The Waste Land*. The outer objective world of Jaliscan geography reflects the inner mental world of his characters, without Rulfo ever reaching out for psychological explanations for the motives and behavior of his people. He doesn't need to, for they "are" the poverty and cruelty of the landscape. *Pedro Páramo* is defined by stones and bleakness, and by the absence of a future. When the novel ends, with the oligarch Pedro Páramo defeated by what he cannot obtain through violence, with his son and heir Miguel dead, and the love of his life, Susana, beyond his reach and mad, he simply returns to the landscape. The last sentence of the novel depicts this becoming stone: "Dio un golpe seco contra la tierra y se fue desmoronando como si fuera un montón de piedras" (129; "He fell to the ground with a thud, and lay there, collapsed like a pile of rocks" [122]).[8] That is, Comala, this fictional village, reverts to the landscape it was constructed from, a ghost town with only the mumbling dead left behind in the cemetery.

History

Rulfo wrote his fiction at a time when the official version of the unique Mexican Revolution had turned into stereotype and lie. All his work must be read against this optimistic backdrop. That there had been a revolution, that its praiseworthy 1917 constitution had been put into practice, and that the people were better off than under the earlier despot Porfirio Díaz, who had enriched his country at the expense of the peasants and indigenous people, stripping them of their land. The novel gives details as to how landownership during the *porfiriato* stayed in the hands of the few, the oligarchs like Pedro Páramo. The proposition was that so much bloodshed and sacrifice had been worthwhile. Possibly Rulfo's most famous short story "Nos han dado la tierra" ("They have given us the land"), published in a magazine in July 1945, reveals the lie in such political optimism. Here, the land the peasants were promised, the *ejido* of self-sufficiency from article 27 of the Mexican constitution, is just dry, hard wasteland. The story opens with a string of negatives as a group of men walk in the sun, without the shade of a tree, not even the seed of a tree, not even the roots of anything ("ni una raíz de nada") to protect them. These "plains" are cracked with dry river beds, with bitter winds, no animal life except for lizards. One raindrop falls like spittle, gobbled up by a thirsty earth in a sentence that epitomizes negativity: "Y a la gota caída por equivocación se la come la tierra y la desaparece en su sed" (16; "And the raindrop fallen by mistake is eaten by the earth and made to disappear in its thirst"). This use of "disappear" is active, the sinister landscape is alive. This is the promised land that the government official gives them, a "costra de tepetate" (17; "crust of mining waste"). The narrator describes this land as "este comal acalorado" (18; "this heated griddle") where nothing will take off, not even vultures (an example of Rulfo's quirky, black humor). This Mexican term "comal" (referring to a stone, or a circular baked earth and later metallic hotplate for cooking maize *tortillas*) leads us to Comala in the novel *Pedro Páramo*, as plains do to "páramo," and the corrupt revolution can only give away this "comal"-land. Alan Riding claimed that, between 1952 and 1981, 85 percent of redistributed land was unsuitable for arable farming.[9] That this part of Jalisco is hellishly hot is made explicit at the start of the novel: "Aquello está sobre las brasas de la tierra, en la mera boca del infierno" (9; "That town sits on the coals of the earth, at the very mouth of hell" [6]).

The official history of Mexico bypassed Comala in the novel *Pedro Páramo*. No land reform, no social justice, no socialist equality, just the powerful "macho" Pedro Páramo, with his obedient priest, the Padre Rentería, and faithful henchman Fulgor Sedano, and Pedro's ability to bribe and force the revolution to go elsewhere. There are scenes where Pedro gets his most trusted "thug," *El Tilcuate*, to take 300 men and join the revolutionaries. Through these encounters with El Tilcuate we learn that nobody knows what the revolution stands for. They are fed up with the rich and with the government, but do not have any instructions (101). They just enjoy the "bulla" (102; "scrap" [97]). Tilcuate later becomes a Pancho Villa supporter, then fights for Carranza and then Obregón, changing sides constantly. But the crucial effect, plotted by Pedro, was to leave his ranch the Media Luna, untouched. Pedro even suggests that they loot a neighboring town, Contla, so as to avoid Comala. In this reactionary village (Rulfo: "They were always a reactionary people"),[10] its complicit women secretly admire Pedro's potency. Nobody rebels against his whimsical, personal authority because all are trapped in religious superstitions and are unwilling to take any responsibility for the abuses of power in their midst. Through Comala, Rulfo has penned a withering but oblique attack on Mexican rural mentality.

Biography

Rulfo was not a professional writer in the sense of dedicating himself exclusively to writing, and making a living out of it (in fact, he held several jobs, from working in the government immigration department, then with Goodrich rubber tyres, then the Instituto Nacional Indigenista from 1962). Neither did he survive as a journalist, nor did he seek sustenance as an academic. In no way was Rulfo a public intellectual in the Octavio Paz mold. He wrote because he was driven to writing. I think that all readers have felt this necessity in Rulfo's fiction, an urgency and density linked to lived and felt experience. But meshed in with his experiences is a literary cunning, based on avid, omnivorous reading. Rulfo learnt how to grasp his peasants from writers like William Faulkner, Thomas Wolfe, James Joyce, and Knut Hamsun; his work flows from such committed reading to ensure classic status for Pedro Páramo because criticism cannot exhaust the meanings on reading the novel.[11] One way into this palpable sense of having written his laconic fiction in his own blood and not ink is to match biography with fiction.

Rulfo was born in Apulco, near Sayula, Jalisco in 1918, and suffered at first hand the reactionary Catholic opposition to the revolution's reforms of the Church. His father was murdered in 1924 (and later his uncle) during the Cristero uprising that lasted from 1926–29, where Catholics took to the hills, armed, to defend their rights (as did his character padre Rentería in the novel Pedro Páramo). The Church had suffered under the revolution's land reform, having all its lands confiscated, even the churches themselves. Priests were not allowed to wear their cassocks in the street, even the president could not enter a church during his presidency.

When his mother died in 1927, Rulfo was effectively an orphan, and brought up partially in an orphanage in Guadalajara from 1928–32, until leaving for Mexico City in 1933. It is tempting to read "orphanhood" into his world along the lines that Octavio Paz developed in the late 1940s in his essay *El laberinto de la soledad* (*The labyrinth of solitude*, 1950).[12] Paz adapted the Parisian "existentialist" debate about twentieth-century man's isolation in cities, severed from religions and gods, a kind of metaphysical orphan embodied in the Mexican "pachuco" (today known as "chicano") who has lost everything Mexican in California except for his body and a defiant way of dressing. In many ways, Rulfo's fiction dramatizes the same debate, at the same time, owing little to Paz's essay. His characters are all "orphans," without roots, or a past that guides them through rituals and traditions; they have no family structure, ignore love, and do not belong to any social groups. They are outsiders, stripped of their human rights, speaking a rural, archaic Spanish, unable to analyze their actions, and even lack conscience when breaking the law and taboos. As Roberto Cantú perceptively noted, normality does not exist in this fiction.[13] The sole exceptions are the pure Indians, who arrive in Comala for market day from the mountains of Apango, sell herbs, and are twice described as chatting away, joking and "soltando la risa" (90 and 91; "laughing" [84 and 85]), where laughter, the joy of living, is depressingly absent in all Comala.

In this sense, orphanhood shifts from being Rulfo's own experience to being that of a rural community where isolation suggests that life itself matters little. And so death matters little. There might be a specific Mexican cultural indifference to death that has grown out of the harsh landscape, analyzed by Paz in his 1950 essay, *El laberinto de la soledad*.[14]

So Rulfo writes from inside the experience of orphanhood and violence. Thus, on the one hand, he sets out to recuperate his geographic area of Mexico and its effect on locals and their dispersal to the cities, all that "música tierna del pasado" (104; "tender music from the past" [99]) of a lost world that the novel *Pedro Páramo* chronicles. On the other hand, Rulfo seems to suggest that this same "lost" world was reactionary and awful, and deserved to become a ghost town. The structure given to this emotional ambivalence, as already noted, is that of a quest of an abandoned son, Juan Preciado, for his father, as stated in the novel's opening line: "Vine a Comala porque me dijeron que acá vivía mi padre, un tal Pedro Páramo" (7; "I came to Comala because I had been told that my father, a man named Pedro Páramo, lived there" [3]). Carlos Fuentes picked up the mythic parallels between Juan Precio and Telemachus in an important early essay.[15] When the quest fails, because Pedro Páramo is already dead, Juan Preciado, his son, also dies but allows us as reader to explore who his father really was, from the inside (especially the slightly conventional pining away for his love Susana).

Rulfo knew this world bitterly from his own experience and wanted to exorcise its grip on him. His working title for the novel was "Los murmullos" ("The whispers"), where voice, especially inner monologue, and dialogue and silence become key terms in trying to make sense of the patriarch in his fiefdom. The reader is simply someone who overhears what is being said from that seemingly timeless place that is memory, the unchangeable past, a chattering cemetery. There are constant references to silence, echoes, rumours, distant songs. From his coffin, Juan Preciado twice says that "me mataron los murmullos" (62; "The murmuring killed me" [57]), an enigmatic phrase that evokes the working title to the novel, "Los murmullos," and blames the ghost voices of the dead, including his mother's false daydreams about Comala in his mind, for having killed him.

Experimental fiction and the reader

What really counts in trying to make sense of Rulfo's novel *Pedro Páramo* is the way it is written and constructed, and what happens to the reader. Rulfo is no believer in realism to convey place and character; he has not written a "costumbrista" sketch of what is typically Mexican. He also appears to fit into what has been called the "regional" novel in Latin America, in vogue over the 1920s and 1930s. These novels dealt realistically with rural issues and emergent nationhood. Mario Vargas Llosa once called them "primitive" novels technically, when contrasted with high modernism in Europe and the United States of the same period. But Rulfo is a modern. Not only was he a close reader of William Faulkner's narrating from the inside of limited characters (as in *As I Lay Dying*, 1930), but he also has adopted some surrealistic motifs (the vivid unpredictability of the dream), as well as highlighting words themselves and rhythms as poems do. Some examples: there are shooting stars "como si el cielo estuviera lloviznando lumbre" (33; "as if the sky were raining fire" [29]); a quiet sobbing passes through "la maraña del sueño, llegando hasta el lugar donde anidan los sobresaltos" (28; "the mesh of sleep and reach the place where his fear lived" [23]); as Juan Preciado dies "daba vueltas a mi alrededor aquel bisbiseo apretado como un enjambre" (63; "circling round me, a constant buzzing like a swarm of bees" [58]), or the wordplay "Enterraron a Susana San Juan y pocos en Comala se enteraron" (121), impossible to translate, with *enterrar* ("to bury") and *enterar* ("to hear about it") ("Susana San Juan was buried and few people in Comala even realized it" [115]). It is an experimental novel that is so carefully and memorably written at the level of words that Gabriel García Márquez once boasted he knew the whole novel by heart.[16] He even might have lifted from Rulfo the name "Melquíades" (55), the phrase that opens *Cien años de soledad* from "El padre rentería se acordaría muchos años después de la noche . . ." (72; "Years later father Rentería would remember the night [67]) and the last inhabitants of Comala as incestuous lovers (as they are in Macondo when the child with a pig's tail is born and Macondo is blown off the map). Most of the inhabitants of Comala have been fathered by Pedro Páramo, and are therefore related. The last couple are brother and sister, and live in guilt and disgust.

From the surrealist exploration of dreams (and nightmares) percolating from Paris in the 1930s and 1940s, Rulfo has taken one constant: his refusal to explain and judge. Carlos Monsiváis underlined Rulfo's not preaching, never openly judging.[17] Dreams happen, without much of a cause and effect exploration; they are emotional and fluid and work inside the dreamer's mind. Rulfo's craft was employed to blend memory and dream, and make the past a bad dream that cannot be explained away. There are many references to a dreamer's loss of control, of being pulled through the fiction and manipulated by time frames, and voices, crossing normal divisions like those of life and death. Juan Preciado does not realize that the first man he meets on his way down into the hell of Comala is a half brother who is already dead. The dead talk to each other in their coffins, walking the streets of Comala like ghosts. All the empirical laws of life and death, and time with its breakdown into present, past, and future are discarded, as in dreams where the living and the dead haunt the dreamer with equal realities, and time loses its forward-arrow momentum. This suspension of time is not magical realism, but simply the esthetics of the dream-experience. The village clock seems, to Pedro Páramo as a boy, to strike the hours at random "como si se hubiera encogido el tiempo" (19; "As if time had telescoped" [15]). That is what dreaming does with clock-time.

The reader is like Juan Preciado and enters the fiction like the latter enters Comala. From then onwards, through the voices, the reader circles around the static hell of memory that is Comala and its guilty inhabitants.

Early on in the novel, Juan Preciado meets up with Eduviges Dyada who had been told by Juan's dead mother that he was arriving. Juan is so puzzled by this that he tells us that "yo no supe qué pensar" (14; "I did not know what to think" [10]); that is, he, like the reader, like any dreamer, has to relinquish thinking, that sequential and causal understanding, and just accept what is happening, as forced to in dreams. His "cada vez entiendo menos" (57; "I understand less by the minute" [52]) is echoed by the reader.

At the end of his dialogue with Eduviges, Juan Preciado describes what is happening to him in these terms:

Yo creía que aquella mujer estaba loca. Luego ya no creí nada. Me sentí en un mundo lejano y me dejé arrastrar. Mi cuerpo, que parecía aflojarse, se doblaba ante todo, había soltado sus amarras y cualquier podía jugar con él como si fuera de trapo (15; "I wondered if she were crazy. But by now I wasn't thinking at all. I felt I was in a faraway world and let myself be pulled along by the current. My body, which felt weaker and weaker, surrendered completely; it had slipped its ties and anyone who wanted could have wrung me out like a rag" [11]).

My point about this self-description is that it is remarkably close to what happens to a dreamer who has to give up predictive thinking, slips into the dream world – "faraway" – along the current of the dream, like a "trapo." This loss of will in both Juan Preciado and the reader has been created by Rulfo's skill in not explaining anything, yet rendering every situation vivid.

This same fluidity of the dream abolishes the frontiers between the past and the future. Early on in the novel, the fifth break (there are no chapters in keeping with dream aesthetics), the reader (like Juan Preciado) overhears a dialogue between a boy and his mother. The boy is daydreaming of Susana, his beloved, and is told to get on and help his grandmother strip the maize. Who are these characters? The reader only realizes two pages later that in fact he has abruptly entered Pedro Páramo's childhood. This technique of delaying making sense continues throughout the novel, and is similar to the way a dreamer can only make sense of a dream after it is over, as an act of hindsight analysis.

In an interview with Fernando Benítez, Rulfo described how he rewrote his novel three times, cutting it down from 300 pages to the 129 pages of the 1964 edition in what he called an exercise of elimination.[18] Another time, Rulfo joked that he cut out so much that even he couldn't understand it.[19] But clearly what was eliminated was padding, connective sequences, explanations, excessive adjectives, the kind of elimination that the discipline and economy of short-story writing induces. The original long manuscript seems to have vanished and what a critic can consult is an earlier variant of the final version, called *Los murmullos* and held at the Centro Mexicano de Escritores in Mexico City.[20] Rulfo told Luis Harss that he waged a war against the Latin American tendency to write in the baroque mode, a proliferating exuberance.[21] Rulfo, over his life, continued to tinker with the novel in each major new edition. The consequence of this reduction was to make it harder for the reader. We reach another aspect of Rulfo's experimental fiction, also derived from surrealism. That is that he makes the reader collaborate in the fiction by baffling him or her. To puzzle the reader, without resolving the puzzle in the detective-story format, has been achieved by elimination. Rulfo was highly aware of this project of involving the reader in the "plot." Again, to Benítez, he said that he wanted the reader to fill in the gaps. In his own words, Rulfo artfully abolished all authorial intrusions and his own views.[22]

Character and plot

Rulfo has broken up the conventions of the traditional novel, based on sequence, plot, and well-rounded characters, E. M. Forster's "tyranny by the plot . . . and by characters," to induce the belief, in the reader, that what is being read is true.[23] There is no way that the novel can be reorganized into a linear narrative. We can piece together only a rough chronology that harks back to the late 1850s (there are no dates in the novel) when Pedro Páramo was born, to somewhere in the 1910s when Susana dies (and the revolution explodes) to when Pedro dies aged sixty-eight, perhaps in 1926 (during the Cristero rebellion), to 1934 when Juan Preciado arrives in Comala at the start of the novel and dies himself. There is an implicit time span of nearly eighty years, thoroughly splintered into some 77 or 78 fragments (according to the *Los murmullos* edition or the final one).

Rulfo's method of characterization links subjectivity to landscape (as already suggested), gives nearly all the information through monologue and dialogue (as voices), and avoids physical description. When Juan Preciado asks Abundio, the muleteer, who Pedro Páramo is, at the start, he is told "Un rencor vivo" (10; "living bile" [6]), a moral quality, for in fact, over the novel, Páramo takes it out on the village for his failure in love. Another time, he's called "la pura maldad" (88; "unmitigated evil" [83]) and "enorme" (71; "towering" [66]), that's all. Pedro establishes the law ("La Ley de ahora en adelante la vamos a hacer nosotros" [44]; "From now on we're the law" [40]) according to his whims. He never went to school and is "ignorante," exemplified in his mispronunciation of "usufruto" for "usufructo" (44) ("usufruct / use"), a legal term that summarizes Pedro Páramo's land-grabbing strategies to become rich and powerful. Pedro Páramo is the archetypal "macho." Again, it is useful to compare his portrayal with Octavio Paz's analysis of the Mexican male in "Máscaras mexicanas," published separately in 1949 (and collected in *El laberinto de la soledad*, 1950). This male locks himself up as a defense; he is mute, polite, hermetic, and never reveals weaknesses. Rather, he is always aggressive ("chingar o de ser chingado"; 66 ["Screw or be screwed"]). Paz linked the landscape with this cactus-like psychology and concluded that this male conceals his humanity so well that he "becomes stone, *pirú*, wall, silence" as if Paz was describing Pedro Páramo.[24] But one thing power cannot obtain is love and Pedro cannot coerce Susana into love. At the heart of this story of power and decline is the love story between

Susana San Juan and Pedro. He daydreams of her as a boy when poor and lonely, but is then separated from her for over thirty years, when she marries another (and she in turn daydreams of her dead husband Florencio). Back in Comala, she is prepared to marry Pedro (who kills off her miner father), but she's "mad," and dies. Bells ring in mourning for three days in Comala, but instead a fiesta develops, and Pedro takes revenge and lets the village fall into ruins: "Me cruzaré de brazos y Comala se morirá de hambre. Y así lo hizo" (121; "I will cross my arms and Comala will die of hunger. And that's what happened" [115]). He is finally murdered by his son Abundio (though this scene is very ambiguous because it is narrated like a dream or in a drunken haze as Abundio is drunk, and Páramo doesn't immediately die when knifed), the muleteer who Juan Preciado meets at the opening of the novel, and the vicious circle closes. Rulfo told Luis Harss that in Mexico "we are stuck in a deadlock."[25] All had begun with Pedro's father's violent death from a stray bullet, which generated more violence as Pedro wipes out all possible assassins (all the wedding guests), until nothing is left but stagnant memories of gratuitous violence.

Further nuanced characters function effectively within the conventions of the realist novel. "Todo comenzó con Miguel Páramo" (25; "It all began with Miguel Páramo" [20]), Eduviges tells us as her sixth sense warns her of Miguel Páramo's death on horseback. He was the only recognized son and heir. His violence, his "machismo" reflect Pedro's, who on hearing of his death realizes that "estoy comenzando a pagar" (72; "I am beginning to pay" [67]). The guilty priest Padre Rentería, whose brother was murdered by Miguel Páramo, and whose niece was raped by him, is the only person who understands. He is educated, can read, but cannot prevent anything until he rides off with the Catholic "Cristero" rebels after being refused absolution from a neighboring priest. We see Susana San Juan from the inside, through her monologues, something Pedro is unable to do. We are asked the question, What is Susana's world? To be answered "Ésa fue una de las cosas que Pedro Páramo nunca llegó a saber" (99; "That was one of the things that Pedro Páramo would never know" [94]). But Susana is also unable to see into Pedro's mind and his yearning for her ("Tan la quiso, que se pasó el resto de sus años aplastado en un equipal, mirando el camino por donde se la habían llevado al camposanto" (84; "He loved her so much, that he spent the rest of his days slumped in a chair, staring down the road where they'd carried her to holy ground" [79]). Susana lives off her erotic memories of her dead husband. She is the sole person who knew "love": "Él me cobijaba entre sus brazos. Me daba amor" (118; "He sheltered me in his arms. He gave me love" [113]). There is Dolores Preciado, with her false memories of Comala resounding in her son Juan's head, who was married off to Pedro to solve his debt. Because she was menstruating, she asked a woman friend to stand in for her on the hastily arranged wedding night (22). And finally, there is Dorotea, with her pretend baby. All of Rulfo's characters are trapped in their false memories, in their daydreams and illusions.

If this haunting, lyrical novel is reduced to themes, it can be easily fitted into the Latin American tradition of the rural novel, dealing with lawless bosses. But what makes it resistant to this kind of reductionism is the way it forces the reader to collaborate in making sense of the dreamy voices and fragments. The novel has become a nostalgic mirror for an inarticulate and rural version of being Latin American, as meaningful for local urban readers as it is for universal readers. I close by invoking the critic and writer Susan Sontag, who calmly claimed that this "multivoiced sojourn in hell" was not only a masterpiece of twentieth-century world literature, but "one of the most influential of the century's books."[26]

NOTES

1. Juan Rulfo, "*Pedro Páramo*, 39 años después," *El País* (January 13, 1986): 14.
2. Juan Rulfo, *Pedro Páramo*, trans. Mararet Sayers Peden (London: Serpent's Tail, 1994), is the translation I have used.
3. In *Contemporáneos*, VIII, n. 26–27 (July–August, 1930): 7–32. Thanks to Tom Boll for a photocopy of this first translation of Eliot into Spanish.
4. See Paz in conversation with Emir Rodríguez Monegal "El surrealismo es uno" in Julio Ortega (ed.), *Convergencias / divergencias / incidencias* (Barcelona: Tusquets, 1973, pp. 176–79).
5. *Contemporáneos*, 16.
6. Reina Roffe, *Juan Rulfo: autobiografía armada* (Buenos Aires: Corregidor, 1973), p. 64.
7. Juan Rulfo, *El llano en llamas* (Mexico City: Fondo de Cultura Económica, 1967), p. 31. Page numbers are inserted in the text. Translations from the stories are my own literal ones.
8. The edition used here is *Pedro Páramo* (Mexico City: Fondo de Cultura Económica, 1969), page numbers inserted in the text. Useful editions are those by José Carlos González Boixo (Madrid: Cátedra, 1983); by Jorge Rufinelli (Caracas: Ayacucho, 1977) and by Claude Fell (Madrid: Archivos, 1991). Glancing at Rulfo's black and white photographs is also recommended; see note 17.
9. Alan Riding, *Mexico. Inside the Volcano* (London: Coronet, 1987), p. 192.
10. Roffe, *Juan Rulfo*, p. 62.
11. James Irby, *La influencia de William Faulkner en cuatro narradores hispanoamericanos* (Mexico City: UNAM, 1956).
12. Octavio Paz, *El laberinto de la soledad* (Mexico City: Fondo de Cultura Económica, 1964), p. 18.
13. Roberto Cantú, "Fragmentos de un sistema discursivo: Juan Rulfo y la literatura mexicana de 1945 a 1965," *Escolios* (May–November, 1979): 86.

14. Octavio Paz, *El laberinto de la soledad*, pp. 48–51.
15. Carlos Fuentes, *La nueva novela hispanoamericana* (Mexico City: Joaquín Mortiz, 1969), p. 16.
16. "Breves nostalgias sobre Juan Rulfo," *El Espectador* (December 7, 1980): 2A.
17. Carlos Monsiváis in *Inframundo. El México de Juan Rulfo* (Hanover, NH: Ediciones del Norte, 1983), p. 30.
18. Fernando B. Benítez, "Conversación con Juan Rulfo," *Inframundo*, 6.
19. "Rulfo en la Universidad Central de Venezuela," *La Gaceta*, 301 (January 1996): 10.
20. The Archivos edition shows the variations between the two versions, but not the cutting down from an earlier typescript that I refer to.
21. Luis Harss, *Los nuestros* (Buenos Aires: Sudamericana, 1968), p. 332.
22. *El país*, 14.
23. E. M. Forster, *Aspects of the Novel* (Harmondsworth: Penguin, 1977), p. 99.
24. Octavio Paz, *El laberinto de la soledad*, pp. 36–37, 66.
25. Luis Harss, *Los nuestros*, p. 312.
26. Susan Sontag, *Where the Stress Falls* (London: Jonathan Cape, 2002), pp. 106 and 108; also the foreword to Margaret Sayers Peden's translation.

FURTHER READING

Blanco Aguinaga, Carlos, "Realidad y estilo de Juan Rulfo," *Revista Mexicana de Literatura* 1 (September–October, 1955): 59–86.
González Boixo, José, *Claves narrativas de Juan Rulfo*, León: Colegio Universitario, 1980.
Luis, Leal, *Juan Rulfo*, Boston: Twayne, 1983.
Roffé, Reina, *Juan Rulfo. Las mañas del zorro*, Madrid: Espasa Calpe, 2003.
Rodríguez Alcalá, Hugo, *El arte de Juan Rulfo*, Mexico City: INBA, 1965.
Rulfo, Juan, *Inframundo, el México de Juan Rulfo*, Hanover, NH: Ediciones del Norte, 1983.
   Toda la obra, ed. Claude Fell, Paris: Colección Archivos, 1992.

13

CLAIRE WILLIAMS

The Passion According to G.H. by Clarice Lispector

Clarice Lispector's fifth novel, *A paixão segundo G.H.* (*The Passion Accord-ing to G.H.*) came out in Rio de Janeiro in 1964. It was the first book-length narrative she published following her definitive return to Brazil after sixteen years of accompanying her husband on diplomatic postings around the world. During her time abroad, she had continued to write and publish in Brazil, contributing short stories and articles to magazines and news-papers. This served to increase her popularity back home and bring her work to a wider circle of readers than her books alone had managed. In fact, a collection of short stories entitled *A Legião Estrangeira* (*The Foreign Legion*) was published the same year as *A paixão segundo G.H.* and threat-ened to overshadow the reception of the novel.[1] But this was a short-lived phenomenon: *The Passion According to G.H.* has since proved to be one of Lispector's best-loved, bestselling, and best-studied works. This disturbing tale of a woman who kills a cockroach differed from her previous books in the dense, intense voice of its first-person narrator and its episodic and fragmented nature. From the outset, it was well received by the critics, espe-cially in Brazil, with several book-length studies and doctoral theses devoted to it.

The Passion is also one of the most translated of Lispector's works: into Spanish (Uruguay, 1970), French (1978), Italian (1982), Japanese and German (1984), Spanish (1979), English (1988), Danish and Norwegian (1989). It is seen by many as her *magnum opus*; the fact that it was cho-sen to be part of the UNESCO-sponsored Archivos series of critical editions of key Spanish American and lusophone works (published in 1988 with a second edition in 1996) attests to this.[2] In Diane E. Marting's extremely thorough and useful *Bio-bibliography of Clarice Lispector*, the chapter on *The Passion* comprises ninety-eight references to critical essays, books, the-ses, and articles in comparison to sixty entries for *A hora da estrela* (*The Hour of the Star*) – Lispector's last and most socially conscious novel, also made into a film – and forty-two for *Perto do coração selvagem* ("Close to the wild heart") – her rapturously praised début –, and critical attention has remained high in spite of, or maybe because of, its complexity.[3]

The plot is minimalist: a woman who kills a cockroach is inspired to take stock of her life and her relationship with the world around her. The form of the narrative is unusual and challenging and it interweaves multiple historical, mystical, philosophical, and religious allusions. Yet trying to identify separate themes or ideas is not straightforward because "everything overlaps."[4] Trying to keep up with the narrator's stream of consciousness, the reader is presented with the dilemmas she faces and witnesses the grotesque act of defilement/redemption/communion that brings her psychological and philosophical wanderings to an apparent conclusion. Hardest of all are the endless unresolved questions she puts to herself, because they open the text up to endless possible answers, defying readers to continue journeys on the trains of thought upon which she herself has embarked. For this is a narrative concerned with searching for the words to describe and thereby come to terms with a traumatic experience. By extension it questions the function and limits of language itself and the implications for the processes of writing and reading.

Plot and structure

In terms of action, very little actually happens in the course of this short narrative of one hundred and sixty pages divided into thirty-three overlapping sections. Instead, a continuous flow of thoughts and meditations is activated by unexpected occurrences, sights, and sensations that trigger repressed memories, thus facilitating revelations, or constructing ideas. These kinds of transforming encounters and experiences that provoke chaos, self-interrogation, or epiphany are a constant presence in Lispector's work, which investigates the formation of identity and the quest for self-knowledge, as Marta Peixoto has shown in her pioneering work on the author: *Passionate Fictions*.[5] The narrator, identified only by her initials, G.H., needs to express and confess the extraordinary experience she underwent on the previous day so she conjures up an interlocutor and addresses her words to a "Tu" ("you"), identified loosely with her ex-lover, but also building up the illusion that she is talking directly to the reader. This interlocutor, who acts as a link with the real world, helps, by holding her hand, to prevent the horrors and delights of the day before from overwhelming her.

The eponymous narrator is a financially independent woman who owns a penthouse apartment and whose maid, Janair, has just resigned. G.H. is a sculptress and control freak who likes to tidy, rearrange, and plan ahead. She is also shallow and superficial, aware that her life is somewhat of a performance for other people. On the day in question, she had planned to clean out the room recently vacated by Janair in preparation for a new maid to move in. But what happens in that room leads her to reevaluate the way she behaves towards others and the means by which she defines her own identity and her finitude.

She feels herself falling: "Caindo séculos e séculos dentro de uma lama – era lama, e nem sequer lama já seca mas lama ainda úmida e ainda viva, era uma lama onde se remexiam com lentidão insuportável as raízes de minha identidade" (61; "Falling through centuries and centuries inside a kind of mud – it was mud, and not even dried mud but mud that was still wet and still alive, it was mud where the roots of my identity moved about unbearably slowly").[6] She feels as though she has been swallowed up by the mud from which life evolved, not like clay that she can sculpt and mould to her wishes, but living matter. Her panic is increased by the fact that she can move only very slowly. This lingering attention to drawn-out suffering returns with the death of the cockroach later in the book and also affects the reader, who is forced to witness extreme pain for most of the duration of the narrative.

The novel begins with a warning to all potential readers that it is a book just like any other (13), about the long and painful process of getting close to something or someone, even an opposite, and that will give to, rather than take from, those who encounter it. This strange statement is followed by an epigraph in English (a quotation from Bernard Berenson) that underlines the notion of an encounter between contrasting entities, ideally leading to "so full identification with the non-self that there is no self to die" (14), in other words a process that would effectively cancel out death. The word "Passion" in the title, alluding to the books of the New Testament that describe Christ's life, death, and resurrection "according to" the Evangelists, provides a clue to the theme of redemption and rebirth which pervade the text. Her retelling of the biblical Passion provides an ironic and sinister alternative that questions the relevance of the original.

The very structure, composed almost musically of sections whereby the last words of one become the first words of the next, emphasizes the idea of resurrection and circularity. Like the cliff-hanging hooks at the end of each of Scheherazade's tales, the words mark the continuity between the sections but allow the text itself to be divided into more palatable pieces, a technique explained by G.H. during the first section: "Uma forma contorna o caos, uma forma dá construção à substância amorfa – a visão de uma carne infinita é a visão dos loucos, mas se eu cortar a carne em pedaços e distribui-los pelos dias e pelas fomes – então ela não será mais a perdição e a loucura: será de novo a vida humanizada" (18; "Form marks the boundaries of chaos, form provides a structure for the amorphous substance – the vision of infinite flesh is the vision of the mad, but if I cut the flesh into pieces and share them among the days and intensities of hunger – then it will no longer be perdition and madness: it will once again be humanized life"). The actual text of the narrative is interrupted, preceded, and followed by dashes that mark the threshold between silence and words (and between punctuation and writing), but that also function like a scar or stitches over a wound, holding in place a story almost too difficult to tell.

The passion of the title, then, is G.H.'s metaphysical journey from ignorance (and innocence) to knowledge and fear, progressing towards confidence through a process that involves tasks and trials, encounters and confrontations, a questioning and ultimate rejection of official discourses (religion and science) and beliefs, and will entail sacrifice and suffering. G.H. learns not to trust blindly absolutes or extremes but to accept the possibilities that lie between them and beyond fixed meanings and values:

> Vou agora te contar como entrei no inexpressivo que sempre foi a minha busca cega e secreta. De como entrei naquilo que existe entre o número um e o número dois, de como vi a linha de mistério e fogo, e que é linha sub-reptícia. Entre duas notas de música existe uma nota, entre dois fatos existe um fato, entre dois grãos de areia por mais juntos que estejam existe um intervalo de espaço, existe um sentir que é entre o sentir [. . .]. A continuidade tem interstícios que não a descontinuam, o milagre é a nota que fica entre duas notas de música, é o número que fica entre o número um e o número dois. (102, 173)

> (Now I'll tell you how I entered the inexpressive, which was always my blind and secret quest. About how I entered what exists between the number one and the number two, about how I saw the line of mystery and fire, which is the secret line. Between two musical notes another note exists, between two facts another fact exists, between two grains of sand, no matter how close together they are, an interval of space exists, a feeling exists that is beyond feeling [. . .]. Continuity has interstices that do not stop it from continuing, the miracle is what there is between two musical notes, it is the number between one and two.)

In fact, the ordeal she undergoes places her in an in-between situation: she is between maids, between lovers, and she sees herself living "entre aspas" ("in, or between, quotation marks"). The dashes that begin and end the text mark the fact that this is an aside, an intrusion, a discrete series of events, within another wider one. This idea is confirmed by G.H.'s references to her temporal location: she wants to capture the present: "uma atualidade que queima [. . .] uma atualidade permanente" (106, 150; "a present that burns, a permanent present"), cut loose from ties to the past and the future. The actual events of the plot, recounted in retrospect, yet still very fresh in her mind, follow the narrator's movements from the breakfast table through her apartment to the tiny storeroom that doubles as the maid's quarters. Full of preconceptions about the working class, G.H. expects the room to be filthy but instead finds it uncluttered and decorated, by its recently departed occupant, with a stark charcoal mural representing three naked figures: a man, a woman, and a dog.[7] Shaken by this invasion of her territory she is further upset when she realizes that crawling out of the wardrobe is a huge cockroach – the insect she fears the most. She is able to muster enough courage to slam the wardrobe door on the creature and crush its shell, although without enough force to kill it outright.

Transfixed by the expiring cockroach, G.H. watches its whitish innards slowly emerging through the crack she has made in its body. Her emotions range from triumph at having committed a determined act, through shock at the insect's beauty, to disgust at herself for having destroyed another living creature. Partly in recompense and to be worthy of redemption, partly to devour and ingest a part of the animal world in order to fill the nagging emptiness inside her, she eats some of the matter oozing from the cockroach's wound. This gesture is at once Eve's transgressive bite at the apple, a rite of initiation into self-knowledge, and an act of communion (another parody of Christian ritual). It reconciles her symbolically with God (the ultimate Other or non-self that the cockroach comes to represent) and the natural world ("A vida se me é"; ["life is itself, does itself to me"]). It cleanses her and strips her of the artificiality and constructed sentiment (*sentimentação*) that had characterized her previously.

The maid's room, the maid, and the mural

The novel's sense of claustrophobia is conveyed by the fact that most of it is set in a very specific enclosed space: the maid's room, which is described in great detail, with close attention to textures, sounds and silence, colors, effects of light and shadow, layout, and décor. Unable to escape from the vigilance of the dying cockroach and move back into her own territory (the main part of her apartment), G.H. stares out of the small window, examines the mural, and uses her imagination to transport herself to faraway places and other eras (like Ancient Egypt). She is an artist who works with shape, and therefore very sensitive to appearances, yet her reaction to two-dimensional images is problematic. Early in the narrative, for example, she considers the reproduction of images, thinking particularly of the emptiness and inexpressiveness of her own eyes when she is photographed. They seem to reflect the fragility and artificiality of her public persona and her enigmatic but silent and meaningless smile ("todos os retratos de pessoas são um retrato de Mona Lisa. [. . .] eu era uma réplica bonita [. . .] mulher que sorri e ri" [31, 35]; "all portraits of people are a portrait of Mona Lisa. I was a beautiful replica, a woman who smiles and laughs").

Part of the shock of seeing the mural is G.H.'s realization that three separate sets of eyes are looking directly at her. After the heat, light, height, and cramped space of the room have led her to imagine herself inside a pyramid, she is surprised that the figures are not in profile like Egyptian wall-paintings but instead face the viewer as in traditional portraits, anatomical drawings, or cave paintings.[8] They all represent the confrontational stare of the absent maid who drew them defiantly on the wall, unable to challenge her mistress whilst in her employ. Caught in their gaze, G.H. suddenly feels herself to be a passive object, rather than an active subject, and thus vulnerable, an effect echoed in the way that she sometimes refers to herself in the first person and sometimes in the third person. She becomes aware that Janair was not "invisível" ("invisible") (45), but a thinking, feeling subject whom she never dreamed of treating as an equal. Having casually stated that her own secret talent (46) is to clean and tidy up, that if she had been born in different circumstances she would be a maid (37), G.H. suddenly finds herself inside the maid's room looking out at the mistress's apartment, seeing from the maid's point of view. She becomes an intruder, an outsider in her own home.

This reversal in positions (which develops into full-blown identification) happens in the confrontation with the cockroach too, echoing encounters with other people, animals, and objects elsewhere in Lispector's work that trigger existential crisis.[9] The insect has multiple eyes all turned on G.H. and it makes her aware of her selfishness and lack of consideration for others in a similar way to Gregor Samsa's physical and emotional transformation in Kafka's *The Metamorphosis*.[10] The eyes, fringed with layers of eyelashes (Lispector uses the technical term "cílio" rather than the more commonly used "pestana"; this is part of her parodying of the sort of technical language that distances readers) are likened to ovaries and, in a reflective kaleidoscopic effect, to dozens of cockroaches, underlining the link between the cockroach and fertility (60). G.H., in contrast, once terminated a pregnancy. Furthermore, she suffers from selective blindness: she has problems seeing beyond the surface of things. During her experiences in the maid's room, though, she learns to see in disturbing but rewarding new ways, as Hélène Cixous explains: "the whole process of *The Passion According to G.H.* consists in letting the reader understand that there is a super-vision, capable of seeing our quotidian organization, the world, appearances, reality in general, everything that the economy of ordinary life prevents us from seeing."[11] G.H. sees new dimensions to the objects inside the room: the dusty suitcases, the stains and hairs on the old mattress that mark the comings and goings of successive maids, the fine segments that make up the cockroach's hard casing. She also stares out of the window over the rooftops of the city and the hills cluttered with slum dwellings, emphasizing her isolation at the top of the building, thus temporarily relieving the claustrophobic atmosphere of the small brightly illuminated room.

G. H. is aware of the temporary nature of her experience in the maid's room and is able to see forwards, past it: "Eu estava vivendo a pré-história de um futuro" (70; "I was living the prehistory of a future"). She often refers to a past so ancient or a future so far ahead that the millions of years she describes lose their force and concentrate into atemporality, defying the finite measurements and chronological advance upon which scientific and narrative discourse rely, as William Paulson explains: "The present of human history and culture thus seems but a coincidental moment in a nested concatenation of self-similar structures and time-frames."[12]

Although the "action" is contained within the frame of one day, G.H.'s thoughts also spill into the recent past and future to situate it between temporal markers, like quotation marks. Her ordeal is told with the benefit of hindsight and the distance necessary to be able to consider its events and embellish them at length rather than blurting them out in panic and relief. She looks back and remembers cozy days spent at home with her lover, and moments of tension with Janair. She plans to go out dancing at the "Top Bambino" club with her friends that very night, buoyed up with the confidence that surviving has given her. This glimpse of the immediate future and the admission that she wants to forget what happened contrast with the references to the superimposition of the many onto the few (the cockroach represents every cockroach that has ever existed since prehistory; Janair symbolizes all the ignored maids in Brazil; G.H. realizes that "Toda mulher é a mulher de todas as mulheres" (178; "Every woman is the woman in all women"). In this way, Lispector plays with notions of individuality and representativeness, identity and anonymity, the self-same and the unique.

Her physical journey through the text is very simple, unlike her psychological trajectory. She moves from the living room, where she eats breakfast, through the kitchen and the utility room and down a dark corridor to the maid's room, the smallest room in her apartment and the one where she usually spends the least amount of time. She describes the process as falling down a horizontal well (49) into the apartment's "cauda" (38; "tail"), its very end (38), as if the building has been tilted sideways. She describes the room in a variety of ways emphasizing its isolation and self-containment, including: a lunatic's cell (41, 42), a minaret (42, 45), the portrait of an empty belly (46), and a cubicle made up only of surfaces with no clear beginning or end (47). It is above all bare and in need of filling, like Janair's hungry stomach and G.H.'s hollow soul. The play of emptiness and plenitude link in with the idea of love as lack that recurs throughout the narrative, as does the cannibal instinct to incorporate the outside world and absorb its qualities.

The room's bleakness and the brilliant white light that floods through its window halt her at the threshold, preventing her entry. She feels excluded and out of place, as if she will not fit into the space. This sense of formlessness almost to the extent of disintegration is evoked again and again in the text as G.H.'s sense of self explodes beyond the boundary of her body or any physical constraint until eventually her "invólucro" ("casing") breaks (182). When she sees the mural she realizes that what was once her territory has been appropriated and marked boldly by her ex-maid, becoming the opposite of what G.H. herself had created within her home (46). She reads it as a defiant message, seeing the nakedness of the figures as intended to confront her with a portrait of herself as an empty shell. Furious, she wants to reclaim her territory, scrape the mural from the wall and erase all traces of the maid, although she identifies herself in the female figure (68). The mural shows only the outlines of three creatures, once again showing the emptiness of two-dimensional images, which is exactly the reason G.H. sees herself reflected there. She describes them as zombies, mummies, and robots – soulless, inhuman creatures. Their nudity is emphasized – perhaps Janair meant to shock her prudish employer, or to remind her of Adam and Eve and the loss of innocence, or maybe to show that even naked bodies are only surfaces and that identity resides beyond the flesh.

Relating to the images of size, shape, space, depth, and containment, architectural, geological, and geographical metaphors abound throughout this novel. Several times G.H. describes her breakdown as the collapse of a building, as someone lost in the desert or sinking into quicksand (48, 61, 72). Likewise, the apartment block where she lives resembles her in its smooth façade that masks an interior with cracks, stains, and shadows (38–40). The building reminds her of the pyramids of Egypt and other ancient civilizations that crumbled over time. The interior heat, dust, and light of the maid's room conjure up images of the desert and biblical settings and references to volcanoes, canyons, and gulches, quicksand, sweeping plains; landscapes which could be prehistoric or post-apocalyptic. But rubble can be cleared, and buildings can be renovated and reconstructed.

The encounter with the cockroach

The cockroach is a creature that has survived the collapse of a succession of civilizations and has a structure so resilient that it has not needed to evolve since ancient times (51–53). G.H. is scared of the cockroach in her wardrobe because it is another unexpected inhabitant of the maid's room, as well being a household pest reminding her of her own disadvantaged childhood. However, once she has overcome the terrifying sadistic elation of destroying the creature by slamming the door on it (reveling in an action diametrically opposed to her favorite activities of sculpting and tidying), the crushed body draws her attention magnetically. She leans closer to appreciate details of its structure: the lush lashes framing many eyes, the twitching antennae, the shiny carapace composed of overlapping layers of fine plated scales. Gradually, G.H. starts to identify with the insect whose bisected "waist" recalls only too vividly the unwanted pregnancy she terminated and the subsequent emotional and physical effects. G.H. admires the creature's resilience and fecundity, attributes she lacks. Instead, she feels the need to slough her skin and begin her life again. The insect becomes a kind of idealized female creature, described both as young bride and even the Virgin Mary.

The decision to eat the matter that issues from the cockroach binds G.H. to the insect in solidarity, and, through incorporation, it will live on inside her – in the same way that the blood and body of Christ are distributed to the faithful worshippers during the Communion service. This notwithstanding the fact that the cockroach is one of the animals forbidden in the Book of Leviticus, which is quoted and paraphrased several times in Lispector's novel. The trial of committing such an act, ingesting the disgusting, is also proof that she can endure extreme suffering and sacrifice in order to achieve redemption. In this she makes connections with Job, and the saints and martyrs who kissed lepers, drank from the wounds of the sick, and endured unbearable torture in the name of their faith. She also voices Lispector's preoccupation with heroism: how one becomes a hero and how this affects one's identity. G.H. espouses depersonalization and deheroization, which makes her no longer an individual but a representative of humankind. Indeed, her initials (G.H.) may stand for "gênero humano" (178–79; "human race").[13]

There are links here to the medieval mystics who dreamed of reaching beyond human limits to attain union with the absolute (Western religions) or complete depersonalization (Eastern religions), in trances or ecstatic visions, later recorded as examples of extreme spirituality.[14] Such a goal could be achieved only once the body had been purified. And Lispector's narrative is pared down to the bare minimum in terms of plot, characterization, and language itself, as is evident in the continual questioning of naming and meaning. She is wary of certain terms and neutralizes them with "o chamado" ("so-called"), or "o que se chama" ("what is known as"). G.H. is suspicious of anything she considers an "acréscimo" ("accretion") because she is searching for authentic matter and meaning, what she calls "o neutro" ("the neutral"), "inexpressivo" ("inexpressive") and "insosso" ("insipid"): "O nome é um acréscimo, e impede o contato com a coisa. [. . .] Não quero a beleza, quero a identidade. A beleza seria um acréscimo, e agora vou ter que dispensá-la. [. . .] O acréscimo é mais fácil de amar" (143, 162, 173; "A name is something additional, and it impedes contact with the thing. I don't want beauty, I want identity. Beauty would be something added, and I'm going to have to do without it. The additional is easier to love").

Language ultimately fails in G.H.'s attempt to describe what she has endured. Lispector's subversion of the rules of grammar and semantics make her text rich in ambiguity, transmitting a sense of "potential language chaos."[15] She uses transitive verbs intransitively, negates usually positive words with the suffixes "de" (de-heroization) or "in" ("indizível" [unsayable]), and thrives on making language contradict itself ("Todo momento de achar é um perder-se a si próprio" [20]; "Every moment of finding is a losing of the self"). She refers to standard oppositions (heaven and hell, dry and wet, hot and cold) only to question why one term has traditionally been valued over the other, eventually and effectively creating a neutral compromise analogous to the "identification with the non" mentioned in the book's epigraph. Through parody and repetition, she problematizes the validity of traditional systems of knowledge. Statements and questions pervade the text but no neat answers are provided, suggesting that sometimes mysteries cannot be solved, or challenging the reader to draw her/his own conclusions. G.H. has always been aware of the difficulty of her task:

> É preciso coragem para me aventurar numa tentativa de concretização do que sinto. É como se eu tivesse uma moeda e não soubesse em que país ela vale. [. . .] Precisarei com esforço traduzir sinais de telégrafo – traduzir o desconhecido para uma língua que desconheço, e sem entender para que valem os sinais. Falarei nessa linguagem sonâmbula que se eu estivesse acordada não seria linguagem. [. . .] Ah, será mais um grafismo que uma escrita, pois tento mais uma reprodução do que uma expressão. (24, 25)

> (I'll need courage to venture out in an attempt to concretize what I feel. It is as if I had a coin and did not know where it has currency. I'll need to force myself to translate telegraph signals – to translate the unknown into a language I don't know, without understanding what the signals mean. I will speak in this sleepwalker's language that would not be language if I were awake. Ah, it will be more making marks on paper than writing, because I'm aiming at reproduction rather than expression.)

What G.H. finds in the maid's room teaches her to see beneath surfaces, masks, and cases to the unadulterated matter of things. Only by appreciating the neutral, tasteless, silent, and meaningless can she come to terms with life. The events that take place there are a series of unanswerable questions, as if during her journey of "approximation" or "identification with the non-self" G.H. is turning back on herself, venturing down paths that turn out to be dead ends, clearing unexpected hurdles only to find herself faced with more, touching heaven and hell, yet ending up as she began – a deconstructed structure rebuilt through language. She is stuck in a vortex of intersecting contradictions, a room with no beginning or end; and the reader has the sense that her search will spiral on forever.

NOTES

1. One of the stories in that collection, "A Quinta História" ("The Fifth Story"), could be seen as a prequel to *The Passion* because it deals with ways of exterminating cockroaches. Its presentation of a selection of titles and successive retellings of the murderous act can also be seen as paving the way for the structure of the novel.

2. *Brazilian Authors Translated Abroad* (Rio de Janeiro: Fundação Biblioteca Nacional, Dept. Nac. do Livro / Seção de Divulgação Internacional, 1994), p. 105; Marting, pp. 116–18.

3. For details of critical attention, see Benjamin Abdala Júnior and Samira Youssef Campedelli "Vozes da Crítica," in *A paixão segundo G.H., Edição Crítica*, coordinated by Benedito Nunes, 2nd edn (Madrid and Paris: ALLCA XX, 1996; Colección Archivos: 13), pp. 196–206; and Diane E. Marting (ed.), *Clarice Lispector: A Bio-bibliography* (Westport, Conn: Greenwood, 1993), pp. 113–32.

4. William Paulson, "Closing the Circle: Science, Literature, and the Passion of Matter," *New England Review and Bread Loaf Quarterly* 12, 1 (1989): 512–26, p. 521. An updated and modified version of this essay, "The Invention of a Non-Modern World," appears in Cláudia Pazos Alonso and Claire Williams (eds.), *Closer to the Wild Heart: Essays on Claire Lispector*, Oxford: Legenda, European Humanities Research Centre, 2002, pp. 198–212.

5. Marta Peixoto, *Passionate Fictions: Gender, Narrative and Violence in Clarice Lispector* (Minneapolis: University of Minnesota Press, 1994).

6. Clarice Lispector, *A paixão segundo G.H.*, 16th edn (Rio de Janeiro: Francisco Alves, 1991). Page numbers refer to this edition. All translations are my own.

7. On the social dimension of this text and others by Lispector, see Marta Peixoto's fascinating essay "'Fatos são pedras duras': Urban Poverty in Clarice Lispector," in Alonso and Williams, *Closer to the Wild Heart*, pp. 106–25. In this article, Peixoto skillfully analyzes Lispector's treatment of class difference, particularly the relationships between her middle-class protagonists and their maids.

8. Ancient Egypt – the desert, scarab beetles, decorated tombs inside the pyramids – is a frequent cultural reference in the text. It represents the depth of G.H.'s experience because she feels transported to an exotic place and a distant time far from

her modern city life, but where cockroaches already existed. Allusions to Egypt also reinforce the contrast between dryness (the desert) and wetness (life) in the novel and recall the theme of death (the tomb, mummified bodies, reincarnation).

9. Well-known examples of these catalysts are a blind man ("Amor," *Laços de família*), a buffalo ("O Búfalo," *Laços de Família*), an egg ("O ovo e a galinha," *A legião estrangeira*), and a clock ("Relatório de uma coisa," *Onde estivestes de noite*).

10. The intertextual link with Kafka's *The Metamorphosis* is explored by Paul B. Dixon in "*A paixão segundo G.H.*: Kafka's Passion According to Clarice Lispector," *Romance Notes* 21, 3 (1981): 298–304.

11. Hélene Cixous, *Readings: The Poetics of Blanchot, Joyce, Kafka, Kleist, Lispector, and Tsvetayeva*, ed., trans., and intr. Verena Andermatt Conley (London: Harvester Wheatsheaf, 1992), p. 97. Cixous was instrumental in bringing Lispector's work to an international audience and has written widely on the Brazilian author's texts, describing them as exemplary of *écriture féminine*. Her most important essays on Lispector are translated and collected in *"Coming to Writing" and Other Essays*, ed. Deborah Jenson, intr. by Susan Rubin Suleiman (Cambridge, Mass.: Harvard University Press, 1991).

12. Paulson, "Closing the Circle," p. 523.

13. Michel Peterson has suggested that G.H. is the "figuration du genre humain (gênero humano) dans sa totalité anonyme" (the figuration of humankind in its anonymous totality); "Les cafards de Clarice Lispector," *Études françaises* 25, 1 (1989): 39–50. José Américo Motta Pessanha offers an alternative interpretation of the letters as standing for "Gente Heróica" (heroic race/people), "O itinerário da paixão," *Remate de Males* 9 (1989): 181–98, p. 198.

14. On the mystical aspects of the novel, see the essays by Krabbenhoft, Nunes, Owen, and Patai cited below in the further reading list.

15. Ronald W. Sousa, "At the Site of Language: Reading Lispector's G.H.," *Chasqui* 18, 2 (1989): 43–48, p. 48. This is an extended version of Sousa's introduction to his translation of the novel, *The Passion According to G.H.* (Minneapolis: University of Minnesota Press, 1988).

FURTHER READING

Castillo, Debra A., "Negation: Clarice Lispector," in her *Talking Back: Towards a Latin American Feminist Literary Criticism*, Ithaca: Cornell University Press, 1992, pp. 185–215.

Diogo, Américo Antonio Lindeza, *A vida das baratas: uma leitura d'A paixão segundo G.H. de Clarice Lispector*, Braga and Coimbra: Angelus Novus, 1993.

Frizzi, Adria, "The Thread of Return: Notes on the Genesis of Literary Discourse in Clarice Lispector's *A paixão segundo G.H.*," *Luso-Brazilian Review* 26 (1989): 24–32.

Hedrick, Tace, "Mother, Blessed be You Among Cockroaches: Essentialism, Fecundity, and Death in Clarice Lispector," *Luso-Brazilian Review* 34 (1997): 41–57.

Krabbenhoft, Kenneth, "From Mysticism to Sacrament in *A paixão segundo G.H.*," *Luso-Brazilian Review* 32 (1995): 51–60.

Nunes, Benedito, "O mundo imaginário de Clarice Lispector," in Benedito Nunes, *O dorso do tigre*, São Paulo: Perspectiva (1969): 93–139.

Oliveira, Solange Ribeiro de, *A barata e a crisálida: O romance de Clarice Lispector*, Rio de Janeiro: José Olympio, 1985.

Owen, Hilary, "Clarice Lispector Beyond Cixous. Ecofeminism and Zen in *A paixão segundo G.H.*," in H. Owen (ed.), *Gender, Ethnicity and Class in Modern Portuguese-Speaking Culture*, Lewiston: Edwin Mellen Press, 1996, pp. 161–84.

Patai, Daphne, "Clarice Lispector: Myth and Mystification," in Daphne Patai, *Myth and Ideology in Contemporary Brazilian Fiction*, London: Associated University Presses, 1983, pp. 76–110.

14

STEVEN BOLDY

One Hundred Years of Solitude
by Gabriel García Márquez

According to many testimonies, like García Márquez's exact contemporary the Mexican Carlos Fuentes or the Colombian critic many years younger than both, Michael Palencia Roth, *Cien años de soledad* (*One Hundred Years of Solitude*, 1967) is the one novel where Latin Americans recognize themselves instantly: their own social, cultural reality, their families, and the history of their countries.[1] It is also the mirror in which a generation of Europeans and North Americans, by the millions, since its publication have discovered the magical reality of an exotic continent, and a taste for its hallucinatory literature.[2] Are they reading the same novel?

One dimension of the "magical realism" which has been seen to characterize the novel is the simultaneous invocation of different mentalities, genres, sorts of truth and experience. The homely and the banal, the content of the hagiographical and the style of the chronicle come together when the priest can levitate only after imbibing drinking chocolate. A similar combination gives Remedios ascending to heaven and Fernanda's annoyance at losing her sheets in the ascension. The conjunction of genres generates synesthesia, the mixing of different senses: "un delicado viento de luz" ("a delicate wind of light").[3] The metaphor and the literal come together when Remedios, as femme fatale, has her suitors die from falls into latrines, kicks to the head from stallions, gun shots. The economic power of the United Fruit Company is translated into meteorological omnipotence when it causes a rainstorm of four years eleven months and two days. One dimension does not cancel or neutralize the other or fuse with it: the prose moves with apparent effortlessness from one to the other, as a Moebius strip.

Cien años de soledad generously invites reading, offers great textual pleasure, but merely tolerates interpretation. One has the impression that weighty motifs which in contemporary modernist texts by Fuentes or Cortázar would cry for analysis and commentary, such as solitude, incest, nostalgia, apocalyptic wind, are here *trompe l'oeil*, simulacra, honey pots for incautious exegetical flies. The uneven fortune of the many interpreters within the novel counsels caution. Aureliano José, who had been destined to live many happy years, is murdered because of an incorrect reading of the cards: "la bala [. . .] estaba dirigida por una mala interpretación de las barajas" (136; "the bullet was directed by a mistaken reading of the cards"). Aureliano Babilonia finally deciphers the manuscript only to read about himself deciphering the manuscript. Like Lonröt in Borges's "La muerte y la brújula," whose investigation shows that the final victim is to be himself, the interpretation is simply a mirror "un espejo hablado" (350; "a spoken mirror"), an image of the same.

Two very disparate models for his prose which García Márquez often mentions in just about the same breath reflect the novel's tight interweaving of different dimensions: the national and the cosmopolitan, the local and the universal, the historical and the mythical. These are the conversational style of his grandmother, Tranquilina Iguarán Cotes, and the text of Franz Kafka's *The Metamorphosis*. When at the age of seventeen he discovered that it was possible to write straightforwardly that one morning Gregory Samsa woke up to find he had been turned into an insect, he knew then that he would become a writer. Kafka used the same method in German as Márquez's grandmother in Spanish: "She would tell me the most atrocious things without batting an eyelid, as if it was something she had just seen."[4] In the established mythology around the genesis of the novel, Tranquilina has another lieutenant in his aunt, known locally to have an answer to every question. When a villager took her a strangely misshapen egg, she calmly judged that it belonged to a basilisk and should be burned; which it was.[5] The novel is the story of a town, Macondo, and six generations of a Colombian family, the Buendías, with a stubborn tendency to incest, to being ravaged by solitude, haunted by the fear of engendering the child with a pig's tail which is born to Aureliano Babilonia and his aunt Amaranta Úrsula in the final pages.[6] It is the story of real Colombian history, not so different from that of other Latin American republics: the struggle between Liberals and Conservatives and the Civil War of 1899–1902, the treaty of Neerlandia, the banana boom of the first decades of the century, the transfer of power from the *criollos* to multinational companies, the strike and massacre of workers in 1928, and the economic ruin of the area by the Caribbean coast. It is also a mythical narration of the original foundation involving murder and incest, exodus (before genesis), the prophetic dream of Macondo, the "ciudad ruidosa con casas de paredes de espejo" (28; "noisy city of mirror-walled houses"), various biblical-style plagues ranging from insomnia to love, and a final apocalyptic hurricane. The focus of the novel slips constantly and deftly between these three planes.

A key apparent dichotomy which the novel handles memorably is that between the referential and the metatextual. The novel has two patriarchs, José Arcadio Buenía, who founded and built the city with his wife and cousin Úrsula Iguarán, and the gypsy Melquíades, master of the occult, who wrote the manuscript in which the whole history of Macondo was predicted: city and text, action and thought. The manuscript is a classic *mise en abyme*, the novel within the novel which is deciphered at the end, and which is similar but probably not identical to the text of *Cien años de soledad*, though some critics follow Vargas Llosa in having Melquíades as the narrator of the whole novel. When the text ends, so does Macondo; it does not exist outside its representation (in this and other novels). Crucially, no opposition is clear-cut in the novel: Buendía moves from action and politics to an obsession with alchemy and science; Melquíades brings practical artifacts such as magnets and false teeth and cures the plague of insomnia. Roberto González Echevarría has persuasively identified Melquíades as an avatar of the Argentine arch-anti-realist writer Jorge Luis Borges. His room contains two works associated with Borges: the encyclopedia and *The Arabian Nights*. It is an image of the novel as an archive of the textual mediations, the authorizing paradigms of Latin American literature such as the chronicles, the *relación*, scientific travel literature, anthropology.[7]

The task of deciphering the manuscript is passed through the generations of Buendía males, but the two most obsessively involved, Aureliano Babilonia and his great uncle José Arcadio Segundo, are also the two figures most linked to censured political and historical knowledge: the massacre of the banana workers by the authorities in connivance with the United Fruit Company. Moreover, Aureliano is the son of the only proletarian to join the family: Mauricio Babilonia. The actual massacre took place at Ciénaga railway station in 1928, and knowledge of it was virtually erased from public knowledge and memory. Márquez reproduces real names of soldiers and words of the official decree. José Arcadio Segundo was involved in organizing a strike and witnessed the killings. He was taken as dead with hundreds of corpses to be dumped into the sea but escaped to discover that the inhabitants of Macondo had mysteriously forgotten about the massacre overnight: magical realism brilliantly used as political satire. He passes on the forbidden knowledge to Aureliano Babilonia. In the final days of dusty and forlorn decadence in Macondo, Aureliano finds a companion who shares his knowledge: the descendent of the liberal general Gerineldo Márquez, called Gabriel. This final pair in a way mirrors the founding patriarchs. While Aureliano is caught up by his destiny in the apocalyptic wind and will never leave the room of Melquíades, Gabriel Márquez exercises his free will and leaves Macondo for the wider world, for Paris to live in a hotel room later occupied by the characters of Cortázar's *Rayuela*, presumably to initiate the literary career which would culminate in the writing of *Cien años de soledad*.[8]

The presence of Borges, whose most influential short stories and essays such as *Ficciones* and *Otras inquisiciones* were written in the forties and fifties, is emblematic of his importance for the generation of the sixties novelists often known as the Boom. Though Márquez, a figure of the left and a strong supporter of the Cuban Revolution, disliked the conservative politics of Borges, he read him constantly. The textual and intellectual sophistication of the Argentine, his whimsical games with literary originality and tradition, the linguistic and the real, provide the tools and consciousness which allow the new novelists to go beyond the old realisms which preceded them, and beyond the Manichaeism of committed versus elitist literature, between the postmodern and historical fiction. In Hutcheon's terms *Cien años* is a "historiographical metafiction."[9] In Borges's "Tema del traidor y del héroe" we already see the history of the IRA being rewritten using plots from Shakespeare.

Another myth about the genesis of Márquez's novel, described by Márquez as "the decisive episode in my life as a writer"[10] introduces us to the central theme of return, recovery of the past, nostalgia. Michael Bell provides a usefully schematic comparison. Just as Cervantes's *Don Quixote* offers a satirical critique of the chivalric romance, yet is also an affectionate recreation of its long-lost values, so García Márquez's characters are destroyed by a negative nostalgia, yet his novel is a wistful celebration of his grandparents' house and world.[11] Another parallel would be the return of Juan Rulfo and his character Juan Preciado in *Pedro Páramo* (1955) to a Comala which at once "huele a miel derramada" ("smells of spilt honey")[12] and is the desolate site of the ghosts of the tormented dead. García Márquez had been brought up in the house of his grandparents at Aracataca, and the house is in many ways the living, and dying, protagonist of the novel. His grandfather Nicolás was the model for José Arcadio Buendía and, together with the liberal General Uribe Uribe, of Coronel Aureliano Buendía. The banana boom, with the exciting influx of strangers and migrant workers, the *hojarasca*, was still a vibrant memory in the town and his family; the house was filled by its ghosts. Aracataca was a rich, peculiar world of folk wisdom, local and family myths. When García Márquez was fifteen, after having lived what he experienced as exile from his luminous Caribbean roots, that is in the boarding school near the cold and inhospitable Bogotá, he accompanied his mother back to Aracataca to sell the family house. He found there his past ruined by the passage of time. "And it was a dusty and stifling place; it was a terrible midday, you breathed the dust."[13] His mother meets an old friend and they silently cry in each other's arms for half an hour.

García Márquez's novel is a literary battle to recover the Aracataca of his childhood from the ravages of time, a battle fought on many fronts, a gloriously undecided war. In the first nine chapters, presided over by the patriarch José Arcadio and the rival matriarchs Úrsula and Pilar Ternera, life is good; the final eleven, presided over by the parallel triad of José Aureliano, Fernanda del Carpio, and Petra Cotes, mirror them darkly as the tide turns in favor of decay. Two sites register the change most memorably. One is the Spanish galleon found in the jungle by the founding patriarch, and revisited many years later by his son the Colonel during one of the thirty-two rebellions he staged and lost. The first experience paradoxically fixes the wreck in a state of pristine and seductive atemporality: "Frente a ellos, rodeado de helechos y palmeras, blanco y polvoriento en la silenciosa luz de la mañana, estaba un enorme galeón español. [. . .] Toda la estructura parecía ocupar un ámbito propio, vedado a los vicios del tiempo y a las costumbres de los pájaros." (18; "Before them, surrounded by ferns and palms, white and dusty in the silent morning light, was an enormous Spanish galleon. [. . .] Its whole structure seemed to occupy a space of its own, immune from the vices of time and the customs of birds.") Viewed by the Colonel with a tired cynicism born of a long fight over power, "lo único que encontró fue el costillar carbonizado en medio de un campo de amapolas" (18; "the only thing he found was the charred rib-cage in the middle of a field of poppies"). The other is the room of Melquíades, perceived by some, in spite of being closed for many years, as luminous and immaculate, while others such as the soldier who comes to capture José Arcadio Segundo see only filth and spiders' webs.

In terms of the biblical book of Revelation Macondo is both Babylon and New Jerusalem, with a typical inversion: New Jerusalem is founded before Babylon is destroyed. The prophesied "city of mirror-walled houses," the "river of diaphanous waters which dashed over a bed of polished stones" (9), evoke the holy city whose light was "like unto a stone most precious, even like a jasper stone, clear and crystal" (Rev. 21:11), the "pure river of water of life, clear as crystal" (Rev. 22:1). It is this New Jerusalem which becomes the final unreal Babylon destroyed by the hurricane. Just as "with violence shall that great city Babylon be thrown down, and shall be found no more at all" (Rev. 18, 21), so in the final lines of the novel, "las estirpes condenadas a cien años de soledad no tendrán una segunda oportunidad sobre la tierra" ("family lines condemned to a hundred years of solitude will not have another chance on earth"). Other similar inversions suggest the perversity of destiny in Macondo. In Revelation the fifth angel and the inhabitants of the bottomless pit torment those who "do not have the seal of God in their forehead" (Rev. 9:4). The seventeen sons of the Colonel who have the indelible crosses on their foreheads after an Ash Wednesday ceremony are hunted and shot one by one by the Conservative troops.

Throughout *Cien años de soledad* time is a protean force. From an original time of creation and energy, for the founding José Arcadio it simply stagnates and stops, and he sinks into madness as every day for him becomes Monday: "La máquina del tiempo se ha descompuesto" (73; "The mechanism of time has gone wrong"), he confusedly laments. For others, especially after returning from a journey or a war, the passing of time becomes intolerably painful. As repetitions of phrases and situations take over from flow, time becomes a meaningless circle: "Es como si el mundo estuviera dando vueltas" (253; "It's as if the world were turning round and round,") exclaims Úrsula. In the second part of the novel, the word nostalgia becomes almost as frequent as solitude throughout. Its power is fatal. The Colonel, for example, hears the noise of a circus and "por primera vez desde su juventud pisó conscientemente una trampa de la nostalgia" (229; "for the first time since his youth he knowingly stepped onto a trap of nostalgia") as he recalls again the founding moment when his father takes him to see the ice. He leans on the chestnut tree and dies with his head between his shoulders like a little chicken.

Two key characters return to their roots and their death drawn by nostalgia: the vivacious and ultramodern Amaranta Úrsula returns to the terminally decaying Macondo only to bleed to death after giving birth to the pig-tailed baby as the first such baby born to the family had died over one hundred years previously at the beginning of the whole cycle. The *sabio catalán* is a bookseller and the intellectual mentor of the group of friends of Aureliano Babilonia, who share the names of García Márquez's friends when he lived in Barranquilla. He is a double of Melquíades, with his own set of manuscripts. After many years in Macondo he returns to the Mediterranean village of his birth, "derrotado por la nostalgia de una primavera tenaz" (336; "defeated by the nostalgia for a tenacious spring"). Once there, he feels the same nostalgia for Macondo and is caught between two facing mirrors: "aturdido por dos nostalgias enfrentadas como dos espejos" (339). This leads him to urge them to leave Macondo and declare that the past is a mirage, that the springs of one's youth are irrecuperable: "en cualquier sitio que estuvieran recordaran siempre que el pasado era mentira, que la memoria no tenía caminos de regreso, que toda primavera antigua era irrecuperable." With this he leads them out of captivity in the spell of Macondo, with the exception of course of Aureliano Babilonia.

The image of the mirrors is a significant and recurring one. For the Catalan it is negative. The twins Aureliano Segundo and his brother use their synchronized movements as a party trick with mirrors, "un artificio de espejos"

(151). They can also be seen to comment, however, on the attraction of the same in the Buendía family. From a literary point if view, it is also a key image of the way in which the novel attempts to capture time and produce a sense of simultaneity. Melquíades seems to achieve this magically in his manuscript: "no había ordenando los hechos en el tiempo convencional de los hombres, sino que concentró un siglo de episodios cotidianos, de modo que todos coexistieran en un instante" (350; "he had not ordered events in conventional human time, but concentrated a century of everyday episodes so that they all came together in one instant"). Gabriel García Márquez has to content himself with sentence and narrative structure.

Many critics have analyzed techniques such as narrative loops, enumeration, hyperbaton, coexistence of the past and the present in key sentences.[14] At the beginning of the sixth chapter, just as the Colonel Aureliano Buendía is embarking on his long military career, one breathtaking, cleverly modulated paragraph lists the most dramatic moments of that career. When we come to read the episodes at length over the next few chapters, it is as if they had already happened, or were destined to happen; being anticipated and later chronicled the events belong to two times, past and future. Other enumerations follow events, as when Úrsula wonders whether José Aureliano Segundo is falling into the Buendía family habit of doing just to undo ("hacer para deshacer" 267). His own actions would belong not so much to the chronology of his own life as to a timeless pattern. Retrospectively, moreover, Amaranta with her shroud, the colonel with his gold fish, José Arcadio Segundo with the parchments, are also inserted into the pattern. Often a single event is briefly mentioned at the beginning of a chapter or section after which the narrative loops back into the past and progresses until the event is reached and fully explained. The chapter closes in on itself as does the Buendía family, or the universal time scale of genesis and apocalypse.

According to Mario Vargas Llosa, the technique used in the memorable first sentence of the novel provides the narrator with a watchtower from which to survey and link all the events of the novel. "Muchos años después, frente al pelotón de fusilamiento, el coronel Aureliano Buendía había de recordar aquella tarde remota en que su padre lo llevó a conocer el hielo." ("Many years later, facing the firing squad, Colonel Aureliano Buendía was to remember that remote afternoon when his father took him to discover ice.") From an undefined present the narrator evokes the future of a past moment, expressed with the ubiquitous "había de" with its hint of inevitability, from which this same past is recalled. We have again the facing mirrors that will reflect and forge the labyrinthine time of the novel. Only in the seventh chapter does the Colonel face the firing squad. Most first-time readers of the novel surely assume that he will die at that point, but he is saved. The predictive function of narrative is subtly evoked and questioned.

The inseparability and complex mirroring of past and the future, of prediction and narration of the past, ultimately, of freedom and destiny make the reading of *Cien años de soledad* a rich and nuanced experience. The warring temporal dimensions are sometimes associated with characters. Úrsula Iguarán is the mother of the legitimate first generation of children born in Macondo; Pilar Ternera bears the following generation, illegitimately, to Úrsula's sons. These rival matriarchs live through almost all the novel, but while Úrsula is the seat of memory for the family, Pilar tells the future by reading cards. Like all oppositions in the novel, this one is gradually undone, inverted, endowed with paradox and complexity. On one occasion Pilar's prediction that Aureliano would face a serious danger connected with his mouth actually changes the future and ensures that she is wrong. Aureliano shoots himself in the chest rather than in the mouth in order to frustrate Pilar's prediction, and in the process fails to die. Úrsula too is wrong on this occasion: when she sees her milk pan full of maggots, she announces that Aureliano has been killed. During the insomnia plague, when the link between sign and thing slips from the people and amnesia sets in, prediction replaces memory when Pilar Ternera must read the cards to discover the past.[15] In her great old age, Pilar realizes that experience is more powerful than telling cards; while in hers, Úrsula lives so exclusively in her memories, that these become "un futuro perfectamente revelado y establecido" (333; "a perfectly revealed and established future").

The narration in the past tense of *Cien años*, which speaks of free will and a creative engagement with history, coexists with various types of prediction which speak rather of determinism, predestination – the prophecies of characters, recurring family traits, and the well-known outcomes of the myths evoked: Oedipus will come to grief, Genesis predicts Apocalypse. The tension is structurally built into the novel, which has in a sense two texts, even if one is more or less virtual: the chronicle of the Buendía family which we read and the text of Melquíades, composed during the action of the novel and finally deciphered, as in Revelation and Daniel, at the end of time. The characters make heroic intellectual efforts to read the parchments, but then it was fated that they should do so.[16]

García Márquez has repeatedly stated that his favorite book is Sophocles's *Oedipus the King*. The unburied corpse from Sophocles's *Antigone*, burial in general, where one is buried, in Colonus or Thebes, Riohacha or Macondo, haunts the Colombian's texts from *La hojarasca*, to *El otoño del patriarca*. In *Cien años* just a couple of examples are the sack with the bones of the

parents of Rebeca and the arrival from Bogotá of the coffin with the putrefy-
ing remains of Fernanda's father. It can be argued that incest in *Oedipus the
King* (Faulkner's *Absalom, Absalom!* and *Pedro Páramo* have a similar role)
seems to attract García Márquez as a force of destiny, a curse, rather than as
a theme in itself. Whereas the themes of solitude and power permeate most
of his texts, incest figures as a major concern only in *Cien años*. Predictions
structure many works: that Santiago would be murdered in *Crónica de una
muerte anunciada*, that the Patriarch's body would be found in such and
such a way. Melquíades's parchment seems to function in a similar way to
the Delphic oracles in Oedipus's case: Oedipus busily goes about trying to
work for the *polis*, discover the murderer of Laius and lift the plague, and
discovers that his own predicted destiny, which he had fought so hard to
avoid, had *already* been fulfilled.[17] His investigation is his own free-willed
action yet reveals his fate fulfilled. Aureliano's deciphering of the manuscript
reveals that he was already destined to suffer the curse brought on by his
destiny of incest and produce the pig-tailed child so persistently evaded
by his family. Destiny and freedom are often two sides of the same coin;
when any life has ended or when a book is completed, what happens within
it becomes destiny. Melquíades's parchment graphically reminds us of this
truism.

When the first Aureliano uses the gold he had been given to go to the
brothel to gild the door keys, his mother laments that children inherit the
idiosyncrasies of their parents and adds that this is as horrendous as a pig's
tail. It is clear that the incest associated with the tail is mostly a metonym
for deterministic inheritance in general. The traits which reappear from generation to generation echo those of Faulkner's Southern families. Some have
positive results, the enterprising streak which builds an ice factory or brings
the train to Macondo; others such as loneliness or the inability to love
do not. Much has been made of the characteristics of the Arcadios and
the Aurelianos in the novel; physical and social, cerebral and withdrawn,
but of course what distinguishes them at birth is not so much parentage,
genes, but an arbitrary name, which takes on ironically magical powers.
Josefina Ludmer works to dissolve such determinism by name, by demonstrating just how extraordinarily complex the mechanism of inherited traits
is. She observes that such are the labyrinthine echoes between disparate situations, characters and periods that rather than any sort of chronological
line, one has a multidirectional movement, a baroque space, infused with
"a sort of cosmic narcissism."[18] Her description echoes Melquíades's notion
of simultaneity.

Cien años de soledad was constantly in García Márquez's mind for some
fifteen years, since the time when he had tried unsuccessfully to write it and

the mythical moment on the road to Acapulco when he had the revelation that he should write it like his grandmother spoke, and he closed himself into his Mexico City flat for a year and a half to write it. It is a novel written with "all the tricks of life and all the tricks of the trade."[19] It compresses or expands all the anecdotic richness of his previous work, giving the impression to the reader of being the tip of a vast iceberg. The reader's experience that in it he can see both sides of the moon at the same time[20] is translated by at least two critics into the aphorism of Gramsci: "pessimism of the intellect, optimism of the will."[21] When one thinks of sex in the novel, the first image is celebratory: Aureliano Babilonia carrying a bottle of beer on his erect "inconceivable masculinity" (328), women clamoring to buy a raffle ticket to win a time in bed with José Arcadio, the riotous "chillidos de gata" (325; "cat-like squeals") of Amaranta Ursula. Then one remembers the misery: the torment by incestuous desire of Amaranta, her fearful rejection of the loves of her life, Pietro Crespi and Gerineldo Márquez. When Aureliano Buendía loses his virginity, he feels "el ansia atolondrada de huir y al mismo tiempo de quedarse para siempre en aquel silencio exasperado y aquella soledad espantosa" (31; "the bewildered urge to flee and at the same time to remain for ever in that exasperated silence and that awful solitude"). When asked what critics had most blatantly missed about his novel, García Márquez answered: "its main quality: the author's immense compassion for all his poor creatures."[22]

NOTES

1. See Carlos Fuentes, "Gabriel García Márquez and the Invention of America," in his *Myself with Others: Selected Essays* (London: André Deutsch, 1988), p. 190, and Michael Palencia-Roth, *Gabriel García Márquez: la línea, el círculo y las metamorfosis del mito* (Madrid: Gredos, 1983), p. 10.
2. See Gerald Martin's excellent study "On 'Magical' and Social Realism in García Márquez," in Bernard McGuirk and Richard Cardwell (eds.), *Gabriel García Márquez: New Readings* (Cambridge University Press, 1987), p. 103.
3. Gabriel García Márquez, *Cien años de soledad* (Buenos Aires: Sudamericana, 1970), p. 205. Page numbers in the text refer to this edition. All translations are my own.
4. Gabriel García Márquez, *El olor de la guayaba: conversaciones con Plinio Apuleyo Mendoza* (Barcelona: Bruguera, 1982), p. 41.
5. See, for example, Mario Vargas Llosa, *García Márquez: historia de un deicidio* (Barcelona and Caracas: Monte Ávila, 1971), p. 24.
6. Similar in many ways to Faulkner's Yoknapatawpha County and Juan Carlos Onetti's Santa María.
7. See Roberto González Echevarría, "*One Hundred Years of Solitude*: The Novel as Myth and Archive," in Robin Fiddian (ed.), *García Márquez* (London and New York: Longman, 1995), pp. 79–99.

8. Characters from other contemporary Latin American novels also stray into the pages of *Cien años de soledad*, such as Carlos Fuentes's Artemio Cruz (254) and Víctor Hugues from Alejo Carpentier's *El siglo de las luces* (84).

9. See Linda Hutcheon, *A Poetics of Postmodernism: History, Theory, Fiction* (New York and London: Routledge, 1991), p. 129.

10. Vargas Llosa, *García Márquez*, p. 90.

11. Michael Bell, *Gabriel García Márquez* (London: Macmillan Press, 1993), p. 67.

12. Juan Rulfo, *Pedro Páramo* (Mexico City: Fondo de Cultura Económica, 1971), p. 22.

13. Vargas Llosa, *García Márquez*, p. 90.

14. The most thorough analysis of the structure of the novel is that of Josefina Ludmer in her *Cien años de soledad: una interpretación* (Buenos Aires: Tiempo Contemporáneo, 1974).

15. In Borges's story "Funes el memorioso" total recall, not amnesia, is the consequence of insomnia.

16. Palencia-Roth has good sections on the apocalyptic dimension of the novel, and the relationship with Sophocles. See also the chapter on Márquez in Lois Parkinson Zamora's *Writing the Apocalypse: Historical Vision in Contemporary US and Latin American Fiction* (Cambridge University Press, 1989).

17. See Bernard Knox's introduction to *Oedipus the King*, in Sophocles, *The Three Theban Plays* (Harmondsworth: Penguin, 1982), esp. p. 150.

18. Ludmer, *Cien años*, p. 145.

19. Gárcia Márquez, *Guayaba*, p. 90.

20. See Ernst Völkening, cit. by Gerald Martin, p. 100.

21. Michael Wood, *Gabriel García Márquez: One Hundred Years of Solitude* (Cambridge University Press, 1990), pp. 6–7.

22. García Márquez, *Guayaba*, p. 111.

FURTHER READING

Bell, Michael, *Gabriel García Márquez*, London: Macmillan Press, 1993.

Fuentes, Carlos, "Gabriel García Márquez and the Invention of America," in Carlos Fuentes, *Myself with Others: Selected Essays*, London: André Deutsch, 1988.

García Márquez, Gabriel, *El olor de la guayaba: conversaciones con Plinio Apuleyo Mendoza*, Barcelona: Bruguera, 1982.

González Echevarría, Roberto, "*One Hundred Years of Solitude*: The Novel as Myth and Archive," in Robin Fiddian (ed.), *García Márquez*. London and New York: Longman, 1995.

Ludmer, Josefina, *Cien años de soledad: una interpretación*, Buenos Aires: Tiempo Contemporáneo, 1974.

Martin, Gerald, "On 'Magical' and Social Realism in García Márquez," in Bernard McGuirk and Richard Cardwell (eds.), *Gabriel García Márquez: New Readings*, Cambridge University Press, 1987.

Palencia-Roth, Michael, *Gabriel García Márquez: la línea, el círculo y las metamorfosis del mito*, Madrid: Gredos, 1983.

Parkinson Zamora, Lois, *Writing the Apocalypse: Historical Vision in Contemporary U.S. and Latin American Fiction*, Cambridge University Press, 1989.

Vargas Llosa, Mario, *García Márquez: historia de un deicidio*, Barcelona and Caracas: Monte Ávila, 1971.

Wood, Michael, *Gabriel García Márquez: One Hundred Years of Solitude*, Cambridge University Press, 1990.

15

STEPHEN HART

The House of the Spirits by Isabel Allende

Isabel Allende's *La casa de los espíritus* (*The House of the Spirits*, 1982) tells the tale of the political struggle between the Left and the Right in twentieth-century Chile which led to Augusto Pinochet's *coup d'état* on September 11, 1973, and the imposition thereafter of a repressive, right-wing military dictatorship. Its novelty is that it does so from the vantage point of the lives of three generations of women – Clara (grandmother), Blanca (mother), and Alba (granddaughter) – though Clara's husband, Esteban Trueba, fulfills an important mediating function within the novel, as we shall see. Like Gabriel García Márquez's *Cien años de soledad* (*One Hundred Years of Solitude*, 1967), the structural impetus of Allende's novel is provided by genealogy rather than plot, though the family line traced is male-centered in the former but feminocentric in the latter. Indeed, the "house" in the title of *La casa de los espíritus* functions paradigmatically as an image of the intrinsically feminine.

The obvious similarities between the two novels, indeed, have led some to question the originality of Allende's novel. In a revealing interview Allende made the following self-deprecatory comment: "Me siento como un pirata que se hubiera lanzado al abordaje de las letras" ("I feel like a pirate who has boarded the ship of letters").[1] There are a number of ways of interpreting this statement. One – the more cynical – is to take it as an admission of plagiarism of Gabriel García Márquez's fiction, with which her work has so often been compared. Isabel Allende – according to the cynical version of events – having illegally entered the "ship of letters" formerly steered by García Márquez, is now guiding it in a new direction. According to Raymond Williams, Allende launched her career as a result of "her initial imitations of Gabriel García Márquez's magic realism in *The House of the Spirits*."[2] Along these lines, Debra Castillo has argued that Allende "arrived belatedly on the 'Boom' scene twenty years after its vogue but with the same assumptions intact."[3] In Verity Smith's influential *Encyclopedia of Latin American Literature*, indeed, Allende is not provided a separate entry; she appears by courtesy of the section on "Best-Sellers," which she shares with the Mexican novelist, Laura Esquivel.[4]

Some critics, however, see the relationship between García Márquez's and Allende's work in terms of a parodic intertextuality. Linda Gould Levine, for example, argues that "Allende's text is a mirror reflection of a female-authored world. Isabel Allende now occupies the seat of García Márquez, while Clara, the spiritual grandmother whose rich imagination and prophetic gifts mirror those of Melquíades, gently pushes the gypsy aside to transcribe her own tale."[5] Robert Antoni, for his part, has emphasized that Allende's fiction is more realist than García Márquez's: "*The House of the Spirits* begins in the tradition of magical realism, but as it continues it becomes less and less Clara's (or García Márquez's) book, and more and more Alba's (Allende's) book, until finally there is no longer magic but only realism, and the novel becomes the tragic political history of Chile."[6] Patricia Hart goes further still and emphasizes the empiric nature of the experience underlying Allende's novel when compared to the Colombian's: "It goes beyond magical realism once more to say that perhaps for Latin America the most important texts are the ones written by real people from their own experience, not imagined by wandering gypsies in a vacuum of time."[7] A more judicious response might be to see the relationship between García Márquez and Allende as somewhere in between these two extreme poles.[8] Although *La casa de los espíritus* does demonstrate significant similarities with *Cien años de soledad*, its feminine perspective, along with its more nuanced use of the interplay between realism and magic, especially as understood in terms of political resonance, set Allende's novel apart, as we shall see.

A fruitful way of addressing the issue of "piracy" is to take a closer look at the social role of the writer and how it has changed over recent years in Latin America and, indeed, elsewhere. This will be clearer if we tie the discussion to three important names: Jorge Luis Borges, Gabriel García Márquez, and Isabel Allende. These three writers can be associated with three different types of literary culture, namely, the genius culture, the professional culture, and the mass-arts culture. According to the conventions of genius culture which had its heyday throughout the nineteenth and early twentieth centuries, the artist saw himself as, in Shelley's words, the "unacknowledged legislator of the world," a godlike creator of new orders of reality based on his powers of imagination. For the genius, the everyday reader is of little direct consequence. Borges, given that he saw the roots of his work in the nineteenth century, and that he made his first literary splash with an art movement of the 1920s, *ultraísmo*, typifies this concept of the writer as genius. The professional writer – like the artist within a genius culture – is also at liberty to express his subjective perceptions, but – unlike the former – his finished work has to be attractive to a large body of readers in order to be financially viable: here the paradigm offered is García Márquez, *primus inter pares* of the Boom novelists, his *Cien años de soledad* being the foundational text of Latin American literature in the modern era. Whereas Borges would sell 1,000 or so copies of his work, the Boom novelists regularly had print runs of 20,000–50,000 in the 1960s. Isabel Allende's fiction overlaps with the notion of the writer common among the Boom writers, but it differs from it in one key respect: her book sales reach hundreds of thousands of copies. Allende can command huge fees for lectures (she was paid $13,000 for a lecture given at the University of Kentucky in the autumn of 1994, and her fees have certainly not decreased since then), and she dabbles in books on food and sex, deliberately courting the popular market.[9] Her work clearly functions within the paradigm of mass-arts culture: any writer who can fill up the Royal Albert Hall, as Allende did in the autumn of 2000, is indisputably part of mass-arts culture.[10]

It is in this sense that we can see Allende as a pirate, but not (according to the cynical version) as someone who has deliberately "stolen" goods from others, and presented them as her own, but rather as an "unwitting pirate" – a writer who, rather surprisingly, has single-handedly changed what it means to be a "Latin American writer." She has jumped astride the ship of letters and changed its coordinates for good. It is because of its mass appeal that Allende's fiction – while not always gaining friends in the academy – attracts a worldwide readership.[11] This is evident in the fact that the reviews of *The House of the Spirits* have been favorable across the board, ranging from the fulsome review in *Cosmopolitan*: "that rarest of successes – a book about one family and one country that is a book about the world and becomes the world in a book" – to *The New York Times Book Review* whose reviewer, Alexander Coleman, described the book as "absorbing . . . moving and compelling."[12]

Perhaps it is best to see Allende as not simply a "pirate" of others' literary goods but a self-made entrepreneur in the world of letters. The shape that Allende's career has taken gives some clue as to why she writes in the way she does: she originally worked as a journalist in Chile, then moved to TV news-reporting, and subsequently to TV chat shows, and finally to fiction.[13] In each case, she has been gradually climbing up the ladder. Fiction has, in effect, been the last rung of the ladder of (literary and commercial) success. For the writer within a genius culture – let us not forget – there are no "rungs" in the ladder: the notion of a writer is hierarchical: you are either a genius or you are not, born to the literary manor or not, and there is no notion of self-betterment. Allende's role as a writer has more to do with a society in which self-advancement is the key.

Source criticism has worked rather unfairly in García Márquez's favor, and with negative consequences for Allende.[14] There is one particularly contentious technique which has often been associated with García Márquez's and Allende's style of magical realism, namely, prolepsis, which is understood here to mean the reference to a future event as if it were already known to have occurred. There are a number of cases of prolepsis in *La casa de los espíritus* and, while their appearance may be seen as an example of borrowing from García Márquez's fiction, there is, I would argue, a more fruitful way of addressing this issue. In Latin America, a world characterized by a mélange of cultures, driven by the cultural dilemmas produced by the violent conquest of the late fifteenth and early sixteenth centuries, that peculiarly Western-Augustinian sense of time – understood as a regular chronological march forward – is often irrelevant.[15] Culture is experienced in Latin America, not as a unitary event but as a clash of past happenings, a trauma. This is how Miguel Ángel Asturias outlined the contours of this cultural trauma in his illuminating Noble Prize acceptance speech delivered in Stockholm in December 1967:

> Cataclysms which engendered a geography of madness and terrifying traumas, such as the Conquest: these cannot be the antecedents of a literature of cheap compromise; and, thus, our novels appear to Europeans as illogical or aberrant. They are not shocking for the sake of shock effects. It is just that what happened to us was shocking. Continents submerged in the sea, races castrated as they surged to independence, and the fragmentation of the New World. As the antecedents of a literature these are already tragic. And from there we have had to extract not the man of defeat, but the man of hope, that blind creature who wanders through our songs. We are peoples from worlds which have nothing like the orderly unfolding of European conflicts, always human in their dimensions. The dimensions of our conflicts in the past centuries have been catastrophic.[16]

Given that culture is experienced in Latin America in terms of what Asturias has called "fragmentation," "cataclysms," and "geographical madness," it should not surprise us that time itself – a Kantian category at the very basis of the specificity of any culture – is also experienced in a way which is at odds with the "orderly unfolding," to use Asturias's words, of the European model. In Latin American culture, as the poet César Vallejo suggests, the past and the present – the archeological past and the modern city – often coexist: "Rotación de tardes modernas / y finas madrugadas arqueológicas!" ("Rotation between modern afternoons / and delicate archeological mornings").[17] Prolepsis – the invasion of the future into the present – is symptomatic of a culture whose origins have been uprooted, whose temporal coordinates turned upside down. Allende uses this technique at certain key junctures in the text but I want to focus on one, that is, when we have a hint of the destruction that Esteban García will bring to the del Valle family, when we witness Old Pedro García's death (the passing away of the old order):

> Pedro García cayó al suelo como una bolsa de huesos. (. . .) Esteban García tomó el clavo y se disponía a pincharle los ojos, cuando llegó Blanco y lo apartó de un empujón, sin sospechar que esa criatura hosca y malvada era su sobrino y que dentro de algunos años sería una tragedia para su familia.   (170–71)

> (Pedro García fell to the ground like a bag of bones. (. . .) Esteban García picked up his nail and was just about to stick it in his grandfather's eye when Blanca arrived and shoved him away, never suspecting that this evil, dark-skinned creature was her nephew and that he would one day be the instrument of a tragedy that would befall her family, 189–90)[18]

One day Esteban García would sexually torture Alba, his half-niece. This event is a central one in the structuring of the novel's message, as we shall see. Prolepsis is not just a neat, novelistic device; it functions in Allende's fiction as a symptom of that catastrophic cultural blindness (see Asturias's mention of the "blind creature" in his Nobel Speech quoted above) which characterizes Latin American reality.

How does feminism play into Allende's portrayal of Latin American culture? An extreme position is that taken by Gabriela Mora who has argued that the women portrayed in *La casa de los espíritus* are not good role models for feminists; because they are invariably presented as either victims or dependent for their identity on the male companions (they are fellow travelers in the revolution, rather than leaders of the cause), Mora argues, Allende's women are always secondary to the main action; Alba, she suggests, in particular is a passive character.[19] Mora charges Allende, as it were, with letting the feminist side down. But it has to be said in Allende's defense that the novels she writes are often concerned with women's rights, and with women's lives, how they have been truncated, destroyed, converted into victims, etc. And she often likes to counter this version of what women are supposed to be like (the angel in the hearth, or the suffering angel, or whatever else), in order to present a dynasty of women who are resourceful, insightful, determined, strong (*pace* Mora). Furthermore, even if we accept that *La casa de los espíritus* falls short of Mora's ideological requirements, it is also important to bear in mind that Allende's fictional works are just that, – namely, they are fiction rather than thesis novels written on behalf of the feminist cause. Their main aim is to tell a story. Likewise, Allende's novels cannot be construed as Marxist manifestos on behalf of Chilean workers' rights. If they are construed as such, they fail. *La casa de los espíritus* is an imaginative projection of Chilean reality rather than a thetic statement about that reality.

But before moving to a wider discussion of the two big issues in Allende's work – feminism and politics – I want to raise one last issue on the Allende–García Márquez interface, and this concerns the use of fantasy and magic in her fiction. The traditional way of looking at the role of fantasy and magic in Allende's work is to see it as an extension – even if a feminist, or feminized, *amplificatio* – of García Márquez's magical realism. The argument goes something like this: the fact that the novel is written from a feminine perspective – Esteban Trueba's recollections are recorded in the text, although they are intercalated within the overriding feminine narrative, and therefore lose preeminence in the overall scheme of things – suggests that Allende's fiction embodies a feminine perspective. And, although magical events are presented in Allende's fiction with the same deadpan style as in García Márquez's fiction, nevertheless, the whole idea is given a feminine twist. A belief in the supernatural (clairvoyance, objects which move as a result of mental processes, premonition, etc.) is often shown to be the province of the female of the species. *La casa de los espíritus* promotes the difference between men and women via a simple contrast between Esteban, who rejects feminism, spiritualism, and Marxism, as non-empiric nonsense, and Clara, who actively pursues and promotes a view of life based on female intuition. Clara's granddaughter, Alba, becomes – by the conclusion of the novel – a symbol of revolutionary resistance which puts all the men to shame. Allende's fiction suggests that it is the women of this world who have the sixth sense, and that the men are the ones who are obtuse and unable to see what is under their noses. Again, it should be pointed out that the spiritual world is not presented in Allende's fiction as a deadly serious matter. Rather there are points at which it is gently mocked and others when it merges with the political. Telepathy, spiritual empathy, female comradeship all melt into each other; the spiritual and the physical are seen as one.

The first chapter, if anything, is a test case in this regard. Beginning with Clara's defiance of masculine authority in the person of Padre Restrepo during Mass ("Si el cuento del infierno fuera pura mentira, nos chigamos todos . . ." (14; "If that story about hell is a lie, we're all fucked, aren't we . . ." [7]) and ending with Rosa's violation at the hands of the autopsy assistant, this chapter is careful to show how in different ways women, and particularly their bodies, are subjected to violation and abuse as a result of the social system of patriarchy. There is a subliminal link between Padre Restrepo's sermons which describe "los tormentos de los pecadores en el infierno, las carnes desgarradas por ingeniosas máquinas de tortura, los

fuegos eternos (. . .), los asquerosos reptiles que se introducían por los orifi-
cios femeninos" (10; "the torments of the damned in hell, the bodies ripped
apart by various ingenious torture apparatuses, the eternal flames [. . .], the
disgusting reptiles that crept up female orifices" [3]) and the humiliating
autopsy which Rosa's body is forced to endure; on tiptoes looking into the
room, Clara "creyó ver una expresion suplicante y humillada" (41; "thought
she saw a supplicating and humiliated expression on her sister's face" [39]).
Perhaps more to the point, the reason for Rosa's death is that she mistakenly
drunk some brandy laced with rat poison intended for her father, Severo del
Valle. This is the first indication of a recurrent theme which will weave its
way through the novel: women pay for men's sins.

It is no coincidence, therefore, that the opening chapter of Allende's novel
should emphasize an unholy alliance of the Church (in the figure of Padre
Restrepo), politics, and the law (epitomized by the autopsy forced upon
Rosa's corpse) as stacked up against women. This explains why the autopsy
is described in terms of a sexual violation; Dr. Cuevas's young assistant "besó
a Rosa en los labios, en el cuello, en los senos, entre las piernas" (41; kissed
Rosa on the lips, the neck, the breasts, and between the legs" [39]). Though
the young assistant's actions are ostensibly motivated by an eroticism which
borders on tenderness, it is important to recall that Rosa is dead at the time,
and thus the epitome of passive victimhood; it is for this reason that Clara
sees "humiliation" on her face during the autopsy (see above). Allende's text
suggests that patriarchal society – even when it appears to adopt a caring
stance – based as it is on the pursuit of power and the use of violence to
achieve the ability to use that power, casts the woman as victim, and uses
forensic science – the discourse of the State – to humiliate womanhood. The
unusual thing about Rosa's death, of course, is that Clara had predicted that
somebody would die, and yet, this prediction in itself – i.e. this superior,
quasi-divine knowledge – was not enough to stop the death. The message is
clear: despite their superior knowledge about life, women are unable to stop
the ravage and carnage that men and politics wreak, although they can –
like modern-day versions of Cassandra – see it coming.

This association is extended in subsequent chapters of the novel. The
reptile in Padre Restrepo's sermon reappears on Clara's plate years later,
once she is married to Count Jean de Satigny; it is a first hint of his
sexual decadence coupled with his mocking complicity with the Indian
servants:

> Blanca encontró en su plato una pequeña lagartija muerta que estuvo a punto
> de llevarse a la boca. Apenas se repuso del susto y consiguió sacar la voz, llamó
> a gritos a la cocinera y le señaló el plato con un dedo tembloroso. La cocinera

se aproximó bamboleando su inmensidad de grasa y sus trenzas negras, y tomó el plato sin comentarios. Pero en el momento de volverse, Blanca creyó sorprender un guiño de complicidad entre su marido y la india.   (223)

(Blanca found a small dead lizard on her plate, which she was about to put in her mouth. When she recovered from the shock and managed to regain her voice, she called for the cook and pointed to the plate with a trembling finger. The cook approached, her mountainous fat and her braids swaying, and picked up the plate without a word. But as she turned round, Blanca could have sworn she caught a wink of complicity between her husband and the cook; 250)

These suspicions are confirmed when Blanca hears, first of all, suspicious creaks around the house at night, then moans and suffocated cries coming from the Count's photography studio, until she discovers the sordid truth; the walls are covered with "acongojantes escenas eróticas que revelaban la oculta naturaleza de su marido" (231; "distressing erotic scenes which revealed her husband's hidden character" [260]). The important point about these pornographic pictures is not only their revelation that her husband had been conducting clandestine orgies with the Indian servants – male and female – or, indeed, that they had dressed up in outlandish theatrical costumes, but also that they reveal a sinister connection with the Incan mummies which had been arriving in the house as a result of Satigny's recent fascination with archeological excavations. One image hints at necrophiliac bestiality: "la llama embalsamada cabalgando sobre la mucama" (231; "the stuffed llama riding atop the lame servant girl" [260]). Once more we perceive a web of association being constructed in the novel: the embalmed mummies and the stuffed llamas are images twinned with the violation of Rosa's corpse portrayed in the opening chapter of the novel. Male sexual perversion is linked to the desire to destroy, embalm, and dress up. Mummification, in effect, becomes a powerful image of the abuse of women's bodies which is at the heart of patriarchy.

This multiple twinning of images comes to its dreadful climax in the anagnorisis scene of the novel (already mentioned, see above) when Alba is sexually tortured by her half-uncle, Esteban García, Old Pedro García's grandson by marriage, but Esteban Trueba's illegitimate grandson by bloodline as a result of the former's rape of Pancha García (the rape had been described in Chapter 2). In a sense, thus, the novel reveals as finally true and paradigmatic the image of degraded humanity which was introduced early on in Las Marías, the ranch in the countryside to which Esteban Trueba took his family. We were treated to three distinct and unforgettable images of the tenants in the ranch, depicting the children, the women, and the men:

Descubrió en la penumbra de uno de ellos, un cajón relleno de papel de periódico donde compartían el sueño un niño de pecho y una perra recién parida. En otro vio a una anciana que estaba muriéndose desde hacía cuatro años y tenía los huesos asomados por las llagas de la espalda. En un patio conoció a un adolescente idiota, babeando, con una soga al cuello, atado a un poste, hablando cosas de otros mundos, desnudo y con un sexo de mulo que refregaba incansablemente contra el suelo. (58)

(He came upon a box filled with newspaper, in which a newborn baby and a puppy lay in a shared sleep. In another he saw an old woman whose shoulder blades were jutting through the open wounds in her back. In a courtyard, moored to a post, he saw a teenage idiot with a rope around his neck, drooling and babbling incoherently as he stood there naked, with a mule-sized penis that he beat incessantly against the ground; p. 58)

This is Allende's vision of humanity: men driven into incoherent frenzies by their sexual instinct, women dying a painful death experienced specifically in their bodies, and children abandoned to a life of animality. It is, of course, not a particularly endearing view of humanity, and Allende presents these three individuals as people simply discovered by Esteban when he visits the tenants' residence, but they can be seen as paradigmatic and, perhaps more important, as causally linked: the novel shows – via the description of Esteban García's pleasure in Alba's sexual torture described in Chapter 14 – that, in a curious twist of Mosaic Law (Exodus 20:5), the sins of the father are visited on the children to the third and fourth generations (in the sense that, by raping Pancha García, Esteban Trueba del Valle was storing up trouble for the future). Male sexuality "punishes" women's bodies and leads to progeny which are little better than animals.

These various images are brought triumphantly together – if triumphant is the right word – when Alba, Clara's daughter and Nivea's granddaughter – is sexually tortured in prison by her half-uncle, now a military officer in the army. The depiction of the torture of females is not a new one in Chilean literature (Fernando Alegría, Dorfman, Donoso, and Eltit have all treated this theme in their fiction), yet it is converted into the very anagnorisis scene of La casa de los espíritus. Whereas incest in García Márquez's novel simply – apocalyptically – leads to the end of the world, and the birth of the progeny with a pig's tail – thereby suggesting that incest is too awful to contemplate and the only option for the writer is to bring about epistemological and ontological meltdown (i.e. apocalypse) – Allende's vision is far tougher. She shows us Alba going through the unimaginable with her half-uncle, coming out of the end of it, and then writing her testimony for the benefit of future generations. Whereas incest had led to apocalypse in *Cien años de soledad*, it leads in *The House of the Spirits* to a sober assessment of the crimes of modern man against others, and concludes on a message of hope for the future.

It is, of course, rather surprising, that despite Alba's experience of incestuous sexual torture – which seemingly confirms a irredeemably bleak view of human existence as characterized by uncontrollable male sexual drives, tortured female bodies, and bastard children who create havoc wherever they go – *La casa de los espíritus* should break its own Gordian knot by concluding on a note of optimism for which the reader is ill-prepared. At the beginning of the novel Esteban is depicted as complicit with the conservative regime but, by its conclusion, he has come to feel a sense of remorse for having supported Pinochet and he changes sides, assisting the people he once despised. The novel, thus, concludes on a note of reconciliation between generations and, perhaps more importantly, between men and women.

Pointing in a similar optimistic direction is the testimony that Alba decides to write. Helped by Ana Díaz in the flesh and then by Clara in spirit, Alba creates "un testimonio que algún día podría servir para sacar a la luz el terrible secreto que estaba viviendo, para que el mundo se enterara del horror que ocurría paralelamente a la existencia apacible y ordenada de los que no querían saber, de los que podían tener la ilusión de una vida normal" (362–63; "a testimony that might one day call attention to the terrible secret she was living through, so that they would know about this horror that was taking place parallel to the peaceful existence of those who did not want to know, who could afford the illusion of a normal life" [414]).

The testimony is, indeed, Allende's version of what González Echevarría has called the Archive in the Latin American novel. Echevarría has argued that the most important Latin American writers use the Archive in their work as a means of pointing to the way in which the New World version of reality is being created in opposition to the European view of things, which held sway for so many years. Thus, in *Cien años de soledad*, for example, the Archive takes the form of the text in Sanskrit which Melquíades is writing, and which Aureliano Segundo is finally able to decipher moments before he dies in the apocalyptic hurricane which occurs at the end of the novel, destroying the Buendías forever. In *La casa de los espíritus*, the role of the Archive is fulfilled by the notebooks produced as a labor of love by a dynasty of tough-minded women. By using Clara's notebooks, Alba in effect reconstructs the untold story of women's oppression in Latin America. It would be very difficult to see García Márquez as the only source of inspiration for this idea; rather García Márquez himself must be seen, like

Allende, as imbibing the same source of cultural re-visionment in which the European view of things is rejected, and a new American version of reality fashioned into shape. Allende, indeed, takes this process one step further since she gives not only a New World but also a feminocentric version of that reality.

There are junctures when Allende appears to have outwitted García Márquez at his own game. A good test case is politics. A number of critics have accused Isabel Allende of making political capital from the use of her uncle's name, Salvador Allende, the president of Chile brutally cut down by Pinochet in his *coup d'état* in September 1973. But if we look at the way in which the political reality of the coup is presented in *The House of the Spirits*, it is surely important to point out that when the political coup is described from Chapter 13 onwards, the magical side of life seems to disappear. As soon as Clara dies, political decline seems inevitable because life loses its meaning and its magic: "La muerte de Clara transformó por completo la vida de la gran casa de la esquina. Los tiempos cambiaron. Con ella se fueron los espíritus . . ." (262; "Clara's death completely transformed life in the big house on the corner. Gone with her were the spirits . . ." [295]). The coup – when it comes in Chapter 13 – is described in anodyne, flat, descriptive sentences, as if to suggest that Pinochet knocked the magic of life out of the window. Surely this is a more responsible way of using the genre of the fantastic in fiction, since it does not thereby trivialize the brutal impact that a *coup d'état* had in real people's lives on September 11, 1973, as arguably García Márquez does in his depiction of the workers' strike in Ciénaga in *Cien años de soledad*, when nobody knows the truth anymore. For Allende, the truth does matter.

Allende's use of political innuendo can be quite subtle, as is evident in the way that Nívea's head functions in *La casa de los espíritus* as a synecdoche of the "desaparecidos" during Pinochet's coup. It is, of course, true that Nívea died in a particularly gruesome car accident in which her head was dislocated from her body, and only found years later by Clara. But – given the way that the rest of the story unfolds, especially from Chapter 13 onwards, and, given that Allende has referred to the awful plight of the "desaparecidos" in other works written at about this time,[20] surely it is not too far-fetched to argue that Nívea's dislocated head – which is disappeared for an inordinately long amount of time in the text – is an arresting image of the trauma of the Southern Cone police state's practice of "disappearing" their victims in the latter half of the 1970s and 1980s. Once more, we note, the victim is a woman. Allende is making the point – though in a displaced form – that it is women's bodies which are victims of state torture and repression.

NOTES

1. *La narrativa de Isabel Allende: claves de una marginalidad*, ed. Adriana Castillo de Berchenko, Marges, 6 (Perpignan: CRILAUP, Université de Perpignan, 1990), p. 21. Translation mine.
2. Raymond Williams, *The Postmodern Novel in Latin America* (New York: St Martin's Press, 1996), p. 71.
3. Debra A. Castillo, *Talking Back: Toward a Latin American Feminist Literary Criticism* (Ithaca: Cornell University Press, 1992), p. 23.
4. "Best-Sellers," *Encyclopedia of Latin-American Literature*, ed. Verity Smith (Chicago: Dearborn, 1997), pp. 115–18.
5. Linda Gould Levine, "A Passage to Androgyny: Isabel Allende's *La casa de los espíritus*," in Noël Valis and Carol Maier (eds.), *In the Feminine Mode: Essays on Hispanic Women Writers* (Lewisburg and London: Bucknell University Press, 1990), p. 166.
6. Robert Antoni, "Parody or Piracy: The Relationship of *The House of the Spirits* to *One Hundred Years of Solitude*," *Latin American Literary Review* 15–16 (1988): 21.
7. Patricia Hart, *Narrative Magic in the Fiction of Isabel Allende* (London and Ontario: Associated University Presses, 1989), p. 91.
8. See Lloyd Davies's reasoned response to this issue: *Isabel Allende: La casa de los espíritus*, Critical Guides Series, 66 (London: Grant and Cutler, 2000); the section at pp. 31–38 discusses similarities and differences.
9. I am thinking specifically of her recent work, *Afrodita: cuentos, recetas y otros afrodisiacos* (Barcelona: Plaza y Janes, 1997).
10. Raymond Williams makes the following point: "The 1980s and 1990s have witnessed the popularity of women writers, a phenomenon begun in Mexico with the mass marketing of the fiction of the Chilean Isabel Allende throughout Latin America by the Plaza y Janés publishing company, a Hispanic arm of the German multinational Bertlesman"; see Williams, *The Postmodern Novel*, p. 22.
11. Her novels consistently outsell those of García Márquez, for example, in Germany; see Meg Brown, *The Reception of Spanish American Fiction in West Germany 1981–1991: A Study of Best Sellers* (Tübingen: Max Niemeyer, 1994).
12. *The House of the Spirits*, trans. Magda Bogin (New York: Bantam, 1986), foreword, pp. i–iii.
13. Allende worked as a journalist, editor, and advice columnist for *Paula* magazine, Santiago from 1967 until 1974, and as an interviewer for Canal 13/Canal 7 television station from 1970 until 1975.
14. The kinds of accusations of plagiarism with respect to Allende could, indeed, also be leveled against García Márquez since *Cien años de soledad* has some similarities with Thomas Mann's novel *Buddenbrooks*, published in 1900 (a similar family structure, the last member of the family will be issueless, etc.). I am grateful to Efraín Kristal for pointing this out to me.
15. In some ways I simplify Augustine's notion of time for the purpose of my argument but it is clear that Augustine saw three distinct phases of time: past, present and future. He associated the past (the "present of past things") with memory, the future (the "present of future things") with expectation, and the "present of present things" with "direct perception." His analysis in Book XI, though

complex in its analysis of the way in which human time differs from eternity, namely God's time, presupposes the notion of an onward march of human time from the point at which it was created by God at the beginning of the world; *Saint Augustine: Confessions*, trans. R. S. Pine-Coffin (Harmondsworth: Penguin, 1961), esp. p. 269.

16. http://www.nobel.se/literature/laureates/1967/asturias-acceptance.html(last consulted on August 25, 2004).
17. "Telúrica y magnética," in *Poemas humanos*; *César Vallejo: Selected Poems*, ed. Stephen Hart (London: Duckworth, 2000), p. 44.
18. References to the Spanish text are to *La casa de los espíritus* (Barcelona: Plaza y Janes, 1988), 27th edn, and to the English text, *The House of the Spirits*, trans. Magda Bogin (New York: Bantam, 1986).
19. Gabriela Mora, "Las novelas de Isabel Allende y el papel de la mujer como ciudadana," *Ideologies and Literature* 2 (1982): 53–61.
20. I am thinking especially of *De amor y de sombra* (1984) which describes the discovery of some Chilean "desaparecidos" in a mine shaft in northern Chile.

FURTHER READING

Antoni, Robert, "Parody or Piracy: The Relationship of *The House of the Spirits* to *One Hundred Years of Solitude*," *Latin American Literary Review* 15–16 (1988): 16–28.

Brown, Meg, *The Reception of Spanish American Fiction in West Germany 1981– 1991: A Study of Best Sellers*, Tübingen: Max Niemeyer, 1994.

Castillo de Berchenko, Adriana (ed.), *La narrativa de Isabel Allende: claves de una marginalidad*, Marges, 6, Perpignan: CRILAUP, Université de Perpignan, 1990.

Davies, Lloyd, *Isabel Allende: La casa de los espíritus*, Critical Guides Series, 66, London: Grant and Cutler, 2000.

Hart, Patricia, *Narrative Magic in the Fiction of Isabel Allende*, London and Ontario: Associated University Presses, 1989.

Mora, Gabriela, "Las novelas de Isabel Allende y el papel de la mujer como ciudadana," *Ideologies and Literature* 2 (1982): 53–61.

Shaw, Deborah A., "Best Sellers," *Encyclopedia of Latin-American Literature*, ed. Verity Smith, Chicago: Dearborn, 1997, pp. 115–18.

Williams, Raymond, *The Postmodern Novel in Latin America*, New York: St. Martin's Press, 1996.

16

MICHELLE CLAYTON

The War of the End of the World by Mario Vargas Llosa

Focused on a cataclysm at the end of an era, Mario Vargas Llosa's monumental 1981 novel, *La guerra del fin del mundo* (*The War of the End of the World*) also appears to want to signal the end of history – or at least the collapse of ideologies that drive it. Furthermore, in its running commentary on the uses of fiction, on the intellectual's place in the interpretation of history, this enormous novel seems to herald an end to storytelling. Vargas Llosa has elsewhere referred to the writer's vocation as "a daily and furious immolation,"[1] and it is notable that he should have chosen a novel about a conflagration to set forth one of his clearest – and most polemical – statements on the force of literature.

The novel has as much to do with storytelling as it is does with history, foregrounding the responsibility of the Latin American writer towards pivotal events. In the wake of his own political realignment – an initial euphoria after the Cuban Revolution followed by a proclaimed loss of faith in political utopias – Vargas Llosa has delineated his position on fiction in stark terms: "I have nothing against fictions [. . .] But there are benign and malign fictions, those that enrich human experience and those that impoverish it and are a source of violence" (*MW*, 300). This very notion has, ironically, polarized criticism of the novel. Where more formally minded readers have placed *La guerra del fin del mundo* in the former camp, politically oriented critics have been made uneasy by a series of assumptions and assertions which structure the novel: among them, the notion that the writer can step outside ideology to comment on history from a vantage point of "common sense." Another sticking point is the question of literature's relation to politics, which Vargas Llosa has approached from somewhat contradictory perspectives. His fiction – frequently insistently historical – seems to want to rehearse certain impasses of history in order to arrive at their solution, or at least their rational rethinking. On the other, he has often proclaimed fiction to be not only entirely autonomous from politics but, moreover, "irresponsible" (citing Bataille in *MW*, 121). *La guerra del fin del mundo* sheds some light on the sense that Vargas Llosa attempts to make, through literature, of what he perceives as the senselessness of history. Early and more recent criticism alike outlined the novel's own pivotal importance within both this writer's trajectory and, more broadly, that of the Latin American novel (particularly the Boom period), hailing it as "Vargas Llosa's greatest work of literature"[2] and as "a work which reveals the maturity of the Latin American novel";[3] Vargas Llosa himself has declared it to be his "most ambitious" novel.[4]

Published in 1981, *La guerra del fin del mundo* had been in gestation and mutation through various forms for almost a decade. In 1972 the Brazilian director Rui Guerra had asked Vargas Llosa to collaborate on a screenplay about the war of Canudos, a peasant uprising with messianic overtones in the "sertões" or backlands of Brazil which took not one but four military expeditions to quell, and which was seen as a pivotal moment in the country's history. As José Miguel Oviedo notes, the subject marked a notable departure for the author, whose earlier novels had all been set in Peru, and were frequently – although not exclusively – based upon his own experiences. In preparation for writing on such a foreign subject, Vargas Llosa immersed himself in contemporaneous newspaper accounts, explicatory treatises written in its aftermath, and of course the most famous source for his novel, Euclides da Cunha's generically monstrous *Os Sertões* (*Rebellion in the Backlands*, 1901), which enveloped sociological and historical analyses in an aura of fiction. Vargas Llosa's screenplay went through a variety of versions and titles only to be abandoned, but shortly after plans for the film had been shelved, he began the task of translating the material into novelistic form. During the next few years he lectured on Da Cunha's work at Columbia University; he underwent a notorious political shift, closing off relations with the Latin American left; and in 1979, with hundreds of pages already in draft form, he visited the setting, interviewing witnesses and their descendants.

The novel narrates an event from Brazil's violent entrance into modernity, mapping this onto modern Latin America in general.[5] In Vargas Llosa's own words: "In the story of Canudos I saw something like a synthesis of the history of our countries, that is, the history of our fanaticism, of our moments of intransigence, of the ideologies which have inflamed us, broken down communications between us, and hurled us into absurd and incomprehensible massacres."[6]

The central event – the "war of the end of the world" – violently pitted a variety of different forces against one another (peasants against the military, guided respectively by religious fanatics and politicians), all of whom had clear investments in determining the country's future, and who manipulated the conflict to their own ends, guided either by cynicism or absolute conviction. The novel does not present these four sectors as monolithic or shadowy agents but rather builds up powerful mini-narratives around representative and complex figures from each one: Antonio the Counselor and his various followers on the one hand, the politician Epaminondas Goncalves and the army colonel Moreira César on the other; on their edges are a variety of other characters, such as the anarchist Galileo Gall, the near-sighted journalist, and the dispossessed Baron of Cañabrava, all of whom comment impotently on events as they progress.[7] Four principal sections, with varying subdivisions, track a different moment or perspective on the central event: the gathering of believers and their movement toward Canudos (section 1), the Republican Party's elaboration of a strategic response (section 2), the military campaign itself (section 3), and a retrospective commentary on its conclusion in a conversation between two of the principal protagonists (section 4).

The novel traces the rise to power of the central character, Antonio the Counselor, from his first sporadic and solitary appearances in small towns of the *sertão*, through his gathering of followers during the 1877 drought, to the cataclysm which would erupt in the town of Canudos, in drawn-out battle between the settlers and the army. Forming the immediate backdrop to the central event is the country's political metamorphosis in 1889 from monarchy to republic, preceded by the abolition of slavery in 1888; understood by the putatively progressive forces (politicians, the army) as a move into modernity, it was comprehended very differently by the peasants, who were taught by their religious leaders to distrust a democratic government which secularized and taxed the nation. The novel also alludes to the shift of power away from the former capital Bahía, while focusing itself on the crucial peasant uprising in Brazil's backlands, giving history a popular rather than a narrowly political grounding.

From the opening section, the narrative follows the trajectories of those characters who make up the Counselor's band – "una variopinta colectividad donde se mezclaban razas, lugares, oficios" (38; "a motley group, a chaotic mixture of races, backgrounds and occupations" [18])[8] – from their lawless early days to their moments of conversion and integration into the makeshift army which will pose such obstacles to rational understanding, political cohesion, and military might alike. As these characters move toward the town of Canudos, they are followed in ever-increasing numbers by actors and observers, soldiers and storytellers. Canudos becomes the location of history, rendered close-up in dizzying, disconcerting immediacy, and it is interpreted at a distance in the capital city of Rio, which itself is pictured as losing its control over events, politics, and the ability to make sense of local or national stories. The intersection between these two spaces points to a salient feature of the novel: that this is a story about storytelling itself, about the requirements and responsibility of narrative.

La guerra del fin del mundo is more deeply a novel about belief: about how to tell a convincing story, but also about how belief can become dogmatic, can distort events, can promote intolerance and occasion violence. Each of the central characters is actively engaged in producing, circulating, or receiving stories, and the differences between them can be ascribed to the way in which they perform these activities as much as to their motivations. Some characters are driven by absolute belief: for example the Counselor, who captivates even the most hardened criminals by appealing to their hearts and minds through language;[9] brigands join his band because "con esa voz cavernosa que sabía encontrar los atajos del corazón . . . [l]es decía cosas que podían entender, verdades en las que podían creer" (36; "in that cavernous voice that unfailingly found the shortest path to their hearts . . . [h]e told them things that they could understand, truths that they could believe in" [17]). The story he tells is of a social utopia, with a specifically religious bent; and he casts his truths in a peculiarly popular form, shaped to resemble not so much biblical teachings as the stories recounted by the wandering minstrels. Galileo Gall is convinced that the content of his and the Counselor's teachings is potentially identical, the only difference residing in the wrapping chosen by the Counselor for the presentation of his truths. Gall's own stories, however, anchored in anarchist ideology and entirely unsugared by esthetics, repeatedly fail to reach their audience; in a supremely ironic contrast, when he interrupts a performance by the circus storyteller the Dwarf, he is in turn interrupted with vitriolic pragmatism by another of his traveling companions, in an oblique comment on the quagmires of Latin American storytelling: "!Estúpido! !Estúpido! !Nadie te entiende! !Los estás poniendo tristes, los estás aburriendo, no nos darán de comer! !Tócales la cabeza, diles el futuro, algo que los alegre!" (305; "You stupid fool! You stupid fool! Nobody's listening to you! You're making them sad, you're boring them, they won't give us money to eat on! Feel their heads, predict their future – do something that'll make them happy!" [231]).

As the novel continually proclaims, Gall literally speaks a different language to those he comes into contact with; and nowhere is this more poignant than in his longed-for encounter with the rebels, which turns into a farce of linguistic disconnection. Gall is starkly contrasted with the master storyteller the Dwarf, who becomes an accidental adherent to the peasants' cause when the circus to which he belongs crosses their path, and who tells entertaining stories which offer escape rather than doctrine. Drawn to these stories are characters like the rebel Satan João, whose first memories are of the wandering minstrels, and who make sense of the world through those traveling tales. Some of those stories, like Gall himself, arrive in the New World from Europe, where they are recast: after forcing himself upon Jurema, the wife of his tracker Rufino, Gall finds himself condemned to death in a narrative which seems to him rationally unintelligible, if not utterly unbelievable, based as it is on the codes of honor and behavior espoused by medieval morality tales and Golden Age drama.

All the characters are interested in elaborating their own versions of stories and events, and in passing those versions off as true, although their motivations and beliefs differ radically. The Counselor's followers believe his teachings to the letter; Gall trusts in and tries to propagate his utopian vision; the Republican candidate Epaminondas Goncalves cynically concocts a story about British and monarchist involvement in the uprising, which the military swallows and upon which it acts; the near-sighted journalist self-servingly begins by hiring his versions out to the highest bidder. And not all the characters accept responsibility for the fictions they try to pass off as truths. When at the end, for example, the Dwarf is asked to elucidate the meaning of his stories, to extract a moral lesson for his listeners, he can only respond: "No sé, no sé . . . No está en el cuento. No es mi culpa, no me hagas nada, sólo soy el que cuenta la historia" (705; "I don't know, I don't know [. . .] It's not in the story. It's not my fault, don't do anything to me, I'm only the one who's telling the story" [557]).

One way of seizing hold of a story is by putting a name on things, and this is one of the dominant tropes in the novel. The shadowy Counselor earns his popular name by learning to communicate with the townspeople; he proceeds to recast the spaces he colonizes – impressing his biblical mark on the streets of Canudos – and he encourages his followers to adopt new Christian names. Several characters in the novel develop appearance-based names; others receive monikers based on the perspective from which they are viewed (Satan João/Abbot João). Galileo Gall, on the other hand, carries an obvious lineage in his name (that of Galileo, the founder of modern science, but also of Gall, founder of the discredited science of phrenology); and he most clearly foresees the structuring potential of names in narrative and history alike:

> En última instancia, los nombres no importaban, eran envolturas, y si servían para que las gentes sin instrucción identificaran más fácilmente los contenidos, era indiferente que en vez de decir justicia e injusticia, libertad y opresión, sociedad emancipada y sociedad clasista, se hablara de Dios y del Diablo.
>
> (345)

> (In the last analysis, names did not matter; they were wrappings, and if they helped uneducated people to identify the contents more easily, it was of little moment that instead of speaking of justice and injustice, freedom and oppression, classless society and class society, they talked in terms of God and the Devil; 264)

For many of the actors in this drama, the imperative to name is not just a matter of control but of life and death: their challenge is to make what surrounds them intelligible. The enemy is perceived by the expeditionary soldiers as pure phantasmatic sound, amplified by the empty plains; Canudos itself is made up of "voces que, mezcladas, integradas, provocaban esa música beligerante que subía al cielo" (41; "voices that mingled and blended into one, producing that belligerent music that was rising heavenward" [21]). The Counselor manages to harmonize those voices, and the identities behind them, in the space of Canudos, soon a center of refuge, fraternity, and community.

Nonetheless, most characters are ironically unaware of what their own experience means, not to mention how it is being interpreted by other groups: the settlers of Canudos believe that their town is being attacked by the army with a view to reinstituting slavery; soldiers are led to believe that they are fighting a rebel group supported by a clandestine coalition of British and Brazilian monarchists; Gall insists right to his bathetic end that Canudos represents not a pseudo-messianic uprising but "la fraternidad universal, el paraíso materialista" (367; "universal brotherhood, a materialist paradise" [282]). And each group contains a character dedicated to documenting its own version of events for posterity. The misshapen Lion of Natuba, for example, records each utterance of the Counselor, in the hope that that collection of sayings will constitute another gospel; he will even begin to record excrescences from his leader's leaking body, in a travesty of the biblical last supper. Gall composes an autobiographical memorandum which he entrusts to the Baron, who is willing but unable to deliver it to its proper address, to return this European's version of history to the Old World. Colonel Moreira César is determined to have his version of events recorded and demands the collusion of the terrified journalist, who worries that he will not be able to live up to the task.

After his close-up experience of Canudos, the journalist is prompted to bear a different kind of witness in writing; if people, as he laments, are "forgetting Canudos," his felt imperative is to keep its memory alive, to press home constantly the reality of its holocaust. His earlier cynicism – his willingness to serve several different editorial masters, writing the story that they wanted in print – dissipates in the face of this real horror; ironically, it is the loss of his glasses which allows him to see more clearly, although the Baron of Cañabrava will mock him for wanting to write a story he didn't see.[10] The journalist responds by immersing himself in reading, mirroring the activities of da Cunha and Vargas Llosa, both of whom could declare "He leído todo lo que se escribió" (459; "I've read everything written about it" [358]). Here, however, he is challenged by another writer-figure, the Lion of Natuba, whose vocal virility betrays his misshapen stature (writers in this novel are significantly either grotesque or physically disabled); pressed by this interlocutor to reevaluate the role of culture in his life, the journalist arrives at a striking conclusion, in which we cannot help catching his author's voice: "Era una cosa que había descubierto en estos meses: la cultura, el conocimiento, mentiras, lastres, vendas. Tantas lecturas y no le habían valido de nada para escapar, para librarse de esta trampa" (617; "That was something that he had discovered in these long months: culture, knowledge were lies, dead weight, blindfolds. All that reading – and it had been of no use whatsoever in helping him to escape, to free himself from this trap" [486]).

Nevertheless, the journalist does manage to escape, and he resurfaces with a different version of events – a different way of telling them – in a long Faulknerian conversation with the Baron of Cañabrava, which both sheds light on the past and displaces the painful present. Whereas the baron repeatedly judges the whole to be an "historia estúpida, incomprensible, de gentes obstinadas, ciegas, de fanatismos encontrados" (676; "a stupid, incomprehensible story of blind, stubborn people, of diametrically opposed fanaticisms" [533]), the journalist insists that "más que de locos es una historia de malentendidos" (587; "it's not so much a story of madmen as a story of misunderstandings" [461]). The Baron's conversation with the journalist – "más que un diálogo, un par de monólogos intocables" (675; "not so much a dialogue as two monologues running side by side without ever meeting" [533]) – is emblematic of the events of this story/history: people talk past one another, misunderstandings are rife, yet both the novel and its characters constantly reiterate the need to try to understand.

The Baron is a somewhat problematic protagonist, as noted not only by various critics but by other characters in the novel; few understand his motives, and even fewer his relative dispassion. An aristocratic landowner who relinquishes his home to the rebels, loses his wife to madness, and makes several attempts at rapprochement with and between his enemies, he is yet placed in a position of quasi-objectivity. His is a sweeping gaze; his thoughts are characterized by greater reason than those of his opponents; even his voice is not strident, booming, or emphatic, as theirs are, but instead murmurs, reflects, and questions. He comes into close contact with every one of the major parties, and his cautious reflectiveness contrasts favorably with their respective fanaticisms.[11] Faced with intransigence, the Baron will resignedly conclude that he no longer understands the situation at hand as it spirals out of control; or rather, he now perceives all too clearly the absurdity of it all: "el mundo entero le pareció víctima de un malentendido sin remedio" (327; "the whole world suddenly seemed to him to be the victim of an irremediable misunderstanding" [251]).

Nonetheless, there is an important distinction to be made here, one central to the politics of the novel. The Baron condemns not actors or agents, caught up and confused by the contingency of events, but rather idealists and, most emphatically, intellectuals: in other words (in his words), the most dangerous are not those who act in accordance with obdurate creeds, but those who impose a dogmatic interpretation on events, who shape understanding of the past, present, and future based on their own hard-bitten beliefs. The Baron will go even further, concluding that events are simply not susceptible to rational interpretation, being ruled jointly by chance and illogic. And yet if the world is, as this novel seems to argue, characterized, even constituted, by chaos, it is still – as the author recognizes – left to both novelist and historian to reorder the entangled stories of history.

Two symbols for this activity are proposed, both tied to the Baron's perceptive and imaginative powers. The first is the chameleon in the garden: a creature notable for its ability to blend into any context, to adopt any position, which is a radical (and, it must be said, unsupported) argument for political maneuverability. The second symbol adduced by the Baron is that of a vulture feasting on putrid flesh, in an image which cogently articulates the self-loathing of a writer forced to fictionalize the failures of history, admitting his lack of faith in a political past and future.

But the novel does propose another avenue for comprehension to counterbalance this, one which takes various forms in the novel: what we might call a bodily connection. This does not mean physical immersion in history, which, as we have seen, is no guarantee of understanding; in fact, the body as such rather gets in the way of the truth, whether in the blinding adrenaline of direct experience, the autopsied cadaver which reveals nothing, or the physical utterances of the Counselor on his deathbed. Rather, this is a question of physical pleasure, which often takes the form of a sexual encounter, gesturing toward an overcoming of disconnection. The novel rehearses three versions of this attempted approach, in scenes which both reflect and deflect one another. The first is given as grotesquely flawed: the formerly celibate Gall, unable to communicate verbally with his tracker's wife Jurema, instead rapes her; and in an attempt to rationalize his actions, he perversely chooses to recast the event as a vehicle for her enlightenment, although he will once again conclude that "tú no me entiendes, yo tampoco te entiendo" (299; "you don't understand me and I don't understand you" [227]). The second version involves the congenitally uncomfortable journalist, who is painfully cognizant of his inadequacy to the events he witnesses, but who comes to a different awareness of the pleasure which can still be derived through connection, even in moments of horror and helplessness; events become for him at once rationally unintelligible and intuitively perceptible with Jurema holding his hand. Jurema, like the plant for which she is named (and which appears in da Cunha's novel where her character does not), has curative or restorative properties, and her contact with each of the central figures of the novel occasions a turnaround in their personal fortunes; the circus performers and writer-figures, whose monstrous bodies effectively alienate them from others, are all made whole by contact with Jurema. She is not merely an untouched agent of their regeneration: rather, in one of Vargas Llosa's rare feminine triumphs, Jurema herself undergoes a transformation in her unlikely relations with the journalist; charged with protecting and complementing the men around her, she finally finds her own happiness, a wholeness which is not mental or emotional but bodily.

In this she forms an interesting counterpart to the Baron, who is notoriously prudish when it comes to discussions of sex, but who ultimately undergoes his own physical awakening in the face of rational despair. Unfortunately, this occurs in a scene which will strike most readers as distasteful.[12] Directly mirroring the two preceding duets, the Baron revokes his own intellectual impotence by asserting his physical potency; he forces his own transformation by forcing himself on his wife's maidservant. This scene appears to push a program of instinct over intellect, and that instinct is itself enmeshed in a cycle of violence for which it problematically provides an alibi. As Rama puts it, in this novel "the irrational impulses of the body are valorized positively, but irrationalism is invalidated when it proceeds from the mind."[13] The novel, in this light, appears to be asserting the power of the senses to supplement the senselessness of history, opposing a doctrine of the physical to the dogma of the intellectual, invalidating any attempt by a writer to respond to history.

And yet even if the novel seems to assert that the responsibility of the intellectual is thrown into crisis in the face of continental carnage, storytelling is not made entirely impossible. In fact, in one of the closing scenes of the novel Vargas Llosa goes so far as to rewrite the ending of the Boom novel most acclaimed for its engagement with the complexities of Latin American history, *Cien años de soledad* (*One Hundred Years of Solitude*). Where García Márquez brought his story to a cataclysmic close, consuming characters and author alike in a literary holocaust, Vargas Llosa reinstalls a survivor in the empty space left by the massacre of Canudos, allowing someone – a storyteller – to live beyond the confines of a narrative which roars along from genesis to apocalypse. This storyteller is captured listening, letting the strains of a story linger long after its protagonists have been exterminated.

en ese mundo ya sin Canudos y sin yagunzos, y que pronto estaría también sin soldados cuando los que habían cumplido su misión acabaran de irse, y esas tierras volvieran a su orgullosa y miserable soledad de siempre, el Enano se había interesado, impresionado, asombrado con lo que Antonio el Fogueteiro refería. (706–707)

(in that world where there was no Canudos any more and no *jagunços*, where soon there would be no soldiers either, when those who had accomplished their mission left at last and the *sertão* returned to its eternal proud and miserable solitude, the Dwarf had been interested, impressed, and amazed to hear what Antonio the Pyrotechnist was relating; 558)

The final scene proclaims more firmly than ever that belief, versions, stories can seep back in through the gaps opened up by misunderstandings. *La guerra del fin del mundo*, for all its uncertainties regarding storytelling and interpretation, ultimately resists closing off either narrative or history; in place of an ending, it offers instead an ambiguous opening, through which warring stories may slip into the echo-chamber of history.

NOTES

1. Vargas Llosa, *Making Waves*, ed. and trans. John King (New York: Penguin, 1998), p. 70. Henceforth *MW*.
2. Efraín Kristal, *Temptation of the Word: The Novels of Mario Vargas Llosa*. (Nashville: Vanderbilt University Press, 1998), p. 124.
3. Ángel Rama, "Mario Vargas Llosa o el fanatismo por la literatura," in Néstor Tenorio Requejo (ed.), *Mario Vargas Llosa: el fuego de la literatura* (Lima: Arteidea, 2001), p. 229; translation mine.
4. "The Author's Favorite of His Novels", in Myron I. Lichtblau (ed.), *Mario Vargas Llosa: A Writer's Reality* (Syracuse University Press, 1991), p. 123.
5. As Douglas Weatherford notes, Vargas Llosa saddles Galileo Gall with all of Euclides da Cunha's Europe-derived theories, in order to let the journalist – a figure for da Cunha himself – elaborate an unadulterated Latin American version of events.
6. Mario Vargas Llosa, "Un escritor y sus demonios," *La Nación*, May 12, 1985; translation mine.
7. Previous treatments had focused upon the narrative of the military victors (seen as the shock-troops of modernization); it was Vargas Llosa who brought the version of the vanquished to the surface, deftly reimagining the stories of this history's losers.
8. References to the Portuguese text and to *La guerra del fin del mundo* (Madrid: Alfaguara/Santillana Ediciones, 1997), and to the English text, *The War of the End of the World*, trans. Helen K. Lane (New York: Penguin, 1997).
9. It is significant that the Counselor is not actually described physically, but rather comes to us through his language, through the stories others tell about him.

10. Baron and journalist alike realize the virtual impossibility of disentangling "esa maraña tan compacta de fábulas y de patrañas que no hay manera de desenredar" ("that whole tangled web of false stories"), and yet they differ over their response to that frustrating, bloodstained inextricability. For the journalist, its maddening complexity is no justification for ignorance, while "tampoco el cinismo es una solución" ("cynicism is no solution, either" [533; 417]).

11. In this attitude the Baron clearly functions as the mouthpiece of the author, who in a 1975 essay called for replacing the fanaticism of a Che Guevara or Frantz Fanon – "prophets of violent adventure and apocalyptic denial" – with Albert Camus' "voice of reason and moderation, of tolerance and prudence" (*MW*, 110).

12. This scene derives from a reading of Bataille's theory of eroticism as "one of those privileged areas of 'Evil and the diabolical,' through which man, by approaching death, can exercise his freedom, rebel and reach fullness" (*MW*, 118); it also, as Efraín Kristal pointed out to me, echoes a scene in Zola's *Thérèse Raquin*.

13. Rama, p. 243 (my translation). The author would clearly reject this charge of contradiction, signaling instead his intention to cross Isaiah Berlin – like Camus, a voice of "reason and moderation" – with the apologist of "unreason" Georges Bataille (*MW*, 147).

FURTHER READING

Bernucci, Leopoldo M., *Historia de un malentendido: un estudio transtextual de La guerra del fin del mundo*, New York: Peter Lang, 1989.

Boldori, Rosa, "*La guerra del fin del mundo*: posmodernidad y transtextualidad," in Hernández de López (ed.), pp. 161–69.

Brown, James W., "Mario Vargas Llosa y la guerra del fin de la inocencia," in Hernández de López (ed.), pp. 171–77.

Castro-Klarén, Sara, *Understanding Mario Vargas Llosa*, Columbia: University of South Carolina Press, 1990.

Cornejo Polar, Antonio, "*La guerra del fin del mundo*: sentido (y sinsentido) de la historia," *Hispamérica* 11, 31 (1982): 3–14.

Gutiérrez, Ángela, *Vargas Llosa e o romance possivel da América Latina*, Rio de Janeiro: Sette Letras, 1996.

Hernández de López, Ana María (ed.), *Mario Vargas Llosa: Opera Omnia*, Madrid: Editorial Pliegos, 1994.

Juzyn-Amestoy, Olga, "La mitificación de la violencia: un estudio del narrador de *La guerra del fin del mundo*," in Hernández de López (ed.), pp. 179–88.

Kristal, Efraín, *Temptation of the Word: The Novels of Mario Vargas Llosa*, Nashville: Vanderbilt University Press, 1998.

Lichtblau, Myron (ed.). *Mario Vargas Llosa: A Writer's Reality*, Syracuse University Press, 1991.

Oviedo, José Miguel, *Mario Vargas Llosa: la invención de una realidad*. Barcelona: Editorial Seix Barral, 1982.

Rama, Ángel, "Mario Vargas Llosa o el fanatismo por la literatura," in Néstor Tenorio Requejo (ed.), *Mario Vargas Llosa: el fuego de la literatura*, Lima: Arteidea, 2001, pp. 229–44.

Skirius, John, "*The War of the End of the World* by Vargas Llosa: A Reconsideration," *Mester* 29 (2000): 116–25.

Vargas Llosa, Mario, *Making Waves*, ed. and trans. John King, New York: Penguin, 1998.

Weatherford, Douglas, "Galileo Gall as Archive in Vargas Llosa's *La guerra del fin del mundo*," *Confluencia* 12, 2 (Spring 1997): 149–59.

Williams, Raymond L., *Mario Vargas Llosa*, New York: Ungar, 1986.

EPILOGUE

17

SUZANNE JILL LEVINE

The Latin American novel in English translation

The earliest translations of the Latin American novel into English were sporadic and haphazard. One of the few nineteenth-century Latin American novels published in the first half of the twentieth century was *Aves sin nido* by the Peruvian Clorinda Matto de Turner, translated as *Birds Without a Nest: a Story of Indian Life and Priestly Oppression in Peru* (1904) by Thyne, a British Protestant press keen on underscoring the "priestly oppression" featured in the novel as the focal point of the defense of an oppressed indigenous people in need of salvation. The most unsavory elements of the novel were removed from the English version and duly restored by Naomi Lindstrom in her Texas University Press 1996 edition of that first translation.

Commercial publishers and small presses in the United States began to venture into the unknown wilds of South American writing in the 1920s and 1930s. New York based publishing houses such as Farrar and Rinehart (soon to be Farrar Straus, and by the 1960s, FS and Giroux) were seriously committed to the publication of some Latin American novels, and London editors such as Constable or Cape, and later on, others such as Faber and Faber tended to follow in the steps of their American counterparts by publishing English editions of the same translations within a year or two. An exception to this tendency occurred in the sixties and seventies when some of the more radical American published translations of experimental Latin American works were rejected, at first, because of the use of colloquial American speech and slang: two such examples were Manuel Puig's *Betrayed by Rita Hayworth* (*La traición de Rita Hayworth*, 1967) and Guillermo Cabrera Infante's *Three Trapped Tigers* (*Tres tristes tigres*, 1965), both published in New York in 1971. It would take decades for British presses to begin significant publishing ventures on their own in the area of Latin American literary translation, most notably in the 1980s with the publication of important Central American writers, and more recently by the initiative of Oxford University Press which has been publishing new scholarly translations of important authors and works from the nineteenth century such as the Chilean Alberto Blest Gana's (*Martin Rivas*, 2000), the Argentine José Marmol's *Amalia*, and the Brazilian Joaquim Maria Machado de Assis's (*Esau and Jacob*, 2000).

In the 1920s and 1930s a realist mode, the so-called *novela de la tierra* (novel of the earth), was dominant in Latin America. On the ground, the literary scene was more diverse and variegated, but the English reading public was limited, by and large, to this mode in the novels that were translated. The novels that circulated included works like Mariano Azuela's *Los de abajo* (*The Underdogs*), translated by Enrique Munguía in 1929 (by Brentano in New York), a novel about the confused aspirations of those who had participated in the Mexican Revolution; or José Eustasio Rivera's *La vorágine* (*The Vortex*), translated by Earle K. James in 1935 (Putnam in New York), the novel of the Latin American jungle in the period of the *caucho* fever, or *Don Segundo Sombra* by Ricardo Güiraldes, published by Farrar and Reinhart as *Don Segundo Sombra: Shadows on the Pampas*, translated by Harriet de Onís in 1935, the gaucho novel par excellence. The publicity surrounding these novels would emphasize elements such as the descriptions of the Latin American landscape, or the translator's ability to render the colorful customs and even the speech of the local characters.

While a variety of houses, large and small, published isolated great works from Spanish and Portuguese, in the 1940s Knopf stood out as the publishing house which most aggressively promoted Latin American literature. Alfred Knopf's press's commitment to publishing works from the region began in earnest when Blanche, his first wife, visited South America in 1942, on a grand tour (co-sponsored by the State Department) of Argentina, Brazil, Colombia, Chile, Peru, and Uruguay. Mrs. Knopf was keen to contact some writers who were respected in the circles that promoted Latin American literature in the United States, and she was also interested in discovering lesser-known talents for the benefit of the American public. Blanche Knopf was looking for novelists who had something to say about the ethos or the customs of Latin America. Her choices had as much to do with her critical instincts as with her sense of an author's local popularity, and other "circumstances" (e.g. writers calling at the publisher's hotel).[1] As Irene Rostagno observes in her book on the promotion of Latin American literature in the United States, Blanche was struck by "the fact that organized publishing in Latin America was all but nonexistent, with the exception of Argentina and, to a lesser degree, Brazil."[2] That being said, during her visit Mrs. Knopf found an extremely lively literary culture. Her initiative would lead, over the years, to numerous works contracted for publication in the United States, including several novels by Jorge Amado, among them *Terras do sem fin* (*The Violent Land*), Eduardo Mallea's *La bahia de silencio* (*The Bay of Silence*) and *Todo verdor perecerá* (*All Green Shall Perish*), Alejo Carpentier's *Los pasos perdidos* (*The Lost Steps*) and *El reino de este mundo* (*The Kingdom of this World*), a now obscure Bolivian author Adolfo Costa du Rels's *Tierras hechizadas* (*Bewitched Lands*), and Graciliano Ramos's *Angústia* (*Anguish*). The publication of these works was intended to generate interest in an American reading public whose curiosity for Latin America might have been partly stimulated by an increase of trade relations with the southern hemisphere during World War II and by the Good Neighbor policy, but they were hardly publishing successes. Interest in the region diminished significantly after the war, but Knopf's commitment to Latin American literature remained strong for decades, even though they did not have a Latin American bestseller until Amado's *Gabriela, Clove and Cinnamon* (*Gabriela, cravo e canela*) appeared in 1962.

Twenty years earlier, during that exploratory 1942 trip, Blanche, who knew a few European languages and was an urbane cosmopolitan in touch with the latest Parisian cultural trends, was especially taken by Eduardo Mallea, the writer of the moment in Buenos Aires, and by his search for the Argentine "national genius" of his alienated bourgeois characters, capturing in novels like *Fiesta en noviembre* (*Fiesta in November*) a local angst with an existentialist bent. (I remember reading this 1938 novel, in Spain during my junior year in college in the mid-sixties, as a serious and representative Latin American work.) Her instincts were ostensibly validated by Mallea's prominence, fame, and sense of relevance with a wide Argentine reading public. There was yet another reason why Mallea mattered to Knopf: he was a key player in the Argentine Spanish language literary publishing business himself, and, since by 1940 Buenos Aires had replaced Barcelona as the publishing capital of the Spanish-speaking world, it was a matter of pride for Blanche Knopf to attach the most prominent Argentine novelist of the time to her husband's press (Rostagno, 32–33).

It never ceases to amaze many of us, as Uruguayan critic Emir Rodríguez Monegal was among the first to note, that when Alfred and Blanche Knopf were offered the works of Jorge Luis Borges in the 1950s, they turned down the metaphysical Argentine fabulist! In his stead they kept on promoting Eduardo Mallea, publishing Mallea's *The Bay of Silence*, which was hardly a critical success when it came out in 1944, and again in 1966, *All Green Shall Perish*. But like most other Latin American works in translation, his books fell through the cracks of a spotty readership; in time Mallea has been relegated to a secondary literary figure in Argentina as well. We can conclude, in hindsight, that Borges, who was a presence in the Argentine literary world at the time, did not "represent" the image of the Latin American writer that would entice American publishers. An appeal to local color was an imperative for a

Latin American novel to be published in the States with or without nods to cosmopolitan trends – and Borges did not bear the folksy marks of a writer regional enough to meet this standard. Knopf's rejection of Borges was symptomatic of a patronizing English-speaking world unable to appreciate that something of great literary significance was brewing on the ground in Latin America, and which was not lost on keener French observers such as Roger Callois or Valery Larbaud. By the late 1930s, Latin American writers – most notably, those surrounding the Argentine journal *Sur* edited by the urbane Victoria Ocampo – had begun incorporating in their innovative works the techniques and experimentation of modernism and surrealism, as well as the concerns of Continental philosophy, and explorations of urban life.[3]

In short, the context that accounted for the literary revolution taking place in Latin America was impossible to appreciate, until the late 1960s, in the United States and Britain where Latin American local-color-type novels were the only kind being translated.

If Knopf was the main publisher of Latin American novels from the 1940s until the 1960s, Harriet de Onís was this publishing press's translator of choice for works in Spanish or Portuguese – following the death of Samuel Putnam, who had translated *Don Quixote*, Amado's *The Violent Land*, and the Brazilian classic *Rebellion in the Backlands* (*Os Sertoes*) by Euclides da Cunha. Onís's career is also symptomatic of her moment. Harriet, the American wife of Federico de Onís – an influential Spanish literary scholar and professor at Columbia University – had been translating Latin American literature since the 1930s. Her status as the premier translator of Latin American literature of her time was consolidated in 1941, when her abridged version of Peruvian author Ciro Alegría's *El mundo es ancho y ajeno* (*Broad and Alien is the World*) won the best Latin American novel competition organized by Farrar and Rinehart.[4] The top prize of this competition reinforced the trend towards realism, regionalism, and local color of Latin America in English translation. *Broad and Alien is the World*, which portrayed the struggle of an Indian community with the white establishment, represented the indigenist current of the earlier literary regionalism.[5] In retrospect, the second prize in the Farrar and Rinehart competition was of greater significance for future developments in the Latin American novel. It was awarded to Uruguayan Juan Carlos Onetti's *Tierra de nadie* (*No Man's Land*, 1941), for its examination of the confusion in Buenos Aires before the war. In *El Boom de la novela latinoamericana* (1972), Rodríguez Monegal avers that, in effect, the jury failed to appreciate what was innovative in Onetti, its hallucinatory style and thematics of moral decadence that foreshadowed a prominent direction of the Latin American novel in subsequent decades, the direction that ultimately culminated in the Boom.[6]

De Onís was characteristic of the early translators of Latin American literature: she was not terribly accurate and tended to normalize (with flowery language) both the regionalisms of some novels, and the original experimental language of others. A glaring example is her translation of *Grande sertão: veredas* (*The Devil to Pay in the Backlands*), which levels the eccentric innovations of the avant-garde Brazilian Guimarães Rosa's into a simple prose. Machado de Assis was yet another great Brazilian writer (doubtlessly the most important South American novelist of the nineteenth century) who was ill-served by mostly uneven translations. Helen Caldwell did decent translations of Machado de Assis, published by Farrar Straus and Giroux (directed by the urbane publisher Roger Straus who later shared his admiration for the Brazilian writer with Susan Sontag) and University of California Press, but the best translator of Machado was, curiously, an economist who had lived in Brazil, William L. Grossman – translating *Memórias póstumas de Brás Cubas*, titled *Epitaph of a Small Winner*, for Farrar Straus and Giroux in 1967. In 1962 he did for Knopf – revising a mediocre translation previously commissioned – the best translation of Jorge Amado's *Gabriela...*

Despite de Onis's shortcomings, however, Mr. Knopf and his editors had a great deal of confidence in her work, and often ran new titles and names of other translators by her for her approval. De Onís's tastes leaned primarily toward the regional and folkloric, which meant, ultimately, that she shared Knopf's bias for the Latin American picturesque. But to her credit, she was also interested in promoting Clarice Lispector, Alejo Carpentier, and José Donoso, whose works were often experimental and – in the case of Lispector – difficult in their introspective hermeticism. Indeed, it was de Onís, herself, in 1952, who brought Jorge Luis Borges to the attention of the press, only to be rejected.[7]

It was not until European publishers awarded the Formentor Prize to both Borges and Samuel Beckett in 1961, as Rodríguez Monegal was the first to point out, that the Argentine's career in the USA – as well as that of the younger innovative Latin American writers – began to take off.[8] France, or more precisely Paris, took the lead in "discovering" Borges, as it would in discovering other Latin American writers, and American publishers, especially those with a deep commitment to literature, felt that if Gallimard thought a writer was worth publishing, then they should take note.

I have been using the term "Latin America" to discuss a corpus of novels, but it is worth noting that this notion was far more important in the United States or Europe than in Latin American nations themselves. Cabrera Infante, the Cuban novelist exiled in London, has insisted that "the Latin American Novel" is a non-referential term invented for publicity – and that we should speak instead of the Cuban, Mexican, or Argentine novel. At the other end of the political spectrum, Jorge Amado, one of Brazil's most popular writers (with deep Marxist affinities) also challenged the idea of a Latin American literature, as a "false and dangerous concept," insisting that there is nothing more different than a Mexican and a Brazilian, and that "we are united by what is negative – misery, oppression, military dictatorship."[9]

The notion of a Latin American writer was championed by novelists and literary critics who claimed that a literary movement was coming into cohesion in the 1960s, and even though the literary quality of such novels is undeniable, the term was underwritten by the area divisions that informed the geopolitical tensions during the Cold War, and which were heightened in the aftermath of the Cuban Revolution. At American universities Latin American studies were officially promoted by the government of the United States in this very period, and this label was not contingent on a precise esthetic definition: it was a designation of a geopolitical area which was also convenient for the business of teaching courses and selling books. As a literary category the term "Latin America" was readily seized upon by the cultural institutions of the recently established Communist state in Cuba earlier and perhaps more forcefully than by its American counterparts: for the rise of a novel of high quality throughout the Southern Hemisphere was taken as a cultural symptom of the revolutionary fervor that had been mounting throughout the hemisphere. And the cultural leaders of the Cuban Revolution were heartened that some of the most prominent Latin American novelists were fervent supporters of a revolutionary process they hoped would spread to other countries. From this perspective, it was often in a reactive mode that the notion of the Latin American novel became popularized in the United States, as Deborah Cohn has underscored:

> Many Latin American writers (Cortázar, García Márquez, Fuentes, Vargas Llosa and others) supported the Cuban government during its first decade . . . It is not surprising, then, that some of the interest in disseminating Latin American literature in the United States was motivated by a desire (1) to make U.S. cultural activity attractive to Latin American intellectuals, and (2) to counter Cuba's influence on the latter by creating alternative, U.S.-based centers of cultural activity.[10]

Cohn's main point here is that the South American novel became important to readers in North America because in 1959, with the Cuban Revolution, "Latin America" became a major player in hemispheric and world politics. Novels such as Carlos Fuentes's *The Death of Artemio Cruz* (1962), Mario Vargas Llosa's *Green House* (1965), and Gabriel García Márquez's *One Hundred Years of Solitude* (1967) became required reading for, at the very least, an educated elite in the United States and the English-speaking world that needed to be knowledgeable. In some quarters, interest in this novel was actively promoted to dispel hostilities and acquire a more positive image – of its "neighbors" to the South. Federal agencies and high-minded publishers alike had a double purpose here, as Harriet De Onis openly noted, as a response to the Cuban Revolution: "Every Latin American writer who receives due recognition at our hands is a potential ally."[11] Deborah Cohn comments on De Onis's assertion in the following:

> Exposure to U.S. culture and values, cultivating the exchange of ideas, and a positive reception in the United States were seen by many as ways of promoting mutual understanding through the Latin American writers who, in their role as public intellectuals, could influence public opinion and ultimately, ideally, lessen hostilities towards the United States.[12]

Of course, what de Onis, naïvely perhaps, could not foresee was that many of the most successful writers promoted by American publishing, such as García Márquez, would continue to maintain strong anti-US positions and lend their prestige to movements such as the Cuban Revolution.

There is also a direct connection between the project of counteracting the influence of Communist sympathies in Latin America in the aftermath of the Cuban Revolution, and the role that university presses played in the dissemination of the Latin American novel; these publications had equally ambiguous results. The Association of American University Presses (AAUP), in fact, organized an ambitious program in the 1960s with assistance from the Rockefeller Foundation – support that allowed the Association to take publishing risks that commercial presses simply could not afford to take. A five-year translation program for literary and scholarly books in the Humanities and Social Sciences was initially proposed to the Rockefeller Foundation in 1958 as a priming operation for developing a market for Latin American books. The Cuban Revolution, certainly, gave a sense of urgency to the project. Although August Frugé, then head of the AAUP and director of the University of California Press, asserted in his proposal that "there is no disposition on the part of the Association of University Presses to embark upon a translation program for the sake of international relations,"[13] Frank Wardlaw, then head of the University of Texas Press, wrote that "we are all convinced that a translation program such as this one could do enormous good in strengthening the cultural ties which bind us to Latin America and helping us as a nation, beginning on a fairly high intellectual level, to understand the complex civilization of our neighbors to the South."[14] The Rockefeller Foundation acknowledged this role in its approval of the program by stating that one of the functions of university presses is the exploration of new areas of scholarly need, "and they now appear ready to act on the belief that significant recent developments in Latin American call for a reorientation of thought in regard to the role this area will play in the future of cultural and intellectual exchange among nations."[15]

The grant allotted $225,000 to the AAUP over the course of five years. The Association set up an Allocation Committee of leading Latin Americanists whose tasks included preparing a list of suggested titles for translation to be distributed to the AAUP's member presses, and reviewing proposals from these presses for grants in aid – payable to translators – to offset the publication costs of specific books. Over the years, the Committee included such distinguished scholars as Enrique Anderson-Imbert and Richard Morse. Between 1960 and 1966, the program approved the publication of eighty-three books; twenty presses were involved. Titles included numerous important literary works, including J. M. Machado de Assis's *The Psychiatrist and Other Stories* and *Esau and Jacob*; *The Invention of Morel*, by Adolfo Bioy Casares; Elena Garro's *Recollections of Things to Come*; Graciliano Ramos's *Barren Lives*; and *The Edge of the Storm* and *The Lean Lands*, by Agustín Yáñez.[16]

Even though the program coincided with the early years of the Latin American novel's entrance into the international mainstream, no Boom novel was ever published through it. Perhaps the factors that kept the university presses' risks down – including smaller editions and lower costs – and made them a good initial vehicle for creating an audience for works from the region ultimately rendered them unsuitable to the "bestsellerism" that defined the Boom. Certainly, many of the translations were less than satisfactory, in part because these presses, to reduce their costs, often hired graduate students, who were beginning their careers in the then fledgling field of Latin American literature, rather than the more experienced and more expensive professional translators. Perhaps, though, the AAUP's failure to tap into the movement may also be ascribed to another contemporary phenomenon: the increasing professionalization of the Latin American writer. As numerous scholars have detailed, the Boom was as much a marketing phenomenon as it was a literary movement, and authors – Fuentes in particular set the standard for his fellow Latin Americans in the USA, as well as opening numerous doors for them – relied increasingly on networking and agents rather than academics to publicize their work. In other words, the AAUP, which drew up its lists of recommended books on the advice of scholars, may well have missed out on the opportunity to publish Boom novels because literary agents started to market them directly to publishers such as Knopf and, as the 1960s progressed and the Boom phenomenon became better-known, Harper and Row, Farrar and Straus, Pantheon, and Grove.

Translating the "Boom"

Between 1960 and 1970 in the European and North American publishing world, the Latin American novel was discovered, translated, and lauded by a new reading public, instigated as much by the experimental sixties – and the era's new engagement with the "Third World" – as by the Cuban Revolution. The floodgates were now opened and a wide range of Latin American literature was to be published in English on both sides of the Atlantic in commercial and academic presses alike; and for the first time, some Latin American writers were deemed among the most innovative in contemporary literature. Miguel Angel Asturias's 1967 Nobel Prize was symptomatic of the acknowledgment that the Latin American novel could be considered world class.

The *nueva novela* was nourished by many influences, not only European and North American modernism but most importantly the synthesizer of those traditions, Jorge Luis Borges, considered by many of the writers, among them Vargas Llosa, García Márquez, and Cabrera Infante, to be the father of the Latin American novel – even though he never wrote a novel himself. Creating a new world literary identity by rewriting the old (European) world, Jorge Luis Borges shaped the "personal geography" of the Latin American writers. Rewriting the Spanish language with the help of French and English literary models meant subverting Spain the motherland and the Spanish language "rhetorical flourishes."[17] Borges drew the line between the old and the new not only by revolutionizing the syntax of the Spanish language through his close readings of an extraordinary range of literary and linguistic influences, but inventing a new – soon to be labeled "postmodern" – concept of fiction. His "ficciones" were indeed a new hybrid genre of the short story – a challenging and dense fusion of detective plot, science fiction, metaphysical treatise, and magical poetry, blurring the ever more tenuous boundaries between reality and fiction within the confines of literature. Through Borges's blind eyes many readers were persuaded that reality is a fiction and that only Borgesian fiction was real!

Borges is and will always be, of course, an impossible act for mortal translators to follow. But in certain ways, some of us who translate from the Spanish have not only been trying to make Latin American works accessible to English readers but have been trying also to bring into the English language the rhythm and pace of the Spanish. Maybe all good translators, bridge-makers in a sense, are trying to work their way back to some common language before Babel, at the same time attempting to follow Ezra Pound's precept about making the old new. What is so difficult to translate in Borges in this context is that he brought English into the Spanish language, so that in a sense he needs to be translated back into the English he was reading; in some ways, the ideal English translator of Borges is Edwardian British in tone but American in wielding with concise economy a spare yet dense literary language. Borges's language in translation, however, can never be matched in translation, precisely because, at least in part, it is his incorporation of English tonality into Spanish which makes the Spanish so original! A similar case in point is García Márquez's brilliantly synthetic magical realist style in *One Hundred Years of Solitude*. Gregory Rabassa did a breathtaking translation of this novel, so vivid that García Márquez himself said he preferred the English version. However intended by the Colombian author, there is great truth in his praise, but Rabassa's *One Hundred Years of Solitude* is not the same as García Márquez's *Cien años de soledad*. The language of the original is an extremely potent Spanish, taut, dense, "synthetic," meaning condensed or compressed, while the English version has a more expansive, relaxed, tall-tale tonality; nonetheless, Rabassa continually finds ingeniously succinct solutions for García Márquez's most inventive metaphors.

Among the translators of the Boom writers, Gregory Rabassa is a household name, the translator most associated with the blockbuster novels, many of them of the magical realist variety but also others which don't fit into that category, like the long political novels of Mario Vargas Llosa. Gregory Rabassa broke the ground for the new Latin American novel in English with his prizewinning translation of Julio Cortazar's *Hopscotch*, published in 1966 by Pantheon Books, Helen and Kurt Wolff's excellent press (with the talented Andre Schiffrin as their senior editor) whose goal, like that of a cluster of more enlightened publishers, was to bring to American readers a select upcoming group of experimental and left-wing writers from Europe and Latin America. Pantheon would eventually (like others) be swallowed up by a larger house, but during those glory years of the late 1960s and early 1970s, like some of the larger literary presses – Knopf, E. P. Dutton, Harper and Row – Pantheon was able to branch out into a literature that might not sell many copies but would receive great critical acclaim and have a pioneering impact on university curricula and intellectual circles.

Hopscotch, among other things a powerful elegy to two other great cities, Paris and Buenos Aires, was a tour de force. Rabassa translated with great creativity all the linguistic experiments that Cortázar embarked on in that novel; speaking of the nonsense language "gliglico," a salient invention in that *roman comique*, Rabassa (taking his inspiration from Lewis Carroll, in turn the wordsmithing mentor of both Cortázar and Cabrera Infante) remarked blithely, "the best way to translate gliglico is to put it into Gliglish."[18] But while *Hopscotch* set the stage, it was Rabassa's masterful rendering of *One Hundred Years of Solitude*, which was published in English, three years after its appearance in Spanish, that crowned him as the leading translator of the Boom writers. And while he earned – a good rate in 1970! – only $25 per thousand words, without royalty or subsidiary rights, for this book which, unlike most translations, would bring considerable earnings to its publisher and make its author a millionaire, Rabassa now had the fame and power to decide not only what books he would or would not translate but also, often, which Latin American books did or did not get translated. The huge success of *One Hundred Years of Solitude* ushered in, again, a seductive new concept for the American reading public: "magical realism." If Borges's fantastic literature made his readers question reality and, indeed, was a foreshadowing of the computer age's "virtual reality," magical realism made its readers suspend disbelief by presenting the marvelous as an everyday reality. Rabassa would continue to bring to readers other, some newer and even older exemplars of this style, for example, another of his favorite writers, whose work had a notable impact on García Márquez, was 1967 Nobel Prizewinner Miguel Angel Asturias, from Guatemala. Among his works, Rabassa translated the marvelous real *Mulata* (1967). A skilled translator from the Portuguese as well, Rabassa brought to readers via Knopf a work even more challenging that Cortázar's *Hopscotch*, Clarice Lispector's most important novel *An Apple in the Dark* (1961), published in English in 1967. Lispector, a Brazilian of Ukrainian origin, was the only woman writer to merit Boom status; a highly original and feminist descendant of the French *nouveau roman*, a true experimenter with language, she was not to Knopf's taste for the more "gutsy" elements of Latin American narrative, and she was an exception to the types of writers Rabassa normally translated (Rostagno, p. 47) But even though her difficult ambiguous prose made her work commercially non-viable, she was doubtlessly a key literary figure, and has been vindicated in the many translations by England-based Giovanni Pontiero, and especially by the Brazilian film of one of her last novellas, *The Hour of the Star*.

When Borges became, at least temporarily, a more commercial success in the early 1970s, this factor encouraged publishers such as E. P. Dutton, in particular, to risk undertaking the translations of the Post-Boom writers, those whose works subverted even more radically literary language by bringing the spoken language and diverse elements of pop culture into the literary text.

An important contributor to the Borgesian opus in English was, in the 1970s, a Harvard student, Norman Thomas di Giovanni, who befriended the Argentine maestro while he was giving the Charles Eliot Norton lectures in Cambridge, Massachusetts in 1967 and proceeded to create a career as Borges's promoter in the United States. The advantage of di Giovanni's translations – as a writer he was a less-than-perfect match because he tended toward the cliché while Borges (particularly the most significant Borges fictions before the writer went blind) was always strikingly original in his choice of vocabulary and casting of sentences – was that Di Gi (as he was called) worked closely with the blind writer. The E. P. Dutton editions, led by editor Jack Macrae, notably *The Aleph and Other Stories* (1970), but also other subsequent works which Di Gi and Borges did together for Dutton, have the virtue of capturing the colloquial verve of the original language, taking liberties because Borges wanted his stories to be more accessible to his readers and was intent on repudiating his earlier style. So that while Borges's earlier translators tried to be more traditionally faithful – hence the language in the 1962 volumes *Ficciones* (translated by Alastair Reid, Anthony Kerrigan, and other English writers) and *Labyrinths* (translated by two American academics, Donald Yates and James Irby) tended to be archaic, in short, more difficult to read – Di Giovanni in collaboration with Borges actually made Borges into a more widely read author in the 1970s, to the extent that, after *One Hundred Years of Solitude* (published in 1970 by Harper and Row), Borges became the writer whose books sold the most copies in the early 1970s! Borges's unexpected success would encourage Macrae at Dutton to take on other lesser-known offbeat or experimental writers, most notably among them another Argentine, and a gay writer to boot, Manuel Puig. It was at this juncture that I began my own career as a translator, initially under the mentorship of Gregory Rabassa who had been my professor at Columbia University. My first experiments with translation led to Harper and Row's publication of Cabrera Infante's *Three Trapped Tigers*, and Puig's first novel *Betrayed by Rita Hayworth*.

While Knopf had started a snowball effect, which eventually brought Dutton, Harper and Row (who published García Márquez and Cabrera Infante), Farrar Straus and Giroux (Carlos Fuentes and Vargas Llosa), Pantheon, and many presses, from the big commercial houses to small poetry presses, into the new world of Latin American literature in English, the institution which single-handedly had a crucial impact on this development was David Rockefeller's foundation, the Center for Inter-American Relations, now called the Americas Society. The center would energetically promote quality Latin American writers through its Literature Program, directed by José Guillermo Castillo, a Venezuelan cultural entrepreneur, who had previous experience as an Inter-American Foundation for the Arts official. Castillo, a cosmopolitan spirit, "was at home both in the New York publishing milieu and in Latin American literary circles," as Rostagno writes, and, "unlike the more cautious Knopfs," he convinced American publishers "that the region was teeming with exciting fiction that anxiously awaited recognition" (107). To overcome the language barrier as well as the "lack of a structured publishing network in South America," both of which discouraged American publishers, "Castillo set up a translation program in 1968" (107).

Working with committees including Rabassa, Latin American literary critics Emir Rodríguez Monegal (also a Yale University professor) and Maria Luisa Bastos (professor at CUNY), New Yorker writer/translator Alastair Reid, Gregory Rabassa, other professors and critics of Spanish American literature such as John Alexander Coleman, American literary critic John Simon and poet Mark Strand, Castillo and his staff sent reports to publishers along with European reviews to encourage the publication of as many books as possible. A crucial aspect of this encouragement was that the Center provided funding to subsidize the translations.[19] A magazine called *Review* – still published by the Americas Society today – now called *Review: Latin American Literature and Arts*, the first magazine in English devoted to the criticism and dissemination of Latin American culture, was founded to help promote the new translations as they appeared in print. Frank MacShane, a writer and professor at the Writing Division at Columbia University, from the late 1960s through the 1970s, ran a translation seminar and co-edited a university-sponsored *Translation Review*, which also contributed to the Center's Latin American campaign by publishing new translations and both well-known and new translators.

Because of "the Center," Gregory Rabassa could readily find publishers for his projects. The same was true for a whole slew of translators, among them myself, Helen Lane (a prolific translator from French and Portuguese as well as Spanish), Thomas Colchie, Margaret "Petch" Peden, Alfred MacAdam, Hardie St. Martin, and Edith Grossman. Also included in this group were translators from England such as Gerald Martin who recreated Miguel Angel Asturias' most magnificent, and also most difficult, work, *Hombres de Maíz* (*Men of Maize*), and Gordon Brotherston, who did the first translation of the Cuban Reinaldo Arenas's most brilliant novel, *El mundo alucinante* (*Hallucinations*). Thomas Colchie not only translated Brazilian poets and novelists but single-handedly as a freelance agent promoted many Brazilian writers from the great "Northeastern" poet Joao Cabral do Melo Neto to Nelida Piñón at an early stage of her career. Helen Lane, like Rabassa, took on many mega-books like Nelida Piñón's *Republic of Dreams* (1989) and Ernesto Sabato's *On Heroes and Tombs* (1981); "Petch" Peden translated many works including those of Carlos Fuentes and the Argentine Abel Posse; Alfred MacAdam, another professor and critic of Latin American literature, has also been prolific, translating the novels of Alejo Carpentier, Carlos Fuentes, and Mario Vargas Llosa.

Not only was the Center the meeting place of publishers and translators but also both Latin American and even North American writers themselves. Carlos Fuentes and José Donoso both played an important role
through their influential friendships and affinities with North American writers like William Styron, Kurt Vonnegut, and Robert Coover. Writers like John
Updike, with his enthusiastic reviews in the *New Yorker* of Borges and García
Márquez, and Susan Sontag, who underscored the importance of Machado
de Assis with a brilliant feature article, also in the *New Yorker*, attracted the
attention of thousands of readers. William Gass, John Barth, John Hawkes,
Donald Barthelme joined the increasing ranks of North American writers
and intellectuals who were fascinated with the brilliant writing from the
South, and prestigious magazines such as the *Hudson Review*, *Fiction* (edited
by Mark Mirsky), the *Paris Review*, *Partisan Review*, and *Triquarterly* frequently devoted features and issues to the new Latin American writers and
participated in the effort to disseminate translations. Carlos Fuentes was a
pivotal figure not only as a novelist but as a generous supporter and promoter
of his fellow writers, most particularly Gabriel García Márquez, or Gabo (as
the Colombian was called by friends), when he was still unknown, and starv-
ing in an attic in Paris, as well as Donoso. Fuentes had great influence in New
York publishing circles and, both as essayist and lecturer, disseminated the
excitement generated by the new literature from South America.

   If in the 1930s there was great interest in social realist and political novelists, in the 1960s, as Deborah Cohn observes, "universal themes and concerns" took the foreground.[20] Hence writers like Cortázar, Donoso, Fuentes,
García Márquez and Vargas Llosa, whose work was both regional and experimental, learning the lessons of modernism and surrealism in their eclectic
readings which respected no national boundaries, then translating these literary ideas into a new Latin American literary universe, were the writers who
would appeal to a broad readership. Indeed what came out of this mixture
of regional realities and European surrealism was a new genre which would
place Latin American literature on the world map: magical realism.

   With the runaway success of *One Hundred Years of Solitude*, magical
realism became equated in many quarters with what was "authentic" in
and about Latin American culture. Not only would it appeal to critics in
the *New York Times* and average readers, but new writers among the formerly marginal groups would soon become the new stars of the magical
realist approach, most notably, women writers like Chilean Isabel Allende
or Mexican Laura Esquivel, and, in the 1980s and 1990s, a whole slew of US
Latino and Latina writers like Julia Alvarez, Ana Castillo, Sandra Cisneros,
and many others. Whether because they "saw the light" in their own cultural
experiences or whether they saw this route as the formula to transcend their

marginality, many of these writers of the 1970s, 1980s, and 1990s got on the now mainstream magical realism bandwagon.

By the early 1970s, North American and to a certain extent European readers knew what they wanted from Latin America: magical realism – the genre which presented the region's realities in hyperbolic surrealist terms, the genre which portrayed the exoticizing image of Latin America that readers found intriguing and entertaining, a wild regressive liberating escape from the humdrum of ordinary progressive overly civilized life. Readers were not looking for introspective or formally subversive or raw realist writing. García Márquez's unreal seemed relatively unproblematic, a joyous and automatic entry into magic. And, after all, this "marvelous real" chimed in perfectly with New Ageism: Latin America represented, again, an exoticized other America where the magical would intermingle with the everyday, with sermonizing priests levitating after sipping hot chocolate, gypsies on flying carpets, men with gigantic penises, women more beautiful than human eyes had ever seen, etcetera.

Magical realism as a door which opened for women writers in Latin America brings us to recent perspectives on the emergence of the new Hispanic narratives. From the 1980s on, the rise of Latino literatures in the United States has taken the foreground over literature actually written in Latin America within the global marketplace, and to the interests of the growing field of cultural studies. It is important to note that most of what is called "Latino" literature is written in English. Now the translator of Latin American literature is becoming less necessary to a new public mostly interested in the Latino experience in English. There is another demographic reason for the changing role of the translator in Hispanic culture: there is now a large bilingual readership (the Hispanic minority is by far the largest in the United States), which was not the case in 1970. And, again, gender, race, and class, the foci of cultural studies, has also impacted on which novels get published.

Translating the new: one translator's view

Aside from the original and eccentric Guillermo Cabrera Infante, it was the "Post-Boom" figures Manuel Puig and Severo Sarduy to whom I, in the late sixties and early seventies, was drawn as a new young aficionado and translator of Latin American writing. What I found most challenging and exciting was the living spoken language that came potently to life in Cabrera Infante and Puig. What I found striking about Puig and Sarduy as gay writers was that they brought to the surface the repressed language of a marginal humanity of women and *folles*, questioning precisely some of the traditional perspectives of the male writers of the Boom toward women and the feminine.

Translators, in conjunction with publishers, make certain critical choices in choosing what they translate. Good translating, as has been said, aims to (re)produce an effect, to persuade a reader, and so it is in the broadest sense, like all rhetorical moves, a political act. I discuss the political function of translation, in my 1991 book on translation titled *The Subversive Scribe: Translating Latin American Fiction* (which retraces the collaborative process of translating specific works with bilingual authors), in the context of the Argentine writer Manuel Puig's *Boquitas pintadas*, which became in translation *Heartbreak Tango*. In this study I discuss some of the difficult choices I faced as a translator. For instance, it was not obvious how to translate the numerous melodramatic tango-lyric epigraphs which set a particular atmosphere for Latin American readers (not just Argentines or Uruguayans) familiar with the popular culture of the River Plate region. To recreate and illuminate Puig's original effects, I transposed the lyrics into Hollywood movie taglines and Madison Avenue advertising jingles. By adding more Hollywood references (a strong element in Puig's imaginary repertoire) than in the original text and substituting some specific Argentine cultural references, Puig and I, working together, gave the American English reader an American English version and, in a literal sense, suppressed some of the local references in the original. On the other hand, if we were to reproduce the original impression of parody upon Argentine readers, a parody that both criticizes and remythifies the uses and abuses of mass and popular culture in people's lives, these changes constituted an unavoidable political as well as poetic act. Historical contexts of course are always changing, and have changed already since my book came out in 1991. Manuel Puig, who died in 1990, is now a figure of history. Translation, again, is a crucial aspect of the historical process because it is one of the ways in which we, his readers, keep alive the writer's spirit and contribution to the dialogue of literature. However, what is important for readers to realize is that even the best translations are another book. For the Argentine reader, Puig's book was very Argentine; for the North American reader, it is Latin American, filled with exotic or "primitive" references (like a maid killing a chicken in the backyard) which are part of what makes it fascinating, a view of a new reality, or a new view of reality.

If as a translator I was drawn less to the magical realists' talking trees than to talking characters, drawn to writers more like Lispector and especially acrobatic wordsmiths, it was because I sensed that for the translator, magic is language itself. For me the last frontier was both a Carrollian and Joycean one, pushing written language to its spoken limits. Guillermo

Cabrera Infante's *Tres tristes tigres* (turned into *Three Trapped Tigers*) was in the way the first work to turn "Cuban" into a literary language – spiked with slang, wordplays, and Joycean dislocutions, a mulatto Spanish marked by both Cuban and Havanan, a specific region and city, but enriched and made polyphonic by diverse cultural and literary references. Severo Sarduy's witty, hallucinatory novel poems or poetic novels took the reader on labyrinthine journeys through civilizations and neologisms, superimposing the Eastern world on the West, juxtaposing the Spanish baroque poet Gongora and the experimental American novelist William Burroughs, trash and the exquisite, resettling Western and non-Western cultures in a utopic or dystopic Cuba that we can find only in his texts. And Manuel Puig went even further in the direction of a hyperrealist language by expanding literary conventions, drawing a thin line between the dime novel and high literary art, as he reproduced and explored popular and mass culture and the spoken Argentine language, and, most especially, our common ground: the movies.

Talking about common ground, Cabrera Infante and I as fellow translooters, or closelaborators, were able to explore something we had in common: Marx, Groucho of course: our shared language was the citywise humor of the American movies, that Marxist verbal non-sense which recalled a more literary antecedent, Lewis Carroll and his looking-glass language. An eccentric Cuban Anglophile – and his Anglophilia has grown with the years spent in the island-city of his exile, exotic London – Cabrera Infante explored the possibilities of inscribing transculturally another kind of humor, enriching Cuban choteo, and expanding the Spanish language through polyglot puns. *Three Trapped Tigers* performs a triple translation act precisely because of the author's and the original's duplicitous relationship to English, beginning with the title whose literal translation would have been "Three sad tigers." Cabrera Infante, living in England by 1965, originally chose a "native," that is an English translator to work with him on the recreation of this novel because he wanted the translator as a collaborator, to work with him close at hand. Cass Canfield, Jr. suggested Donald Gardner, who had previously translated the Mexican essayist and poet Octavio Paz. While Gardner did not have an extensive knowledge of Spanish, his contribution to the sections of *Three Trapped Tigers* containing Lewis Carrollian nonsense poetry and wordplays were very helpful and creative. But British speech was not what Cabrera Infante was seeking as a substitute for the spoken Cuban in the book.

Returning to English, one of the sources of the source, signifies betraying the original's critique of the language of the exploiter but also, finally, results in exploiting or cannibalizing the exploiter. Cabrera Infante, in explaining the process of translating *TTT* (his acronym for the book) told an interviewer that I brought to *TTT*:

> that sense of humor characteristic of New York Jews, which is based on play upon words and confronts reality with strict verbal logic. Nothing was closer to my purpose in TTT than the philosophy of life expressed by the Marx brothers, and in Jill Levine my three Marxistigers had met their Margaret Dumont! While by day Jill Levine-Dumont was busy destroying with alice aforethought the remains of the stiff-upper-and-underlips, the sometimes metaphrastic construction of the English version of TTT, by night I went on building my construction of a phrase, of a word, of a phoneme – and even went so far as to treat proper names as subjects of linguistic experiments, as I did in Spanish.[21]

As he made clear, translation follows the original's subversive act by undermining the sacred unicity of names and the semantic role of titles. Gaining access into the mind of an exemplary explorer of language and its possibilities such as Cabrera Infante's shows us that one of the most valuable ways in which a translator enriches his or her own language is by being a good critic, that is, by choosing wisely (or wildly) the writers s/he translates.

Among the Latin American writers, Cabrera Infante stands as a brilliant recreator of his own works into English, on the same level as Nabokov or Beckett in this regard. Puig, too, shared such polyglot talents, as revealed in the novel he wrote first in English, *Maldición eterna a Quien lea estas páginas* (*Eternal Curse on the Reader of These Pages*, 1980). Like Cabrera Infante, a number of writers, many of them bilingual such as the Puerto Rican Rosario Ferré, would undertake the challenge of self-translation, with varying degrees of success. A particularly lamentable case was that of Maria Luisa Bombal in the 1940s, who "translated" but really rewrote her fine novella *La ultima niebla* into *House of Mist*, a conventional sentimental English novel, adding characters and providing a happy ending.[22] This work was fortunately given a second chance in English in the 1980s.[23]

Beyond magical realism, finally?

Magical realism captured a rural reality – for the next three decades, a trail of imitators, mostly the new Latino writers took up the García Márquez (or as people insist on calling him, Márquez) banner and recovered in English (or Spanglish) their grandmothers' tales and folkloric founts of superstitions. But which writers are being translated as well as published in English now? Maybe we've come full circle: the new urban Latin American novel, notably younger Colombian writers Mario Mendoza, Hector Abad, Juan Carlos Botero, Jorge Franco, and others (not to mention the new urbane

Mexican writers such as Jorge Volpi and Ignacio Padilla, co-founders of what they call, partly in jest, the "Crack" generation, a metaphoric sequel to the Boom) is returning to that noble staple: realism. Mario Mendoza observed in a recent article by Juan Forero titled "New Generation of Novelists Emerges in Colombia" published in the *New York Times* (April 6, 2003: 11) that "the long shadow of Gabriel García Márquez has begun to fade": "the literature of García Márquez is . . . imminently rural, and we, as writers, developed in an environment where our references were urban . . ." Drug trade and street violence are current themes of these novels; Juan Carlos Botero, another Colombian, who resides in Miami, explains: "When García Márquez began writing, 70 percent of the country was in the countryside, 30 percent was in the cities, but now it is the other way around."

What the future of the Latin American novel translated into English is, it is difficult to say. Even though, with the shrinking of the globe and a heightened awareness of the relations among different cultures which began to take the foreground in the 1960s, today's publishers no longer cultivate isolationism, they still often exclude from their lists – at the mercy of cultural-political as well as market pressures (maybe two sides of the same coin?) – the most worthy writers. But perhaps the question to ask is: in the global marketplace, will the novel (and not only the Latin American novel) as innovation and not mere commodity survive technology's vertiginous spin into the future?

NOTES

1. See Maria Eugenia Mudrovcic, "Reading Latin American Literature Abroad: Agency and Canon Formation in the Sixties and Seventies," in Daniel Balderston and Marcy E. Schwartz (eds.), *Voice-overs: Translation and Latin American Literature* (SUNY University Press, 2002), p. 131.
2. Irene Rostagno, *Searching for Recognition: The Promotion of Latin American Literature in the United States* (Westport, Conn. and London: Greenwood Press, 1997), p. 31. Henceforth "Rostagno" in the text plus page references in parentheses.
3. See John King's book on *Sur* Magazine, *Sur: A Study of the Argentine Literary Journal and its Role in the Development of a Culture 1931–1970* (Cambridge: Cambridge University Press, 1986).
4. Ciro Alegría, *Broad and Alien is the World*, trans. Harriet de Onis (New York: Holt, Rienhart and Winston, 1963).
5. See the essays by Márquez and Goldnick in this volume.
6. Emir Rodríguez Monegal, *El boom de la novela latinoamericana* (Caracas: Tiempo Nuevo, 1972), pp. 76–77.
7. De Onis persuaded Herbert Weinstock, Knopf's executive editor, that Borges was a writer of high quality, but he refused to recommend the publication of his short stories. He doubted "that a book of them in English translation could be sold to the American public." Cited from a manuscript in the Alfred A. Knopf, Inc.

Records held by the Harry Ransom Humanities Research Center at the University of Texas at Austin Library, box 112, folder 11. I would like to acknowledge, with enormous gratitude, Professor Deborah Cohn for contributing generously to this essay with her groundbreaking research and perspectives on the promotion of Latin American literature in the USA: the sections here dealing with the history of Knopf and the translations of de Onis as well as the Association of American University Presses are tantalizing glimpses of her work-in-progress: Dr. Cohn's book promises to make an important contribution to the fields of American and Latin American studies.

8. See, for example, Rodríguez Monegal's introduction to Borges in his two-volume *Borzoi Anthology to Latin American Literature* (New York: Knopf, Inc, 1977), p. 499.
9. Thomas Colchie (ed.), "Introduction," *A Hammock Beneath the Mangoes: Stories from Latin America* (New York: Dutton, 1991), p. xi.
10. "Introduction," *The Promotion of Latin American Literature in the United States* (1960–1979), ms., p. 2.
11. Quoted in Deborah Cohn, "Retracing the Lost Steps: The Cuban Revolution, the Cold War, and Publishing Alejo Carpentier in the United States," *The New Centennial Review* 3, 1 (Spring 2003): 96.
12. Cohn, "Retracing the Lost Steps," p. 102.
13. Cited from "General Statement and Justification," by August Frugé, dated February 16, 1960, in the Rockefeller Foundation Archives, record group 1.2, series 200r, box 292, folder 2738, held by the Rockefeller Archive Center.
14. Cited from a letter from Frank Wardlaw to John P. Harrison, dated March 11, 1959, in the Rockefeller Foundation Archives, record group 1.2, series 200r, box 292, folder 2737, held by the Rockefeller Archive Center.
15. Cited from a resolution on "Yale University Press – Latin American Translations," dated April 6, 1960, in the Rockefeller Foundation Archives, record group 1.2, series 200r, box 292, folder 2738, held by the Rockefeller Archive Center.
16. Cited from the "Projects Approved" list for the Association of American University Presses, Inc.'s Latin American Translation Program, dated April 1, 1966, in the Rockefeller Foundation Archives, record group 1.2, series 200r, box 293, folder 2743, held by the Rockefeller Archive Center.
17. Mario Vargas Llosa, "Borges's Fictions," in Myron Lichtblau (ed.), *A Writer's Reality* (Syracuse University Press, 1991), p. 10.
18. Gregory Rabassa, "Words Cannot Express . . . The Translation of Cultures," in Balderston and Schwartz, *Voice-Overs*, p. 85.
19. See Rostagno, p. 107: "Often the center covered half of the translating expense. On rare occasions it would pay the whole cost, a sum ranging between $2000 and $5000."
20. Cohn, "Retracing the Lost Steps . . .", p. 82.
21. Rita Guibert, "Interview: Guillermo Cabrera Infante," in *Seven Voices: Seven Latin American Writers Talk to Rita Guibert* (New York: Knopf, 1973), p. 414.
22. Published by Farrar, Straus & Co. in 1947, reprinted in England by Cassell in 1948.
23. *The New Islands and Other Stories*, trans. Lucia Guerra and Richard Cunningham (Ithaca: Cornell University Press, 1988).

FURTHER READING

Balderston, Daniel and Marcy Schwartz (eds.), *Voice-Overs: Translation and Latin American Literature*, Albany: State University of New York Press, 2002.

Boyd, Robert, "Bibliography of Translations of the Latin American Novel: 1900–1970," *Revista de Estudios Hispanicos* 7 (1973): 139–44.

Levine, Suzanne, Jill, *The Subversive Scribe: Translating Latin American Fiction*, Saint Paul: Graywolf Press, 1991.

Rostagno, Irene, *Searching for Recognition: The Promotion of Latin American Literature in the United States*. Westport, Conn. and London: Greenwood Press, 1997.

Shaw, Bradley A., *Latin American Literature in English Translation: An Annotated Bibliography*, New York University Press, 1976.

Wilson, Jason, *An A to Z of Modern Latin American Literature in English Translation*, London: Institute of American Studies, 1989.

BIBLIOGRAPHY

COMPILED BY KELLY AUSTIN AND RYAN KERNAN

General works: Histories, guides, handbooks, encyclopedias and companions

Alegría, Fernando, *Breve historia de la novela hispano-americana*, Mexico City: De Andrea, 1959; expanded as *Historia de la novela hispanoamericana*, Mexico City: Ediciones de Andrea, 1965 (expanded again in 1966 and 1974). *Nueva historia de la novela hispanoamericana*, Hanover NH: Ediciones del Norte, 1986.

Bethell, Leslie (ed.), *A Cultural History of Latin America: Literature, Music and the Visual Arts in the Nineteenth and Twentieth Centuries*, Cambridge University Press, 1998.

Boudon, Lawrence and Katherine D. McCann (eds.), *Handbook of Latin American Studies (HLAS Online)*, Austin: University of Texas Press, http://lcweb2.loc.gov/hlas/hlashome.html.

Brotherston, Gordon, *The Emergence of the Latin American Novel*, Cambridge University Press, 1977.

Brushwood, John S., *The Spanish American Novel: A Twentieth-Century Survey*, Austin: University of Texas Press, 1975.

Dinneen, Mark, Annual Bibliographic Reports, *Year's Work in Modern Language Studies*, Vol. 62 (2001): 327–33; Vol. 61 (1999): 366–72; Vol. 60 (1998) 341–48; Vol. 59 (1997): 461–68, London: Modern Humanities Research Association.

Foster, David William (ed.), *Handbook of Latin American Literature*, New York and London: Garland Publishing, 1987.

Franco, Jean, *An Introduction to Spanish-American Literature*, Cambridge University Press, 1969.

Goic, Cedomil, *Historia de la novela hispanoamericana*, Universidad de Valparaíso, 1972.

Goic, Cedomil (ed.), *Historia y crítica de la literatura hispanoamericana*, Barcelona: Editorial Crítica, 1988.

González Echevarría, Roberto and Enrique Pupo Walker (eds.), *The Cambridge History of Latin American Literature*, Cambridge University Press, 1996.

Grossman, Rudolph, *Historia y problemas de la literatura latino-americana*, trans. Juan C. Probst, Madrid: Revista de Occidente, 1972.

Hart, Stephen, *A Companion to Spanish-American Literature*, London: Tamesis, 1999.

Hart, Stephen and Richard Young (eds.), *Contemporary Latin American Cultural Studies*, Oxford University Press, 2003.

Henríquez Ureña, Max, *Literary Currents in Hispanic America*, Cambridge, Mass.: Harvard University Press, 1945.

Joséf, Bella, *História da literatura hispano-americana*, Rio de Janeiro: Francisco Alves, 1982.

King, John (ed.), *The Cambridge Companion to Modern Latin American Culture*, Cambridge University Press, 2004.

Klein, Leonard S. (ed.), *Latin American Literature in the Twentieth Century*, New York: Ungar, 1986.

Lindstrom, Naomi, *Twentieth-Century Spanish American Fiction*, Austin: University of Texas Press, 1994.

Luis, William (ed.) *Modern Latin American Fiction Writers, First Series*, Detroit: Gale Research, 1992.

with Ann González (eds.) *Modern Latin American Fiction Writers, Second Series*, Detroit: Gale Research, 1994.

McMurray, George, *Spanish American Writing Since 1941: A Critical Survey*, New York: Ungar, 1987.

Martin, Gerald, *Journeys through the Labyrinth: Latin American Fiction in the Twentieth Century*, London and New York: Verso, 1989.

Puccini, Dario and Saúl Yurkiévich (eds.), *Storia Della Civilta' Letteraria Ispanoamericana*, Vols. I and II, Turin: UTET, 2000. This collective work will be issued in Spanish by the Fondo de Cultura Económica in Mexico City.

Shaw, Donald (ed.), *A Companion to Modern Spanish-American Fiction*, Rochester: Tamesis, 2002.

Shaw, Donald, *Nueva narrativa hispanoamericana: Boom, Postboom, Posmodernismo*, Madrid: Cátedra, 1999.

The Post-Boom in Spanish American Fiction, Saratoga Springs: State University of New York Press, 1998.

Antonio Skármeta and the Post Boom, Hanover, NH: Ediciones del Norte, 1994.

Smith, Verity (ed.), *Encyclopedia of Latin American Literature*, London and Chicago: Fitzroy Dearborn, 1997.

Swanson, Philip, *Latin American Fiction: A Short Introduction*, Oxford: Blackwell Publishing, 2005.

Swanson, Philip (ed.), *The Companion to Latin American Studies*, London: Arnold, 2003.

Sánchez, Luis Alberto, *Proceso y contenido de la novela hispanoamericana*, Madrid: Editorial Gredos, 1968.

Solé, Carlos A. and María Isabel Abreu (eds.), *Latin American Writers*, New York: Charles Scribner's Sons, 1989.

Williams, Raymond Leslie, *Postmodernidades latinoamericanas: la novela postmoderna en Colombia, Venezuela, Ecuador, Perú y Bolivia*, Santafé de Bogotá, Colombia: Fundación Universidad Central, 1988.

The Postmodern Novel in Latin America: Politics, Culture, and the Crisis of Truth, New York: St. Martin's Press, 1995.

The Twentieth-Century Spanish American Novel, Austin: University of Texas Press, 2003.

Williamson, Edwin, *The Penguin History of Latin America*, London: Penguin Books, 1992.

Zum Felde, Alberto, *Indice crítico de la literatura hispanoaméricana*, Mexico City: Editorial Guarania, 1959.

La narrativa en hispanoamérica, Madrid: Aguilar, 1964.

Specialized works: On authors, topics and national literatures

Alonso, Carlos, *The Burden of Modernity: The Rhetoric of Cultural Discourse in Spanish America*, Oxford University Press, 1998.

Boland, Roy and Sally Harvey (eds.), *Magical Realism and Beyond: The Contemporary Spanish and Latin American Novel*, Special issue of *Antipodas* 3 (July 1991).

Boldy, Steven, *The Narrative of Carlos Fuentes: Family, Text, Nation*, Durham (UK): University of Durham, 2002.

The Novels of Julio Cortázar, Cambridge University Press, 1980.

Brushwood, John, *Mexico in its Novel*, Austin: University of Texas Press, 1965.

Campanella, Hebe N., *La novela histórica argentina e iberoamericana hacia fines del siglo XX, 1969–1999*, Buenos Aires: Vinciguerra, 2003.

Cohn, Deborah N., *History and Memory in the Two Souths: Recent Southern and Spanish American Fictions*, Nashville: Vanderbilt University Press, 1999.

Cornejo Polar, Antonio, *La novela peruana*, Lima: Editorial Horizonte, 1989.

Cortínez, Verónica (ed.), *Albricia: la novela chilena del fin de siglo*, Providencia, Santiago: Cuarto Propio, 2000.

D'Lugo, Carol Clark, *The Fragmented Novel in Mexico: The Politics of Form*, Austin: University of Texas Press, 1997.

Dill, Hans-Otto, Carola Gründler, Inke Gunia, and Klaus Meyer-Minnemann, *Apropiaciones de realidad en la novela hispanoamericana de los siglos XIX y XX*, Frankfurt: Vervuert, 1994.

Fiddian, Robin, *The Novels of Fernando del Paso*, Gainsville: University Press of Florida, 2000.

Fishburn, Evelyn, *The Portrayal of Immigration in Nineteenth-Century Argentine Fiction (1845–1902)*, Berlin: Colloquium Verlag, 1981.

Follain de Figueiredo, Vera Lúcia, *Da profecia ao labirinto. Imagens da História na ficçao latino-americana contemporânea*, Rio de Janeiro: Imago, 1994.

Franco, Jean, *The Decline and Fall of the Lettered City: Latin America in the Cold War*, Cambridge, Mass.: Harvard University Press, 2002.

Critical Passions, ed. Pratt, Mary Louise, and Kathleen Newman, Durham: Duke University Press, 1999.

Fuentes, Carlos, *Valiente Mundo Nuevo: épica, utopia y mito en la novela hispanoamericana*, Madrid: Mondadori España, 1990.

González, Aníbal, *Killer Books: Writing, Violence and Ethics in Modern Spanish American Narrative*, Austin: University of Texas Press, 2001.

González Echevarría, Roberto, *Alejo Carpentier: The Pilgrim at Home*, Ithaca: Cornell University Press, 1977.

Crítica práctica / práctica crítica, Mexico City: Fondo de Cultura Económica, 2002.

Myth and Archive: A Theory of Latin American Narrative, Cambridge University Press, 1990.

La ruta de Severo Sarduy, Hanover, NH: Ediciones del Norte, 1987.

The Voice of the Masters: Writing and Authority in Modern Latin American Literature, Austin: University of Texas Press, 1985.

Johnson, Randal (ed.), *Tropical Paths: Essays on Modern Brazilian Literature*, New York: Garland, 1993.

Juan-Navarro, Santiago, *Archival Reflections: Postmodern Fiction of the Americas (Self-reflexivity, Historical Revisionism, Utopia)*, Lewisberg: Bucknell University Press, 2000.

Kadir, Djelal, *Questioning Fictions: Latin America's Family Romance*, Minneapolis: University of Minnesota Press, 1986.

Kerr, Lucille, *Reclaiming the Author: Figures and Fictions from Spanish America*, Durham: Duke University Press, 1992.

King, John (ed.), *On Modern Latin American Fiction*, New York: Noonday Press, 1987.

Klahn, Norma and Wilfrido H. Corral (eds.), *Los novelistas como críticos Vols. I and II, Tomo 1 & Tomo 2*, Mexico City: Fondo de Cultura Económica, 1991.

Levine, Suzanne Jill, *Manuel Puig and the Spider Woman: His Life and Fictions*, New York: Farrar, Straus, and Giroux, 2000.

López Kimberle, *Latin American Novels of the Conquest*, Columbia and London: Univeristy of Missouri Press, 2002.

Lindstrom, Naomi, *The Social Conscience of Latin American Writing*, Austin: University of Texas Press, 1998.

Ludmer, Josefina, *Onetti: Los procesos de construcción del relato*, Buenos Aires: Editorial Sudamericana, 1977.

Mac Adam, Alfred J., *Modern Latin American Narratives: The Dreams of Reason*, University of Chicago Press, 1977.

Textual Confrontations: Contemporary Readings in Latin American Literature, University of Chicago Press, 1987.

McGuirk, Bernard and Richard Cardwell (eds.), *Gabriel García Márquez: New Readings*, Cambridge University Press, 1987.

Magnarelli, Sharon, *The Lost Rib. The Female Character in the Spanish-American Novel*, Lewisburg: Bucknell University Press, 1985.

Menton, Seymour, *Caminata por la narrativa latinoamericana*, Mexico City: Fondo de Cultura Económica, 2002.

Latin America's New Historical Novel, Austin: University of Texas Press, 1993.

Prose Fiction of the Cuban Revolution, Latin American Monographs, 37, Austin: University of Texas Press, 1975.

Ortega, Julio, *Una poética del cambio*, Caracas: Ediciones Ayacucho, 1991.

Payne, Judith A. and Earl E. Fitz, *Ambiguity and Gender in the New Novel of Brazil and Spanish America: A Comparative Assessment*, Iowa City: University of Iowa Press, 1993.

Pérez-Firmat, Gustavo, *The Cuban Condition: Translation and Identity in Modern Cuban Literature*, Cambridge University Press, 1989.

Prieto, René, *Body of Writing: Figuring Desire in Spanish American Literature*, Durham: Duke University Press, 2000.

Rama, Ángel, *Transculturación narrativa en américa latina*, Mexico City: Siglo XXI, 1982.

La ciudad letrada, Hanover, NH: Ediciones del Norte, 1984.

Los dictadores latinoamericanos, Mexico City: Fondo de Cultura Económica, 1976.

Restrepo, Darío Henao, *O fáustico na nova narrativa latino-americana*, Rio de Janeiro: Leviatã, 1992.

Rowe, William and Vivian Schelling, *Memory and Modernity: Popular Culture in Latin America*, London and New York: Verso, 1991.

Santí, Enrico Mario, *Bienes del siglo: sobre cultura cubana*, Mexico City: Fondo de Cultura Económica, 2002.

Schneider, Luis Mario, *La novela mexicana entre el petróleo, la homosexualidad y la política*, Mexico City, Nueva Imagen, 1997

Sklodowska, Elzbieta, *La parodia en la nueva novela hispanoamericana*, Amsterdam: Benjamins, 1991.

Sommer, Doris, *Foundational Fictions: The National Romances of Latin America*, Berkeley and Los Angeles: University of California Press, 1991.

Proceed with Caution when Engaged by Minority Writing in the Americas, Cambridge, Mass.: Harvard University Press, 1999.

Sommers, Joseph, *After the Storm: Landmarks of the Modern Mexican Novel*, Albuquerque: University of New Mexico Press, 1968.

Sosnowski, Saúl (ed.), *Augusto Roa Bastos y la producción cultural americana*, Buenos Aires: Ediciones de la Flor, 1986.

Steele, Cynthia, *Literatura indigenista en los Estados Unidos y México*, Mexico City: Instituto Nacional Indigenista, 1985.

Swanson, Philip, *The New Novel in Latin America: Politics and Popular Culture after the Boom*, New York: St. Martin's Press, 1995.

(ed.), *Landmarks in Modern Latin American Fiction*, London and New York: Routledge, 1990.

Unruh, Vicky, *Latin American Vanguards*, Berkeley and Los Angeles: University of California Press, 1994.

Unzueta, Fernando, *La imaginación histórica y el romance nacional en hispanoamérica*, Lima: Latinoamericana Editores, 1996.

Villanueva, Darío and José María Viña Liste, *Trayectoria de la novela hispanoamericana actual: del "Realismo Mágico" a los años ochenta*, Spain: Colección Austral, 1991.

Williams, Raymond Leslie, *The Colombian Novel 1844–1987*, Austin: University of Texas Press, 1991.

Zamora, Lois Parkinson, *Writing the Apocalypse: Historical Vision in Contemporary U.S. and Latin American Fiction*, Cambridge University Press, 1989.

The Usable Past: The Imagination of History in Recent Fiction of the Americas, New York: Cambridge University Press, 1997.

Zamora, Lois Parkinson and Wendy B. Farris (eds.), *Magical Realism: Theory, History, Community*, Durham and London: Duke University Press, 1995.

INDEX

Bayly, Jaime
  No se lo digas a nadie (Don't Tell Anyone) 213
  La noche es virgin 96–97
Bazán, Osvaldo
  La más maravillosa música, una historia de amor peronista 211
Beckett, Samuel 314
Beleño, Joaquín
  Luna verde 167
Bell, Michael 261
Bellatín, Mario
  Salón de belleza 203, 207, 214, 215
Belli, Gioconda
  La mujer habitada (The Inhabited Woman) 174
Bencastro, Mario
  Odisea del Norte 178
Benítez, Fernando 240
Benítez Rojo, Antonio 36, 125
Berg, Mary G. 39
Berman, Marshall 76
Bernadet, Jean-Claude
  Aquel rapaz 211
Bianco, José 66
  La pérdido del reino 207
  Las Ratas 207
  Sombras suele vestir (Shadow Play) 207
Billini, Francisco G.
  Engracia y Antoñita 129
Bioy Casáres, Adolfo 66
  La invención de Morel (The Invention of Morel) 304
Blanco, José Joaquín 203
Blest Gana, Alberto
  Martín Rivas 28, 298
Bolívar, Simón
  Carta de Jamaica ("Jamaica letter") 26
Bombal, María Luisa 9, 49–50, 185, 188–189, 194
  La amortajada (The Shrouded Woman) 50, 188–189
  La última niebla (The House of Mist) 50, 188, 314
Borges, Jorge Luis 8, 62, 63, 64, 65–66, 74, 97, 260, 271, 301, 305–306, 307
  El Aleph (The Aleph and Other Stories) 65, 308
  Ficciones 65, 261, 308
  Labyrinths 308
  Otras inquisiciones 261

Bosch, Juan
  La mañosa ("The clever woman") 139
Botero, Juan Carlos 314, 315
Brañas, César
  Alba América 164
Brandão, Ignácio Loyola
  Não verás país nenhm (And Still the Earth: An Archival Narration) 116
  Zero 116
Brau, Salvador
  Lejanías 128
  La pecadora 128
Breton, André 77
Brotherston, Gordon 309
Brushwood, John S. 26, 30
Bryce Echenique, Alfredo 11, 150–151
  Un mundo para Julius (A World for Julius) 151
Buarque, Chico
  Budapest 11
Burgos-Debray, Elisabeth 92
Burroughs, William 313

Cabello de Carbonera, Mercedes 185
  El Conspirador 9
Cabezas, Omar
  La montaña es algo más que una inmensa estepa verde (Fire From the Mountain: The Making of a Sandinista) 172
Cabral do Melo Neto, Joao 309
Cabrera Infante, Guillermo 6, 129, 135, 301, 305, 308, 311
  Ella cantaba boleros 132
  La Habana para un Infante difunto (Infante's Inferno) 131
  Holy Smoke 132
  Tres tristes tigres (Three Trapped Tigers) 71, 86, 131, 297, 308, 313–314
Calcagno, Francisco
  Aponte 127
  Los crímenes de Concha 127
  Romualdo, uno de tanto 127
Caldwell, Helen 301
Callado, Antônio
  Bar Don Juan 116
  Quarup 116
Callois, Roger 300
Calva, José Rafael 203
  El jinete azul 210
  Utopía gay 210
Cambaceres, Eugenio
  Sin rumbo 36–37

CAMBRIDGE COMPANIONS TO LITERATURE

The Cambridge Companion to Harriet
Beecher Stowe
edited by Cindy Weinstein

The Cambridge Companion to Theodore
Dreiser
edited by Leonard Cassuto and Claire
Virginia Eby

The Cambridge Companion to Willa Cather
edited by Marilee Lindemann

The Cambridge Companion to Edith
Wharton
edited by Millicent Bell

The Cambridge Companion to
Henry James
edited by Jonathan Freedman

The Cambridge Companion to
Walt Whitman
edited by Ezra Greenspan

The Cambridge Companion to
Ralph Waldo Emerson
edited by Joel Porte and Saundra
Morris

The Cambridge Companion to
Henry David Thoreau
edited by Joel Myerson

The Cambridge Companion to Mark Twain
edited by Forrest G. Robinson

The Cambridge Companion to Edgar
Allan Poe
edited by Kevin J. Hayes

The Cambridge Companion to Emily
Dickinson
edited by Wendy Martin

The Cambridge Companion to
William Faulkner
edited by Philip M. Weinstein

The Cambridge Companion to Ernest
Hemingway
edited by Scott Donaldson

The Cambridge Companion to F. Scott
Fitzgerald
edited by Ruth Prigozy

The Cambridge Companion to
Robert Frost
edited by Robert Faggen

The Cambridge Companion to
Ralph Ellison
edited by Ross Posnock

The Cambridge Companion to Eugene
O'Neill
edited by Michael Manheim

The Cambridge Companion to
Tennessee Williams edited by Matthew
C. Roudané

The Cambridge Companion to
Arthur Miller
edited by Christopher Bigsby

The Cambridge Companion to
Sam Shepard
edited by Matthew C. Roudané

CAMBRIDGE COMPANIONS TO CULTURE

The Cambridge Companion to Modern
German Culture
edited by Eva Kolinsky and
Wilfried van der Will

The Cambridge Companion to Modern
Russian Culture
edited by Nicholas Rzhevsky

The Cambridge Companion to Modern
Spanish Culture
edited by David T. Gies

The Cambridge Companion to Modern
Italian Culture
edited by Zygmunt G. Barański
and Rebecca J. West

The Cambridge Companion to Modern
French Culture
edited by Nicholas Hewitt

The Cambridge Companion to Modern
Latin American Culture
edited by John King

The Cambridge Companion to Modern Irish
Culture
edited by Joe Cleary and Claire Connolly